GOODWILL

# WORD POWER
# MADE EASY

**D.S. PAUL**

# GOODWILL PUBLISHING HOUSE®

**B-3 RATTAN JYOTI, 18 RAJENDRA PLACE**
**NEW DELHI-110008 (INDIA)**

*Published by:*

**GOODWILL PUBLISHING HOUSE®**

B-3 Rattan Jyoti, 18 Rajendra Place
New Delhi–110 008 (INDIA)
Tel: 25820556, 25750801
Fax: 91-11-25764396
E-mail: goodwillpub@vsnl.net
        ylp@bol.net.in
Website: www.goodwillpublishinghouse.com

**Printed at** Rajiv Book Binding House, Delhi

# About the Author

**D.S. Paul** is former Lecturer in English, Guru Nanak Dev University, Amritsar. He also worked as Manager in a nationalised bank. He has authored and edited many books and published articles in journals of repute. His regular columns, like 'How to Write Correct English', 'Wordsmith' and 'Descriptive Topics' in career magazines have earned him laurels from the readers.

# PREFACE

In Shakespeare's *Hamlet,* when Polonius asks: "What do you read, my lord?" Hamlet replies: "Words, words, words." Forgetting the context and taking the remark at its face value we dawn upon a great reality: What we read in any write-up are just words—nothing else. And words, mind you are the most difficult things to control. Every writer has the experience of the bemusing wilfulness of words which invariably tend to wander off into obscurity. Even the erudite scholars and senators miss the meaning of a word or two. When in a congressional meeting Mr. Taft told Mr. Connally that the senator wanted to know the meaning of the word *supererogation*, the latter said that the senator can look in the dictionary for it and that he did not have the time to educate the senator.

If men in position can be set aside like this, the commoners cannot expect a better treatment. If you are an employee, your seniors do not have the time or compulsion to rectify your reports; rather they have the authority to tell you how ignoble your ideas are and how imbecile have you been projected by your poor selection of words. If you are a Civil Services or Management aspirant and are taking a 'make or break test', nobody will tell you the meanings of words like *evanescent, refulgent, hegemony, egregious, inexorable, inebriated* or phrases like *fait accompli, ultra vires, sui generis,* etc. should they appear in the question paper. Your chances of getting past others in the present day high voltage competition are anybody's guess.

The fact of the matter is that the necessity of possessing a decent English vocabulary with a wide range cannot be overemphasized. English is unarguably the most dominant language in academics, professions, communication, computers, websites and mass media. Globalisation and widespread application of technology has led to an increased use of English in business, services, conferences, sports, print media and verbal communication. The development of backward regions within nations is synonymous with learning and adopting English in education and vocation along with indigenous languages. Less developed countries are realising the need to develop English language skills among their population to adopt modern ways in farming, industry and trade and thereby pave the way for broad-based and sustainable development.

The book *Word Power Made Easy* gives you different new ways to learn and remember words, and puts punch, pertinence and perspicuity into your speech and writing. It is not just a collection of a few words and their meanings; nor does it attempt to get hold of a limited range of key words and delve into their etymology. It is a super collection of a wide range of words for every profession, occasion and need. Synonyms, antonyms, doublets, words often confused, one word substitutes, foreign words and terms frequently appearing in English write-ups, word formation, prefixes, suffixes and expressive words have been painstakingly arranged from authentic sources. Review tests and comprehensive tests have been included to help the readers check their progress periodically.

The book will prove immensely beneficial to students, professionals, businessmen, writers, reporters, media persons and all those aspiring to strengthen their expression and communication through the power of words.

**D.S. PAUL**

# CONTENTS

# IMPORTANCE OF VOCABULARY

## English — a Dominating Language

English is unarguably the most dominating language in the world today. Over 500 million people speak English as their mother tongue, and another 500 million or so use it as a second language. It is used in over hundred countries as an official or semi-official language. It is the main world language of books, newspapers, periodicals, computer information storage, internet, websites, advertisements, international conferences, seminars, treaties, and office work in general in major parts of the world. The bottom line is that you cannot ignore English.

One of the chief reasons of its widespread use and acceptability has been its vast vocabulary. It is believed that there are over one lac words in English. The number is increasing further as some prominent words from other major languages are being absorbed and assimilated into English. The words are the building blocks with which the empire of English language has been built. There are several words to convey the same or similar idea. Still there are shades of difference in these synonyms. There are antonyms to convey the exactly opposite notion.

## The Role of Vocabulary

A decent knowledge of vocabulary can work wonders for anyone—whether a student, a professional, a researcher, an employee or a Civil Services aspirant.

A student pursuing an academic course can easily comprehend the text and grasp the ideas if he is equipped with a good vocabulary, and fare better in the examination. An aspirant of a challenging competitive examination like Civil Services, MBA entrance to a reputed Business School, or GRE to seek admission with scholarship in a foreign university can outcompete others if he/she has a better vocabulary. Reading Comprehension (RC) which forms an integral part of many academic as well as competitive examinations is all about properly understanding the given passage and answering the questions that follow it. If the candidate taking such an examination does not know the meaning of a couple of words in a paragraph, we can well imagine that the quality of his answers and the chances of his getting a high score will be negligible. Needless to say that the candidate who has worked on his vocabulary remains one up on those who haven't.

Acquiring effective vocabulary proves to be an asset in any examination where written or spoken English is tested. It offers the candidate a wide range of words to choose from to write his answers. The write-up of candidate having a limited vocabulary suffers from improper use of words, and/or repetition of words. The examiners are too experienced not to detect such weaknesses. On the other hand a candidate with a good vocabulary has several distinct advantages. He invariably chooses the right word, avoids repetition and shows a range of words in his expression. Evidently, such an expression never fails to create an impression.

In a Group Discussion (GD), it is necessary to have a clear idea of what other speakers are saying, which of course is not possible without having at least a reasonably good vocabulary. More often than not, each topic has its key terms. For example, in a discussion on terrorism, the words like militancy, outfit, disruption, desecration, extortion, harbouring, human bombs, mines, fundamentalism, ethnicim, infiltration, bloodbath, hideout, mainstream, alienation, lethal, etc. would be used by various participants. A knowledge of these words would not only enable the candidate to properly understand the arguments and contentions of others but also present his own ideas coherently and effectively. A knowledge of the topic and the ideas around which the discussion is to be built is of course necessary. But such knowledge cannot take a proper shape without commensurate vocabulary.

Similarly, an interview, particularly for a lucrative job like that in Civil Services, or for admission for MBA in a reputed Management Institute (IIM, etc.) demands an elaborate preparation by the candidate including a nice build-up of vocabulary. To-the-point and pert answers to the questions, using key words and terms often do the job.

In the present age of high voltage competition the student/candidate who presents himself/herself better even though having nearly the same level of knowledge manages to nudge past the others. An effective vocabulary and mastery of the English language often prove to be the key.

Not only the students and the aspirants, but also the professionals engaged in different jobs need to build an effective vocabulary. The competition that exists in the present age is not only confined to schools, colleges and qualifying/entrance examinations. It has creeped into the corporate world, and is becoming more intensified there. Globalisation and expansion of trade, business and services within the country and internationally have opened floodgates of opportunities for various kinds of jobs. The entrepreneurship has brought new dimensions in management and performance functions with the introduction of new techniques like conferences, surveys, sending delegations abroad, interacting with foreign functionaries, regular research, market studies, adoption of latest technology, exploring diversification and mergers and acquisitions, etc. These functions need qualified, smart and efficient employees in all the departments of the company. The employees need to acquire more knowledge to enhance their chances of promotion and/or getting regular raises in salary. Acquiring an emphatic word power helps them perform better and make an impressive career graph.

## How to Build an Emphatic Vocabulary

Building an emphatic vocabulary with a wide range is not an easy affair. In fact, there is no magic mantra whereby you can suddenly or in a short span of time build a decent vocabulary. It is pertinent to mention here that those books which guarantee to make you a vocal champion in six weeks or those institutions which claim to make you a prolific writer or impressive speaker in a month or two are trying to market their products rather than providing you with what you need. If that were the case, none of us would be deficient in vocabulary. The fact of the matter is that building a vocabulary from an ordinary to an excellent level requires a systematic approach. There are certain basic requirements which must be fulfilled before you can embark on the art and skill of having a vast vocabulary in your repertoire and also know the art of using the right word at the right place. Such requirements are discussed below:

## 1. Keenness

First and foremost, you must be very keen to build a decent vocabulary. And this keenness must be sustained till you have reached the objective and even beyond because words need to be retained in the memory with regular use. All those who have interest in English language or whose academic or professional pursuits necessitate to have a reasonable word power, at some stage, develop an urge to enhance their vocabulary. At times, this urge is felt after a student fails an examination or gets much lower marks or rank than expected, or a professional is unable to present a paper properly and fails to impress others including his/her boss, or when his write-up is improved by others to his chagrin, bordering on disappointment. But in most cases, this urge and the resultant enthusiasm is not sustained beyond a few days. The students, aspirants and professionals put the idea of improving their vocabulary on the back burner when things begin to fall in place, or when they begin to accept their mediocrity.

It must be kept in mind that mediocrity and average performance are only for those who accept them as their fate. In order to rise above this level and reach higher echelons it is necessary to keep the fire burning in the belly. This is as true of acquiring word power as of achieving anything else in life. What the sustenance of enthusiasm will do is to exhort you to do what it takes to acquire a high word power.

## 2. Putting in Efforts

The foregoing leads us to the other key requirement in this regard, viz. putting in the efforts to achieve this objective. One has to garner all available material and human resources to acquire a decent vocabulary. The material resources include standard newspapers, magazines and books that one must read to improve one's English and know more and more words—the meaning and usage thereof. Reading well-written articles, news items, editorials, stories and other standard write-ups always improves English. This habit of reading should be regular even though for a limited time daily. Between thirty minutes to an hour's reading of such exclusive material everyday will work wonders in building a good vocabulary. Such reading should be apart from academic and vocational reading, if any, by the students and professionals respectively. It is advisable to choose topics, magazines and other sources which benefit academic/professional pursuits but the focus during such reading should be on vocabulary. This objective should not be made subservient to the contents or topic.

The material source must be supplemented by a standard word power book and the plan must be followed sincerely, diligently and systematically. Internet is another great material source which can prove immensely helpful in knowing the meanings of words and getting written material to read and understand expressions, vocabulary and word usage.

The available human resources can also be utilized for building a decent vocabulary. These include one's teachers, parents, peers, colleagues and even an erudite neighbour. A serious person will always try to get his/her problem relating to words/usage removed by consulting whosoever is readily available at a given situation.

## 3. Usage

Words have limited use until they are used in conversation or write-ups. They also help us in properly and completely comprehending a passage while reading but this use is confined to the words given in a particular piece of writing. The real, or shall we say, the proper way of maintaining a good vocabulary is using various words in our sentences while we write or speak as per demands of the situation. It is advisable to read one's own written draft and improve it with better and more appropriate words. Knowing the proper use of words must always be accompanied by their meaning. Using different words— their synonyms, antonyms, avoiding repetition, not hesitating to make experiments, willing to learn different expressions, emulating established writers, newspaper editorials and other important columns and articles in magazines of repute are some of the ways through which one can constantly improve one's vocabulary. It must be understood clearly that acquiring a good vocabulary and maintaining and improving it further are interdependent processes— one cannot be accomplished without the other. If you don't maintain the acquired level of vocabulary by regular usage, several words will slip out of your mind, their meaning will get dimmed, and in some cases completely forgotten. So nurture your vocabulary with regular use.

## 4. Spellings

Learning new words is not complete unless you know the correct spellings thereof. The effort of using a better, more appropriate and beautiful word comes to naught if its spellings are incorrect. Linguists like Thorstein Veblen feel that "English spellings are archaic and cumbersome." They need earnest efforts and careful observation to learn and master. One must also be careful about American spellings and use them only where they are allowed. The spellings accepted by standard dictionaries should be used.

"The secret of strength in speech and writing lies," as Frank Vizetelly says, "in the art of using the right word in the right place." Therefore, careful speakers and writers should aim to command not only a large vocabulary but wide and correct knowledge of the meaning of words as well. "The golden rule", according to Ernest Gowers "is not the rule of grammar or syntax. It concerns not the arrangement of words but their choice. Only the right words can convey the right meaning. The golden rule is to pick those words and use them."

# 2

## TESTING YOUR PRESENT LEVEL OF VOCABULARY

After having understood the crucial role a decent word power plays in one's career, profession and interaction with others generally, the next logical step is to embark on a strategy to increase your vocabulary as planned in this book.

At the onset, it is necessary to assess your present level of vocabulary. In order to realise our aim it is necessary to know where we stand and what amount of effort is actually required.

There is a consensus of opinion among educationists, linguists and other scholars that the students upto the age of 15 years or so have a great urge to learn new words. As soon as their schooling is finished, they become less enthusiastic about building a vocabulary. Most of them confine their studies to textbooks of courses they pursue. Their work schedule is so tight that they rarely think about word power. Those who ease into some job or enterprise remain so busy with their projects and career plans that increasing their word power is no longer among their priorities. Whatever increase ensues in their vocabulary is through browsing the internet and sites—which is a part of most jobs these days—or through whatever amount of written work they have to undertake.

The fast pace of life in modern times is dictating human activities. People have limited time for even as important things as enhancing their vocabulary. However, there are those who recognize the role of word power in taking them to higher echelons and are willing to make sincere efforts in this regard.

This chapter will put you to a series of challenging tests regarding vocabulary and word responsiveness. Take these tests sincerely, strictly following the allotted time. Answers to each of the given tests have been provided. Grading has been given after the answers for self-assessment.

It is pertinent to mention that the spellings of words that you write as your answer, wherever required should be correct. Give yourself half a mark, not one, in case your word is right but spellings are wrong. In case your score falls in high category, do not conclude that you need not improve your vocabulary. Remember the following:

● There is always a room for improvement whatever your present level of vocabulary.

● Without proper follow up, even a decent vocabulary slips out of memory. Hence, there is no room for complacency.

So let us get going.

**Test 1:** Given below are some important words. Write their meanings on a sheet of paper. Take a maximum of 10 minutes. Match your answers with those given after this test to know your score. One correct meaning = 1 mark.

| | | |
|---|---|---|
| 1. abandon | 2. accretion | 3. agony |
| 4. allure | 5. astonishment | 6. banter |
| 7. bestow | 8. betray | 9. betwixt |
| 10. camouflage | 11. chide | 12. clientele |
| 13. cliffhanger | 14. competence | 15. contentious |
| 16. culminate | 17. daunt | 18. decorous |
| 19. destitution | 20. detour | 21. detract |
| 22. detente | 23. disclaimer | 24. discomfiture |
| 25. earnest | 26. ecology | 27. efficacious |
| 28. effervescent | 29. eminent | 30. empirical |
| 31. enviable | 32. entreaty | 33. evacuate |
| 34. exhaustive | 35. extensive | 36. exude |
| 37. facade | 38. facilitate | 39. farsighted |
| 40. fettle | 41. fickle | 42. fillip |
| 43. flamboyant | 44. fluster | 45. flagrant |
| 46. fizzle | 47. fortitude | 48. fulminate |
| 49. gargantuan | 50. gamut | 51. grievance |
| 52. grit | 53. hostile | 54. ignominy |
| 55. inherent | 56. largesse | 57. libido |
| 58. litigation | 59. obligation | 60. parity |

## ANSWERS (Test 1)

| | | |
|---|---|---|
| 1. abandon | : | to leave somebody esp. somebody you are responsible for. |
| 2. accretion | : | addition to something. |
| 3. agony | : | extreme physical or mental pain. |
| 4. allure | : | the quality of being attractive, exciting. |

5. astonishment : great surprise.

6. banter : friendly remarks and jokes.

7. bestow : to give something to somebody.

8. betray : to hurt somebody who trusts you.

9. betwixt : between, in a middle position.

10. camouflage : behaviour that is deliberately meant to hide the truth.

11. chide : to rebuke or reprimand.

12. clientele : customers as a whole

13. cliffhanger : a situation (in a story, etc.) in which you cannot guess what will happen next.

14. competence : the ability to do something well.

15. contentious : likely to cause disagreement between people—*a contentious issue.*

16. culminate : to end, conclude (a meeting, show).

17. daunt : to make somebody feel nervous, intimidate.

18. decorous : proper, appropriate to a particular situation.

19. destitution : a state/situation without money, food and other necessary things.

20. detour : a longer route that you take to avoid a problem.

21. detract : take away from

22. detente : an improvement in relation between nations

23. disclaimer : a statement not claiming right or

accepting responsibility for something.

24. discomfiture : a state of being embarrassed or confused.

25. earnest : serious—*earnest endeavour.*

26. ecology : the relation of plants and living creatures to each other in their environment.

27. efficacious : effective, producing the intended results (things).

28. effervescent : bubbly, excited, enthusiastic.

29. eminent : famous and respected.

30. empirical : based on experiments and experiences rather than theories and ideas—*empirical data.*

31. enviable : something that others want to have too—*enviable position.*

32. entreaty : a serious and emotional request.

33. evacuate : to move people from a place of danger.

34. exhaustive : including everything possible, thorough.

35. extensive : covering a large area, far-reaching— *extensive damage.*

36. exude : to give out a feeling or quality— *exude confidence/smell.*

37. facade : the front of a building; the way something appears to be.

38. facilitate : to make an action or process possible or easier.

39. farsighted : having a vision about future.

40. fettle : in good condition—*in fine fettle*.

41. fickle : changing often, suddenly.

42. fillip : boost, a thing that causes something to improve.

43. flamboyant : (people) who are different, confident, exciting.

44. fluster : to make somebody nervous.

45. flagrant : blatant—*flagrant abuse of human rights*.

46. fizzle : to gradually become less affective and end poorly—*fizzle out*.

47. fortitude : bravery, courage.

48. fulminate : to criticize somebody/something angrily.

49. gargantuan : enormous, extremely large.

50. gamut : a complete range of a particular kind of things—*a whole gamut of human emotions*.

51. grievance : something you think is unfair and complain about.

52. grit : courage and determination.

53. hostile : unfriendly, aggressive.

54. ignominy : public shame, loss of honour.

55. inherent : intrinsic, basic or permanent part of something.

56. largesse : the act or quality of being generous with money.

| 57. libido | : sexual desire. |
|---|---|
| 58. litigation | : the process of making or defending a claim in the court. |
| 59. obligation | : commitment, something you must do because you have promised it. |
| 60. parity | : the state of being equal. |

**Score:** one mark for each correct meaning.

## Assessment

| 0-12 | : below average |
|---|---|
| 13-32 | : average |
| 33-42 | : above average |
| 43-52 | : very good |
| 53-60 | : excellent |

**Test 2:** Given below are 60 brief phrases each containing one italicized word. Out of the given four options (*a*), (*b*), (*c*) and (*d*) mark the one that gives the correct meaning of italicized word. Refrain from making wild guesses in case you do not know the meaning of some words. It will help in arriving at the valid score and assessment. Take upto 10 minutes:

1. *intimidating* manner
   - (*a*) frightening
   - (*b*) friendly
   - (*c*) confident
   - (*d*) straightforward

2. *invaluable* contribution
   - (*a*) worthless
   - (*b*) of little value
   - (*c*) valuable
   - (*d*) uncertain

3. *nascent* stage
   - (*a*) final
   - (*b*) not fully developed
   - (*c*) middle
   - (*d*) profitable

4. *overblown* matter
   - (*a*) secret
   - (*b*) clear
   - (*c*) impressive
   - (*d*) exaggerated

5. *earnest* endeavour
   - (*a*) total
   - (*b*) serious
   - (*c*) half-hearted
   - (*d*) with outside help

6. *moot* point
   - (*a*) unlikely
   - (*b*) bringing disagreement or confusion
   - (*c*) basic
   - (*d*) main

7. *ominous* form
   - (*a*) foreboding
   - (*b*) excellent
   - (*c*) inconsistent
   - (*d*) invisible

8. *copious* flow
   - (*a*) limited
   - (*b*) polluted
   - (*c*) intermittent
   - (*d*) abundant

9. *lackadaisical* approach
   - (*a*) careful
   - (*b*) dismal
   - (*c*) judicious
   - (*d*) lacking enthusiasm

10. *desultory* conversation
    - (*a*) angry
    - (*b*) dull, uncertain
    - (*c*) important
    - (*d*) certain

11. liquid *effluents*
    - (*a*) solutions
    - (*b*) petrol, etc.
    - (*c*) wastes, sewage
    - (*d*) beverages

12. *utopian* society
    - (*a*) perfect
    - (*b*) ancient
    - (*c*) modern
    - (*d*) civilised

**13.** *hegemonic* control
- (a) economic
- (b) control by one country/organisation over other nations
- (c) colonial
- (d) political

**14.** *ostensible* reason
- (a) stated and true
- (b) unstated but true
- (c) stated but false
- (d) unclear

**15.** *malafide* intention
- (a) genuine
- (b) good
- (c) undisclosed
- (d) bad

**16.** *perceptible* change
- (a) visible
- (b) hidden
- (c) insignificant
- (d) great

**17.** without *compunction*
- (a) zeal
- (b) clarity
- (c) guilty feeling
- (d) plan

**18.** *astounding* increase
- (a) normal
- (b) expected
- (c) low
- (d) astonishing

**19.** *wanton* disregard
- (a) amorous
- (b) deliberate
- (c) causing harm without reason
- (d) childish

**20.** forced *abnegation*
- (a) endowment
- (b) exile
- (c) denial to self
- (d) acceptance

21. *hurtling* along
    (a) causing damage
    (b) moving fast in one direction
    (c) hurting
    (d) hurling

22. going *astray*
    (a) far away
    (b) near the objective
    (c) away from the target, point
    (d) to an island

23. *arrogant* style
    (a) showing anger and pride
    (b) new
    (c) latest
    (d) fashionable

24. shorn of *embellishments*
    (a) brightness       (b) decoration
    (c) clarity          (d) depth

25. resource *crunch*
    (a) excess           (b) utilisation
    (c) constraint, shortage (d) wastage

26. imaginative *empathy*
    (a) enmity
    (b) ability to understand others' feelings
    (c) scorn
    (d) pity

27. *austerity* after war
    (a) hostility
    (b) cold war

    (c) rehabilitation

    (d) ordinary life with limited provisions

**28.** *overbearing* manner

    (a) uneducated     (b) indecent

    (c) domineering     (d) pleasing

**29.** *contingent* liability

    (a) collective     (b) real

    (c) unspecified     (d) possible

**30.** *tantalisingly* out of reach

    (a) irritatingly     (b) obviously

    (c) totally     (d) partially

**31.** *mitigate* the effect

    (a) increase     (b) reduce

    (c) change     (d) hide

**32.** *haphazard* manner

    (a) irregular     (b) harmless

    (c) harmful     (d) immaculate

**33.** strong *contender*

    (a) rival     (b) likely winner/receiver

    (c) enemy     (d) concept

**34.** *contemptuous* look

    (a) affluent     (b) stylish

    (c) hateful     (d) full of love

**35.** *defiant* message

    (a) disobeying     (b) disturbing

    (c) definite     (d) difficult to understand

**36.** *defer* the decision

    (a) convey

    (b) postpone

(c) take on somebody's behalf

(d) infer

37. *estranged* wife

(a) abnormal

(b) second

(c) behaving strangely

(d) separated from husband

38. *triumphant* look

(a) defeatist      (b) enthusiastic

(c) angry      (d) victorious

39. *feasible* project

(a) possible, viable      (b) unviable

(c) expensive      (d) unmanageable

40. *generous* offer

(a) kind      (b) liberal

(c) sympathetic      (d) genuine

41. *slender* margin

(a) double-sided      (b) uncertain

(c) narrow, small      (d) big, huge

42. *indomitable* spirit

(a) unenthusiastic

(b) profound

(c) which cannot be dominated

(d) slovenly

43. *radical* change

(a) exterior      (b) unimportant

(c) fundamental      (d) complete

44. *menial* job

(a) involving manual work

(b) involving mental work
(c) honorary
(d) not skilled or important

45. *valiant* attempt
   (a) wasteful           (b) half-hearted
   (c) brave, courageous   (d) futile

46. *commercially* oriented
   (a) relating to banking
   (b) relating to property
   (c) relating to money/business
   (d) relating to export

47. *marginalised* sections
   (a) edgy             (b) influential
   (c) middle class     (d) ordinary, unimportant

48. *implicit* idea
   (a) suggested, not directly expressed
   (b) apparent
   (c) imperfect
   (d) irrelevant

49. patterns to be *discerned*
   (a) discarded      (b) seen, understood
   (c) derived        (d) discussed

50. *garner* support
   (a) refuse         (b) accept
   (c) gather, collect   (d) provide

51. *emphasizing* the need
   (a) ignoring       (b) stressing
   (c) misjudging     (d) assessing

**52.** *reveal* the truth
   (a) disclose    (b) hide
   (c) transform   (d) respect

**53.** *subjective* approach
   (a) fair    (b) personal
   (c) academic   (d) creating

**54.** *indigenous* language
   (a) undeveloped   (b) difficult
   (c) local   (d) vernacular

**55.** *synthesis* of concepts
   (a) separation
   (b) contemporary
   (c) deciphering
   (d) combining separate ideas

**56.** *resonant* frequencies
   (a) unclear   (b) resolved
   (c) resounding   (d) resistible

**57.** *subtle* variations
   (a) uncanny   (b) not very obvious
   (c) indeterminate   (d) numerous

**58.** emotional *upheaval*
   (a) contentment   (b) concord
   (c) upliftment   (d) disruption

**59.** *upbeat* note
   (a) optimistic   (b) frightening
   (c) indifferent   (d) suitable

**60.** racially *segregated*
   (a) separated   (b) combined
   (c) classified   (d) marked

## Answers (Test 2)

(One mark for each correct option)

| | | | | | |
|---|---|---|---|---|---|
| 1. (a) | 2. (c) | 3. (b) | 4. (d) | 5. (b) | 6. (b) |
| 7. (a) | 8. (d) | 9. (d) | 10. (b) | 11. (c) | 12. (a) |
| 13. (b) | 14. (c) | 15. (d) | 16. (a) | 17. (c) | 18. (d) |
| 19. (c) | 20. (c) | 21. (b) | 22. (c) | 23. (a) | 24. (b) |
| 25. (c) | 26. (b) | 27. (d) | 28. (c) | 29. (d) | 30. (a) |
| 31. (b) | 32. (a) | 33. (b) | 34. (c) | 35. (a) | 36. (b) |
| 37. (d) | 38. (d) | 39. (a) | 40. (b) | 41. (c) | 42. (c) |
| 43. (c) | 44. (d) | 45. (c) | 46. (c) | 47. (d) | 48. (a) |
| 49. (b) | 50. (c) | 51. (b) | 52. (a) | 53. (b) | 54. (c) |
| 55. (d) | 56. (c) | 57. (b) | 58. (d) | 59. (a) | 60. (a) |

## Assessment

| | | |
|---|---|---|
| 0-12 | : | below average |
| 13-32 | : | average |
| 33-42 | : | above average |
| 43-52 | : | very good |
| 53-60 | : | excellent |

**Test 3:** Given below are 60 pairs of words in two columns X and Y. Taking not more than 6 minutes, mark whether the word in column Y conveys the exactly or approximately *same, opposite* or *different* meaning to its matching word in column X. You can tick (S) (O) or (D) for the answer, respectively.

| Column X | Column Y | Answer |
|---|---|---|
| 1. delusive | deceptive | S O D |
| 2. succumb | overcome | S O D |

| | Column X | Column Y | Answer |
|---|---|---|---|
| 3. | contemplate | escalate | S O D |
| 4. | obnoxious | injurious | S O D |
| 5. | anguish | elation | S O D |
| 6. | raze | devastate | S O D |
| 7. | accentuate | underscore | S O D |
| 8. | delinquent | peremptory | S O D |
| 9. | intimate | close | S O D |
| 10. | obvious | apparent | S O D |
| 11. | ebullient | despondent | S O D |
| 12. | profound | deep | S O D |
| 13. | contemplate | mull | S O D |
| 14. | turpitude | wickedness | S O D |
| 15. | descendant | ancestor | S O D |
| 16. | dilemma | predicament | S O D |
| 17. | historical | ahistorical | S O D |
| 18. | substantial | futile | S O D |
| 19. | chagrin | annoyance | S O D |
| 20. | furious | enraged | S O D |
| 21. | denote | indicate | S O D |
| 22. | spurious | genuine | S O D |
| 23. | fount | source | S O D |
| 24. | perturbed | calm | S O D |
| 25. | affluent | wealthy | S O D |
| 26. | exacerbate | aggravate | S O D |
| 27. | surrogate | substitute | S O D |

| | Column X | Column Y | Answer |
|---|---|---|---|
| 28. | obviate | accrue | S O D |
| 29. | mundane | worldly | S O D |
| 30. | ecstasy | rapture | S O D |
| 31. | progress | retrogress | S O D |
| 32. | awesome | awful | S O D |
| 33. | benevolent | malevolent | S O D |
| 34. | ambiguous | vague | S O D |
| 35. | disparate | equal | S O D |
| 36. | vociferous | equitable | S O D |
| 37. | comity | association | S O D |
| 38. | heinous | adultery | S O D |
| 39. | nominate | intend | S O D |
| 40. | questionable | debatable | S O D |
| 41. | gratitude | gratefulness | S O D |
| 42. | finance | accounts | S O D |
| 43. | penitent | remorseful | S O D |
| 44. | disband | join | S O D |
| 45. | frequent | occasional | S O D |
| 46. | pertinent | relevant | S O D |
| 47. | peruse | search | S O D |
| 48. | downsize | reduce | S O D |
| 49. | rebuke | commend | S O D |
| 50. | precedence | priority | S O D |
| 51. | spiteful | specific | S O D |
| 52. | torrent | deluge | S O D |

|     | Column X  | Column Y  | Answer  |
|-----|-----------|-----------|---------|
| 53. | secure    | sedate    | S  O  D |
| 54. | contrive  | contrite  | S  O  D |
| 55. | fringe    | extra     | S  O  D |
| 56. | fright    | scare     | S  O  D |
| 57. | acquit    | introduce | S  O  D |
| 58. | befitting | peculiar  | S  O  D |
| 59. | pacify    | placate   | S  O  D |
| 60. | scurry    | scuttle   | S  O  D |

## Answers (Test 3)

(One mark for each correct option)

| | | | | | |
|---|---|---|---|---|---|
| 1. (S) | 2. (O) | 3. (D) | 4. (S) | 5. (O) | 6. (S) |
| 7. (S) | 8. (D) | 9. (S) | 10. (S) | 11. (D) | 12. (S) |
| 13. (S) | 14. (S) | 15. (O) | 16. (S) | 17. (O) | 18. (D) |
| 19. (S) | 20. (S) | 21. (S) | 22. (O) | 23. (S) | 24. (O) |
| 25. (S) | 26. (S) | 27. (S) | 28. (D) | 29. (S) | 30. (S) |
| 31. (O) | 32. (O) | 33. (O) | 34. (S) | 35. (O) | 36. (D) |
| 37. (S) | 38. (D) | 39. (D) | 40. (S) | 41. (S) | 42. (S) |
| 43. (S) | 44. (O) | 45. (O) | 46. (S) | 47. (D) | 48. (S) |
| 49. (O) | 50. (S) | 51. (D) | 52. (S) | 53. (D) | 54. (D) |
| 55. (S) | 56. (S) | 57. (D) | 58. (D) | 59. (S) | 60. (S) |

## Assessment

|       |   |               |
|-------|---|---------------|
| 0-12  | : | below average |
| 13-32 | : | average       |
| 33-42 | : | above average |
| 43-52 | : | very good     |
| 53-60 | : | excellent     |

**Test 4:** Take a sheet of paper and write 40 different words starting with letter *s* and 40 different words starting with the letter *r*. Write either a root word or any of its derivatives in each case, avoiding repetition.

### Answers (Test 4)

The 40 words starting with the letter *s* are given below;

| | | |
|---|---|---|
| 1. season | 2. security | 3. scenario |
| 4. shabby | 5. sentiment | 6. shipment |
| 7. shoddy | 8. saturation | 9. sneak |
| 10. snatch | 11. saving | 12. sustain |
| 13. smother | 14. shelve | 15. schedule |
| 16. stable | 17. slight | 18. separate |
| 19. saviour | 20. sanitary | 21. significant |
| 22. secular | 23. scale | 24. scarcity |
| 25. sibling | 26. secondary | 27. scrambling |
| 28. scourge | 29. showdown | 30. scan |
| 31. scrupulous | 32. solemn | 33. settle |
| 34. scream | 35. shameful | 36. shanty |
| 37. surround | 38. standard | 39. shocking |
| 40. stimulate. | | |

The 40 words starting with the letter *r* are given below;

| | | |
|---|---|---|
| 1. reason | 2. rest | 3. rascal |
| 4. relevant | 5. reminiscent | 6. raise |
| 7. refuse | 8. regiment | 9. renounce |
| 10. rivalry | 11. reader | 12. rustic |
| 13. reserve | 14. resist | 15. rogue |
| 16. rusty | 17. rhetoric | 18. revise |

| **19.** reflect | **20.** restore | **21.** ravenous |
| **22.** react | **23.** reference | **24.** reduction |
| **25.** regard | **26.** refute | **27.** remorse |
| **28.** rotten | **29.** rugged | **30.** rumbling |
| **31.** riparian | **32.** ridiculous | **33.** reveal |
| **34.** radical | **35.** reality | **36.** rational |
| **37.** remarkable | **38.** rarity | **39.** recreation |
| **40.** represent | | |

### Assessment

|       |   |               |
|-------|---|---------------|
| 0-20  | : | below average |
| 21-35 | : | average       |
| 36-50 | : | above average |
| 51-64 | : | good          |
| 65-80 | : | excellent     |

**Test 5 (Verbal Responsiveness):** Given below are two sets of words—*Set A* and *Set B*. Each word is followed by a blank space. Write words therein giving same or nearly same meaning to the given word. All the answer words should begin with letter *b* in case of set A, and with letter *e* in case of set B.

### Set A

| **1.** very strange | _____ |
| **2.** courageous | _____ |
| **3.** width | _____ |
| **4.** occupied | _____ |
| **5.** trade | _____ |
| **6.** cruel | _____ |

7. large and heavy _____
8. moneyless _____
9. intimidate _____
10. purchase _____
11. phrase _____
12. onlooker _____
13. apart from _____
14. prejudiced _____
15. confusion _____
16. very attractive _____
17. improvement _____
18. divide/separate _____
19. sully _____
20. faith _____
21. yell _____
22. possessions _____
23. aggressive/violent _____
24. kind _____
25. advantage _____
26. give _____
27. woe _____
28. empty _____
29. flagrant _____
30. bragging _____

**Set B**

1. mistake _____

2. serious         _____
3. curious         _____
4. additional      _____
5. bliss           _____
6. nervous         _____
7. effective       _____
8. sewage          _____
9. excited         _____
10. choose         _____
11. basic          _____
12. raise/promote  _____
13. set free       _____
14. thin and weak  _____
15. explain        _____
16. awkward        _____
17. avoid          _____
18. feeling/passion _____
19. authorise      _____
20. increase       _____
21. extraordinary  _____
22. showdown       _____
23. strive         _____
24. huge           _____
25. trap           _____
26. zealous        _____
27. venture        _____

**28.** totally     _____

**29.** envision     _____

**30.** era     _____

## Answers (Test 5)

### Set A

| | | |
|---|---|---|
| **1.** bizarre | **2.** brave | **3.** breadth |
| **4.** busy | **5.** business | **6.** brutal |
| **7.** bulky | **8.** broke | **9.** browbeat |
| **10.** buy | **11.** buzzword | **12.** bystander |
| **13.** besides | **14.** biased | **15.** bewilderment |
| **16.** bewitching | **17.** betterment | **18.** bifurcate |
| **19.** besmirch | **20.** belief | **21.** bellow |
| **22.** belongings | **23.** bellicose | **24.** benign |
| **25.** benefit | **26.** bestow | **27.** betide |
| **28.** blank | **29.** blatant | **30.** boastful |

### Set B

| | | |
|---|---|---|
| **1.** error | **2.** earnest | **3.** eager |
| **4.** extra | **5.** ecstacy | **6.** edgy |
| **7.** efficacious | **8.** effluent | **9.** elated |
| **10.** elect | **11.** elementary | **12.** elevate |
| **13.** emancipate | **14.** emaciated | **15.** elucidate |
| **16.** embarrassed | **17.** elude | **18.** emotion |
| **19.** empower | **20.** enhance | **21.** exceptional |
| **22.** encounter | **23.** endeavour | **24.** enormous |
| **25.** ensnare | **26.** enthusiastic | **27.** enterprise |
| **28.** entirely | **29.** envisage | **30.** epoch |

## Assessment

| | | |
|---|---|---|
| 0-12 | : | below average |
| 13-32 | : | average |
| 33-42 | : | above average |
| 43-52 | : | very good |
| 53-60 | : | excellent |

If you have attempted these tests honestly, without resorting to guesswork or exceeding the given time limit, your score would be a true reflection of your present level of vocabulary. The assessments on all tests will allow you to place yourself in any one of the given categories and exhort you to plan and work accordingly.

# 3

# TESTING YOUR GRAMMAR

Words carry their own importance. But without correct usage and adequate knowledge of grammar, a decent vocabulary gets inhibited and fails to make the desired impact. Wrong use of words mars the prospects of a good score in academic as well as competitive examinations. In write-ups—articles, papers, reports the wrong usage of words will create a bad impression.

Grammar is a vast term. It can be defined as the rules in a language for changing the form of words and joining them into meaningful sentences. Simply speaking, grammar is a person's knowledge and use of language. In English language the generative grammar gives a set of rules which can be used to produce all the possible sentences. It encompasses parts of speech, use of tenses, non-finites, modals, determiners, clauses, phrases, prepositions, nouns, pronouns, adjectives, verbs, adverbs, transformation and synthesis of sentences and much more. It will not be pertinent to discuss these aspects of grammar here. But it is necessary to test your grammar before proceeding further. It will also help you assess yourself in the knowledge of grammar and plan accordingly. It is not possible to put all aspects of grammar in a single test or even in number of small tests. Laying emphasis on usage of words within the framework of basic rules of grammar, we have prepared the following tests. The assessments given after the answers of each test will help you know your present knowledge in grammar. The answers will also help you know some important rules.

**Test 1:** Given below are 30 sentences each of which has been segregated into four parts (*a*), (*b*), (*c*) and (*d*). You have to judge if an error exists in any of the parts. That part will be your answer. If you think that there is no error, mark your answer as (*e*).

1. You can cut / glass only / by /
      (*a*)              (*b*)          (*c*)
   a diamond tipped tool. / No error.
            (*d*)                         (*e*)

2. Never for / a moment / I suspected that /
      (*a*)            (*b*)                (*c*)
   I would be cheated. / No error.
          (*d*)                      (*e*)

3. The British empire / was the last /
         (*a*)                        (*b*)
   of the great empire to have /
                (*c*)
   left its mark on Delhi. / No error.
            (*d*)                       (*e*)

4. Scarcely had the door opened / than the people /
                  (*a*)                              (*b*)
   rushed / out of the hall. / No error.
     (*c*)            (*d*)              (*e*)

**5.** It is time / the Government / has banned rigging /
    (a)         (b)          (c)

in educational institutions. / No error.
     (d)         (e)

**6.** The judge asked the man / if the bag he had lost /
        (a)            (b)

contain five thousand rupees. /
       (c)

The man replied that it did. / No error.
      (d)         (e)

**7.** Just laws are no restraint with /
        (a)

the freedom of the good /
      (b)

for the good man desires nothing /
        (c)

which a just law interfere with. / No error.
      (d)         (e)

**8.** Important Articles are /
     (a)

amended by a majority of two-third /
        (b)

of the members / present and voting. / No error.
    (c)        (d)       (e)

**9.** Indian agriculture is dependent /
       (a)

to a large extent on the monsoons /
       (b)

which are uncertainly, irregularly /
      (c)

and are not equally distributed. / No error.
                        (*d*)                              (*e*)

**10.** The young girl / sang / quiet a / beautiful song. /
        (*a*)            (*b*)      (*c*)         (*d*)

No error.
  (*e*)

**11.** Sometimes / you are not / motivated enough /
        (*a*)              (*b*)                      (*c*)

to do the job. / No error.
      (*d*)                (*e*)

**12.** The house / was costing me / over /
        (*a*)              (*b*)              (*c*)

ten lakh rupees. / No error.
      (*d*)                    (*e*)

**13.** I suppose you have / heard the latest news /
                    (*a*)                        (*b*)

that the boss is / marrying with the secretary. /
        (*c*)                          (*d*)

No error.
  (*e*)

**14.** I have told you / many a times / that I do not like /
        (*a*)                  (*b*)                    (*c*)

such movies. / No error.
      (*d*)                (*e*)

**15.** Learning from his failure / he is working hard /
                    (*a*)                            (*b*)

lest he should not fail / again. / No error.
        (*c*)                      (*d*)            (*e*)

**16.** When the university was established / he was /
                    (*a*)                                    (*b*)

yet studying at / the law college./ No error.
        (*c*)                    (*d*)                (*e*)

**17.** I met / a close friend of mine / whom I did not see /
        (*a*)                (*b*)                            (*c*)

for many years. / No error.
            (*d*)                (*e*)

**18.** My brother will / return back / from Singapore /
                (*a*)                (*b*)                        (*c*)

next week. / No error.
        (*d*)                (*e*)

**19.** I am certain / that Anita can be able /
                (*a*)                        (*b*)

to do this job / without much difficulty. / No error.
        (*c*)                        (*d*)                            (*e*)

**20.** She sang / beautifully / at the occasion /
            (*a*)                (*b*)                        (*c*)

Did she? / No error.
    (*d*)                (*e*)

**21.** I am one of / the boy /
                (*a*)                (*b*)

who need constant guidance / from the elders. /
                    (*c*)                                    (*d*)

No error.
    (*e*)

**22.** No sooner did the thief / see the policeman /

                            (*a*)                                    (*b*)

that he jumped over the wall / and ran away. /
                 (*c*)                            (*d*)

No error.
  (*e*)

**23.** Had he done / his homework well /
       (*a*)              (*b*)

he would not have / suffered this embarrassment. /
      (*c*)                 (*d*)

No error.
  (*e*)

**24.** He told me / that he cannot get / qualifying marks /
    (*a*)          (*b*)           (*c*)

and was thus rejected. / No error.
     (*d*)          (*e*)

**25.** Neither Peter / or anybody else in the class /
     (*a*)              (*b*)

could answer the question / properly. / No error.
       (*c*)          (*d*)    (*e*)

**26.** It was Prashant / a sepoy /
      (*a*)        (*b*)

in Armed Police who had / the last laughter. /
       (*c*)            (*d*)

No error.

**27.** When somebody acquires a bad habit /
            (*a*)

even the members of his own family /
          (*b*)

begin to keep him / at a distance. / No error.
    (*c*)         (*d*)     (*e*)

**28.** In India the era of / national-level parties /
     (*a*)                              (*b*)

is over and it is the regional parties /
                              (*c*)

that are calling the shooting. / No error.
     (*d*)                              (*e*)

**29.** Life on the earth may last / as far as /
     (*a*)                              (*b*)

available stock of foodstuff /
                    (*c*)

and other necessaries are there. / No error.
     (*d*)                              (*e*)

**30.** Hardly had / we moved out / of the house /
     (*a*)              (*b*)                  (*c*)

than it began to rain heavily. / No error.
     (*d*)                              (*e*)

## Answers and Explanations

**1.** (*c*)  with in place of by
**2.** (*c*)  did I suspect
**3.** (*c*)  of the great empires
**4.** (*b*)  when the people
**5.** (*c*)  delete *has*
**6.** (*c*)  contained five ....
**7.** (*d*)  interferes with
**8.** (*b*)  two-thirds
**9.** (*c*)  uncertain, irregular
**10.** (*c*)  quite a
**11.** (*e*)  No error

**12.** (*b*)  cost me/was to cost me
**13.** (*d*)  marrying the secretary
**14.** (*b*)  many a time
**15.** (*c*)  lest he should fail
**16.** (*c*)  still studying
**17.** (*c*)  whom I had not seen
**18.** (*b*)  delete *back*.
**19.** (*b*)  will be able
**20.** (*d*)  Didn't she?
**21.** (*b*)  the boys
**22.** (*c*)  than he
**23.** (*e*)  No error
**24.** (*b*)  that he could not
**25.** (*b*)  nor anybody else
**26.** (*d*)  the last laugh
**27.** (*e*)  No error
**28.** (*d*)  calling the shots
**29.** (*b*)  as long as
**30.** (*d*)  when it began

## Assessment

| | | |
|---|---|---|
| 0-7 | : | below average |
| 8-16 | : | average |
| 17-21 | : | above average |
| 22-26 | : | excellent |
| 27-30 | : | superior |

**Test-2**

**A.** *Fill in the blanks of the following sentences, with correct form of verbs given in the brackets:*

1. Sam was not _____ (select) in the team.

2. In whatever profession you _____ (be) work honestly.

3. The news of the coup was _____ (broadcast) in all TV channels.

4. The boss rejected whatever we _____ (propose).

5. It was difficult _____ (go) uphill.

6. He sometimes _____ (lose) his temper.

7. It is better to _____ (starve) than beg.

8. Time is _____ (change).

9. Hard work is always _____ (reward).

10. If it _____ (begin) to rain don't take the baby out.

### Answers

1. selected; 2. are; 3. broadcast, 4. proposed, 5. to go; 6. loses; 7. starve; 8. changing; 9. rewarded; 10. begins.

**B.** *Fill in the blanks of following sentences with suitable phrase prepositions:*

1. Parents always work hard _____ their children.

2. We express our thoughts _____ words.

3. _____ rules we have to pay service tax on the transactions.

4. He boarded the train _____ being late.

5. _____ power failure, the work remained held up for several hours.

6. She couldn't have succeeded _____ her teacher's help.

7. People carry credit card _____ cash these days.

8. The clerk worked _____ the officer who was on leave.

9. Everything worked _____ plans.

10. They succeeded _____ their hard work.

### Answers

1. for the sake of; 2. by means of; 3. According to; 4. inspite of; 5. Owing to; 6. but for; 7. instead of; 8. in place of; 9. as per; 10. by dint of.

**C.** *Fill in the blanks of following expressions with suitable prepositions:*

1. indifferent _____ pain/pleasure

2. infested _____ vermin

3. convulsed _____ laughter

4. committed _____ the task

5. abstain _____ smoking

6. beset _____ problems

**7.** trifle _____ trivials

**8.** look _____ the matter

**9.** fast _____ death

**10.** remain _____ reproach

### Answers

1. to; 2. with; 3. with; 4. to; 5. from; 6. with; 7. over; 8. into; 9. until, 10. above.

## Assessment (A + B + C)

| | | |
|---|---|---|
| 0-7 | : | below average |
| 8-16 | : | average |
| 17-21 | : | above average |
| 22-26 | : | excellent |
| 27-30 | : | superior |

## Test-3

**A.** *Make a proper choice in the following sentences:*

**1.** The stuff is so expensive that there are _____ buyers. (few, a few).

**2.** _____ I borrow your magazine please. (Can, May)

**3.** My sister speaks French _____ English. (beside, besides)

**4.** He was shaken _____ by the news of his mother being sick. (a little, little)

**5.** My sister is older than _____ (me, I)

6. Between Tom and Sam, _____ is better at creating new designs. (latter, later).

7. My sister told me that she _____ help me. (will, would)

8. The sky is overcast, it _____ rain pretty soon. (may, might)

9. This belief is held by _____ of people. (lot, a lot)

10. The man _____ we saw talking to the chief guest is our principal. (who, whom)

11. Smoking _____ our health. (affects, effects).

12. What _____ person your cousin is! He left the party early without informing anyone. (a kind of, kind of a)

13. Bad weather _____ for trekking. (prevented us from going, prevented us to go)

14. Walk fast lest _____. (we should miss the train, we shall miss the train)

15. You ought to have known _____. (better, well)

## Answers

1. few; 2. May; 3. besides; 4. a little; 5. me; 6. latter; 7. would; 8. might; 9. a lot; 10. who; 11. affects; 12. kind of a; 13. prevented us from going; 14. we should miss the train; 15. better.

**B.** *There are grammatical errors in each of the following sentences. Re-write them as correct sentences.*

1. They are true to their words.

2. He has completed two-third of the book.

3. She gave me a ten rupees note.

4. He has two brother-in-laws.

5. There is no place in the compartment.

6. The scissor is lying on the table.

7. The number of students are increasing.

8. We have a good cause for fighting.

9. He has no wish for food.

10. Who is greater—Ashoka or Akbar?

11. May I know who is he?

12. The servant refused that he had broken the plate.

13. He has left smoking.

14. Either you or I are there.

15. Last night I went to bed lately.

16. See this word in the dictionary.

17. The students gave a test in Mathematics.

18. The child can rarely walk.

19. I want few books.

20. He is stronger than anybody.

21. If I will go to Agra I will see Taj Mahal.

22. He died from cholera.

23. Her hairs are curly.

24. You cannot get this book for such a price.

25. Unless you do not work hard you will not get through.

## Answers

1. They are true to their word.

2. He has completed two-thirds of the book.

3. She gave me a ten rupee note.

4. He has two brothers-in-law.

5. There is no room in the compartment.

6. The scissors are lying on the table.

7. The number of students is increasing.

8. We have a good reason for fighting.

9. He has no desire for food.

10. Which is greater—Ashoka or Akbar.

11. May I know who he is?

12. The servant denied that he had broken the plate.

13. He has given up smoking.

14. Either you or I am there.

15. Last night I went to bed late.

16. Look up this word in the dictionary.

17. The students took a test in Mathematics.

18. The child can hardly walk.

19. I want a few books.

**20.** He is stronger than anybody else.

**21.** If I go to to Agra I will see Taj Mahal.

**22.** He died of cholera.

**23.** Her hair is curly.

**24.** You cannot get this book at such a price.

**25.** Unless you work hard you will not get through.

## Assessment (A + B) T/40

|       |   |               |
|-------|---|---------------|
| 0-12  | : | below average |
| 13-22 | : | average       |
| 23-28 | : | above average |
| 29-35 | : | excellent     |
| 36-40 | : | superior      |

You must have got a fair idea now, about your grammar and how much effort you need to put in to improve it. If your scores are below excellent, you must get hold of an established grammar book like Wren Matrin's and work on your grammar. If your score is excellent or superior you may continue your reading habits.

# 4

# TALKING ABOUT PERSONALITY TRAITS

Personality includes the various aspects of a person's character that combine to make him/her different from other people. Every human being is, in some way unique having a combination of different characteristics.

In society we constantly judge others around us—even those who are far away from us. All of us have to describe somebody to someone else at some time or the other—what type of person he or she is! In the absence of proper words it is not easy to say exactly what personality traits a particular person—your close friend, a relative, even your boss possesses. A wrong choice of words can mislead others. For example calling one of your friends *arrogant* when he is just *proud* of having achieved some laurel will be absolutely out of sorts. Similarly, calling your boss *critical* instead of *watchful* or *eager* in place of *curious* may even cause serious problems.

In this chapter we will describe various personality traits of people through appropriate words and the usage of these words. Small tests have been added for quick review of what you have learnt and also to revise your newly acquired vocabulary.

Since a person is the sum total of the ideas he holds—which govern his actions and attitudes, we will take them first.

## IDEAS – ATTITUDES

### Egoist – Egotist – Altruist – Compassionate

An *egoist* is a person who thinks that he is better than other people and talks about himself. For him, self is most important. His positive sentences start with I or end with me/myself. If he talks about others it is only to compare them with himself and accentuate their inferiority in some way.

*Egotist* on the other hand is a person who highlights his achievements and capabilities. He wants appreciation and accolades all the time.

What about *altruist*? Well, he is a person who thinks that the other people's needs and happiness are more important than his own.

*Compassionate* is someone who shows feelings of sympathy for people who are suffering (*compassionate feelings/grounds*).

### Introvert – Extrovert – Ambivert – Ambivalent

An *introvert* is a quiet person who prefers to remain in his own thoughts and feelings rather than spending time with other people.

An *extrovert* is exactly opposite to an *introvert*. He is lively, confident and enjoys being with people rather than remaining in his world of thoughts.

An *ambivert* is someone who is both introverted and extroverted in different situations at different times. Most of the people belong to this category.

It is necessary to distinguish the word *ambivalent* which means—having good and bad feelings about something, *e.g. feeling ambivalent about new job.*

## Misanthrope – Misogynist – Misogamist – Ascetic – Austere

*Misanthrope* is a person who hates and avoids people. He is suspicious of others and is always embittered. *Anthrop/anthrope* means relating to human beings. Since mis is a negative prefix, one can easily judge the meaning of the word *misanthrope* (one who hates and avoids other people).

One may also recall the word *anthropology*—the study of human race, its origin, race and development.

*Misogynist* is a man who hates women. *Gynae* means women. *Miso* is again a negative prefix. It is believed that such persons may have been very badly treated by a woman (aunt, cousin, sister, etc.) and develop this attitude as a fence against further or more rough treatment.

*Misogamist* is a person who does not want to tie the nuptial knot. He/she may accept the members of opposite sex as great companions, lovers, roommates but is not ready to go for any deeper legal commitment through the institution of marriage.

*Ascetic* is a person who denies himself physical pleasures because of religious reasons. You can associate the words self-denial, loneliness, contemplation with such persons—an abstinence from fleshy, mundane pleasures— their aim is spiritual perfection.

*Austere* is simple and plain person. He cannot afford any luxuries or even comforts, but only bare necessities. He is strict and serious in conduct and appearance.

## Vain – Conceited

*Vain* is a person who is too proud of his/her appearance, abilities and achievements.

*Conceited* is one who takes too much pride in oneself and whatever they do.

You have been introduced to 15 important words to express people's ideas. The next step is to pronounce these words correctly. Learn the correct pronunciation thereof as given below and say them aloud several times till you are comfortably using them in your conversation.

| | | | |
|---|---|---|---|
| 1. | Egoist | — | ee'gōisot |
| 2. | Egotist | — | ee'gōtist |
| 3. | Altruist | — | al'trōoist |
| 4. | Compassionate | — | kəm'pæfənət |
| 5. | Introvert | — | intrə'vərt |
| 6. | Extrovert | — | ekstrə'vərt |
| 7. | Ambivert | — | am'bivərt |
| 8. | Ambivalent | — | am'bivələnt |
| 9. | Misanthrope | — | mis'ənthrōp |
| 10. | Misogynist | — | mi'soj'ənist |
| 11. | Misogamist | — | misog'əmist |
| 12. | Ascetic | — | a'setik |
| 13. | Austere | — | ə:stiə(r) |
| 14. | Vain | — | vein |
| 15. | Conceited | — | kən'siitid |

## Review Test

*Match these words with the important personality trait they denote:*

| | | | |
|---|---|---|---|
| **1.** | egoist | *a.* | hates marriage |
| **2.** | egotist | *b.* | hates people |
| **3.** | altruist | *c.* | turns thoughts inwards |
| **4.** | compassionate | *d.* | cannot afford luxuries/comforts. |
| **5.** | introvert | *e.* | proud of his/her appearance, etc. |
| **6.** | extrovert | *f.* | takes too much pride in whatever he does. |
| **7.** | ambivert | *g.* | hates women |
| **8.** | ambivalent | *h.* | turns thoughts outwards |
| **9.** | misanthrope | *i.* | interested in others' welfare |
| **10.** | misogynist | *j.* | talks about his accomplishments |
| **11.** | misogamist | *k.* | believes in self advancement |
| **12.** | ascetic | *l.* | having mixed feelings for something |
| **13.** | austere | *m.* | has sympathy for those who suffer |
| **14.** | vain | *n.* | does not pursue fleshly pleasures |
| **15.** | conceited | *o.* | turns thoughts both outwards and inwards. |

## Answers

1. k; 2. j; 3. i., 4. m; 5. c; 6. h; 7. o; 8. l; 9. b; 10. g; 11. a; 12. n, 13. d; 14. e; 15. f.

## Roots and Derivatives of These words

Both words *egoist* and *egotist* have the same Latin root—*ego*—a pronoun meaning your own value and importance.

*I* is the main concern of an egoist's mind (Remember the word matching the *i* with ego*t*ist's *ti*.

*Egotist* talks a lot about himself. Distinguish this word with egoists's *i*.

*Egoism* is thinking that you are better or more important than anyone else.

*Egoistical* is a tendency to think on these lines.

*Egocentric* is thinking only about yourself and not about what other people think or want.

*Egomania* is a mental condition in which somebody is interested in themselves in a way that is not normal.

*Ego-surfacing* is a relatively new term often humorously used to denote activity of reaching the internet to find places where one's own name has been mentioned. Similarly, there are derivatives like *egotism, egotistical*.

The word *altruism* has the Latin root word *alter*—meaning *other*. As you know, *altruistic* actions benefit others.

There are several words in English vocabulary which have been formed with the root word *alter*. Having a look at them will immensely help your vocabulary.

*Alteration* to change to something that makes it different, e.g. *alteration to a house, dress*, etc.

*Altercation* is, however, a noisy argument or disagreement, a row.

*Alter ego* is a person whose personality is different from your own but who shows or acts as another side of your personality. The word is also used to denote a close friend who is like yourself.

*Alternate* is happening or following the regular pattern. of taking one skipping the other and again taking the next, *e.g.* alternate dark and pale strips.

*Alternative* is a thing that you can choose to do or have out of two or more possibilities; something that can be used instead of the other, e.g. *alternative medicine*.

The root word of *introvert* is intra—meaning inside or within.

The root word for *extrovert* is *extra*—meaning outside, beyond.

While many words start with intra, most of them denote negative sense of the prefix *in* such as *intractable*—very difficult to deal with; *intransigent*—unwilling to change one's opinion; and *intransitive*—a verb used without direct object.

Here the prefix *in* is to be kept in mind, not the root *intra*.

The words made with extra are many:

*Extra-curricular*—not part of (beyond) usual course or work.

*Extradite*—to send a criminal (outside) to the country where the crime was committed.

*Extrajudicial*—happening outside the normal power of law.

*Extramarital*—happening outside marriage.

*Extraordinary*—exceptional, far above others in any quality.

**Review Test 2**

*Match the following words with their explanatory terms:*

| | | | |
|---|---|---|---|
| **1.** Egotistical | | *a.* | a change to make something different. |
| **2.** Egomaniacal | | *b.* | a noisy disagreement. |
| **3.** Egocentric | | *c.* | a close friend who is like yourself. |
| **4.** Alteration | | *d.* | talking about oneself quite abnormally. |
| **5.** Altercation | | *e.* | talking a lot about oneself. |
| **6.** Alternate | | *f.* | self, not others. |
| **7.** Alternative | | *g.* | unwilling to change one's opinion. |
| **8.** Alter ego | | *h.* | something that can be used instead of another. |
| **9.** Intransigent | | *i.* | very difficult to deal with. |
| **10.** Intractable | | *j.* | take one skip one. |

**Answers**

1. e; 2. d; 3. f; 4. a; 5. b; 6. j; 7. h; 8. c; 9. g; 10. i.

Extending the roots of certain words used to describe the personality traits, the Latin verb *verts*—meaning to turn, is the root for words *introvert*, *extrovert* and *ambivert*. If your thoughts are turned inwards, you are an *introvert*, if outwards you are an *extrovert*, if both inwards and outwards, you are an *ambivert*.

The prefix *ambi* means something that refers to both or two. It is used for words *ambivalent*—having mixed feelings about the same thing, and *ambidextrous*—

someone who is able to use both his right and left hand equally well.

Incidently, *deterous* means skilful with hands (and mind). Actually, *dexter* is the Latin word for right hand. Ambidextrous is someone who can use both his hands like the right hand. Left hand is considered *awkward* and *sinister*. The word *sinister* means evil or dangerous, making you think something bad will happen.

The French word for the left hand is *gauche*. In English vocabulary, the word *gauche* means awkward while dealing with people—often doing or saying wrong things. A *gauche* remark is tactless, a gauche offer of sympathy is overdone, exaggerated and becomes embarrassing. The gauche person, we can say in a nut-shell, lacks *finesse*.

The French word for the right hand *droit* is used to form the English word *adroit* which, like dexterous, means skilful (skillful) and clever, especially in dealing with people, e.g. an *adroit negotiator*.

*Adept* is good at something that is quite difficult like *adept in painting/sketching*.

We must differentiate these words from the word *immaculate*—meaning clean and tidy, spotless.

Let us now turn to the words relating to marriage, love, hate, relationship. The Greek root word *misein*—meaning—to hate has been used to form the words *misanthrope, misogynist* and *misogamist* which have already been discussed. *Anthropos*—meaning—mankind, is also found in anthropology—the study of development of human race; and philanthropist—one who loves mankind, a rich person who helps the poor and those in need.

The root word *gamos*—meaning—marriage which occurs in words like *monogamy*, *bigamy* and *polygamy* means nuptial relations with one, two and many respectively.

The word *andros* (Greek) means male. Thus, a form of marriage of a woman with two or more males is called polyandry.

### Derivatives

1. misanthrope – misanthropy – misanthropic – misanthropist
2. misogamist – misogamy – misogamous
3. monogamist – monogamy – monogamous
4. misogynist – misogyny – misogynous
5. gynaecologist – gynaecology – gynaecologist
6. bigamist – bigamy – bigamous
7. polygamist – polygamy – polygamous
8. polygynist – polygyny – polygynous
9. polyandrist – polyandry – polyandrous
10. philanthropist – philanthropy – philanthropous
11. anthropologist – anthropology – anthropological

## Review Test of Prefixs, Suffixes, Roots – 1

*Given below are certain prefixes, suffixes, roots alongwith their meanings. You have to mention two words each for them:*

| Prefix/Suffix/Root | Meaning | Words |
|---|---|---|
| 1. ego | self | _____ |
| 2. alter | other | _____ |
| 3. extro/extra | outside | _____ |

| 4. | intro | inside | _____ |
| 5. | verto | turn | _____ |
| 6. | ambi | both | _____ |
| 7. | misein | hate | _____ |
| 8. | poly | more than two | _____ |
| 9. | anthropos | mankind | _____ |
| 10. | gyne | woman | _____ |
| 11. | gamos | marriage | _____ |
| 12. | mania | madness | _____ |
| 13. | dexter | skill/right hand | _____ |
| 14. | ist | person who | _____ |
| 15. | y | custom, practice | _____ |

## Answers

1. egoist, egotist; 2. alteration, altruist; 3. extrovert, extra-judicial; 4. introvert, inter-religious; 5. introvert, extrovert; 6. ambivert, ambidextrous; 7. misogamist, misogynist; 8. polygamy, polyandry; 9. anthropology, misanthrope; 10. misogynist, gynaecology; 11. monogamous, polygamy; 12. egomania, kleptomania; 13. ambidextrous, dexterity; 14. gynaecologist, monogamist; 15. philanthropy, polygony.

## Test of Vocabulary/Usage – 2

*Mention the word that means the same as the words/ terms given below:*

1. awkward _____
2. one who engages in charitable work _____
3. skill, cleverness _____

4. evil, threatening          _____

5. women's doctor          _____

6. living a lonely, austere life          _____

7. study of human development          _____

8. capable of using both hands with equal skill          _____

9. hatred of marriage          _____

10. a close friend like yourself          _____

11. female with two or more husbands          _____

12. A noisy row or argument          _____

13. Hating mankind          _____

14. Hatred of women          _____

15. Skip one take one          _____

### Answers

1. gauche; 2. philanthropist; 3. adroitness; 4. sinister; 5. gynaecologist; 6. ascetic; 7. anthropology; 8. ambidextrous; 9. misogamy; 10. alter ego; 11. polyandrist; 12. altercation; 13. misanthrope; 14. misogyny; 15. alternate.

## Test of Distinguishing the Key Words – 3

*Words and their meanings often get confused in the mind. Given below are the meanings relating to similar words. You have to mention the correct words:*

1. one thing instead of the other          _____

2. taking one skipping the other in a regular pattern          _____

3. change to something different          _____

4. a noisy argument                    _____

5. hatred of women                     _____

6. hated of marriage                   _____

7. evil, threatening                   _____

8. skillful (skilful)                  _____

9. male with a plurality of wives      _____

10. female with a plurality
    of husbands                        _____

11. capable of using both hands
    equally well                       _____

12. having mixed feelings
    about the same thing/situation     _____

13. denial of physical pleasures       _____

14. denial of luxuries/comforts        _____

15. someone lacking finesse            _____

16. spotless, clean and tidy           _____

## Answers

1. alternative;      2. alternate;       3. alteration;

4. altercation;      5. misogyny;        6. misogamy;

7. sinister;         8. adroit;          9. polygamist;

10. polyandrist;    11. ambidextrous;

12. ambivalent;     13. asceticism;    14. austerity;

15. gauche;         16. immaculate.

# 5

# SOME EMPHATIC WORDS–I

There are as many different ideas as there are people. Learning a few words is not sufficient to describe a variety of situations or ideas. A person with limited vocabulary is easily exposed. He either repeats the words again and again in his conversation and write-up or keeps reserved and hesitates in taking up challenging assignments. If he has time he gets his work down through a colleague or friend. But, in today's fast paced life colleagues and friends don't have much time for others. Moreover, who will complete other's task again and again? Another problem is that many jobs are to be done then and there. What will help you out is your own strength. So instead of being a dependent on others or shying away from demanding tasks and thus restricting your chances of rising higher in life, you should begin to fortify yourself with a powerful vocabulary in right earnest. Let us get going.

In this chapter we are giving 60 powerful words alongwith their meanings and purports. These are highly emphatic words and can be used in various situations. They make an immediate impact and more often than not evince the desired response.

1. *resonant* — resounding; deep, clear and continuing for a long time — *resonant voice, frequencies*. Its noun is *resonance* and verb *resonate*.

2. *abjure* — to renounce, publicly promise to give up or reject a belief or way of behaving.

3. *avaricious* — greedy, having extreme desire for wealth; noun — *avarice*.

4. *desultory* — unfocused, going from one thing to another without any plan or enthusiasm — a *desultory conversation*.

5. *diffident* — shy; not having much confidence in oneself, not wanting to talk about oneself — *a diffident manner, smile*; noun *diffidence*.

6. *gregarious* — sociable; liking to be with other people; (of animals and birds) living in groups.

7. *inarticulate* — not able to express ideas or feelings clearly or easily; not using clear words — *an inarticulate speech*.

8. *abominable* — extremely unpleasant and causing disgust; appalling, disgusting — *abominable crime; treated him/her abominably*.

9. *pariah* — outcast; a person who is not acceptable to society and is avoided by everyone. These days the word is also used for countries — *pariah states; pariah status of a country*.

10. *pragmatic* — realistic; solving the problem in a practical and sensible way rather than sticking to fixed ideas — *pragmatic approach*.

11. *preposterous* — outrageous; completely unreasonable especially in a way that is shocking or annoying — *preposterous war*.

12. *redoubtable* — formidable — having strong qualities that make you respect him/her.

13. *ebullient* — full of confidence, energy and good humour — *in an ebullient mood.*

14. *succinct* — concise; expressed clearly and in a few words — *a succinct explanation.*

15. *sinecure* — a job that you are paid for even if it involves little or no work.

16. *aegis* — protection or support of a particular person or organization — *under the aegis of something/somebody.*

17. *apocryphal* — well-known stories about someone but probably not true.

18. *coterie* — a small group of people who have the same interests and do things together but do not like to include others. (used disapprovingly)

19. *menagerie* — a collection of wild animals kept at a place.

20. *tirade* — a long, angry speech criticizing, accusing somebody of something.

21. *vituperative* — abusive; making angry and cruel criticism — *vituperative attack.*

22. *abstruse* — very complex (situation/argument), difficult to understand.

23. *bellwether* — something that is used as a sign of what will happen in the future — *bellwether of change.*

24. *benchmark* — something that can be measured and used as a standard for comparing other things — *benchmark index, test,* etc.

25. *burgeoning* — growing or developing rapidly — India's burgeoning private sector.

26. *chauvinistic* — having aggressive and unreasonable belief that one's own country or class is better than all others — *male chauvinism.*

27. *emancipation* — setting free, especially for legal, political or social restrictions — *women's emancipation.*

28. *esoteric* — likely to be understood or employed only by a few people with a special knowledge or interest.

29. *euphemism* — an indirect word or phrase that people often use to refer to something unpleasant or embarrassing.

30. *ignominy* — public shame and loss of honour — disgrace — *ignominy of defeat in the elections.* Adj. *ignominious.*

31. *lachrymose* — tearful, having a tendency to cry easily.

32. *obfuscate* — obscure; to make something less clear and more difficult to understand. Noun *obfuscation.*

33. *obtuse* — slow or unwilling to understand something.

34. *obtrusive* — noticeable in an unpleasant way.

35. *nefarious* — criminal, immoral—*nefarious activities.*

36. *panegyric* — a speech or piece of writing praising somebody/something.

37. *pantheon* — all the gods of a nation or people. Also a group of people who are famous within a particular area of activity.

38. *pristine* — immaculate; fresh, clear as if new — *The bike is in pristine condition.* Unspoiled, left in its original condition — *pristine, pollution-free beaches.*

39. *recondite* — obscure, not known about or understood by many people.

40. *serendipity* — the fact of something pleasant or interesting happening by chance — *serendipitous discovery*.

42. *tenuous* — so weak or uncertain that it hardly exists — *a tenuous hold on life*.

43. *transitory* — temporary, fleeting — continuing for a short period of time.

44. *vernal* — connected with the season of spring — *the vernal equinox*.

45. *mendicant* — a member of religious group living by asking people for money and food.

46. *affluent* — rich, wealthy—*the affluent class*.

47. *effluent* — liquid wastes, especially chemicals produced by factories.

48. *penultimate* — last but one — *the penultimate chapter; penultimate day of Test match*.

49. *adulatory* — showering praise that is more than necessary.

50. *assiduous* — diligent, working very hard and taking care that everything is done as well as can be.

51. *execrable* — terrible, very bad.

52. *imprecation* — a curse; an offensive word that is used to express extreme anger.

53. *nemesis* — punishment or defeat that is deserved and cannot be avoided.

54. *impudent* — impertinent; not showing respect for other people — *an impudent remark*.

55. *imprudent* — unwise, not sensible — *It would be imprudent to invest all the money in one company's shares.*

56. *derided* — mocked or treated as ridiculous and not worth considering seriously — *His views were derided as old-fashioned.*

57. *deference* — behaviour that shows that you respect something or somebody.

58. *defiant* — refusing to obey — sometimes in an aggressive way — a defiant teenager.

59. *precocious* — having developed particular abilities and ways of behaving at a younger age than usual.

60. *cohort* — a group of people who share a common feature or aspect of behaviour.

You have just been introduced to a set of 60 powerful and extremely useful words. You must have read them carefully and learnt the meanings thereof. It is pertinent to mention here that just one or two readings of these words will not take these words in the reportoire of your vocabulary. You have to read them again and again, know their meaning and the context in which each of these words can be used. In order to assimilate these words you need to use them in your write-ups, speeches, conversations. If you come across any of these words while reading a newspaper, magazine or book, mark the connotation it carries.

Another harder but equally rewarding exercise would be to replace the words used in a text by the words given above wherever possible—without changing the meaning or intensity of expression.

The following review tests will enable you to assess how well you have understood these words.

**Review Test 1**

*Find the words that match the following expressions. The first letter of the correct word has been provided to help you:*

1. treated ridiculously      d_____

2. greedy for wealth      a_____

3. shy, unwilling to talk about himself/herself      d_____

4. formidable, respectful      r_____

5. expressed clearly in a few words      s_____

6. showing future trends      b_____

7. long angry speech      t_____

8. slow to understand something      o_____

9. noticeable in an unpleasant way      o_____

10. very weak or uncertain      t_____

11. all the gods of a nation/people      p_____

12. very hardworking      a_____

13. something interesting happening by chance      s_____

14. temporary, fleeting      t_____

15. crying easily      l_____

16. developing very rapidly      b_____

17. full of confidence      e_____

**18.** protection of a particular group  a_____

**19.** developing abilities at a
young age                              p_____

**20.** refusing to obey                  d_____

## Answers

1. derided; 2. avaricious; 3. diffident; 4. redoubtable;
5. succinct; 6. bellwether; 7. tirade; 8. obtuse; 9. obtrusive;
10. tenuous; 11. pantheon; 12. assiduous; 13. serendipity;
14. transitory; 15. lachrymose; 16. burgeoning; 17. ebullient;
18. aegis; 19. precocious; 20. defiant.

## Review Test 2

*Do you understand these words? Say yes or no to the
statement that says something about the word.*

**1.** Is desultory conversation a dull conversation?
Yes     No

**2.** Does a diffident person have much confidence?
Yes     No

**3.** Is preposterous totally unreasonable?
Yes     No

**4.** Is aegis a support or protection of somebody?
Yes     No

**5.** Do you have natural respect for a redoubtable
person?                               Yes     No

**6.** Is bellwether something that can be used as a
standard for comparisons?             Yes     No

**7.** Is obtrusive complex?              Yes     No

**8.** Is tirade a long angry speech?     Yes     No

**9.** Does obfuscation make something
easy to understood?                   Yes     No

10. Are nefarious activities criminal?    Yes    No

11. Is pristine condition just like new, unspoiled?    Yes    No

12. Is tenuous robust and strong?    Yes    No

13. Is transitory evanescent, fleeting, fugacious?    Yes    No

14. Is vernal a disease of the skin?    Yes    No

15. Is re-condite easy to understand?    Yes    No

16. Do we bow to a pantheon?    Yes    No

17. Is an assiduous person an asset for a company?    Yes    No

18. Do affluent people enjoy luxuries?    Yes    No

19. Is adulatory excessive praise?    Yes    No

20. Is impudent unwise and insensible?    Yes    No

## Answers

1. Yes; 2. No; 3. Yes; 4. Yes; 5. Yes; 6. No; 7. No; 8. Yes; 9. No; 10. Yes; 11. Yes; 12. No; 13. Yes; 14. No; 15. No; 16. Yes; 17; Yes; 18. Yes; 19. Yes; 20. No.

# 6

# SOME EMPHATIC WORDS–II

Continuing the vein of the previous chapter we are giving 60 more powerful words. They pertain to a variety of ideas and can be used at various places and occasions—either in conversation or in writing some paper or article.

Read these words and their meanings carefully and try to use them in your sentences. If you happen to read them in newspapers and magazines, note the meaning they convey. It is necessary to assimilate them in your thinking and expression, so that they start coming to you naturally in your speech and writing at appropriate occasions.

Another equally important factor is that you must not forget the words learnt in previous chapters as you gain access to new and more words. For this you have to read this book again and again. The rewards will be higher even than your own expectation. Let us proceed.

1. *abnegation* — the act of not allowing yourself something that you want; the act of rejecting something.

2. *atonement* — the act of doing something to make amends for some wrong done in the past.

3. *dichotomy* — the separation that exists between two groups or things that are different from each other. *Dichotomy between advanced and poor nations.*

4. *ephemeral* — short lived; lasting for a short period.

5. *travail* — an unpleasant experience or situation that involves a lot of hard work.

6. *myriad* — an extremely large number of something. *Myriad of stars in the sky.*

7. *decimate* — to destroy a large number of something. *The rabbit population was decimated by the disease.*

8. *attenuate* — to make something weak or less effective. *This medicine attenuates the effects of virus.*

9. *evanescent* — short-lived, fleeting, fugacious.

10. *propriety* — appropriateness or relevance to a situation.

11. *germane* — relevant, pertinent (ideas, remarks, etc.), connected with something in an important and appropriate way.

12. *insipid* — dull; having no taste or flavour—*Insipid conversation.*

13. *audacious* — bold, usually in a negative sense; risky, doing something shocking. Noun — *audacity.*

14. *dilatory* — causing delay; not acting quickly enough.

15. *furtive* — stealthy; keeping something secret.

16. *appurtenance* — a thing that forms part of something larger or more important.

17. *turpitude* — wickedness; very immoral behaviour.

18. *excoriate* — to criticise somebody/something severely. Also (*medical*) to irritate a person's skin harshly.

19. *importunate* — very demanding; asking for things many times in a way that becomes annoying; to pester.

20. *ribaldry* — low and abusive language.

21. *didactic* — designed to tell people moral lessons.

22. *prehensile* — able to hold things. *Prehensile trunk of the elephant.*

23. *comprehensible* — easily understand; simple, clear.

24. *disseminate* — to spread information, knowledge so that it reaches many people.

25. *invective* — rude language and unpleasant remarks shouted in anger.

26. *erudite* — learned; having great academic knowledge gained from study.

27. *dilapidated* — ramshackle; (of buildings and furniture) old and in very bad condition.

28. *viscous* — thick and sticky, not flowing freely.

29. *scurrilous* — very rude and insulting, intended to damage somebody's reputation.

30. *scrupulous* — meticulous, careful about giving attention to every detail.

31. *affront* — to insult or offend someone. Also an act/remark that does so.

32. *apposite* — very appropriate for a particular situation or in relation to something.

33. *atrocious* — terrible; bad and unpleasant; cruel and shocking—*atrocious act, weather, accent.*

34. *bastion* — a group or people that protect a thought or way of life that may disappear — *bastion of male superiority.*

35. *complicity* — collusion, connivance; the act of taking part in a crime with another person.

36. *convoluted* — complicated and difficult to follow—*a convoluted argument/explanation.*

37. *effulgent* — shining brightly (literary).

38. *dolorous* — feeling or showing great sadness.

39. *inveigle* — to achieve control over somebody in a clever and dishonest way.

40. *exegis* — the detailed explanation of a piece of religious writing.

41. *expiate* — to accept punishment for something done wrong to show that you are sorry.

42. *insinuate* — imply; to suggest indirectly that something unpleasant is true. To succeed in gaining somebody's respect, affection so that you can use it to your advantage. Noun—*insinuation.*

43. *invidious* — unpleasant and unfair; likely to offend or make others jealous. *An invidious position.*

44. *laconic* — using only a few words to say something. Adverb — *laconically.*

45. *plaudits* — praise and approval. *His work won him plaudits even from his critics.*

46. *pre-emptive* — act done to prevent something bad/harmful from happening.

47. *jettison* — discard, to get rid of something you no longer need. Also to reject an idea.

48. *pretext* — a false reason that you give for doing something, usually something bad.

49. *orient* — to direct somebody/something towards something; to find your position in relation to your surroundings.

50. *quixotic* — having or involving ideas that show some imagination but are not very practical.

51. *pretentious* — trying to appear important, intelligent, etc. in order to impress other people.

52. *redolent* — making you think of the thing mentioned. *An atmosphere redolent of hot, dry deserts.*

53. *prurient* — having or showing too much interest in things connected with sex.

54. *rubric* — a title or set of instructions written in a book, an exam or paper.

55. *tenor* — the general character or meaning of something.

56. *frisk* — to search people's bodies for hidden weapons, drugs, etc.

57. *quibble* — to complain or argue about a small matter or an unimportant detail.

58. *lincentious* — behaving in a way that is sexually immoral.

59. *disparage* — to suggest that something is not important or valuable.

60. *veteran* — a person who has a lot of experience in a particular activity.

## Review Test 1

*Find the word that matches the meaning mentioned below:*

1. short-lived, fleeting     e_____
2. stealthy, secretive     f_____
3. weaken the effect of     a_____

4. very immoral behaviour            t_____
5. low, abusive language             r_____
6. very appropriate to a situation   a_____
7. ramshackle                        d_____
8. rude and insulting                s_____
9. self denial                       a_____
10. collusion, connivance            c_____
11. accept punishment                e_____
12. to suggest that something is
    not important or valuable         d_____
13. complain about a small matter    q_____
14. libidinous                       p_____
15. trying to appear important,
    intelligent                      p_____

## Answers

1. evanescent; 2. furtive; 3. attenuate; 4. turpitude;
5. ribaldry; 6. apposite; 7. dilapidated; 8. scurrilous;
9. abnegation; 10. complicity; 11. expiate; 12. disparage;
13. quibble; 14. prurient; 15. pretentious.

## Review Test 2

*If you have understood the words, you will be able to answer Yes or No to the following questions correctly:*

1. Is abnegate to abjure something?
                                    Yes      No
2. Does ephemeral last long?        Yes      No
3. Is travail a hilarious experience?   Yes      No

**4.** Does attenuate weaken something?

                                   Yes     No

**5.** Is an audacious person prone to risks?

                                   Yes     No

**6.** Does germane pertain to Germany?

                                   Yes     No

**7.** An effulgent character shines brightly?

                                   Yes     No

**8.** Do plaudits please you?         Yes     No

**9.** Quixotic is not practical?      Yes     No

**10.** Is laconic terse, brief?       Yes     No

**11.** Invidious is fair and pleasant?  Yes     No

**12.** Is myriad limited in quantity?   Yes     No

**13.** Is dichotomy a separation between
two ideas?                  Yes     No

**14.** Is propriety appropriateness?  Yes     No

**15.** Is an insipid conversation lively?  Yes     No

## Answers

1. Yes; 2. No; 3. No; 4. Yes; 5. Yes; 6. No; 7. Yes; 8. Yes; 9. Yes; 10. Yes; 11. No; 12. No; 13. Yes; 14. Yes; 15. No.

## 7

# SOME DIFFICULT WORDS

English language has a marvellous range. There are words that are easy, and others that are not so easy. Any decent write up is a combination of easy and difficult words as per demands of the topic and expression. Actually no word is difficult once it is learnt and used confidently. By difficult, here we mean those words which are used in write-ups of scholars and those who have acquired a high standard, e.g. editorials of newspapers and journals of repute. Use of such words testifies to a decent word power.

If you have to reach that level you have to learn uncommon, difficult and even very difficult words so that a lack of knowledge thereof—whenever you encounter them—does not become a stumbling block in your goal of achieving academic excellence or professional brilliance.

Read and learn the following set of very powerful words:

1. *abashed* — embarrassed and ashamed for having done something wicked.

2. *actuarial* — relating to statistical calculation.

3. *adjunct* — addition to something larger or more important.

4. *arraign* — to bring somebody to court in order to formally accuse them of a crime.

5. *attrition* — a process of making your enemy weaker by repeatedly attacking them or creating problems for them.

6. *bespoke* — made especially according to the needs of the customer; tailor-made. *Bespoke software.*

7. *blatant* — flagrant, done in an open, obvious way without caring if people would be shocked.

8. *capitulate* — surrender, agreeing to do something that you have been refusing to do for a long time.

9. *comity* — a group, especially of nations.

10. *commensurate* — matching something in quality, strength, etc. *Salary commensurate with work.*

11. *contiguous* — adjacent, as adjoining countries.

12. *corollary* — consequence, result of some course of action.

13. *crass* — totally, absolute. *Crass cacophony* (sheer, noise, without meaning).

14. *deleterious* — harmful and damaging.

15. *diurnal* — active during day time. Opposite to *nocturnal* which means active during night time.

16. *segacious* — bold, having courage to say what is right.

17. *flippant* — not serious about things.

18. *fugacious* — short-lived, fleeting, evanescent.

19. *fecundity* — ability to produce new and useful ideas.

20. *histrionic* — emotional behaviour intended to attract attention that does not seem sincere.

21. *incarcerate* — imprison, put somebody in a place from where they cannot escape.

22. *iterative* — repeating, emphasizing an idea or equation.

23. *insuperable* — insurmountable, e.g. difficulties, problems that cannot be dealt with easily.

24. *immanent* — present everywhere; present as a natural part of something.

25. *livid* — furious, extremely angry.

26. *levity* — frivolty; behaviour that shows a lack of respect for something serious and treats it lightly.

27. *mollify* — placate; to make somebody feel less angry or upset.

28. *mayhem* — confusion and fear usually caused by a sudden violent event.

29. *myopic* — shortsighted, narrow-minded.

30. *palpable* — something that is easily noticed. *Tension in the room was easily palpable.*

31. *palatable* — having a pleasant or acceptable taste, relishable.

32. *perfunctory* — done as a duty, without real interest, attention or feeling.

33. *pertinacious* — determined to achieve a particular aim despite difficulties or opposition.

34. *profligacy* — wastefulness, careless spending of money, time, resources.

35. *raucous* — sounding loud and rough—*raucous laughter*.

36. *quagmire* — bog, an area of soft wet ground; a difficult or dangerous situation.

37. *reprehensible* — deplorable, morally wrong and deserving criticism.

38. *purblind* — lacking understanding.

39. *reproof*—reprimand, rebuke; the art of telling somebody that you don't like something they have done.

40. *rhapsodic* — expressing extreme happiness or ecstasy.

41. *sequestered* — (of places) far away from people.

42. *subsume* — to put it in a group and not consider it separately.

43. *supercilious* — behaving as if you are better than others.

44. *symbiotic* — (of people and companies) having relations with others that are to the advantage of each other.

45. *upbraid* — reproach; to speak angrily with or criticize somebody.

46. *insoucient* — nonchalant, not worried about anything.

47. *inexorable* — relentless, a process that cannot be changed or stopped — *inexorable decline*.

48. *swindle* — to cheat others of their money.

49. *virulent* — (of disease and poison) dangerous, harmful and quick to have an effect.

50. *vitreous* — shiny, hard and transparent.

51. *volition* — free will, the power to choose freely or make one's own decision.

52. *mountebank* — a person who tries to trick people especially to get their money.

53. *obsequious* — servile, trying hard to please somebody.

54. *procrastinate* — delay action due to too much pondering over the issue.

55. *unctuous* — friendly or giving praise that is not sincere.

56. *ostentatious* — showy, expensive or noticeable in a way that is intended to impress others.

57. *innuendo* — hint, suggestion, a nuance.

58. *indocrinate* — brainwash, to doctrinate partisan or subversive ideas.

59. *specious* — deceptive.

60. *puerile* — childish, immature.

If you have read the above words and noted their meanings carefully, you will be able to take the following review tests successfully.

## Review Test 1

*Find the words that match the meanings given:*

1. tailor-made — b _____
2. flagrant — b _____
3. relating to statistical calculation — a _____
4. matching in quality, etc. — c _____
5. harmful and damaging — d _____
6. emotional behaviour — h _____
7. present everywhere — i _____
8. tough and dangerous situation — q _____
9. lacking understanding — p _____
10. careless spending of time, money, resources — p _____
11. speak angrily, criticize — u _____
12. nonchalant — i _____
13. quick to have an effect, dangerous — v _____

**14.** deceptive     s_____

**15.** childish, immature     p_____

### Answers

1. bespoke; 2. blantant; 3. actuarial; 4. commensurate;
5. deleterious; 6. histrionic; 7. immanent; 8. quagmire;
9. purblind; 10. profligacy; 11. upbraid; 12. insoucient;
13. virulent; 14. specious; 15. peurile

## Review Test 2

*Answer the following questions relating to the words in Yes or No:*

| | | | |
|---|---|---|---|
| **1.** | Is adjunct an additon? | Yes | No |
| **2.** | Is capitulate to be adament? | Yes | No |
| **3.** | A comity is a group? | Yes | No |
| **4.** | Crass means partially? | Yes | No |
| **5.** | Is segacious bold? | Yes | No |
| **6.** | Histrionic is objective? | Yes | No |
| **7.** | Is livid cool and calm? | Yes | No |
| **8.** | Is myopic farsighted? | Yes | No |
| **9.** | Does palatable lack taste? | Yes | No |
| **10.** | Is reprehensible deplorable? | Yes | No |
| **11.** | Perfuntory is feeling? | Yes | No |
| **12.** | Purblind lacks understanding? | Yes | No |
| **13.** | Is inexorable sporadic? | Yes | No |
| **14.** | Is ostentatious showy? | Yes | No |
| **15.** | Is mountebank a cheat? | Yes | No |

### Answers

1. Yes; 2. No; 3. Yes; 4. No; 5. Yes; 6. No; 7. No; 8. No;
9. No; 10. Yes; 11. No; 12. Yes; 13. No; 14. Yes; 15. Yes.

# 8

# SPECIAL WORDS/ USAGE FOR SPECIAL OCCASIONS

There are some special words/usage for special occasions. If you don't know their meaning or usage, you will have no idea what others are saying. Naturally, in such case you will hesitate to participate in discussion or conversation. Others will think that you are either an introvert, a dullard or simply arrogant. Your friends, acquaintances and others around may find you boring, depressing, or just distracted or off-colour. If your boss is around, your chances of promotion or a pay rise may be as good as gone. To help you out of such a mire, given below are four sets of such words, their meanings and usage explained through meaningful sentences:

## 1. Holidays – Vacations

**crib:** a house, apartment. Come on over to my *crib* and we'll watch the match on TV.

**chill:** to relax. After working hard during the week days, the weekend is a time to *chill out*.

**down:** willing, in agreement with. We're *down* for a road journey at spring break.

**hooptie:** old car that's in a bad shape. My Maruti-800 may be a *hooptie* but it's better than nothing at all.

**player:** a person who dates many people at the same time. Peter is such a *player*. He has a different girl every weekend. (The word is also spelled as *playa*).

**tight:** fantastic, cool, interesting. The new CD containing numbers (songs) from Marina is really *tight*.

**homey:** a close friend. I'm going skiing with my *homeys* next month.

**whatevs:** short for whatever, no comments, what will be, will be. We're going for a world tour next year, *whatevs*. (Also *whatev*).

**jet:** leave in a hurry. I'd better *jet* lest my friends waiting for me should think I'm not going with them to the beach.

**phat:** excellent, great, well put-together. That shot by Mark was a real *phat*.

**dis:** to insult, dishonour or disrespect. Rita said, that she would meet us at the cafe, but she *dissed* us and never showed up.

**wack:** weird or strange, unacceptable. Breaking up with a sincere friend is *wack*.

**yo:** an attention getter, hey or hello! *Yo*, Janet, are you joining us to the party?

**bling-blang:** expensive jewellery, diamonds; also flashy. Modern girl friends are all about *bling-blang*.

**my bad:** my mistake or fault. It's *my bad* that the guests have started arriving and there is no wine in the house.

**peace out:** see you later, good bye. Gotta go out for dinner. *Peace out* for now.

## 2. Personal – General

**trousseau:** a collection of linen and clothing collected for a bride. My grandmother's handmade shawl was a part of my cousin's *trousseau.*

**evocate:** drawing forth, tending to evoke. The rich smell of cakes was evocative of my childhood days at Goa.

**cortege:** a procession, especially for a ceremony. The *corteges* across busy streets often prove a traffic hazard.

**prevaricate:** to speak falsely so as to avoid the truth. Embarrassed by his own mistake, the doctor *prevaricated* about the operation, blaming a nurse.

**hassock:** thick cushion; ottoman. My aunt's den was so cluttered that I stepped on a *hassock* on my way out.

**effeminate:** having traits, habits and tastes traditionally considered feminine. As a young boy, he was rather *effeminate* and often suffered taunting from the bulleys.

**garrote:** execution by strangling; collar worn for such an execution. It was a heart-rending scene when the executioners put a *garrote* around Saddam's neck.

**cannonade:** an attack, as of continuous cannon fire. During the debate he unleashed a *cannonade* of criticism against his rivals.

**ostensibly:** with a professed appearance. He approached the beautiful model *ostensibly* to praise her, but actually he wanted her mobile number.

**pathological:** displaying an unhealthy obsession or compulsion. The lie-detector proved that the accused was a *pathological* liar.

**flaxen:** pale yellow, the colour of flax or straw. Ashwarya's *flaxen* lair glistened in the sunshine as she walked on the beach.

**stevedore:** a person or company responsible for unloading a ship's cargo. Before joining the coast guard, my cousin worked as a *stevedore* at the Vasakhapatnam port.

**edifice:** large or imposing building. Buckingham Palace is a beautiful *edifice* in the heart of London.

**impish:** pertaining to an imp — a mischievous child or demon. Even the *impish* characters of Shakespeare's plays have a charm about them.

**substantiate:** affirm or establish by evidence. The public prosecutor's detailed report *substantiated* the charges against the accused.

**reciprocity:** positive or favourable response. Trust and reciprocity are the bases of social development.

**unseemly:** unacceptable, unpalatable, not pleasing to the eye. Fierce competition in sports has led to many unseemly occurrences on the field.

## 3. Film, Play & TV Programmes

**cameo:** brief appearance, especially by a notable actor. Mel Gibson has a *cameo* in *Father's Day*.

**pedestrian:** lacking imagination, rather ordinary. Because of poor story of the film, even the famous stars looked *pedestrian*.

**swashbuckling:** impressive, exceptional. The small child actress, Kapur gave a *swashbuckling* performance in Bhansali's *Black*.

**raucous:** loud and rowdy. The peaceful processions of the yesteryears have turned *raucous* these days.

**spinoff:** secondary or derived product. The remix of old songs sometimes produces very attractive *spinoffs*.

**oeuvre:** an artist's entire body of work. The film festival focused on the *oeuvre* of Spielberg and Attenborough.

**deadpan:** expressionless. The play's climax was marred by some *deadpan* dialogue.

**repartee:** quick-witted dialogue or reply. Shakespeare's court jesters have a great sense of *repartee*.

**purport:** to profess. The movie *Gladiators* clearly *purports* to depict the barbarity of ancient rulers.

**kitsch:** artistic work that is tasteless or sentimental. The films that have a *kitsch* style do not go well with the common viewers.

**incisive:** sharp, penetrating. The performance of superstar Amitabh Bachchan in almost all his films is *incisive*.

**idiosyncratic:** strongly individual. Some of fictional characters are so *idiosyncratic* that the readers identify themselves with them.

**protagonist:** lead character. The *protagonist* of Salman Rushdie's novel, *The Midnight's Children* was born on the night of India's independence.

**poignant:** evoking sadness. Rabindranath Tagore's stories are heart-warming and *poignant*.

**flashback:** replay of earlier events. The technique of *flashback* is used by the filmmakers to connect past events with the present times.

**vignette:** short memorable scene. Some plays have a series of *vignettes*.

**resonance:** prolonged, intense effect or sound. The *resonance* of the main actor's voice stood out in this film.

**swashbuckling:** swaggering. Sudha Chandran gave a *swashbuckling* dance performance at Mumbai despite her handicap.

4. **Words with Stress**

**detritus:** debris. The municipal workers had to remove *detritus* from the ground after some miscreants went on rampage and indulged in brickbatting.

**schism:** plan or diagram in the form of an outline or model. Before robbery, the villains prepared a detailed *schism* of the jewellery showroom.

**curmudgeon:** bad tempered or surly person, often old and male. One is sure to find a *curmudgeon* or two in a town bar.

**mischievous:** playful, teasing, sometimes maliciously so. Cats are *mischievous* little creatures.

**sieve:** a utensil containing wire or plastic mesh; strainer. Pass the gravy through a *sieve* to remove lumps.

**acquiesce:** agree, accept without protest. Sometimes it is better to *acquiesce* than argue.

**convalesce:** to recover from illness. My uncle who has been ill for some time, is *convalescing* now.

**delour:** sorrow or state of great distress. The terrorists activities bring *delour* in the lives of many.

**elegiac:** mournful, in the manner of lament for the dead. Some of Grey's poems are *elegiac*.

**lambaste:** upbraid, criticize harshly. Musharraf's act of declaring an emergency in Pakistan was *lambasted* worldwide.

**slough:** to cast off or shed. The snakes *slough* after regular intervals.

**riposte:** retort; quick, clever reply. A quick *riposte* is the comedian's forte.

**lachrymose:** tearful, sad. In an Indian marriage, the bride's *lachrymose* appearance is understandable.

**crevasse:** deep crack. The Himalayan mountains have several *crevasses*. Also *crevace* or *crevice*.

**continuum:** a series of books on some subject. These publishers have brought a *continuum* on Environment.

**accomplice:** partner. The gangster has been nabbed but his *accomplice* is still at large.

# 9

# CHECKING YOUR PROGRESS
## COMPREHENSIVE TEST—1

**(Chapters 4-8)**

You must have read these chapters carefully and learnt many new words about different personality traits, some emphatic words that can be used on different occasions and also some special words used in the modern-day conversations.

Before proceeding further, it is necessary to check your progress. Given below are 4 simple vocabulary tests. Take them sincerely and match your answers with those given in the end to know your score. The assessment is also given to enable you to know whether you need to read these chapters again before going further.

## TEST 1

*Find words that correctly match the given statement:*

1. a person who prefers to remain in his   i_____ thoughts.

2. both open and reserved      a_____

3. one who hates women      m_____

4. a conceited person      v_____

5. a noisy argument      a_____

6. unwilling to change his opinion      i_____

7. good at something      a_____

8. tendency to steal small articles, things      k_____

9. evil, threatening      s_____

10. an outcast      p_____

11. unfocused, wavering      d_____

12. greedy, having extreme desire for wealth      a_____

13. outrageous, unreasonable      p_____

14. very confident      e_____

15. public shame      i_____

16. clear as if new      p_____

17. diligent, working hard      a_____

18. refusing to obey      d_____

19. respectful behaviour      d_____

20. relevant, pertinent      g_____

# TEST 2 (A)

*Match the words with their synonyms in the two columns:*

1. furtive      (*a*) ramshackle

2. insipid      (*b*) dull

3. decimate      (*c*) furious

| 4. dilapiated | (d) complicated |
| 5. convoluted | (e) stealthy |
| 6. jettison | (f) nonchalant |
| 7. sagacious | (g) placate |
| 8. mollify | (h) destroy |
| 9. livid | (i) discard |
| 10. insoucient | (j) bold |

## TEST 2 (B)

*Match the words with their antonyms :*

| 1. austere | (a) permanent |
| 2. veteran | (b) impertinent |
| 3. ignominy | (c) laud |
| 4. transitory | (d) earnest |
| 5. tenuous | (e) affluent |
| 6. germane | (f) hazy |
| 7. eflulgent | (g) novice |
| 8. disparage | (h) mature |
| 9. flippant | (i) stout |
| 10. puerile | (j) adulation |

## TEST 3

*Choose the option that correctly matches the given statement:*

1. A simple plain person
   (a) mendicant          (b) austere
   (c) affluent           (d) ambivert

2. Takes too much pride in whatever he/she does
   - (*a*) conceited
   - (*b*) proud
   - (*c*) affable
   - (*d*) altruist

3. A noisy argument
   - (*a*) alteration
   - (*b*) scuffle
   - (*c*) altercation
   - (*d*) intractable

4. Stealthy, secretive
   - (*a*) apparent
   - (*b*) furtive
   - (*c*) dilatory
   - (*d*) ribald

5. Very demanding:
   - (*a*) importunate
   - (*b*) opportune
   - (*c*) atavistic
   - (*d*) defiant

6. Short-lived
   - (*a*) euphemism
   - (*b*) evanescent
   - (*c*) audacious
   - (*d*) livid

7. Insult or offend someone
   - (*a*) jettison
   - (*b*) oppose
   - (*c*) arraign
   - (*d*) affront

8. Having much interest in things connected with sex
   - (*a*) sexy
   - (*b*) vulgar
   - (*c*) prurient
   - (*d*) womanish

9. Done in open, obvious way without caring if people would be shocked
   - (*a*) ostensible
   - (*b*) flippant
   - (*c*) adjunct
   - (*d*) flagrant

10. Embarrassed for having done something wicked
    - (*a*) abashed
    - (*b*) harassed
    - (*c*) uncomfortable
    - (*d*) fugacious

11. A group of nations
    - (*a*) cronies
    - (*b*) comity
    - (*c*) peer
    - (*d*) enjoin

12. To make somebody feel less angry :
   (a) volition              (b) enrage
   (c) mollify               (d) stratify

13. Relentless, unstoppable
   (a) constant              (b) exorable
   (c) inexorable            (d) supercilious

14. Done as duty, not interest
   (a) palatable             (b) palpable
   (c) lividity              (d) perfunctory

15. Deplorable, morally wrong and deserving criticism
   (a) comprehensive         (b) comprehensible
   (c) apprehensive          (d) reprehensible

16. Deceptive
   (a) spacious              (b) peurile
   (c) specious              (d) ostentatious

17. Brief appearance :
   (a) cameo                 (b) entry
   (c) dramatics             (d) edifice

18. Loud and rowdy
   (a) vocal                 (b) raucous
   (c) incisive              (d) poignant

19. Prolonged intense effect or sound :
   (a) octave                (b) resonance
   (c) reverberation         (d) sonorous

20. Quick, clever reply :
   (a) ribaldry              (b) curt
   (c) riposte               (d) laconic

## TEST 4

*Say whether the following pairs of words are Synonyms
(S), Antonyms (A) or Different (D) from each other:*

1. desultory – unfocused          S   A   D
2. desultory – wary               S   A   D
3. abjure – accept                S   A   D
4. abominable – unpleasant        S   A   D
5. chauvinistic – emancipation    S   A   D
6. preposterous – outrageous      S   A   D
7. pristine – spoiled             S   A   D
8. adulatory – critical           S   A   D
9. abjure – renounce              S   A   D
10. imprecation – blessing        S   A   D
11. impudent – unwise             S   A   D
12. succint – concise             S   A   D
13. deferential – imprudent       S   A   D
14. obfuscate – obscure           S   A   D
15. pristine – immaculate         S   A   D
16. turpitude – veracity          S   A   D
17. accentuate – underline        S   A   D
18. assiduous – diligent          S   A   D
19. attenuate – aggrevate         S   A   D
20. chill – relax                 S   A   D

## ANSWERS

**Test 1**

1. introvert          2. ambivert
3. misogynist         4. vain
5. altercation        6. intransigent
7. adept              8. kleptomania
9. sinister          10. pariah

11. desultory                    12. avaricious
13. preposterous                 14. ebullient
15. ignominy                     16. pristine
17. assiduous                    18. defiant
19. deference                    20. germane

**Test 2 (A)**

| | | | | |
|---|---|---|---|---|
| **1.**–(*e*) | **2.**–(*b*) | **3.**–(*h*) | **4.**–(*a*) | **5.**–(*d*) |
| **6.**–(*i*) | **7.**–(*j*) | **8.**–(*g*) | **9.**–(*c*) | **10.**–(*f*) |

**Test 2 (B)**

| | | | | |
|---|---|---|---|---|
| **1.**–(*e*) | **2.**–(*g*) | **3.**–(*j*) | **4.**–(*a*) | **5.**–(*i*) |
| **6.**–(*b*) | **7.**–(*f*) | **8.**–(*c*) | **9.**–(*d*) | **10.**–(*h*) |

**Test 3**

| | | | | |
|---|---|---|---|---|
| **1.**–(*b*) | **2.**–(*a*) | **3.**–(*c*) | **4.**–(*b*) | **5.**–(*a*) |
| **6.**–(*b*) | **7.**–(*d*) | **8.**–(*c*) | **9.**–(*d*) | **10.**–(*a*) |
| **11.**–(*b*) | **12.**–(*c*) | **13.**–(*c*) | **14.**–(*d*) | **15.**–(*d*) |
| **16.**–(*c*) | **17.**–(*a*) | **18.**–(*b*) | **19.**–(*b*) | **20.**–(*c*) |

**Test 4**

| | | | | |
|---|---|---|---|---|
| **1.**–(S) | **2.**–(D) | **3.**–(A) | **4.**–(S) | **5.**–(D) |
| **6.**–(S) | **7.**–(A) | **8.**–(A) | **9.**–(S) | **10.**–(A) |
| **11.**–(D) | **12.**–(S) | **13.**–(D) | **14.**–(S) | **15.**–(S) |
| **16.**–(A) | **17.**–(S) | **18.**–(S) | **19.**–(A) | **20.**–(S) |

---

**ASSESSMENT**

**Test 1, 2, 3 & 4**

| | |
|---|---|
| *Upto 10* | *not up to the mark* |
| *11–13* | *average* |
| *14–16* | *good* |
| *17–18* | *excellent* |
| *19–20* | *superior* |

# 10

# EXPRESSIVE WORDS

Expressive words are exclusive words that convey some specific meaning in a given context. They form phrases and expressions which are used to convey some special meaning. Knowing these words enhances one's vocabulary and docorates conversation and write-ups. In some cases the use of expressive words becomes necessary to covney the intended meaning otherwise the expression is deemed to be incorrect. For example, the expressions 'group of lions' or 'herd of lions' is wrong. The correct expression is 'pride of lions'. Pride in this case is an expressive word.

The regime of expressive words is very vast. It encompasses collective names, specific names of places, movements, sounds, appropriate comparisons, among others. Some important expressive words in different categories are given below:

## I. Collective Names

An *anthology* of poems.

A *band* of musicians.

A *batch* of boys.

A *bench* of judges/magistrates.

A *bevy* of girls/ladies.

A *board* fo directors.

A *bouquet/nosegay* of flowers.

A *budget* of news.

A *bunting* of flags.

A *brace* of pistols.

A *caravan* of merchants.

A *cellar* of wine.

A *clank* of hired applauders.

A *cloud* of locusts.

A *clowder* of cats.

A *cluster of* islands.

A *constellation/galaxy* of stars.

A *clutch* of eggs.

A *congregation* of worshippers.

A *consignment* of goods.

A *council* of advisors.

A *course* of lectures.

A *crew* of soldiers.

A *crowd/throng* of people.

A *fleet* of ships.

A *flotilla* of boats.

A *gain* of whales.

A *gang* of thives.

A *gallery* of pictures.

A *grove* of trees.

A *heap/mass* of ruins.

A *herbarium* of dried plants.

A *hive/swarm* of bees.

A *horde* of pirates.

A *kennel* of dogs.

A *leap* of leopards.

A *legion* of devils.

A *litter* of pigs, pups.

A *museum* of art.

A *muster* of peacocks.

A *pack* of wolves.

A *panel* of jurymen.

A *peal* of bells.

A *pencil* of rays.

A *posse* of constables.

A *pride* of lions.

A *quiver* of arrows.

A *regiment* of soldiers.

A *retinue* of followers.

A *rookie* of penguins/seals.

A *rope* of pearls.

A *school* of whales.

A *sheaf* of corn/grain.

A *shaol* of fish.

A *squadron* of cavalry.

A *string* of pearls.

A *stud* of horses.

A *suite* of rooms.

A *syndicate* of merchants.

A *tissue* of lies.

A *troop* of monkeys.

A *troupe* of artists.

## II.  Collective Names in Basic Science

A *pile* of nuclear physicists.

A *grid* of electrical engineers.

A *set* of pure mathematicians.

A *field* of theoretical physicists.

An *amalgamation* of metallurgists.

A *line* of spectroscopists.

A *coagulation* of celluloid chemists.

A *galaxy* of cosmologists.

A *cloud* of theoretical meteorologists.

A *shower* of applied meteorologists.

A *litter* of geneticists.

A *knot* of nautical engineers.

A *labyrinth* of communication engineers.

An *exhibition* of Nobel Prize winners.

An *intrigue* of Council Members.

A *dissonance* of faculty members.

A *stack* of librarians.

A *complex* of psychologists.

A *wing* of ornithologists.

A *branch* of fermentation chemists.

A *colony* of bacteriologists.

## III. Words Indicating Sounds Made by Objects

| Object | Sound | Object | Sound |
|--------|-------|--------|-------|
| Aeroplanes | zoom | Bells | peal |
| Bugles | blow/call | Chains | clang |
| Clocks | tick | Coin | clinks |
| Coins | jingle | Fire | crackles |
| Flags | flutter | Guns | roar |
| Hinges | creak | Hoofs | clatter |
| Horns | toot | Leaves | rustle |
| Rain | patters | Shoes | creak |
| Streams | purl | Telephones | buzz |
| Trumpets | blare | Waves | ripple |
| Wind | howls | Wings | flutter |
| Hood | crackles | | |

## IV. Appropriate Comparisons

As *alert* as a chamois.

As *angry* as a wasp.

As *bald* as coot/egg.

As *bare* as a stone.

As *bitter* as wormwood/gall.

As *black* as coal/crow/devil/ink/jet/pitch starless night/
thunder.

As *blind* as bat/beetle/thunder/mole/harper.

As *blithe* as butterfly.

As *bold* as brass.

As *boundless* as the ocean.

As *bright* as day/noon-day/light/silver.

As *brisk* as flea.

As *brittle* as glass.

As *brown* as bun/berry.

As *busy* as a bee.

As *careless* as the wind.

As *changeable* as the moon/a woman.

As *chaste* as Minerva/a lily.

As *cheap* as dirt/lies.

As *cheerful* as a lark.

As *clean* as a whistle.

As *clear* as a bell/crystal/daylight.

As *close* as wax.

As *clumsy* as a bear.

As *coarse* as fustian.

As *cold* as key/marble/ice/stone.

As *complacent* as a cat.

As *confident* justice.

As *conscientious* as a dog.

As *cool* as cucumber.

As *countless* as the stars/hair.

As *crafty* as crow.

As *cross* as a bear.

As *cruel* as media/death.

As *cunning* as a fox.

As *dead* as door nail/herring.

As *deaf* as an adder/beetle/door post.

As *deep* as sea/well.

As *dirty* as hog.

As *dismal* as a hearse.

As *distant* as the horizon.

To *drink* like a fish.

As *drunk* as a beggar/fiddler/fish.

As *dry* as a biscuit/bone/stick.

As *dull* as dishwater/lead.

As *dumb* as oyster/statue.

As *easy* as pie.

As *elusive* as quicksilver.

As *fair* as rose/dawn.

As *familiar* as an oath.

As *fat* as hen/pig/butter.

As *soft* as silk.

To *spread* like wild fire.

As *straight* as an arrow/die/ramrod.

As *strong* as lion/horse.

As *supple* as a snake.

As *surly* as a bear.

As *swift* as lightning/wind.

As *talkative* as a magpie.

As *tall* as a steeple/maypole.

As *thin* as a wafer/rake.

As *transparent* as glass.

As *true* as the gospel.

As *ugly* as a toad/sin.

As *unreal* as a dream.

As *vague* as future.

As *vast* as eternity.

As *white* as snow/lily.

As *yielding* as wax.

## V. Masculine – Feminine

| *Masculine* | *Feminine* |
| --- | --- |
| Abbot | abess |
| Administrator | administratix |
| Ambassador | ambassadress |
| Bachelor | maid |
| Baron | baroness |
| Beau | belle |
| Boar | sow |
| Bullock | heifer |
| Colt | filly |
| Czar | czarina |
| Drake | duck |
| Duke | duchess |
| Earl | countess |

| | |
|---|---|
| Executor | executrix |
| Friar/Monk | nun |
| Hart | roe |
| Stallion | mare |
| Marquic | mistress |
| Mayor | mayoress |
| Ram | ewe |
| Seamester/Tailor | seamstress |
| Signor | signora |
| Sloven | hut |
| Stag | hind |
| Swain | nymph |
| Viceroy | vicerine |
| Wizard | witch |

## VI. Important Diminutives

| *Word* | *Diminutive* |
|---|---|
| ankle | anklet |
| Animal | animalcule |
| Arm | armlet |
| Art | article |
| Ass | foal |
| Babe | baby |
| Ball | bullet |
| Baron | baronet |
| Bill | billet |

| Bird     | birdie, nestling |
|----------|------------------|
| Book     | booklet          |
| Brook    | brooklet         |
| Bull     | bullock          |
| Cage     | cageling         |
| Cabin    | cabinet          |
| Car      | chariot          |
| Cask     | casket           |
| Cat      | kitten           |
| Church   | chapel           |
| Cigar    | cigarette        |
| Circle   | circlet          |
| City     | citadel          |
| Cock     | cockerel         |
| Cow      | calf, heifer     |
| Crown    | coronet          |
| Dame     | damsel           |
| Dear     | darling          |
| Deer     | fawn             |
| Dog      | puppy            |
| Duck     | duckling         |
| Eagle    | eaglet           |
| El       | elver            |
| Elephant | calf             |
| Eye      | eyelet           |
| Face     | facet            |

| | |
|---|---|
| Flower | floweret |
| Fourth | farthing |
| Fowl | chicken |
| Fox | cub |
| Frog | tadpole |
| Globe | globule |
| Goat | kid |
| Goose | gosling |
| Hare | leveret |
| Hawk | bowet |
| Hen | pillet |
| Hill | hillock |
| Home | hamlet |
| Hump | hummock |
| Horse | colt, foal |
| Ice | icicle |
| Isle | islet |
| Lamb | lambkin |
| Lance | lancet |
| Latch | latchet |
| Leaf | leaflet |
| Lion | cub |
| Lock | locket |
| Lord | lordling |
| Mare | filly |
| Mode | model |

| | |
|---|---|
| Maid | maiden |
| Man | manikin |
| Moth | caterpillar |
| Mouth | muzzle |
| Nesting | nozzle |
| Nurse | nursling |
| Owl | owlet |
| Pack | packet |
| Pad | paddock |
| Part | particle |
| Pile | pillow |
| Pill | pilule |
| Peg | riglet |
| Puss | pussy |
| Pipe | pipkin |
| Ring | ringlet |
| River | rivulet |
| Sack | satchel |
| Salmon | parr |
| Seat | saddle |
| Seed | seedling |
| Shade | shadow |
| Sheep | lamb |
| Sign | signet |
| Spark | sparkle |
| Star | asterisk |

| | |
|---|---|
| Statue | statuette |
| Stream | streamlet |
| Suck | suckling |
| Swan | cygnet |
| Table | tablet |
| Throat | throttle |
| Thumb | thimble |
| Top | tip |
| Tower | turret |
| Trout | fry |
| Verse | verselet |
| Whale | calf |
| Weak | weakling. |

# ONE-WORD SUBSTITUTES

One-word substitutes are those special words which say a whole term or detail relating to some characteristic, person, branch of science or art form in one word.

Knowledge of such words proves highly useful in writing precis of a passage, summary/abstract of a write-up or explaining the gist of an article. These words are also helpful in Reading Comprehension (RC) because the questions following a passage for RC have to be answered in a few words. One-word substitutes are also the words which lend brevity to writing and terseness to conversation. There are specific words relating to trades, professions, characteristics, arts, sciences, theories and concepts. A knowledge thereof broadens one's horizon and increases word power.

Given below are certain important one-word substitutes along with the meanings they carry—the statements they can replace.

## I. Words Denoting Places

Nest of a bird of prey            : eerie

| | |
|---|---|
| Place of keeping bees | : apiary |
| Artificial tank for keeping live fish | : aquarium |
| Place where public/govt records are kept | : archives |
| Wide road with trees on each side | : avenue |
| A place where birds are kept | : aviary |
| A covered place for storing gram, hay | : barn |
| A covered stall at the market | : booth |
| Shelter for a cow | : byre |
| Kitchen of a shop | : caboose |
| Place where provisions/treasure/arms are hidden | : cache |
| Place where soldiers are quartered | : cantonment |
| A building where plants are kept from cold | : conservatory |
| A street closed at one end | : cul-de-sac |
| A place where ships are loaded/unloaded/repaired | : dock |
| A place where silk is reeled from cocoons | : filature |
| A place for preserving sculpture | : glyptotheca |
| A place for storing grain | : granary |
| Building where aeroplanes are housed | : hangar |
| A theatre providing variety entertainment | : hippodrome |
| A cage for keeping rabbits | : hutch |

| | |
|---|---|
| School for very young children | : kindergarten |
| Residence for monks | : monastery |
| Place for making astronomical observations | : observatory |
| Place where fruit trees are grown | : orchard |
| Place where ships can be tied | : quay |
| A place where public revenues are kept | : treasury |

## II. Words Denoting Trades/Professions

| | |
|---|---|
| Commander of country's warships | : admiral |
| One who studies the evolution of mankind | : anthropologist |
| One who makes a scientific study of antiquities | : archeologist |
| One who draws plans for buildings, etc. | : architect |
| One who is engaged in space travel | : astronaut |
| One who studies heavenly bodies | : astronomer |
| One who sells goods to the highest bidder at public sale | : auctioneer |
| One who draws maps and charts | : cartographer |
| One who deals in candles, oil, paint, etc. | : chandelier |
| Woman hired to clean offices | : charwoman |
| One employed to drive a privately owned vehicle | : chauffeur |

| | |
|---|---|
| One who mends shoes | : cobbler |
| One who works in a coal mine | : collier/miner |
| One who performs magical tricks | : conjurer |
| One who makes tubs, casks, barrels | : cooper |
| An official incharge of a museum or art gallery | : curator |
| One who deals in dress material | : draper |
| One who draws plans in engineering and architecture | : draughtsman |
| One who deals in cattle | : drover |
| One who makes a scientific study of insects | : entomologist |
| One who shoes horses | : farrier |
| One who deals in fish | : fishmonger |
| One who deals in flowers | : florist |
| One who studies earth's crust, rocks, etc. | : geologist |
| One who sets glass in windows | : glazier |
| One who deals in small articles like ribbons, tape, pins, etc. | : haberdasher |
| One who deals in hardware goods | : ironmonger |
| One hired to take care of building or office | : janitor |
| One who cuts, polishes precious stones | : lapidary |
| One who writes a dictionary | : lexicographer |
| One who studies the elements of weather | : meteorologist |

| One who makes and sells eye-glasses | : optician |
| One who attends to horses at an inn | : ostler |
| One who lends money on the security of goods, etc. | : pawnbroker |
| One who collects stamps | : philatelist |
| One who loads/unloads ships in a harbour | : stevedore |
| One who manages funerals | : undertaker |
| One who deals in carpets, curtains, beds, etc. | : upholsterer |
| One who lends money at an excessive rate of interest | : usurer |

## III. Persons with Special Characteristics

| One who studies art or plays a game for love not for money | : amateur |
| An awkward person with unpolished manners | : bumpkin |
| One who pretends to know a great deal about everything, particularly medicine | : charlatan |
| One well-versed in art, etc. | : connoisseur |
| A girl/woman who flirts with boys/men | : coquette |
| One who is critical of others' motives/actions | : cynic |
| A coward who is brutal when there is no risk to him | : dastard |

| | |
|---|---|
| A person who has the ability to make impressive public speeches | : orator |
| A political leader who can stir up people with his oratory | : demagogue |
| One who is ready to do any reckless or criminal act | : desperado |
| One who dabbles in matters of art | : dilettante |
| One given to the pleasures of eating and drinking | : epicure |
| One having excessive and often mistaken enthusiasm, especially about one's religion | : fanatic |
| One who believes in fate | : fatalist |
| One who champions the cause of women | : feminist |
| One who flees from danger/justice | : fugitive |
| One who believes that pleasure is the highest objective in life | : hedonist |
| One who pretends to be what he is not | : hypocrite |
| One who has little knowledge | : ignoramus |
| One who passes himself off as someone else | : imposter |
| One who maliciously sets fire to property | : incendiary |
| One who has a compelling desire to steal small things | : kleptomaniac |
| One who indulges in immoral pleasures | : libertine |

| | |
|---|---|
| One who lays down his life for a noble cause | : martyr |
| One who obeys his master slavishly in order to win favour | : minion |
| One who hates mankind | : misanthrope |
| One who hates women | : misogynist |
| One who is new/beginner/untrained | : novice |
| One who is journeying on foot | : pedestrian |
| One who loves people/humanity | : philanthropist |
| An uncultured person whose interests are purely material | : philistine |
| One making a journey to a holy place | : pilgrim |
| An inspired preacher, godly person | : prophet |
| One who prefers to stay alone and avoids people | : recluse |
| One who ridicules others on the basis of their social position, etc. | : snob |
| One who has the habit of walking in their sleep | : somnambulist |
| One who talks in their sleep | : somniloquist |
| One who uses clever but false arguments | : sophist |
| One who spends money extravagantly | : spendthrift |
| One who is indifferent to pleasure and pain | : stoic |
| One devoted to luxury | : sybarite |

| | |
|---|---|
| One who never touches alcoholic drinks | : teetotaller |
| One who betrays one's country/friends | : traitor |
| One who has suddenly risen to wealth and importance | : upstart |
| One who wanders without a settled home | : vagabond |
| One who has high technical skill in an art, particularly in music | : virtuoso |
| One who does not believe in God | : atheist |
| One who is ostentatious about learning | : pedant |
| One who is very fond of good food | : gourmet |
| One who bootlicks rich men | : sycophant |
| One who always expects failure | : defeatist |
| One who is indifferent to virtue and decency | : profligate |
| One who aggressively believes that his country/class is the best | : chauvinist |
| One who takes a gloomy view of things | : pessimist |
| One who keeps a positive outlook and remains hopeful | : optimist |
| One who lives and acts for the welfare of others | : altruist |
| One who hates marriage | : misogamist |
| One who accompanies a lady for protection | : chaperon |

| | |
|---|---|
| A person detained in custody | : detainee |
| One who is displaced from home | : refugee |
| Person under legal guardianship | : ward |
| One whose thoughts are turned inward | : introvert |
| One whose interests/thoughts are turned outward | : extrovert |
| One who loves to be the centre of attention | : exhibitionist |
| Idealistic but impractical | : quixotic |
| Mentally and physically handicapped | : inhibited |
| Gloomy and dull person | : saturnine |
| A person who buys or uses a particular product or service | : punter |
| Habitually moving in company of others | : gregarious |
| Shy and timid | : diffident |

## IV. Words Pertaining to Arts and Sciences

| | |
|---|---|
| The science of sound | : acoustics |
| The science of aviation | : aeronautics |
| The science of land management | : agronomics |
| The science of the structure of animal bodies | : anatomy |
| Art of designing buildings | : architecture |
| The art of interpreting the influence of the stars on humans | : astrology |

| | |
|---|---|
| Science/study of heavenly bodies | : astronomy |
| Study of physical condition of the heavenly bodies | : astrophysics |
| The science of launching projectiles into space | : ballistics |
| The chemistry of living matter | : biochemistry |
| The science of making small living replicas of animals human types | : clones |
| The art of making pottery | : ceramics |
| The science of colours | : chromatics |
| The study of crime, etc. | : criminology |
| Study of births, deaths, population, etc. in an area | : demography |
| The science of morals | : ethics |
| The science of origin and history of words | : etymology |
| The science of good eating | : gastronomy |
| The science of family descent | : genealogy |
| The science of physical characteristics that are passed by parents to their children | : heredity |
| The science which deals with the condition and structure of the earth | : geology |
| The art of cultivating and managing gardens | : horticulture |
| The science dealing with the maintenance of cleanliness and good health | : hygiene |

| | |
|---|---|
| The art of growing plants in chemical solution, without soil | : hydroponics |
| The science of dealing with the extraction of metals from ores | : metallurgy |
| Science of weather and climate | : meteorology |
| The art of communicating with the dead and revealing the future | : necromancy |
| The study of coins and coinage | : numismatics |
| The study of eggs | : oology |
| The study of birds | : ornithology |
| The study of mountains | : orology |
| The study of ancient modes of writing | : palaeography |
| The science of teaching | : pedagogy |
| The science of language, its nature and development | : philology |
| The science of speech, sounds, etc. | : phonetics |
| The art of judging character from the facial features | : physiognomy |
| The art of making fireworks | : pyrotechnics |
| The art of representing on a map the physical features of a place | : topography |
| The science of poisons | : toxicology |

## V. Words Denoting Theories and Concepts

| | |
|---|---|
| Interest in the welfare of fellowmen, not in one's own | : altruism |

| | |
|---|---|
| Belief that nothing is likely to be known of the existence of God | : agnosticism |
| Belief that fun and happiness are the most important things in life | : hedonism |
| Scientific study of communication and control | : cybernetics |
| Belief that everything is pre-destined | : fatalism |
| A belief/statement that your own country is the best especially when at war against another country | : jingoism |
| The fact of not showing how you are feeling while suffering | : stoicism |

## VI. Political Words

| | |
|---|---|
| Government by the nobility | : aristocracy |
| Government by an absolute ruler | : autocracy |
| The right of the self-government, especially the partial government | : autonomy |
| Government behaviour/way of working of the officials | : bureaucracy |
| Town or district represented by a member of parliament, assembly, etc. | : constituency |
| Government formed by the representatives chosen by the people | : democracy |
| Territory under one ruler or government | : dominion |

| The right of voting at the elections | : franchise/ suffrage |
| Leadership of one state in a group of states | : hegemony |
| The time between two reigns | : interregnum |
| Government by a small class | : oligarchy |
| Government by the wealthy | : plutocracy |
| Deciding a political issue by the direct vote of the citizens | : referendum |
| A state which is governed by the Constitution | : republic |
| Betrayal of the government, etc. | : treason |
| A government in which many political parties join to reach the majority | : coalition |

## VII. Literary Words

| The repetition of sounds in the lines of a poem bringing musical quality | : alliteration |
| A short narrative about some person or event | : anecdote |
| Unknown authorship of a book | : anonymous |
| A collection of choice poems or articles in book form | : anthology |
| A short pithy saying | : aphorism |
| Some additional information given at the end of the book | : appendix |
| Author's introductory write up about the book | : preface |

The introductory write up about the book by some other eminent person than the author, given at the beginning of the book : foreword

A speech by a player at the beginning of the play : prologue

A speech by a player at the end of the play : epilogue

A story of a person's life written by himself : autobiography

A story of a person written by someone else : biography

A literary composition or dramatic representation that mocks at its original : burlesque

An exaggeration/distortion/ridicule of a character/person, etc. : caricature

The final unravelling of the plot in a drama/story : denouement

A funeral song : dirge

A sad poem mourning the death of a person : elegy

A book containing information on all aspects of a subject or on all branches of knowledge : encyclopaedia

A perfect example of something : epitome

A speech or writing in praise— generally excessive praise : eulogy

A passage taken from a book : excerpt

| A passage/small part taken from a poem | : stanza |
| Remove improper or objectionable portion from a book | : expurgate |
| Speech, etc. made without previous preparation | : extempore |
| An illustration facing the title page of the book | : frontispiece |
| List giving explanations of rare, technical words, etc. used in the book | : glossary |
| A long loud speech, often scolding | : harangue |
| An exaggerated statement made to bring a comic effect | : hyperbole |
| A detailed list of articles/stock | : inventory |
| Words or expressions used by people of some particular profession which are difficult for others to understand | : jargon |
| A piece of writing, attacking and ridiculing somebody | : lampoon |
| Author's hand-written or typed copy of the book | : manuscript |
| A record of events for future use, note to help the memory | : memorandum |
| To write a given passage in slightly different language/expression | : paraphrase |
| The culminating part of a speech | : paroration |
| The main character in a play or novel | : protagonist |

| | |
|---|---|
| Speaking one's thought alone on the stage (in a play) | : soliloquy |
| Collection of views of several persons on a topic | : symposium |

## VIII. Legal and Commercial Words

| | |
|---|---|
| A written statement given on oath | : affidavit |
| The plea in a criminal charge claiming to be somewhere else at the time of crime | : alibi |
| Allowance due to wife from husband on separation | : alimony |
| An accomplice in crime committed to give evidence against the co-accused/prisoner | : approver |
| One who files a suit in a court of law | : plaintiff |
| The person who is sued | : defendant/ respondent |
| One who gives a statement in the court relating to the case | : witness |
| A temporary order that prevents arrival and departure of ships | : embargo |
| Relating to state finances/ public revenue | : fiscal |
| A written malicious statement | : libel |
| The act of altering a written document by fraud | : forgery |
| Suspension of payments of debts temporarily by Government | : moratorium |

| | |
|---|---|
| Propaganda or talk urging people to revolt | : sedition |
| A judicial decision in favour of somebody | : decree |
| A document produced in court as evidence | : exhibit |
| Connected with scientific tests used by the police while solving a crime | : forensic |
| Bungle public money by fraud to one's own use | : embezzle |
| A legal inquiry to ascertain a fact in some matter | : inquest |
| One who is unable to repay his debts | : insolvent |
| A sum of money given by a will | : legacy |
| Something held or given in trust | : fiduciary |
| A call to appear before a judge or magistrate | : summon |
| To conform a statement/fact/ contention by signature | : ratify |
| To indulge in counter charges/ allegation | : recriminate |
| The right to keep possession of a particular property/balance in an account, etc. till a debt is repaid | : lien |
| A person under legal guardianship | : ward |
| To leave property, etc. by will to somebody | : bequeath |
| A supplement to a will | : codicil |

| | |
|---|---|
| The seizure of goods by orders of a court | : attachment |
| Settling disputes through disinterested parties | : arbitration |
| Redemption of public debt | : amortisation |
| An undertaking to make good any possible loss or damage | : indemnity |
| List of topics to be discussed at a meeting | : agenda |
| Brief summary of the proceedings of an official meeting | : minutes |
| Money paid to a shareholder from company's profit | : dividend |
| A document signed by a shareholder authorising another person to vote on his behalf at company's annual meeting | : proxy |
| Offer to supply certain goods at a particular (offered) rate | : tender |
| Shares held in a person's demat account in a depository | : holding |
| Fixed sum of money paid annually for a fixed term | : annuity |
| The area over which an official has control | : jurisdiction |

## IX. Words of Military Warfare

| | |
|---|---|
| An unprovoked act of hostility | : aggression |
| A general pardon given by an authority | : amnesty |

| | |
|---|---|
| An agreement during a war to stop fighting | : armistice |
| A manufactory or stockpile of military warfare | : arsenal |
| Heavy guns mounted on carriages, etc. | : artillery |
| Army unit consisting of several troops | : battalion |
| A barrier formed by heavy, continuous gunfire | : barrage |
| A short sharp sword fixed on the end of a firearm | : bayonet |
| A nation which engages itself in a war | : belligerent |
| To surround a place with armed soldiers | : besiege |
| The resting of soldiers at night in the open air | : bivouac |
| The surrounding of a place by troops to keep the goods/people from entering/leaving | : blockade |
| To surrender on certain conditions | : capitulate |
| Soldiers mounted on horse | : cavalry |
| Compulsory enrolment for military service | : conscription |
| Ships of war under escort | : convoy |
| Speedy warship meant to locate and destroy enemy ships | : cruiser |
| To release from military service | : demobilise |

| | |
|---|---|
| The practice of spying or using spies to know enemy's plans, etc. | : espionage |
| To remove people from a place or district to avoid destruction of war | : evacuate |
| Military force stationed in a fortress | : garrison |
| Causing destruction to both the sides | : internecine |
| Foot soldiers in the army | : infantry |
| Military supplies | : munitions |
| Heavy guns and military store | : ordnance |
| The activity of getting information about an area for attacking it, etc. | : recce |
| Military examination of a tract to locate army | : reconnaissance |
| to go near enemy territory to learn about their territory | : reconnaitre |
| A newly enlisted soldier | : recruit |
| A large permanent unit of the army | : regiment |
| Return to one's native land | : repatriate |
| Simultaneous discharge of firearms to mark an occasion | : salvo |

## X. Words Pertaining to Marriage

| | |
|---|---|
| An engagement to marry | : betrothal |
| Having two wives or husbands at one time | : bigamy |
| One who is unmarried/has taken a vow not to marry | : celibate |

| | |
|---|---|
| To run away with a lover to get married secretly | : elope |
| One with who one is engaged to marry | : fiancee |
| A hater of marriage | : misogamist |
| Being married to more than one person at a time | : polygamy |

## XI. Miscellaneous Words

| | |
|---|---|
| The boy in the stage of growth between boyhood and youth | : adolescent |
| The science or philosophy of beauty | : aesthetics |
| One who holds the belief that nothing can be known about God | : agnostic |
| One having the faculty of using both his hands equally well | : ambidextrous |
| Having the power of living in two elements, air and water | : amphibious |
| One who excites disorder in a state | : anarchist |
| A substance which has the power of depriving one of feeling or sensation | : anaesthetic |
| Any error which implies the misplacing of persons or events in time | : anachronism |
| A plant that grows in water | : aquatic |
| One who does not profess faith in God | : atheist |

| | |
|---|---|
| Personal observation in medical science, post-mortem examination | : autopsy |
| A lover of books | : bibliophile |
| A person blindly attached to any opinion | : bigot |
| Impiously irreverent or reproachful towards God/religion | : blasphemous |
| A woman of very fair complexion with light hair and light blue eyes | : blonde |
| A man, with brown or dark complexion with dark eyes and dark hair | : braggart |
| A human being that eats human flesh; a man-eater | : cannibal |
| One who is well-versed in the facts relating to the heart | : cardiologist |
| An animal that eats or feeds on flesh | : carnivorous |
| A roundabout way of speaking | : circumlocution |
| Morbid fear of confined spaces | : claustrophobia |
| One competent to pass critical judgement upon anything | : connoisseur |
| One living at the same time | : contemporary |
| The gradual recovery of health and strength after disease | : convalescence |
| One who is at home everywhere; a citizen of the world | : cosmopolitan |
| Anything which has lost its force, by lapse of time or any other cause, and has ceased to be acted on | : dead-letter |

| | |
|---|---|
| One who believes in the existence of God but denies revelation, generally implying a certain antagonism to Christianity | : deist |
| One who is well-versed in the science which treats the skin and its diseases | : dermatologist |
| A place where one lives permanently | : domicile |
| That which is fit to be eaten | : edible |
| One having the qualities of woman instead of those of a man | : effeminate |
| One who is hard to please | : fastidious |
| The murder of a brother | : fratricide |
| One who talks excessively | : garrulous |
| Killing of a whole race | : genocide |
| Medicine that kills germs | : germicide |
| (Animals) subsisting on plants | : herbivorous |
| The killing of one man by another | : homicide |
| Possessing a title, or post, without performing services or without receiving benefit or reward | : honorary |
| One characterised by exaggerated uneasiness or anxiety, mainly as to what concerns one's health | : hypochondriac |
| One who makes attacks upon established beliefs | : iconoclast |
| A personal peculiarity of constitution or temperament | : idiosyncrasy |

| | |
|---|---|
| (A writing) incapable of being read | : illegible |
| Incapable of being moved by force | : impregnable |
| Something that is not likely—impossible | : improbable |
| That which cannot be heard | : inaudible |
| Incapable of being corrected or amended | : incorrigible |
| That which cannot be believed | : incredible |
| Incapable of being fatigued; untiring | : indefatigable |
| Incapable of being effaced, or cancelled, or obliterated | : indelible |
| That which cannot be explained | : inexplicable |
| Something which is relentless, continuous | : inexorable |
| Not capable of erring or falling into error | : infallible |
| Capable of being set on fire; combustible | : inflammable |
| That which cannot be imitated | : inimitable |
| That which is harmless | : innocuous |
| That which comes at the wrong time | : inopportune |
| That which cannot be defeated; unconquerable | : invincible |
| Incapable of being seen | : invisible |
| One who knows several languages | : linguist |
| A continual talker; garrulous | : loquacious |
| The state of being married | : matrimony |

| | |
|---|---|
| One who is greedy of gain | : mercenary |
| One who is too careful or fastidious | : meticulous |
| A substance which relieves pain, produces sleep, and in large doses brings stupor, coma and even death | : narcotic |
| One versed in neurology, the branch of science which treats disorder of the nerves | : neurologist |
| Out of fashion | : obsolete |
| One skilled in the art of midwifery or the delivery of women in childbed | : obstetrician |
| One skilled in the disease of the eyes | : oculist |
| One who is all powerful—used generally for God | : omnipotent |
| One who is present everywhere —God | : omnipresent |
| A government official whose job is to examine the complaints of people | : ombudsman |
| suggesting that something bad is going to happen | : ominous |
| One having knowledge of everything | : omniscient |
| Impervious to the rays of light; not transparent | : opaque |
| One versed in the branch of science which deals with the eyes | : opthalmologist |
| Showy; intended for vain display | : ostentatious |

| | |
|---|---|
| One favouring the policy of peace | : pacifist |
| A remedy for all diseases | : panacea |
| The doctrine that the universe, taken or conceived of as a whole, is God, and that all things are simply modes or manifestations of God | : pantheism |
| A utopian community in which all the members are equal in rank and social position | : pantiscracy |
| One that frequents the tables of the rich and earns his welcome by flattery: a hanger-on | : parasite |
| One versed in the nature of diseases, their causes and symptoms | : pathologist |
| A person who makes a vain display of his learning, but is devoid of taste; one devoted exclusively to system of rules | : pedant |
| The act of wilfully making a false oath in a judicial proceeding; the act of violating an oath or solemn promise | : perjury |
| One who flirts with ladies | : philanderer |
| One who exerts oneself in doing good to one's fellowmen; a person of general benevolence | : philanthropist |
| A person of narrow views and tastes | : philistine |
| The crime of literary theft; stealing the words or ideas of others and passing them off as one's own | : plagiarism |

| | |
|---|---|
| The power or rule of wealth | : plutocracy |
| An examination of a body made after death | : post-mortem |
| A child born after the death of his father | : posthumous |
| Something, e,g. water that is suitable for drinking | : potable |
| A child that is developed or matured before time | : precocious |
| A name assumed by a writer; a false or assumed name | : pseudonym |
| Four children born at the same time, to the same mother | : quadruplets |
| Five children born at the same time, to the same mother | : quintuplets |
| One who defies and seeks to overthrow the authority to which he is rightfully subject | : rebel |
| A person who adheres pedantically to the forms and routine of office | : red-tapist |
| The murder, or murderer, of a king | : regicide |
| The violation or profaning of sacred things; the stealing of goods out of any church or chapel | : sacrilege |
| One who takes pleasure in the cruel treatment of the companion; a sexual pervert | : sadist |
| An ill-tempered woman | : shrew |
| Any office which has revenue without employment | : sinecure |

| | |
|---|---|
| Taking place or happening at the same time | : simultaneous |
| One who is skilled in the science which investigates the laws that regulate human society in all its grades | : sociologist |
| A disease which consists of an eruption tubercles on the bearded portion of the face and on the scalp | : sycosis |
| One who is habitually silent | : taciturn |
| One who believes in the existence of God | : theist |
| That which transmits rays of light, but not so as to render the form or colour of objects beyond distinctly visible | : translucent |
| Of one voice; of one mind | : unanimous |
| A person of infirm body or sickly constitution | : valetudinarian |
| Wilful or ignorant destruction of works of art or literature; hostility to art or literature | : vandalism |
| That may be forgiven; excusable | : venial |
| Word for word | : verbatim |
| Abounding in words—using more words that are necessary | : verbose |
| Something done of one's own accord or free will; spontaneous | : voluntary |

# 12

## WORD FORMATION

English is a vast language with a large vocabulary. It is, however, neither feasible nor necessary to mug up all kinds of words. What is required is to have a decent range and the art of to use the right words in the right context to express ourselves. In this regard, a knowledge of nature of words, the prefixes and suffixes that form words proves extremely useful in written as well as spoken English.

In English we have (i) primary words and (ii) derived words. The primary words are not derived from or compounded with other words. The derived words are formed in the following ways:

(i) By combining two or more words, as: cottonseed, greenhouse, breakaway, classroom, silkworm, etc. They are called compound words.

(ii) By changing the forms of words such as: clarity from clear, success from succeed, national from nation, statement from state, etc. They are known as primary derivatives.

(iii) By adding some prefix or suffix to other words like: predict, non-entity, counteract, withdraw, boyhood, sidelong, hopeful, etc. They are known as secondary derivatives.

## 1.  Compound Words

They are mostly nouns, adjectives or verbs. They are formed by the following combinations:

(i)   Noun + noun as:
      tea-pot, inkpot, goalkeeper, anthill, spiderweb, screwdriver.

(ii)  Noun + verb as:
      nightfall, snowfall, earthquake, headache.

(iii) Noun + gerund, as:
      horse-riding, shoe-making, net-surfing, policy-making, sky-diving.

(iv)  Adjective + noun, as:
      redcross, sweetmeat, blacksheep, whitehouse, darkroom.

(v)   Verb + noun, as:
      drawback, push-button, cut-piece

(vi)  Gerund + noun, as:
      cutting-edge, living-being, flying-saucer, booking-window.

(vii) Adverb + noun, as:
      backyard, front-door, overtone.

(viii) Adverb + verb, as
      outcome, output, outlive, outline, withstand.

## 2.  Primary Derivatives

The knowledge of primary derivatives is necessary for the right use of words in written as well as spoken English. Using *practise* as a noun and *advice* as a verb is a common pitfall because of lack of such knowledge and creates an unfavouarble impression at any mode or level of conversation. Some important primary derivatives are therefore listed below:

## (i)  Formation of Nouns from Verbs

| Verb | Noun | Verb | Noun |
|------|------|------|------|
| abide | abode | abound | abundance |
| admit | admission | agree | agreement |
| attend | attendance | bind | bound |
| break | breach | chop | chip |
| deceive | deceipt | dig | ditch |
| envelop | envelope | expel | expulsion |
| float | fleet | flight | flight |
| lend | loan | live | life |
| move | motion | offend | offence |
| parctise | practice | prove | proof |
| speak | speech | strive | strife |
| succeed | success | think | thought |
| trace | track | urge | urgency |
| wake | watch | write | writ |
| weigh | weight | | |

## (ii)  Formation of Nouns from Adjectives

| Adjective | Noun | Adjective | Noun |
|-----------|------|-----------|------|
| able | ability | adequate | adequacy |
| civil | civility | cowardly | cowardice |
| ferocious | ferocity | frequent | frequency |
| high | height | liberal | liberty |
| necessary | necessity | notorious | notoriety |
| pious | piety | prudent | prudence |
| real | reality | rival | rivalry |

| | | | |
|---|---|---|---|
| rigid | rigidity | round | roundness |
| royal | royalty | scarce | scarcity |
| secret | secrecy | solitary | solitude |
| splendid | splendour | true | truth |
| vain | vanity | vacant | vacancy |
| wide | width | wise | wisdom |
| young | youth | | |

## (iii) Formation of Verbs from Nouns

| Noun | Verb | Noun | Verb |
|---|---|---|---|
| advice | advise | apology | apologize |
| bath | bathe | blood | bleed |
| brass | braze | breath | breathe |
| brood | breed | cloth | clothe |
| deity | deify | food | feed |
| glass | glaze | grass | graze |
| heir | inherit | island | insulate |
| knot | knit | mass | amass |
| practice | practise | utility | utilize |
| vice | vitiate | wreath | wreathe |

## (iv) Formation of Verbs from Adjectives

| Adjective | Verb | Adjective | Verb |
|---|---|---|---|
| able | enable | hale | heal |
| abundant | abound | clear | clarify |
| civil | civilize | clean | cleanse |
| deep | deepen | double | duplicate |
| fine | refine | foul | defile |

| cool | chill | full | fill |
| hale | heal | public | publish |
| rare | rarefy | right | rectify |
| special | specialize | stupid | stupefy |
| just | justify | | |

## (v) Formation of Adjectives from Nouns

| Noun | Adjective | Noun | Adjective |
|------|-----------|------|-----------|
| advice | advisable | anger | angry |
| bound | binding | brass | brazen |
| courage | courageous | example | exemplary |
| essence | essential | fame | famous |
| friend | friendly | fury | furious |
| heat | hot | heir | hereditary |
| hour | hourly | industry | industrious |
| machine | mechanical | transparency | transparent |

## (vi) Formation of Adjectives from Verbs

| Verb | Adjective | Verb | Adjective |
|------|-----------|------|-----------|
| abound | abudnant | advise | advisable |
| account | accountable | eat | eatable |
| move | movable | succeed | successful |

## 3. Secondary Derivatives

The secondary derivatives are formed by adding prefixes or suffixes as simple words. The prefixes and suffixes can be English, Latin or Greek. The major words with them are given below:

## (i) English Prefixes

A — (on, in) adrift, ajar, akin, asleep.

A — (out, from) alight, abound, arise.

Be — (by) beside, besides, besmirch, beguile.

For — (thoroughly) forsake, forbear, forward.

Fore — (before) forecast, forebode.

In — (in) income, instil, inland, inseminate.

Mis — (wrong) misappropriate, miscarriage, misuse, misdeed, misjudge, misdemeanour, mismatch.

Over — (above) overcast, overload, overflow, overthrow.

To — (this) today, tonight, towards, together.

Un — (not) unhealthy, unkind, unkempt, unbecoming.

Un — (reverse action) undo, unfold, unwind.

Under — (below, beneath) undergo, undercharge, underperform, underestimate.

## (ii) Greek Prefixes

A, An — (without) abate, atheist, anarchy.

Amphi — (around) amphibian, amphitheatre.

Anti — (against) anti-clockwise, antidote.

Apo—, Ap— (from) apology, apposition.

Arch—, Archi— (chief) archbishop, arch-rival, architect.

Auto—(self) autobiography, autocrat, auto-cut, automatic.

Cata—(down) cataract, catalogue, catapult.

Di—(double) dilemma, diurnal.

Dia—(through) diameter, diaphragm, diagonal, diaspora.

En—, Em (in) encyclopaedia, embodiment, emblem.

Epi — (upon) epidermis, epilogue, epitaph.

Ex–, Ec — (out of) exodus, eccentric, exigency.

Hemi–, (half) hemisphere.

Homo–, Hom — (like) homogenous, homogeneity.

Hypo — (under) hypodermis, hypocrite, hypothesis.

Meta, Met — (denoting change) metaphor, metaphysical.

Para — (beside) parabola, parallel, parable, paradox.

Peri — (round) periphery, period, perimeter, periscope.

Philo, Phil — (love) philosophy, philology.

Pro — (before) proactive, probable, prophecy, programme, pronoun.

Syn, Sym Sy, Syl — (together) synonym, symbol, sympathy, system, syllabus, syllable.

## (iii) **Latin Prefixes**

Ab (away) : abuse, across, abound, abstraction.

Ad-Ac-Af-Ap-As-Ar (to): adjoining, account, affect, appoint, assert, arrive.

Ambi-Amb-Am (around): ambition, ambivalent, ambiguity, amass.

Ante–, Anti, An (before): ante chamber, antecedents, anticipate.

Bene– (well): benedict, benefit, benevolent.

Bi– (two): biscuit, bisect, binoculars, bi-focal.

Circum, Circu (around): circumstances, circumspect, circumnavigate, circular.

Con-Col, Com, Cor (together): content, collection, comrade, correction.

Contra, -Counter- (against): contraband, counteract, contradict, countermand.

De – (down): debase, depose, defect, deregulate, derail, destabilise.

Dis, Di, Dif (apart): disband, differ, disgust, divide.

Demi (half): demigod.

Extra (beyond): extra-curricular, extra-mural, extraordinary, extravagant.

In– Il, Im, Ir, En, Em (into): instil, infiltrate, illusion, illustration, irrigation, enrich, embark.

In–Il–Im–Ir (not): invalid, illiterate, impractical, immature, irrational, irrelevant.

Inter–, Intro–, Enter–(within, among): interact, introduce, intertwine, internecine, entertain.

Male–, Mal– (bad): maladjustment, maladvice, malcontent, malevolence.

Post– (after): postgraduate, post-date posthumous, postpone, post-independence, post-colonial.

Pre– (before): predated, predict, pre-ordainted, pre-planned, prefix, premature, pre-natal.

Pro– (for): propound, promote, pronoun, progeny, propel.

Re– (again, back): rebuild, recount, redress, research, rebound, rellocate, regain, rejoin, remind.

Semi (half): semi-circle, semi-colon.

Sub (under): subdue, subject, subordinate, sub-judge, sub-inspector, submissive, subvert.

Super (above): superannuation, superfine, supervision, superfluous.

Trans (across): transport, trans-world, transgress, transcription.

Vice (in place of): vice-chairman, vice-chancellor, vice-president, viceroy, vice-principal.

## (iv) **English Suffixes**

— er- (agent or doer): painter, teacher, lawyer, banker, creeper, sweeper, sculptor.

— ter: father, mother, sister, daughter.

— dom: freedom, wisdom, serfdom.

— hood: boyhood, childhood, manhood, godhood.

— ock, lock: wedlock, padlock, hillock.

— ledge: acknowledge, knowledge.

— ness: goodness, badness, wickedness, selfishness, boldness, frankness, business.

— ship: hardship, friendship, partnership, kinship, authorship.

— th: health, wealth, growth, stealth.

— el, le: mentel, satchel, kernel, handle, ramble.

— en: maiden, kitten, chicken.

— let: drumlet, booklet, leaflet.

— ling: duckling, sapling, inkling, weakling.

— ed (having): talented, gifted, renowned, learned, planned, armed.

— en (made of): golden, wooden, brazen, silken, frozen, woollen, earthen.

— ful (full of): hopeful, mirthful, joyful, fruitful, lawful, spiteful, wilful, hateful.

— less (without): baseless, careless, fearless, shameless, hopeless, senseless, treeless, waterless, leafless, sleeveless, priceless.

— ly- (like): manly, motherly, godly, happily, gaily, freely, blindly.

— some (with the quality of): burdensome, lonesome, wholesome, meddlesome, quarrelsome.

— ward (inclined to): inward, outward, homeward, forward, wayward.

— en (forming verbs): awaken, broaden, weaken, gladden, quicken, widen, sweeten.

— ly (like): cutely, boldly, firmly, slyly, shyly, wisely.

— way, ways (towards): always, anyway, straightway, subway, highway, sideways.

— wise (manner): serialwise, likewise, page-wise, otherwise.

Of all the English suffixes, *er, hood, ness, ship, full, less, some and ward* are the most powerful as a large number of derivatives are formed with them.

## (v) Greek Suffixes

— ic: angelic, poetic, civic, cynic.

— ique: beautique, critique, unique.

— ist: artist, racist, chemist, alchemist, dentist.

— ism, asm: despotism, patriotism, racism, enthusiasm.

— ize: civilize, criticize, synchronize, synthesize.

— sis: crisis, nemesis, analysis, paralysis, dialysis.

— sy: poesy, heresy.

## (vi) Latin Suffixes

(a) *those denoting Doer of Something*

— ain, an, en, on: captain, chieftain, artisan, citizen, surgeon.

— ar, er: scholar, polar, teacher, preacher, engineer, baker.

—or: emperor, warrior, governor.

(b) *those denoting a State or Action*

— age: breakage, brokerage, bondage, cartage, leakage, marriage, carriage.

— ance, ence: abundance, askance, attendance, assistance, brilliance, pretence, dependence.

— cy: accuracy, accountancy, lunacy, fallacy.

— ion: action, motion, notion, portion, opinion.

— ment: merriment, judgement, astonishment, shipment.

— ty: civility, brutality, frailty, ability, nobility.

— ure: curvature, brochure, pleasure, venture.

— y: bribery, rosary, missionary, visionary.

(c) *those denoting Place*

— ary-ery-ry: library, treasury, dispensary, colliery.

— ter-tre: cluster, theatre.

(d) *those forming Verbs*

— ate: vacate, oscillate, captivate, vitiate, placate

— fy: signify, qualify, magnify, testify.

— ish: banish, punish, nourish, astonish.

(e) *those forming Adjectives*

— al: accrual, national, legal, regal, penal.

— ar: circular, polar, regular.

— ary: customary, stationary, visionary, binary.

— ate: fortunate, obstinate.

— able-ible, ble: capable, enviable, viable, lovable, sociable, serviceable, gullible.

— id: livid, vivid, candid.

— ine: combine, feminine, divine, proline.

— ous: dangerous, vicious, porous.

**13**

# CHECKING YOUR PROGRESS
## COMPREHENSIVE TEST—2

### (One-Word Substitutes, Word Formation)

If you have read carefully Chapters No. 11 and 12 you have learnt the following:

1. One-word substitutes of various sciences, arts, personality traits, concepts, places, trades.

2. Political, literary, legal, military and several miscellaneous words.

3. Formation of various words having English, Greek and Latin prefixes, and suffixes.

Your score in the test that follows shall be an indication of your progress. Answers are given at the end.

**I.** ***A.*** *Fill in the blanks with one word that can replace the statement.*

   1. Wide road with trees on each end _____

   2. A street closed at one end     _____

3. Place where public/govt. records are kept

_____

4. Place where public revenues are kept

_____

5. One who studies the evolution of mankind

_____

6. One who sells goods to the highest bidder at public sale     _____

7. Woman hired to clean offices     _____

8. An official incharge of a museum

_____

9. One who writes a dictionary     _____

10. One who attends horses at an inn

_____

11. One who loads/unloads ships in a harbour

_____

12. One who deals in carpets, curtains, etc.

_____

**B.   Fill in the blanks with one-word substitute.**

13. A coward who is brutal when there is no risk to him.     _____

14. One who dabbles in matters of art

_____

15. One who passes himself off as someone else

_____

16. One who hates mankind     _____

17. One who prefers to stay alone and avoids people

_____

18. One who is indifferent to pain and pleasure

_____

19. An uncultured person whose interests are purely material _____

20. One who bootlicks rich men _____

21. One who is indifferent to virtue and decency

_____

22. One who always expects failure _____

23. One who lives and acts for the welfare of others

_____

24. Idealist but impractical _____

II. **A.** *Find the correct option that matches the given statement:*

1. A person who buys or uses a particular product or service
   - (a) punter
   - (b) curator
   - (c) ward
   - (d) philistine

2. One whose thoughts are turned inward
   - (a) extrovert
   - (b) entrovert
   - (c) introvert
   - (d) quixotic

3. The science of sound
   - (a) ballary
   - (b) acoustics
   - (c) verbose
   - (d) screech

4. The science of colours
   - (a) astronomy
   - (b) ballistics
   - (c) genealogy
   - (d) chromatics

5. Science of morals
   - (a) morality
   - (b) ethics
   - (c) amorology
   - (d) moralism

6. The art of growing plants in chemical solution, without soil:
   - (a) hydrology
   - (b) floriculture
   - (c) faunery
   - (d) hydroponics

7. The study of mountains
   - (a) oology
   - (b) hillogy
   - (c) orology
   - (d) topology

8. The science of teaching
   - (a) pedagogy
   - (b) philology
   - (c) professorship
   - (d) readership

9. The art of making fireworks
   - (a) pyrotechnics
   - (b) pyrology
   - (c) litology
   - (d) firology

10. Belief that one's nation is the only good nation in the world
    - (a) jargon
    - (b) nationalism
    - (c) stoicism
    - (d) jingoism

11. Leadership of one state in a group of states
    - (a) leadership
    - (b) hegemony
    - (c) oligarchy
    - (d) annexation

12. The time between two reigns
    - (a) interval
    - (b) interregnum
    - (c) recluse
    - (d) nexus

13. A speech by a player at the end of a play
    - (a) prologue
    - (b) index
    - (c) epilogue
    - (d) appendix

14. To remove improper or objectionable portion from a book
    - (a) edit
    - (b) rectify
    - (c) depurgate
    - (d) expurgate

15. One who files a suit in a court of law
    - (a) plaintiff
    - (b) dependent
    - (c) respondent
    - (d) witness

**16.** Something held in trust
- (a) legacy
- (b) inquest
- (c) fiduciary
- (d) liar

**B.** *Fill in the blanks with suitable words:*

17. He voted in the meeting on _____

18. I had to prepare an _____ for the meeting.

19. The two warring nations reached an _____.

20. The soldiers laid a _____ on the town.

21. The girl _____ with her lover.

22. My brother is an _____; he bowls left-handed and bats right-handed.

23. Gandhi and Nehru were _____.

24. My brother is _____; it is difficult to please him.

25. _____ oils are no longer cheap.

26. This remedy is a _____ for many ills.

**III. A.** *Mention nouns of the following verbs:*

1. abide
2. abound
3. float
4. dig
5. urge
6. solitary
7. chop
8. wake
9. move
10. envelop

**B.** *Mention at least two words each with the following English prefixes.*

1. be (by)
2. for (thoroughly)
3. over (above)
4. un (not)
5. under (below)

*C.* *Mention at least two words each with the following Latin suffixes:*

1. ain (doer of things)
2. age (state or action)
3. ion (state)
4. er/re (place)
5. ure (state)

## ANSWERS

I.  (A)  1. avenue; 2. cul-de-sac; 3. archives; 4. treasury;
5. anthropologist; 6. auctioneer; 7. charwoman;
8. curator; 9. lexicographer; 10. ostler,
11. stevedor; 12. upholsterer.

(B)  13. dastard; 14. dilettante; 15. imposter;
16. misanthrope; 17. recluse; 18. stoic;
19. philistine; 20. sycophant; 21. profligate;
22. defeatist; 23. altruist; 24. quixotic.

II.  (A)  1. a; 2. (c); 3. (b); 4. (d); 5. (b); 6. (d); 7. (c); 8. (a);
9. (a); 10. (d); 11. (b); 12. (b); 13. (c); 14. (d).
15. (a); 16. (c)

(B)  17. proxy; 18. agenda; 19. armistice; 20. besiege;
21. eloped; 22. ambidextrous; 23. contemporaries;
24. fastidious; 25. Edible; 26. panacea.

III. (A)  1. aboad; 2. abundance; 3. fleet; 4. ditch;
5. urgency; 6. solitude; 7. chip; 8. watch; 9. motion;
10. envelope.

(B)  1. beside, besmirch; 2. forgo, forbear; 3. overcast,
overload; 4. unkind, unkempt; 5. undergo,
underperform.

(C)  1. captain, chieftain; 2. brokerage, bondage;
3. notion, opinion; 4. theatre, cluster; 5. pleasure,
venture.

# 14

## SYNONYMS
### (Words Similar in Meaning)

English language has a vast vocabulary. There are several words to express different shades of similar meaning—which brings variety in expression and enables us to convey exactly what is intended.

Given below are some important words and their synonyms. A knowledge thereof will help you in the following ways:

- Reinforce your word power.

- Help you better comprehend speeches, lectures, conversations, dialogues, news, write-ups, texts—whatever you listen or read in English.

- Help you avoid repetition in your writing.

- Make your conversation influential.

- Make your write-ups—whether academic or professional—precise and emphatic.

## A

**Abandon**    :    relinquish, forsake, renounce, desert

| | | |
|---|---|---|
| **Abnormal** | : | unusual, exceptional, irregular |
| **Ability** | : | capability, skill, competence |
| **Abstain** | : | refrain, avoid |
| **Abridge** | : | shorten, summarise, condense |
| **Accuse** | : | indict, charge, arraign |
| **Assent** | : | agreement, consent |
| **Allow** | : | permit |
| **Avenge** | : | revenge, retaliation |
| **Anger** | : | wrath, fury, indignation, rage |
| **Attain** | : | acquire, get, gain |
| **Ancient** | : | old, antique |
| **Accomplish** | : | achieve, fulfil, complete, execute |
| **Actual** | : | real, tangible |
| **Abstruse** | : | occult, obscure, recondite |
| **Accommodate** | : | adopt, adjust, oblige |
| **Authentic** | : | real, actual, genuine |
| **Active** | : | agile, smart, industrious, hustling |
| **Adequate** | : | proper, sufficient, commensurate |
| **Admire** | : | applaud, appreciate, praise, extol |
| **Advantage** | : | benefit, gain, usefulness |
| **Ambition** | : | aim, aspiration, goal, objective |
| **Amiable** | : | amicable, pleasing, friendly |
| **Announce** | : | proclaim, declare, herald |
| **Applicable** | : | suitable, appropriate, apt, fit |
| **Ardent** | : | fervent, eager, intense |
| **Arrogant** | : | proud, haughty, presumptuous, impudent |

| | | |
|---|---|---|
| **Assurance** | : | confidence, ensurance, pledge |
| **Assign** | : | give, allot, consign |
| **Average** | : | ordinary, common |
| **Auspicious** | : | propitious, favourable, fortunate |
| **Awful** | : | terrible, poor, ugly |
| **Awesome** | : | extraordinary, awe-inspiring, excellent |
| **Awkward** | : | clumsy, uncouth, ungainly |
| **Astonishment** | : | surprise, wonder |
| **Amuse** | : | entertain, please, regale, enliven |
| **Amorous** | : | sexual, loving |
| **Attack** | : | invade, assault, assail |
| **Adversity** | : | calamity, disaster, misery |
| **Aversion** | : | hatred, dislike, abhorrence |

## B

| | | |
|---|---|---|
| **Bad** | : | wicked, evil, malicious |
| **Baffle** | : | confuse, confound, foil, puzzle |
| **Bashful** | : | shy, diffident, coy |
| **Barbarious** | : | savage, cruel, uncivilized |
| **Bear** | : | endure, tolerate, suffer, undergo |
| **Beat** | : | defeat, vanquish, thrash, pound, spank |
| **Behaviour** | : | conduct, manners, demeanour |
| **Benefactor** | : | patron, helper, friend |
| **Benevolent** | : | generous, charitable, liberal, kind |
| **Betray** | : | reveal, exhibit, manifest, show |
| **Bewildered** | : | confused, perplexed, dazed, befuddled |

| Bewitching | : | captivating, charming, fascinating, attractive |
| Blame | : | condemn, accuse, convict |
| Bold | : | daring, audacious, valiant, courageous |
| Boisterous | : | noisy, vociferous, blatant |
| Boundless | : | vast, magnanimous |
| Bounty | : | generosity, liberality, magnanimity |
| Brevity | : | briefness, terseness, conciseness |
| Boastful | : | bragging, vainglorious |
| Bias | : | prejudice, preordain, bent |

# C

| Calm | : | peaceful, cool, tranquil, quiet |
| Capacity | : | competence, capability, skill |
| Calamity | : | catastrophe, disaster, vagary, adversity |
| Caprice | : | whim, fantasy, freak |
| Celebrated | : | distinguished, famous, known, noted |
| Celestial | : | divine, heavenly, angelic |
| Childish | : | silly, puerile, unwise |
| Choice | : | preference, selection |
| Coherent | : | constant, connected |
| Colossal | : | huge, monumental, enormous |
| Commodious | : | roomy, spacious, accommodating |
| Companion | : | mate, friend, comrade |
| Complain | : | grumble, growl, remonstrate |
| Complete | : | finish, conclude |

| | | |
|---|---|---|
| **Complex** | : | complicated, intricate |
| **Component** | : | element, ingredient, part, constituent |
| **Conceit** | : | egoism, egotism, vanity |
| **Conflict** | : | strife, skirmish, encounter |
| **Conformity** | : | concurrence, compliance, agreement |
| **Conjecture** | : | guess, supposition, hint |
| **Conscientious** | : | scrupulous, moral |
| **Conscious** | : | aware, cognizant |
| **Consequence** | : | outcome, result, effect |
| **Correspond** | : | agree, answer, harmonise |
| **Corrupt** | : | depraved, vile, vicious |
| **Creditable** | : | praiseworthy, meritorious, honourable |
| **Crude** | : | unripe, unrefined, immature, raw |
| **Cite** | : | quote, refer |
| **Compulsion** | : | obligation, necessity |
| **Confer** | : | bestow, give |
| **Character** | : | conduct, nature, temper, disposition |
| **Contagious** | : | infectious |
| **Cool** | : | cold, relaxed, carefree |
| **Clever** | : | smart, sharp, adroit, crafty, cunning |
| **Caution** | : | warning, watchfulness |
| **Civil** | : | affable, polite, courteous |
| **Comprehend** | : | understand, know, grasp |
| **Comprehensive** | : | detailed, wide |
| **Contrary** | : | opposite, reverse, against |
| **Couple** | : | pair, duo |
| **Customary** | : | usual, conventional, normal |

# D

| | | |
|---|---|---|
| **Decent** | : | decorous, honest, fair, nice |
| **Defiant** | : | stubborn, rebellious, insolent, flagrant |
| **Dark** | : | dismal, gloomy, sad, sombre |
| **Debatable** | : | disputable, questionable, doubtful |
| **Declaration** | : | announcement, assertion, statement |
| **Decrease** | : | diminish, reduce, wane, lessen |
| **Defence** | : | protection, security, resistance, justification |
| **Deficient** | : | lacking, wanting, insufficient |
| **Definite** | : | exact, precise, defined, distinct |
| **Delicious** | : | tasty, palatable, pleasing |
| **Destroy** | : | devastate, demolish, raze, annihilate |
| **Despotic** | : | tyrannical, autocratic, domineering |
| **Detrimental** | : | injurious, harmful, obnoxious |
| **Desire** | : | wish, want, need, longing |
| **Difficult** | : | hard, tortuous, trying, troublesome |
| **Discord** | : | dispute, disagreement, dissonance, dissension |
| **Disease** | : | illness, ailment, malady, sickness |
| **Distinct** | : | clear, definite, marked, separate |
| **Distinguished** | : | noted, illustrious, famous, eminent |
| **Droop** | : | drop, bend, pine |
| **Deceit** | : | trickery, deception, fraud, guile, vile |
| **Dirty** | : | shabby, untidy, slovenly, filthy, dusty |
| **Dull** | : | slow, stupid, insipid, sluggish |

| | | |
|---|---|---|
| **Despair** | : | disappointment, frustration |
| **Dangerous** | : | hazardous, perilous |
| **Despise** | : | hate, scorn, disdain |
| **Delusion** | : | illusion, misunderstanding |
| **Disaster** | : | calamity, mishap |
| **Daring** | : | bold, courageous, lion-hearted |
| **Discriminate** | : | distinguish, separate |

## E

| | | |
|---|---|---|
| **Eager** | : | keen, enthusiastic, ardent, fervent, impetuous |
| **Ease** | : | repose, rest, relax |
| **Endeavour** | : | attempt, try, strive, task |
| **Encourage** | : | inspire, hearten, motivate, stimulate, cheer, buck up |
| **Endless** | : | boundless, infinite, limitless, countless |
| **Endowed** | : | gifted, talented |
| **Ephemeral** | : | transient, fleeting, temporary, evanescent, short-lived |
| **Equivocal** | : | questionable, doubtful, dubious |
| **Esteem** | : | regard, pride, honour, value |
| **Eternal** | : | everlasting, perpetual, infinite, undying, immortal |
| **Evidence** | : | proof, testimony, sign |
| **Explicit** | : | clear, evident, obvious, definite |
| **Extraordinary** | : | exceptional, unusual, remarkable |
| **Extravagant** | : | wasteful, prodigal, excessive |

| **Exultation** | : | joy, cheerfulness, gaiety, mirth, happiness |
| **Enough** | : | sufficient, adequate, ample |
| **Earthy** | : | wordily, mundane, corporeal, terrestrial, material |

# F

| **Frank** | : | candid, free, open, straightforward |
| **Fear** | : | dread, scare, fright, horror, awe, terror |
| **Flatter** | : | coax, wheedle |
| **Fault** | : | defect, weakness, flaw, demerit, blemish, transgression |
| **False** | : | untrue, fictitious, counterfeit, spurious |
| **Face** | : | countenance, look, appearance, visage, mien |
| **Force** | : | compel, constrain, oblige, strength, power |
| **Faithfulness** | : | fidelity, loyalty, constancy |
| **Fabulous** | : | incredible, fantastic, unbelievable |
| **Fame** | : | glory, reputation, greatness |
| **Favour** | : | goodwill, boon, privilege |
| **Fickle** | : | capricious, oscillating, changing, unconstant |
| **Fervour** | : | zeal, enthusiasm, spirit |
| **Foresight** | : | prudence, forethought |
| **Fortitude** | : | courage, heroism, boldness, endurance |
| **Futile** | : | fruitless, useless, vain, ineffectual |

## G

| | | |
|---|---|---|
| **Gallant** | : | courageous, bold, venturesome |
| **Generous** | : | liberal, benevolent, munificent, kind |
| **Garrulous** | : | talkative, chatterbox, verbose, loquacious |
| **Genial** | : | warm, cordial, hearty |
| **Gorgeous** | : | showy, sexy, splendid, magnificent |
| **Grant** | : | allow, concede, permit |
| **Grudge** | : | ill will, malice, spite, animosity |
| **Gentle** | : | kind, mild |
| **Grateful** | : | indebted, thankful |
| **Grand** | : | magnificent, superb, majestic, stately, lofty, sublime |
| **Greedy** | : | avaricious, rapacious, covetous |

## H

| | | |
|---|---|---|
| **Haste** | : | hurry, dash, spurt, rush, scramble |
| **Harbour** | : | shelter, support, a port |
| **Hate** | : | scorn, despise, abominate, abhor, detest |
| **Hinder** | : | hamper, obstruct, impede, thwart |
| **Habitual** | : | regular, customary, usual |
| **Handy** | : | convenient, useful, dexterous, convenient |
| **Harmony** | : | concord, agreement, consent, unison |
| **Heedful** | : | careful, mindful, prudent |

| | | |
|---|---|---|
| **Hesitation** | : | reluctance, doubt, uncertainty |
| **Holy** | : | sacred, pure, divine, saintly, godly |
| **Honesty** | : | fairness, sincerity, integrity |
| **Huge** | : | big, enormous, colossal, monumental, immense |

# I

| | | |
|---|---|---|
| **Idle** | : | lazy, futile, unoccupied, unemployed |
| **Ignorant** | : | illiterate, uneducated, unknowing |
| **Idiocy** | : | foolishness, imbecility, stupidity |
| **Illusive** | : | misleading, deceptive, deceitful |
| **Imminent** | : | near, at hand, close, impending |
| **Imperative** | : | urgent, pressing, essential, necessary |
| **Implore** | : | beseech, request, pray, entreat, beg |
| **Imposter** | : | deceptive, fraud, fake |
| **Impudent** | : | insolent, arrogant, impertinent |
| **Incentive** | : | encouragement, motivation |
| **Incense** | : | inflame, irritate, exasperate |
| **Incomparable** | : | matchless, unrivalled, unequal |
| **Indecorous** | : | indecent, unbecoming |
| **Industrious** | : | diligent, persevering, hardworking |
| **Inference** | : | deduction, conclusion, hint, idea |
| **Insolence** | : | arrogance, rudeness |
| **Intrepid** | : | bold, fearless, dauntless |
| **Inviting** | : | charming, tempting, alluring, captivating, enthralling |

| **Irksome** | : | wearisome, tedious, irritating, vexatious |
| **Ironic** | : | satirical, sarcastic, unjustified |

## J

| **Jeer** | : | mock, scoff, joke, snear |
| **Joy** | : | happiness, merriment, |
| **Judgment** | : | decision, opinion |
| **Judicious** | : | wise, prudent, thoughtful |
| **Justice** | : | equity, fairness |
| **Juvenile** | : | youthful, childish |

## K

| **Kill** | : | slay, assassinate, murder, decimate |
| **Know** | : | understand, comprehend |
| **Keepsake** | : | souvenir, memento, remembrance |

## L

| **Lag** | : | linger, delay, lax |
| **Latent** | : | hidden, implicit, dormant |
| **Leave** | : | quit, abandon, desert, renounce, relinquish |
| **Legendary** | : | mythical, fabulous |
| **Let** | : | allow, permit |
| **Likely** | : | probable, presumable, credible |
| **Liking** | : | fondness, attraction, inclination |
| **Lofty** | : | high, elevated, soaring, towering |

| Little | : | small, petty, insignificant, diminutive, meagre, wee, tiny |
| Logical | : | reasonable, consistent, fair |
| Lonely | : | solitary, forlorn, single, alone, sequestered, secluded |
| Low | : | mean, base, ignoble, contemptible, indecent, coarse, disgraceful, stooping |
| Ludicrous | : | funny, laughable, comical, droll |
| Linger | : | loiter, stray, wander |
| Libel | : | slander, abuse |
| Luxurious | : | rich, voluptuous, affluent |

# M

| Mad | : | crazy, insane, lunatic, deranged, demented, maniac, rapid |
| Modest | : | shy, bashful, diffident |
| Manifest | : | clear, lain, contained, evident |
| Marriage | : | matrimony, wedding, wedlock, nuptuals |
| Maxim | : | precept, adage, proverb |
| Mediocre | : | average, ordinary, commonplace, inferior |
| Memory | : | recollection, remembrance, reminiscence, retrospection |
| Miserable | : | wretched, woebegone |
| Motive | : | purpose, object, aim |
| Mourn | : | bemoan, lament, grieve, bewail |
| Misfortune | : | affliction, suffering, hardship, adversity, reverse |

## N

| | |
|---|---|
| **Nascent** | : initial, beginning, developing |
| **Necessary** | : needed, needful, required, imperative, essential, requisite, indispensable |
| **News** | : information, tidings, communication |
| **New** | : fresh, modern, recent, novel, neo |
| **Notation** | : idea, coneption, remark |
| **Novice** | : neophyte, beginner, raw, tyro, greenhorn |

## O

| | |
|---|---|
| **Obscure** | : unknown, dark, unintelligible |
| **Observe** | : watch, note, see |
| **Obstacle** | : impediment, roadblock, hindrance, obstruction |
| **Obstinate** | : stubborn, obdurate, headstrong, unyielding, staunch |
| **Occasion** | : time, opportunity, need |
| **Odd** | : strange, curious, eccentric |
| **Opinion** | : idea, view, impression |
| **Ostentation** | : show, display, vaunt, parade |
| **Outrage** | : assault, insult, indignity |
| **Overlook** | : ignore, pardon, condone |
| **Objection** | : opposition, dissent, demur |

## P

| | | |
|---|---|---|
| **Partake** | : | participate, act |
| **Patience** | : | relaxation, resignation, calmness, coolness |
| **Peace** | : | calm, quiet, tranquility, amity, harmony |
| **Please** | : | gladden, amuse, gratify, delight, charm |
| **Poverty** | : | destitution, penury, indigence, want |
| **Praise** | : | laud, applause, appreciation, plaudit |
| **Predict** | : | foretell, prophesise |
| **Pretend** | : | feign, show, dissemble |
| **Pride** | : | arrogance, vanity, haughtiness |
| **Prohibit** | : | forbid, ban, check, stop |
| **Partial** | : | incomplete, imperfect, biased, inclined, prejudiced |
| **Pattern** | : | design, scheme, model, type |
| **Penalty** | : | fine, punishment, forfeiture |
| **Penetration** | : | insight, acumen, discernment |
| **Penitent** | : | repentant, remorseful |
| **Perfect** | : | complete, faultless, sound |
| **Perfume** | : | scent, odour, fragrance, aroma |
| **Period** | : | time, term, era, duration, season |
| **Perceive** | : | comprehend, understand, grasp |
| **Persuade** | : | induce, convince, urge, advise |
| **Pert** | : | impudent, impertinent, saucy, irrelevant |
| **Perverse** | : | wayward, petulant, polluted |
| **Pollute** | : | contaminate, defile, profane, spoil |

| Populous | : | thronged, crowded, populated |
| Posterity | : | progeny, descendants, offspring |
| Precarious | : | uncertain, risky, hazardous |
| Precise | : | exact, definite, firm, to the point |
| Prejudicial | : | inclined, biased, preordained, rigid |
| Preposterous | : | unreasonable, absurd, monstrous |
| Preserve | : | safeguard, save, uphold, protect, maintain |
| Prevalent | : | prevailing, widespread, universal |
| Previous | : | former, prior, preceding |
| Price | : | cost, worth, value |
| Primitive | : | ancient, early, original |
| Principal | : | chief, major, prime, prominent |
| Proclaim | : | announce, declare |
| Profound | : | deep, abstruse |
| Profuse | : | abundant, copious, lavish, munificent, copious |
| Prolong | : | extend, lengthen, delay |
| Prosaic | : | dull, unattractive, humdrum |
| Protect | : | guard, defend, shelter, safeguard |
| Prudent | : | discreet, wise, circumspect |
| Purchase | : | buy, barter, bargain, obtain, procure |

## Q

| Qualify | : | clear, pass, become eligible |
| Quantify | : | measure, number, amount |
| Quack | : | fake, unqualified |

| Quarrel | : | dispute, altercation, dissension |
| Queer | : | curious, strange, quaint, unusual |
| Quit | : | leave, resign, abandon |

# R

| Radiant | : | shining, gleaning, gleaming, dazzling, brilliant, bright |
| Rapacious | : | greedy, ravenous |
| Redress | : | address, solve, relief |
| Rob | : | steal, divest, cheat |
| Regret | : | sorrow, repentance |
| Rash | : | reckless, impetuous, thoughtless |
| Rustic | : | lout, clown, uncivilised, boorish |
| Rapture | : | glee, ecstasy, bliss, exultation |
| Rational | : | logical, reasonable, sane |
| Refresh | : | revive, recreate, regale, invigorate |
| Repress | : | suppress, check, stifle |
| Romantic | : | fanciful, imaginative, sentimental |
| Ruthless | : | apathetic, pitiless, cruel, relentless |

# S

| Scandalous | : | defamatory, libellous, scurrilous |
| Scorn | : | hate, mock, despise, disdain, scoff |
| Shake | : | quiver, shiver, tremble, shudder |
| Sharp | : | incisive, smart, clever, intelligent, shrewd |

| | | |
|---|---|---|
| **Sagacious** | : | bold, courageous, audacious |
| **Shine** | : | brighten, illuminate, glitter, glisten, gleam, glimmer, sparkle |
| **Smooth** | : | even, polished, sleek, glossy |
| **Sublime** | : | splendid, serene |
| **Substitute** | : | replacement, alternative |
| **Singular** | : | unique, matchless |
| **Sovereign** | : | regal, supreme, absolute |
| **Sprightly** | : | vivacious, active |
| **Stable** | : | smooth, firm, constant, unwavering |
| **Sumptuous** | : | rich, expensive, costly, luxurious |
| **Spite** | : | malice, ill will, rancour, grudge |
| **Stern** | : | strict, severe, rigid, stiff, harsh |
| **Size** | : | bulk, volume |
| **Shame** | : | dishonour, disgrace, humiliation |
| **Serene** | : | calm, tranquil, unruffled |
| **Significant** | : | important, main, major |
| **Surplus** | : | excessive, abundant, copious |
| **Suspicion** | : | doubt, mistrust |
| **Symptom** | : | sign, indication, token |
| **System** | : | method, arrangement, order, scheme |

## T

| | | |
|---|---|---|
| **Think** | : | reflect, muse, deliberate, ponder, contemplate, ruminate |
| **Thrift** | : | frugality, economy, parsimony |
| **Tired** | : | exhausted, weary, fatigued, jaded |

| Trick | : | guile, ruse, trickery, subterfuge |
| Trade | : | business, commerce |
| Truce | : | treaty, agreement |
| Transpire | : | happen, occur |
| Trifling | : | trivial, insignificant |
| Talent | : | ability, skill, gift, prowess |
| Terse | : | condensed, brief, pithy, succinct |
| Thrive | : | prosper, flourish, succeed |
| Triumph | : | victory, win, success |

## U

| Understand | : | comprehend, grasp, know, perceive |
| Usage | : | custom, fashion, practice |
| Urbane | : | polished, civilized, courtly |
| Uphold | : | support, sustain, maintain |
| Unanimity | : | accord, consent |

## V

| Vanity | : | pride, arrogance, haughtiness, conceit |
| Vengeance | : | revenge, retaliation, retribution, avenge |
| Villain | : | rogue, rascal, scoundrel, knave, scamp |
| Vulgar | : | coarse, indecent, ribald, low, indecorous |
| Vague | : | undefined, indefinite, wayward, uncertain |
| Valid | : | cogent, weighty, strong |

| Vanquish | : | defeat, conquer, overcome, overpower |
|---|---|---|
| Vehement | : | forceful, strong, impetuous |
| Veneration | : | respect, reverence, adoration |
| Verbose | : | wordy, prolix |
| Verdict | : | decision, judgment, sentence |
| Verification | : | checking |
| Vindicate | : | justify, prove |
| Virile | : | manly, strong, capable |
| Virtual | : | unreal |

# W

| Waver | : | falter, vacillate, hesitate |
|---|---|---|
| Waive | : | exonerate, remit, clear |
| Wayward | : | digressing, off target, irrelevant |
| Weak | : | infirm, feeble, languid, debilitated |
| Warlike | : | militant, belligerent, bellicose, combative, contentious |
| Wise | : | prudent, discreet, sensible, judicious |
| Wane | : | lessen, diminish, decrease |
| Wrong | : | incorrect, erroneous, mistaken |
| Wild | : | savage, rash, uncivilised, untamed |
| Wicked | : | evil, perverse, sinful, villainous |
| Whimsical | : | fantastic, capricious, assuming |

## Y

| **Yield** | : | agree, succumb, submit, surrender, concede |
| **Young** | : | juvenile, youthful, immature, callous |
| **Yummy** | : | delicious, palatable |

## Z

| **Zealous** | : | enthusiastic, ardent, eager |
| **Zenith** | : | summit, elevation, height |
| **Zest** | : | appetite, excitement |

# 15

# ANTONYMS
## (Words Opposite in Meaning)

Antonyms of words give opposite meaning thereof. Knowledge of antonyms is extremely important for various reasons. Apart from enhancing one's vocabulary and strengthening the expression, they offer variety and range in write-ups and conversation—official or personal. Antonyms are especially helpful in presenting counter arguments to a given view. In answering argumentative questions, participating in a Group Discussion, a high level of performance is not possible without adequate knowledge of antonyms.

Broadly, antonyms can be divided into two categories, viz. (i) different words, and (ii) by Prefixes. Different words are those antonyms which are not similar to the words in spellings, pronunciation or tenor. Borrow-Lend; Scarcity-Abundance; Economy-Extravagance; Bravery-Cowardice are the examples of antonym pairs of this category. The second category of antonyms are formed by certain prefixes, for example: Like-Dislike; Ability-Inability; Kindness-Unkindness; Moral-Immoral; Regular-Irregular, Associate-Dissociate, Connect-Disconnect, etc.

It should be kept in mind that the part of speech to which a word belongs, i.e. noun, adjective, verb, adverb should not be changed while writing its antonym. Necessary changes must be made in the sentence, if required, while using an antonym.

Some important words and their antonyms are given below:

## I.  Different Words

| Word | Antonym |
|------|---------|

### (A)  *Nouns*

| | |
|------|---------|
| Abduction | restoration |
| Abundance | scarcity, dearth, shortage |
| Acquisition | relinquishment |
| Adversity | prosperity |
| Alien | native |
| Ancestor | descendant |
| Arrival | departure |
| Ascent | descent |
| Assent | dissent |
| Attraction | repulsion |
| Audacity | reservation |
| Beauty | ugliness |
| Benefactor | malefactor |
| Bravery | cowardice |
| Brevity | detail |
| Boastfulness | modesty |
| Beginning | culmination |
| Care | neglect |

| Word | Antonym |
| --- | --- |
| Civility | rusticity |
| Comfort | distress |
| Concord | discord |
| Contrast | comparison |
| Credit | debit |
| Complaint | thanksgiving |
| Compliance | defiance |
| Danger | safety |
| Deficit | surplus |
| Discount | premium |
| Esteem | degradation |
| Ebb | flow |
| Economy/Frugality | extravagance |
| Elevation | depression |
| Enmity | friendship |
| Enthusiasm/Concern | indifference, apathy |
| Entrance | exit |
| Exterior | interior |
| Fact | fiction |
| Falsehood | truth |
| Fame | notoriety |
| Friend | foe, enemy |
| Gain | loss |
| Gaiety | sadness |
| Glory | shame |
| Happiness | woefulness |
| Haste | delay |

| Word | Antonym |
|------|---------|
| Honour | dishonour |
| Hope | despair |
| Ignorance | knowledge |
| Interest | indifference |
| Leniency | severity |
| Merit | flaw |
| Moderation | excess |
| Optimism | pessimism |

**(B) Verbs**

| | |
|------|---------|
| Abandon | adopt |
| Accept | reject |
| Affirm | deny |
| Accuse | acquit |
| Advance | retreat |
| Agree | differ |
| Allow | forbid |
| Attract | repel |
| Avenge | condone |
| Baffle | solve |
| Bequeath | disown |
| Borrow | lend |
| Collect | disperse |
| Conceal | reveal |
| Confess | deny |
| Condemn | extol |
| Contract | expand |

| Word | Antonym |
|------|---------|
| Converge | diverge |
| Combine | separate |
| Cure | infect |
| Diminish | enhance |
| Defy | yield |
| Destroy | preserve |
| Debilitate | invigorate |
| Despise | love |
| Encourage | discourage |
| Enthrone | dethrone |
| Enchant | depress |
| Exult | bemoan |
| Endow | divest |
| Ease | harden |
| Flatter | condemn |
| Free | enslave |
| Falsify | justify |
| Gain | lose |
| Gather | scatter |
| Grant | withhold |
| Guard | endanger |
| Hide | seek, expose |
| Harass | assist |
| Hurt | heal |
| Hinder | facilitate |
| Include | exclude |
| Induce/Persuade | dissuade |

| Word | Antonym |
| --- | --- |
| Inhale | exhale |
| Indict | acquit |
| Implore | order |
| Incense | cool |
| Join | leave, separate |
| Lead | follow |
| Lessen | increase, extend |
| Lower | lift |
| Magnify | reduce |
| Make | mar |
| Mourn | exult |
| Murmur | shriek, shout |
| Oppose | yield |
| Overlook | accuse, indict |
| Object | acquiesce |
| Praise | criticize |
| Prohibit | permit |
| Pardon | punish |
| Place | remove |
| Precede | succeed |
| Pursue | avoid |
| Recollect/Remember | forget |
| Recognize | ignore |
| Refuse | allow |
| Rejoice | lament |
| Repress | encourage |
| Resist | submit, yield |

| Word | Antonym |
|------|---------|
| Reward | punish |
| Shorten | lengthen |
| Sink | swim |
| Smile | frown |
| Solidify | liquify |
| Strengthen | weaken |
| Teach | learn |
| Triumph | fail |
| Unite | separate |
| Unsurp | relinquish |
| Vanish | appear |
| Wane | wax |
| Wed | divorce |
| Yield | resist |

**(C)** *Adjectives*

| | |
|------|---------|
| Absent | present |
| Abreast | away |
| Acute | mild |
| Ample | scanty |
| Amorous | dull, dry |
| Angry | pleased |
| Attractive | repulsive |
| Attuned | awry |
| Awkward | graceful |
| Base | noble |
| Barren | fertile |

| Word | Antonym |
| --- | --- |
| Blunt | sharp |
| Boisterous | melodious |
| Calm | disturbed |
| Coherent | inconsistent |
| Commodious | narrow |
| Conscientious | unscrupulous |
| Celestrial | terrestrial |
| Cheerful | gloomy |
| Coarse | fine |
| Defensive | offensive |
| Different | similar |
| Explicit | implicit |
| Extravagant | frugal |
| Faithful | treacherous |
| Famous | notorious |
| Flimsy | substantial |
| Final | initial |
| Frequent | occasional |
| Frank | reserved |
| Fresh | stale |
| General | particular |
| Genuine | counterfeit |
| Hopeful | despondent, defeatist |
| Hostile | friendly |
| Humane | ruthless |
| Humble | proud |
| Ideal | actual |

| Word | Antonym |
| --- | --- |
| Idle | busy |
| Important | trivial |
| intentional | accidental |
| Injurious | beneficial |
| Lenient | harsh |
| Liberal | conservative |
| Natural | artificial |
| Numerous | few, scanty |
| Plain | obscure |
| Permanent | temporary, transient |
| Progressive | retrogressive |
| Rash | cautious |
| Real | imaginary |
| Repulsive | attractive |
| Rough | smooth |
| Rude | polite, gentle |
| Sacred | profane |
| Savage | civilized |
| Severe | gentle |
| Stout | thin |
| Straight | curved, transverse |
| Strange | familiar |
| Superior | inferior |
| Tame | wild |
| Timorous | bold |
| Transparent | opaque |
| Uniform | variable |
| Vague | definite |

| Word | Antonym |
| --- | --- |
| Vertical | horizontal |
| Virtuous | vicious, wicked |
| Voluntary | compulsory |
| Vulgar | refined |
| Virile | sterile |
| Wayward | focused |
| Wonderful | lousy, awful |

### (D) *Adverbs and Prepositions*

| | |
| --- | --- |
| Above | beneath, below |
| Also | only |
| Down | up |
| Early | late |
| For | against |
| Frequently | occasionally |
| Here | there |
| In | out |
| Now | then |
| Off | on |
| Often | seldom |
| Slowly | quickly |
| To | from, fro |
| Too | only, solely |

## II. By Prefixes

### (A) *Nouns*

| | |
| --- | --- |
| Ability | inability |
| Agreement | disagreement |

| Word | Antonym |
| --- | --- |
| Advantage | disadvantage |
| Belief | disbelief |
| Concord | discord |
| Decency | indecency |
| Equality | inequality |
| Gratitude | ingratitude |
| Honour | dishonour |
| Kindness | unkindness |
| Like | dislike |
| Merit | demerit |
| Obedience | disobedience |
| Pleasure | displeasure |
| Purity | impurity |
| Quietude | disquietude |
| Regularity | irregularity |
| Repute | disrepute |
| Real | unreal |
| Romantic | unromantic |
| Sense | nonsense |
| Use | abuse, misuse |

**(B)** *Verbs*

| | |
| --- | --- |
| Account | discount |
| Agree | disagree |
| Appear | disappear |
| Arm | disarm |
| Allow | disallow |

| Word | Antonym |
| --- | --- |
| Believe | disbelieve |
| Close | disclose |
| Continue | discontinue |
| Enthrone | dethrone |
| Encourage | discourage |
| Honour | dishonour |
| Include | exclude |
| Inhale | exhale |
| Like | dislike |
| Obey | disobey |
| Please | displease |
| Tie | untie |
| Unite | disunite |

## (C) *Adjectives*

| Word | Antonym |
| --- | --- |
| Active | inactive |
| Animate | inanimate |
| Attentive | inattentive |
| Correct | incorrect |
| Certain | uncertain |
| Decent | indecent |
| Different | indifferent |
| Equal | unequal |
| Explicit | implicit |
| Fazed | unfazed |
| Firm | infirm |
| Frequent | infrequent |

| Word | Antonym |
| --- | --- |
| Fortunate | unfortunate |
| Honest | dishonest |
| Holy | unholy |
| Kind | unkind |
| Lawful | unlawful |
| Legal | illegal |
| Limited | unlimited |
| Literate | illiterate |
| Loyal | disloyal |
| Manly | unmanly |
| Moderate | immoderate |
| Moral | immoral |
| Mortal | immortal |
| Necessary | unnecessary |
| Noble | ignoble |
| Obedient | disobedient |
| Ordinary | extraordinary |
| Parallel | Unparallel |
| Possible | impossible |
| Perfect | imperfect |
| Proper | improper |
| Prudent | imprudent |
| Pure | impure |
| Polite | impolite |
| Rational | irrational |
| Real | unreal |
| Relevant | irrelevant |

| Word | Antonym |
|------|---------|
| Reverent | Irreverent |
| Religious | irreligious |
| Regular | irregular |
| Repressible | irrepressible |
| Romantic | unromantic |
| Safe | unsafe |
| Scrupulous | unscrupulous |
| Sufficient | insufficient |
| Viable | unviable |
| Visible | invisible |
| Voluntary | involuntary |
| Worthy | unworthy |
| Well | unwell |
| Yielding | unyielding |

# 16

## PARONYMS
### (Words Similar in Sound)

Paronyms are words that are similar in sound but entirely different in meaning. They are also called homophones. It is extremely important to distinguish these words so that the right word is used while writing or conversing. While listening to others when they speak—whether in a lecture, meeting, conference or taking a dictation—it is necessary to know which word is intended by the speaker. In the absence of skill to do so, one can face embarrassing situations. Sometimes the consequences can be as serious as losing a pay rise, promotion, an important assignment, and even a job. An employee who writes: "My boss is also a "liar" instead of a 'lawyer' is not likely to escape a severe action. Similarly, someone who writes the word 'wreck' (to destroy) in place of reck (to care) or raze (to pull down) instead of raise (to lift) is likely to present an entirely wrong picture.

Some important paronyms are given below. Note their spellings and mark their meanings:

1. **Air,**      atmosphere
   **Er,**       before
   **Heir,**     one who inherits

| 2.  | **Ail,**     | to be sick                        |
|     | **Ale,**     | alcoholic beverage                |
| 3.  | **Altar,**   | gallows, place of sacrifice       |
|     | **Alter,**   | to change                         |
| 4.  | **Aught,**   | anything                          |
|     | **Ought,**   | should                            |
| 5.  | **Accede,**  | agree                             |
|     | **Exceed,**  | go beyond                         |
| 6.  | **Ball,**    | a dance, a round, plaything       |
|     | **Bawe,**    | to shout                          |
| 7.  | **Bare,**    | naked                             |
|     | **Bear,**    | a wild animal                     |
|     | **Beer,**    | a drink                           |
|     | **Bier,**    | frame for a dead body             |
| 8.  | **Beach,**   | shore                             |
|     | **Beech,**   | a tree                            |
| 10. | **Berry,**   | a fruit                           |
|     | **Bury,**    | to put below the ground           |
| 11. | **Brake,**   | that which checks                 |
|     | **Break,**   | to dismantle into pieces          |
| 12. | **Bridal,**  | relating to a bride               |
|     | **Bridle,**  | that which controls a horse       |
| 13. | **Cask,**    | a barrel                          |
|     | **Casque,**  | a tramlet                         |
| 14. | **Cast,**    | to set or throw                   |
|     | **Caste,**   | social class                      |
| 15. | **Ceiling,** | inner part of roof                |
|     | **Sealing,** | fixing with wax, etc.             |
| 16. | **Check,**   | to stop                           |
|     | **Cheque,**  | order to pay money                |

17. **Cord,**     a string
     **Chord,**     musical note

18. **Cue,**     a sign, a stick in billiards
     **Queue,**     a line of people

19. **Dose,**     of medicine
     **Doze,**     light nap

20. **Dual,**     double
     **Duel,**     a combat

21. **Fain,**     gladly
     **Feign,**     to pretend

22. **Fair,**     just, white complexioned
     **Fare,**     cost of journey

23. **Floor,**     surface
     **Flour,**     ground wheat

24. **Gage,**     pledge
     **Gaze,**     look
     **Gauge,**     to measure

25. **Gift,**     covered with gold
     **Guilt,**     crime

26. **Hale,**     healthy
     **Hail,**     frozen raindrops

27. **Hoard,**     to store
     **Horde,**     a crowd

28. **Hue,**     colour
     **Hew,**     to cut

29. **Idle,**     not occupied with any work
     **Idol,**     an image

30. **Key,**     a lever to open the lock
     **Quay,**     a place for landing

31. **Lain,**     participle of 'lie'
     **Lane,**     a narrow street

| 32. | **Lessen,** | to decrease |
| | **Lesson,** | something to learn |
| 33. | **Liar,** | one who tells a lie |
| | **Lyre,** | a musical instrument |
| 34. | **Lightening,** | illuminating, making less |
| | **Lightning,** | flash from the clouds |
| 35. | **Main,** | major, chief |
| | **mane,** | hair on neck (of a horse/tiger) |
| 36. | **Marshal,** | to arrange, the high army officer |
| | **Martial,** | heroic, warlike |
| 37. | **Mean,** | to intend, low |
| | **Mien,** | to look, bearing |
| 38. | **Moat,** | ditch |
| | **Mote,** | dust particle |
| 39. | **Naught,** | nothing |
| | **Nought,** | zero |
| | **Not,** | in the negative |
| 40. | **Naughty,** | badly behaving |
| | **Knotty,** | complicated |
| 41. | **Pain,** | suffering |
| | **Pane,** | a glass |
| 42. | **Peer,** | noble |
| | **Pear,** | a fruit |
| | **Pier,** | jetty |
| 43. | **Plain,** | simple, clear |
| | **Plane,** | even surface |
| 44. | **Plum,** | a fruit |
| | **Plumb,** | to find depth |
| 45. | **Pray,** | to implore |
| | **Prey,** | a hunted animal |

46. **Pour,**   cause to flow
    **Pore,**   small hole in the skin

47. **Rain,**   downpour
    **Rein,**   for driving a horse
    **Reign,**   rule

48. **Rays,**   beams
    **Raise,**   lift
    **Raze,**   destroy

49. **Reck,**   to care
    **Wreck,**   to destroy

50. **Rack,**   place to keep books, etc.
    **Rake,**   search

51. **Right,**   correct
    **Write,**   to scribble
    **Rite,**   ceremony

52. **Sail,**   of a ship or boat
    **Sale,**   act of selling

53. **Cite,**   quote
    **Site,**   place
    **sight,**   seeing

54. **Cede,**   to give up
    **Seed,**   of plants, etc.

55. **Soar,**   fly high
    **Sore,**   painful
    **Sour,**   a particular taste

56. **Sole,**   singular
    **Soul,**   spirit

57. **Story,**   tale
    **Storey,**   of a house

58. **Straight,**   direct
    **Strait,**   narrow

59. **Tear,**      drop from the eye, to do pieces
    **Tier,**      a row

60. **Team,**      group of players
    **Teem,**      to abound

61. **Throne,**    for kings
    **Thrown,**    past participle of 'throw'

62. **Vain,**      useless, proud
    **Vane,**      weather cock, proud
    **Vein,**      blood vessel

63. **Vale,**      valley
    **Veil,**      veneer, curtain
    **Wail,**      cry

64. **Wait,**      to stay
    **Weight,**    heaviness

65. **Waste,**     to squander
    **Waist,**     the middle part of human body

66. **Wave,**      to move, of the water
    **Waive,**     to condone, give up

67. **Weak,**      feeble
    **Week,**      seven days

68. **Whether,**   if
    **Weather,**   climate

69. **Whet,**      to sharpen
    **Wet,**       moist

70. **Whit,**      a small particle
    **Wit,**       intelligence

71. **Wrath,**     anger
    **Worth,**     angry

72. **Yew,**       a tree
    **Ewe,**       female sheep

73. **Yoke,**      sway, not for an ox
    **Yolk,**      yellow of an egg

# 17

# DOUBLETS

Doublets are pairs of words that differ in form and meaning but may have the same derivation. They are neither synonyms nor antonyms of each other. In some cases, the pronunciation may be similar (Accede, Exceed; Assent, Ascent), in others the connotation may appear the same (Price, Value; Tenor, Tenure; Elder, Older) but the meaning of each word in a doublet is different from the other; one cannot be substituted for the other.

Given below are certain important doublets. The meaning of each word has been given. The usage has also been explained wherever necessary.

| | | |
|---|---|---|
| **Abjure** | : | renounce, abandon |
| **Adjure** | : | beg, entreat, implore |
| **Accede** | : | to give assent to a view |
| **Exceed** | : | surpass, go beyond |
| **Accidental** | : | happening unexpectedly |
| **Occidental** | : | belonging to the West |
| **Accomplice** | : | an associate, particularly in a crime |
| **Accomplish** | : | to achieve or fulfil |
| **Adapt** | : | to make suitable |

| Adopt | : | to take a child voluntarily |
| Adept | : | skilled in something |
| Addition | : | the process of adding |
| Edition | : | form of publication of a book, etc. |
| Admission | : | permission to enter |
| Admittance | : | right to enter/act of entering a building/an institution |
| Advice | : | (noun) a given opinion or counsel |
| Advise | : | (verb) to offer counsel |
| Affect | : | to make an impact, influence, generally negative (used as a verb, e.g. Regular bouts of drinking have affected his health). |
| Effect | : | (noun) impact better or worse; (verb) to bring about |
| Allusion | : | indirect reference (allude to something) |
| Illusion | : | a false impression, deception |
| Alternate | : | happening by turns (e.g. fever every alternate day) |
| Alternative | : | one in place of the other (e.g. reading a book is a better alternative than watching a movie) |
| Amiable | : | friendly persons, nature |
| Amicable | : | in a friendly spirit (amicable settlement of dispute) |
| Anticipate | : | to forestall, guess |
| Expect | : | to look forward to something which is likely to happen |
| Antic | : | odd, disagreeable gestures (foolish antics) |
| Antique | : | ancient, old (antique coins) |

| | | |
|---|---|---|
| **Apposite** | : | appropriate, suitable for the purpose. |
| **Opposite** | : | contrary, against, rival. |
| **Ardent** | : | eager, yearning (ardent desire). |
| **Arduous** | : | strenuous, tortuous |
| **Artist** | : | skiled in some fine art. |
| **Artiste** | : | a performer on stage, etc. (cine artiste) |
| **Assent** | : | agreement, consent, concurence. |
| **Ascent** | : | an upward movement (ascent of sap in plants). |
| **Auger** | : | a boring instrument. |
| **Augur** | : | foreboding, to predict by sign (augur well). |
| **Attenuate** | : | to make thin. |
| **Extenuate** | : | lessen the effect by an excuse |
| **Aught** | : | anything. |
| **Ought** | : | past tense of 'owe' ('should' and 'ought to' indicate moral obligation or desirability, e.g. we ought to respect our elders) |
| **Beneficial** | : | useful (applicable to things only). |
| **Beneficient** | : | good and kind (persons) |
| **Born** | : | took birth, brought forth. |
| **Borne** | : | carried (airborne); met the expenditure, etc. (The expenses will be borne by the company) |
| **Canon** | : | a legal clause or a church decree. |
| **Cannon** | : | a heavy artillery gun |

| Canvas | : | a kind of white coarse cloth used to paint on, or used as sails. |
| Canvass | : | to solicit for votes, charity, contributions, membership, etc. |
| Casual | : | occasional or accidental (casual leave, casual labour). |
| Causal | : | demoting cause of something. |
| Cermonial | : | formal gesture or action (applied to persons and behaviour). |
| Ceremonious | : | formal gesture or action (applied to procedures, etc. in state matters). |
| Childish | : | silly, immature (negative sense). |
| Childlike | : | innocent, like a child (positive sense). |
| Chord | : | string of musical instrument; a line in geometry joining the extremities. |
| Cord | : | a thin rope. |
| Collision | : | crash, striking together. |
| Collusion | : | a secret plan/agreement with someone to deceive others. |
| Comity | : | courtesy, friendly recognition by nations of one another's laws (comity of nations). |
| Committee | : | a body of persons formed to perform some special functions. |
| Confirm | : | to establish firmly, to ratify a title or treaty. |
| Conform | : | to comply with a rule, to go as per given pattern. |
| Conscious | : | aware (of attributes, defects, etc.). |
| Conscience | : | moral and ethics governing a fair mind. |

| | | |
|---|---|---|
| **Considerable** | : | much, sufficient, worth considering. |
| **Considerate** | : | thoughtful of others, kind. |
| **Contemptible** | : | hateful, despicable (person). |
| **Contemptuous** | : | scornful, haughty (look). |
| **Contiguous** | : | adjoining (states, countries). |
| **Contagious** | : | infectious (disease). |
| **Corporal** | : | bodily, physical (corporal punishment). |
| **Corporeal** | : | material (not spiritual). |
| **Corps** | : | (pron. core) organised body of men. (National Cadet Corps) |
| **Corpse** | : | a dead body of a human being. |
| **Credible** | : | something which can be believed. |
| **Credulous** | : | someone who easily believes what others say, gullible (used in negative sense). |
| **Critic** | : | judge of literary/artistic works. |
| **Critique** | : | a critical assessment/essay on some work/book. |
| **Council** | : | an assembly of persons. |
| **Counsel** | : | to advise, also advice (noun). |
| **Currant** | : | dried grape. |
| **Current** | : | present, flow of water, transmission of electric power. |
| **Definite** | : | precise, specific. |
| **Definitive** | : | unconditional, final, (e.g. an offer in which the terms cannot be changed). |
| **Deference** | : | respect, regard (a deferential person). |
| **Difference** | : | disagreement (difference of opinion). |

| Dairy | : | a place/shop where milk and milk products are sold. |
| Diary | : | a book/note book for making daily records. |
| Deprecate | : | to plead against; to pray to prevent evil. |
| Depreciate | : | to decline in value. |
| Depose | : | dethrone, remove from a high position. |
| Dispose | : | deal, finish, place suitably (dispose of work). |
| Desert | : | sandy waste land; to leave or forsake. |
| Dessert | : | a sweet dish served after meals. |
| Desecrate | : | to profane (something sacred). |
| Dessicate | : | dry up. |
| Desperate | : | reckless owing to frustration or failure. |
| Disparate | : | diverse, diverging. |
| Dissent | : | disagree (disagreement). |
| Descent | : | going down. |
| Decent | : | nice, reasonably good. |
| Economic | : | relating to economics (e.g. economic condition); saving expenditure. |
| Economics | : | the study of finances, etc. The profitability or otherwise of a venture, policy. |
| Elder | : | denotes seniority among members of a family (e.g. my elder brother). |
| Older | : | comparatively aged (older than I). |

| | | |
|---|---|---|
| **Eligible** | : | one who fulfils the prescribed conditions; fit to be chosen. |
| **Illegible** | : | difficult to read (illegible hand). |
| **Emigrant** | : | one who leaves his native country to live in another country. |
| **Immigrant** | : | one who goes into one country from another country. |
| **Eminent** | : | distinguished (person). |
| **Imminent** | : | near, at hand (occurrence, event). |
| **Enquiry** | : | probe (applies for a question). |
| **Inquiry** | : | probe (applies for an investigation). |
| **Ensure** | : | to make certain. |
| **Assure** | : | give word/promise. (He assured me of his help). |
| **Insure** | : | to cover the risk (insurance policy). |
| **Epidemic** | : | spreading of a disease, affecting a great number of people. |
| **Endemic** | : | a disease constantly or generally present in an area. |
| **Eruption** | : | breaking out (volcanic eruption). |
| **Irruption** | : | breaking into, barging in (the irruption of American soldiers in Iraq). |
| **Expatiate** | : | to speak at length. |
| **Expiate** | : | pay the penalty of (sinful act). |
| **Expedient** | : | advantageous. |
| **Expeditious** | : | done promptly. |
| **Faint** | : | languid, pale, weak. |
| **Feint** | : | pretence. |

| **Fatal** | : | deadly, accident, etc. which leads to death. |
| **Fateful** | : | time or period which brings illuck, misery or mishap. |
| **Fewer** | : | less in number. |
| **Less** | : | insufficient; used for uncountable nouns (e.g. less sugar, etc.) |
| **Facilitate** | : | to make easy, affect. |
| **Felicitate** | : | congratulate, celebrate. |
| **Flagrant** | : | glaring, open (flagrant disregard). |
| **Fragrant** | : | sweet-smelling (fragrance of flowers). |
| **Forcible** | : | done by force (forcible occupation of the house). |
| **Forceful** | : | energetic, full of strength. |
| **Funeral** | : | burial, last rites of a dead body. |
| **Funereal** | : | gloomy, relating to a funeral. |
| **Gentle** | : | refined, well-behaved. |
| **Genteel** | : | well-bread, fashionable; mockingly used for false refinement. |
| **Gaol** | : | jail, prison (sent to the gaol). |
| **Goal** | : | destination, aim. |
| **Graceful** | : | elegant, majestic. |
| **Gracious** | : | merciful (God is gracious). |
| **Hygienic** | : | pertaining to the rules of health. |
| **Sanitary** | : | of conditions affecting health like dirt, filth, etc. |
| **Imperial** | : | kingly, majestic; of empire or emperor. |
| **Imperious** | : | haughty, commanding. |

| | | |
|---|---|---|
| **Industrial** | : | relating to an industry. |
| **Industrious** | : | hard-working. |
| **Insight** | : | penetration into or a grasp of circumstances or situation. |
| **Incite** | : | to stir up or exhort someone to do something. |
| **Ingenious** | : | skillful to invent something. |
| **Ingenuous** | : | frank, open-minded. |
| **Intense** | : | strong, vehement (intense heat). |
| **Intensive** | : | strenuous (strenuous training). |
| **Irrelevant** | : | not relating to the matter in hand. |
| **Irreverent** | : | disrespectful, not showing due regard. |
| **Judicial** | : | relating to law, legal (judicial review). |
| **Judicious** | : | sensible (judicious approach). |
| **Loath** | : | unwilling (we want to catch the fish but are loath to wet our feet). |
| **Loathe** | : | (verb) to hate (I loathe people with double standards). |
| **Luxuriant** | : | rich in growth (luxuriant hair or vegetation). |
| **Luxurious** | : | rich in finance/money/assets (luxurious apartment). |
| **Masterful** | : | commanding, majestic (Sachin's masterful square drive). |
| **Masterly** | : | skilful, showing talent of a champion. |
| **Mendacity** | : | falsehood, suppression of truth. |
| **Mendicity** | : | begging, state of penury. |

| | | |
|---|---|---|
| **Meritorious** | : | having great merit, praiseworthy. |
| **Meretricious** | : | showily attractive. |
| | | |
| **Metal** | : | elements like iron, copper, gold. |
| **Mettle** | : | skill, talent. |
| | | |
| **Middle** | : | point or time in between beginning and end of something (middle of the night). |
| **Centre** | : | middle part of something (centre of a circle); also main part of a city or town. |
| | | |
| **Miner** | : | one who works in a mine. |
| **Minor** | : | one who has not attained majority. |
| | | |
| **Miserable** | : | unhappy, sad. |
| **Wretched** | : | sick, ill, awful, pitiful. |
| | | |
| **Momentary** | : | short-lived, lasting only a moment (momentary pleasure). |
| **Momentous** | : | important (momentous occasion). |
| | | |
| **Monastic** | : | of monks and monasteries. |
| **Monistic** | : | those who believe that there is only one God; a belief in one God. |
| | | |
| **Necessaries** | : | all the things required in order to live. |
| **Necessities** | : | things that must be done (necessity of employing more staff). |
| | | |
| **Notable** | : | worthy of note, remarkable. |
| **Notorious** | : | known for bad acts and behaviour. |
| | | |
| **Observance** | : | keeping the custom, heeding, paying attention. |
| **Observation** | : | remark after watching a situation or perceiving a condition. |

| | | |
|---|---|---|
| **Official** | : | pertaining to office, having government sanction (official declaration). |
| **Officious** | : | meddlesome (officious character, fellow). |
| **Persecute** | : | harass; treat someone badly because of their religious belief. |
| **Prosecute** | : | start legal proceedings against somebody. |
| **Popular** | : | of the people (popular government); liked by people (popular actor). |
| **Populous** | : | populated, full of people (populous city). |
| **Precede** | : | come before in time or turn. (The dance preceded the song). |
| **Proceed** | : | go forward (proceed on leave). |
| **Principal** | : | chief; head of a school/college; money given on interest. |
| **Principle** | : | rule; a fundamental truth. |
| **Quote** | : | repeat words spoken or written, verbatim. |
| **Cite** | : | refer in general terms. |
| **Recourse** | : | resort for aid, protection or action (legal recourse). |
| **Resource** | : | source of help or production (India is rich in resources). |
| **Reverend** | : | worthy of reverence or respect. The word is prefixed to clergymen's names. |
| **Reverent** | : | expressing respect (reverent behaviour). |

| | | |
|---|---|---|
| **Sceptic** | : | one who has doubts, a disbeliver. |
| **Septic** | : | causing putrefaction. |
| **Seize** | : | lay hold of (seized of fever). |
| **Cease** | : | to stop, giver over (ceased to work). |
| **Shear** | : | to cut with scissors or shears. |
| **Sheer** | : | utter (sheer nonsense); steep (sheer fall). |
| **Slake** | : | to quench (slake the thirst). |
| **Slack** | : | loose, idle, sluggish (slack season). |
| **Site** | : | place where some construction work is going on. |
| **Sight** | : | scene (strange sight); ability to see (eye sight). |
| **Spacious** | : | roomy (spacious room). |
| **Specious** | : | plausible having a fair appearance. |
| **Stationary** | : | still, not moving (stationary star). |
| **Stationery** | : | writing material—pen, pencils, note books, etc. |
| **Suit** | : | petition (law suit); a set of clothes; to be convenient or useful. |
| **Suite** | : | retinue, a set of double rooms in a hotel. |
| **Symbol** | : | sign (a symbol of peace, love). |
| **Cymbal** | : | a musical instrument. |
| **Supplementary** | : | additional (supplementary sheet). |
| **Complementary** | : | (used in Mathematics) complementary angles. |
| **Complimentary** | : | conveying greetings; concessional (complimentary passes). |

| | | |
|---|---|---|
| **Team** | : | a set of players. |
| **Teem** | : | abundantly stocked with (This lake is teeming with fish). |
| **Temporal** | : | pertaining to time; also spiritual (contrary to physical). |
| **Temporary** | : | for a limited time only (opp. permanent). |
| **Tenor** | : | purport; general character of something. |
| **Tenure** | : | term, period of time someone holds an important job or position. |
| **Torrid** | : | extremely hot (Southern Africa is in the torrid zone). |
| **Torpid** | : | dull, sluggish. |
| **Troop** | : | a group of soldiers; a herd of animals (a troop of monkeys). |
| **Troupe** | : | a group of performers (A troupe of ballet dancers). |
| **Union** | : | combination, joining together (labour union). |
| **Unison** | : | joint sound/singing (the group sang in unison). |
| **Value** | : | The worth of a thing. |
| **Price** | : | What you pay to buy something. |
| **Venue** | : | meeting place for official purpose (venue of conference). |
| **Place** | : | Any spot for going or meeting unofficially. |

| **Veracious** | : | truthful (a veracious statement). |
| **Voracious** | : | greedy, having unsatiable desire for something (voracious reader or eater). |

| **Variety** | : | diversity, range |
| **Verity** | : | truthfulness (verity of statement). |

| **Variance** | : | disagreement (at variance with). |
| **Variation** | : | change, variety, range. |

| **Verbal** | : | spoken, uttered by mouth (opp. written). |

| **Verbose** | : | containing more words than are necessary (speech containing high sounding words). |

| **Vocation** | : | profession, trade, work |
| **Avocation** | : | leisure, minor occupation as hobby, etc. |

| **Zealous** | : | enthusiastic, having vigour and vitality to do something. |
| **Jealous** | : | envious. |

# 18

# WORDS OFTEN CONFUSED

There are many words in English vocabulary which appear to have the same meaning, though there are significant differences in their purport and one often cannot be used for the other. Students, aspirants and even professionals at times find it difficult to find the most appropriate word to be used in the given context.

It is necessary to understand sets of words conveying a similar meaning and to distinguish the words that often cause confusion. Given below are sets of important words, their exact meaning and usage. Reading them and putting them in use would help you in the following ways:

○ Increasing your vocabulary.

○ Enhancing your knowledge of synonyms.

○ Enabling you to distinguish words that have a similar meaning, e.g. near/close; above/over; ask/demand; rise/raise; beside/besides, etc.

○ Gaining knowledge of usage of words.

## 1. Above – Over

**Above** and **over** both can be used to describe a position higher than something. *We built a loft above/over the kitchen.* However, for movement from one side of something, we use only **over**.

**Above** and **over** can also mean more than. Above is used in relation to a minimum level or fixed point: *1000 feet above sea level* ○ *temperature above 15ºC.* **Over** is used with numbers, age, time and money: *She is over 40. This watch costs over $150.*

## 2. Act – Deed – Feat – Move

**Act** is a thing that somebody does: *an act of kindness.* **Deed** is more formal and literary. It denotes a thing that somebody does that is usually very good or very bad: *heroic deed/evil deed.*

**Feat** is an action or piece of work that needs skill, courage or strength: *a brilliant feat of designing.*

**Move** used more in journalism, it is an action that you do or need to do to achieve something: *a political move.*

## 3. Current – Present

**Current** and **Present** both mean existing or happening now. However, **current** suggests that the situation is temporary: *Current situation* ○ *current level of output.*

**Present** is used in a particular place or thing: *level of pollution present in the atmosphere* ○ *present context* ○ *present government.*

## 4. Admit – Acknowledge – Concede – Confess

**Admit** is to agree, often unwillingly that something is true: *I admit it was my mistake.*

**Acknowledge** is rather formal; to accept that something exists, is true or has happened: *to acknowledge receipt of a letter.*

**Concede** is to admit, often unwillingly that something is true or logical: *She was forced to concede that the plan may not work.*

**Confess** is to admit something that you feel ashamed, embarrassed about: *Confession of crime, guilt, ignorance.*

### 5. Affect – Effect

**Affect** (verb) is to have an influence on somebody or something: *Cinema affects young minds.* It is never a noun.

**Effect** (verb) to achieve or produce: *effect a compromise.*

**Effect** (noun) result or influence: *good effect, bad effect, effect of TV on children's behaviour.*

### 6. Afraid – Frightened – Apprehensive – Sacred – Paranoid

**Afraid:** feeling fear; worried that something bad will happen: *Afraid that you'll fail.*

**Frightened:** feeling intense fear due to some happening: *The sound of gunshots frightened the people.*

**Apprehensive:** slightly afraid: *I was a little apprehensive about the effect of my remarks.*

**Sacred** (informal) feeling fear; worried: *The thief got scared and ran away.*

**Paranoid** (informal) afraid or suspicious of other people—believing that they will harm you.

## 7. Agree – Approve – Consent – Acquiesce

**Agree:** to agree that you'll do what somebody wants.

**Approve:** to officially agree to a plan, request or suggestion.

**Consent** (formal) to agree to give you permission to something: *The minister finally consented to consider our proposal.*

**Acquiesce** (formal) to accept something without arguing even if you have your reservations: *At times it is better to acquiesce than to disagree.*

## 8. Almost – Nearly – Practically

**Almost** is used in positive sentences with certainly, every, all, entirely, impossible, empty.

**Nearly** is used with numbers, and words like all, every, always, died, finished.

**Practically** is used with all, every, no, impossible, nothing, anything.

**Almost** and **Practically** are used before words like any, anything, anybody, etc. **Almost** is also used to say that one thing is similar to another: *The girl looked almost like a doll.*

## 9. Alone – Lonely

**Alone:** single, separated from others. It does not mean unhappy: *I like being alone in the house* ○ *He alone could solve this sum.*

**Lonely** (American—lonesome) alone and sad.

### 10. Also – Too – As Well

**Also** (more formal) usually comes before the main verb or after *be*.

**Too** is more common in spoken and formal English.

**As well** is used more in British English. Americans consider it old fashioned.

### 11. Although – Even Though – Though

**Although** and **Even though** can be used at the beginning of a sentence or clause that has a verb. The words are used basically to show a contrast between two clauses.

**Though** is used more in spoken English. Avoid using 'but' in the second clause if the first starts with any of these three words. Either use 'yet' or simply follow the first clause by the second.

### 12. Angry – Mad – Indignant – Cross – Irate – Furious – Enraged

**Angry:** feeling or showing anger.

**Mad:** (not before noun) informal word for angry. It means very angry.

**Indignant:** showing anger and surprise at being ill-treated.

**Cross:** means angry and rather annoyed: *She was cross with me for being late.*

**Irate:** very angry: *irate customers; an irate letter.* It is not usually followed by any preposition.

**Furious:** extremely angry.

**Enraged:** made very angry by some undesirable action or behaviour by something or somebody.

### 13. Answer – Reply – Respond

**Answer:** we *answer* a person, question or letter but *reply to* somebody or something.

**Answer** can be used with or without an object: *She hasn't answered my e-mail yet.*

**Answer** used as a noun, may be followed by *to*: *Your answer to this question is wrong.*

**Reply** is often used with actual words spoken: *"I will initiate an enquiry," the boss replied to a question.*

**Respond** is more formal but less common.

### 14. Around – Round – About

**Around** and **round** can be used with the same meaning, but **around** is more formal: *The earth goes around/round the sun.* In American English only **around** is used for these meanings.

**About** can also be used in the same context: *running about/around/round.*

**About** and **around** are also used to mean approximately.

### 15. As – Like

**As** is a conjunction and an adverb and is used before another adverb, a clause: *I enjoy continental food, as my brother does.*

**Like** is a preposition used before nouns and pronouns: *My sister has brown hair like me.*

However, in informal English, **like** is also used as a conjunction: *Nobody bats like Sachin does.*

## 16. Ask – Demand – Enquire/Inquire – Query

These words are used to say or write something in the form of a question, to get some information.

**Ask** is simply used to get information.

**Demand** is used to ask a question firmly: *demand an explanation.*

**Enquire/Inquire** is used to get some official information: *enquire about flight schedule.*

**Query** is also more formal and official and is used to ask a further question in a discourse.

## 17. Avenge – Revenge – Retaliate

People **avenge** themselves on somebody or **avenge** something: *He avenged himself on his father's killers. He vowed to avenge (not revenge) his brother's death.*

You take **revenge** on a person. You cannot **revenge** something. Revenge can also be used as a verb. People **revenge** themselves on somebody.

## 18. Awake – Awaken – Wake up – Waken

**Awake** is used in writing; usually past tense of **awake** is used.

**Awake** is also an adjective, meaning *not asleep.*

**Awaken** is more used in literature: *She awakened her lover with a kiss.*

**Wake up** is most common of these: *What time you usually wake up? (Wake-up call).*

**Waken** is more formal: to wake or make somebody wake from sleep.

## 19. Behind – At the Back – At the Rear

**Behind** means after, at the back, or also lagging: *behind someone in score/marks.*

**At the back** and **at the rear** have similar meaning, but **at the rear** is more formal and official: *back door* of the house but the *rear exit* of the aircraft.

## 20. Bad – Unpleasant – Wicked, etc.

**Bad** means not good, of poor quality: *bad news/health/weather/dream/habit,* etc.

**Unpleasant** is full of problems: *unpleasant smell*

**Appalling:** dreadful (weather).

**Terrible/serious/horrific** (accident).

**Wicked/Evil/Immoral** (person).

**Awkward/Embarrassing/Difficult** (situation).

## 21. Luggage – Baggage

**Luggage** is the usual word in British English.

**Baggage** is used in the context of bags and cases that passengers take in a flight. Both are uncountable nouns.

## 22. Base – Basic – Foundation

**Base** is an idea or a situation from which something is developed: *economic base.*

**Basic** denotes a principle, idea or fact that supports something.

**Foundation** is used to denote larger or more important things than **basis**.

## 23. Beat – Batter – Lash, etc.

**Beat:** to hit somebody or something repeatedly, especially hard; also defeat in a game/match.

**Batter** is hit hard in a way that causes damage.

**Lash** is to hit somebody/something with a lot of force.

**Pound** is to hit hard, especially in a way that makes a lot of noise: *Heavy downpour pounded on the roof.*

**Pummel** to hit something/somebody with fists.

**Hammer** to hit in a manner that is noisy and violent.

## 24. Beautiful – Pretty – Attractive ..., etc.

**Beautiful:** very pleasant to look at (especially, girl or woman).

**Pretty:** good looking—used for girls. When used for a woman it suggests that she is like a girl, with small delicate features.

**Handsome:** (used for men) pleasant to look at—having large, strong, features.

**Attractive:** pleasant to look at (in a sexual way).

**Lovely:** beautiful, very attractive. The word is used when you also have a strong feeling of affection for someone: *lovely little girl.*

**Gorgeous:** extremely attractive in a sexual way.

**Charming:** very pleasant or attractive: *charming person.*

## 25. Become – Get – Go – Turn

All these are verbs and are used usually with the following adjectives:

**Become:** accustomed, clear, involved, pregnant, famous.

**Get:** used to, better, worse, pregnant, angry, dark, well.

**Go:** bad, bald, blend, crazy, wrong.

**Turn:** bad, blue, cold, sour, red.

## 26. Begin – Start – Commence

There is not much difference between these words. However, **begin** is used when you describe a series of events: *The play begins with mysterious sounds.*

You **start** a journey not begin.

The ing forms of begin and *start* are followed by the preposition *to* i.e. *beginning to/starting to*

**Commence** means to begin to happen — a meeting, financial year, etc.

## 27. Beside – Besides – Except – Apart from

**Beside:** means next to something: *He sat beside me.*

**Besides:** The adverb besides is used to give another reason to the argument.

**Except** is used to mention the only thing that is not included in a statement.

**Apart from:** can be used in the sense of besides and except.

## 28. A bit – A little – Little

**A bit** means slightly or to small extent: *These shoes are a bit tight.*

**A little** or **a little bit** means slightly, just.

**Little** means small, less than required.

### 29. Boring – Tedious – Dry – Uninteresting

**Boring:** something that makes you feel tired: *boring job*.

**Tedious:** something taking too long and not interesting, making you impatient: *tedious journey.*

**Dry:** boring, lacking human interest: *dry reading.*

**Dull** is not interesting or exciting: *dull place.*

**Uninteresting:** something that does not attract your interest or attention.

### 30. Rest – Respite – Breather

**Rest:** a period of relaxing, sleeping or not working.

**Respite:** a short break from something difficult or unpleasant: *respite from pain.*

**Breather:** a short pause in an activity to relax a little: *a five minute breather.*

### 31. Call – Exclaim – Cry out – Blunt

**Call:** to shout or say something loudly to attract somebody's attention.

**Exclaim** is to say something suddenly or loudly expressing emotion or reaction to something.

**Cry out:** to shout something loudly, especially when you need help.

**Blurt** is to say something loudly without thinking carefully enough, e.g. *blurt out a secret.*

**Divulge** is to give out some secret information under threat or pressure.

## 32. Battle – Fight – Struggle – War

**Battle:** a competition or argument between people or groups of people trying to win power or control: *legal battle*.

**Fight:** trying to stop or prevent something bad or achieve something good: *fight to stop retrenchment*.

**Struggle:** efforts/collective action to achieve power or control: *struggle for independence*.

**War:** effort over a long period of time to stop something bad: *war against crime/terrorism*. Also military engagement of two or more countries against each other.

## 33. Can – May

**Can** is used to say that somebody knows how to do something: *I can drive this car.* ○ *I can hear someone shouting.*

Can is to be able to.

**May** is used as a polite and formal way to ask or give permission: *May I borrow your magazine?* ○ *You may go now*.

## 34. Take care of – Look after – Care for

You **take care of** someone who is old or sick. Look after is used in the sense of bringing up children. It is also used to denote the work one is engaged in: *I am looking after the credit card portfolio*.

## 35. Cautious – Careful

**Cautious** is someone who is nervous that something bad may happen through him, and goes slowly in his actions.

**Careful** is also apprehensive but takes extra precautions to ensure that everything goes on smoothly.

## 36. Certain – Definite – Assured – Bound

**Certain** is something you can rely on to happen or be true.

**Definite** is certain to happen, something that is not going to change.

**Assured** is more formal — certain to happen (something sensitive): *victory is assured.*

**Bound** is only used in the phrase bound to be/do: *bound to pass; bound to be changed.*

## 37. Cheap – Affordable – Inexpensive – Reasonable

**Cheap** means costing little or less amount of money than you had anticipated. (It may also mean of low quality).

**Affordable** is cheap enough for most people to be able to buy.

**Inexpensive** means something is good value for its price.

**Reasonable** is not too expensive but not cheap either.

## 38. Check – Examine – Inspect – Probe

**Check** is to look something closely to ensure that everything is correct, in good condition.

**Examine** is to look closely to see if there is anything wrong, or to find the cause of the problem.

**Inspect:** is to look closely to make sure that everything is satisfactory: *official inspection of school, college, bank branch,* etc.

**Probe:** is to ask questions to know the truth.

## 39. Claim – Allegation – Assertion – Contention

**Claim** is a statement that something is true though not proved.

**Allegation** is a public statement made without giving proof accusing someone of something.

**Assertion** is a statement about something that you strongly believe.

**Contention** is a belief or opinion that you give in an argument.

## 40. Choice – Favourite – Preference – Option

**Choice** is a thing or person that is chosen: *the obvious choice*.

**Favourite:** a person or thing that you like more than others: *favourite actor*.

**Preference:** a thing that is liked better or best.

**Option:** is a course of action — to take or not to take a particular course of action.

## 41. Clear – Apparent – Obvious – Evident

**Clear** is easy to see or understand: *It is quite clear that....*

**Apparent** (not before noun) clear from some situation/ position: *It was apparent from his face that he was tense.*

**Obvious:** clear from some statement, situation: *obvious choice*.

**Evident:** some clearly visible fact from a situation: *obvious/evident reluctance*.

Some expressions: *obvious reasons; no apparent reason; clear plan; obvious case; evident enjoyment.*

## 42. Close – Shut

We close or shut doors, windows, our mouth, eyes.

**Shut** suggests more noise and is usually used with the words/phrases slammed shut, snapped shut and banged shut.

**Closed** is generally used about airports, roads, market: *The road is closed for repair.*

## 43. Cold, Cool, Freezing, etc.

**Cold:** having a temperature that is lower than usual or lower than human body. Also used for indifferent response or behaviour.

**Cool:** fairly cold, in a pleasant way.

**Freezing:** extremely cold — temperature below 0° C.

**Chilly** (formal) too cold to be comfortable.

**Tepid:** slightly warm, sometimes in an unpleasant way.

**Lukewarm** (often disapprovingly) not warm enough. Also lukewarm response.

## 44. Collect – Gather – Accumulate – Amass

**Collect** is to bring things or information together from different places/people/sources: *collecting data.*

**Gather** is to bring things together that have been spread around. Both these words can be used for data, information, evidence.

**Accumulate** is to gradually get more and more of something over a period of time: *She accumulated the shares of Reliance Industries. ○ Debts began to accumulate.*

**Amass** is to collect something in large quantities.

## 45. Complain – Object — Protest, etc.

**Complain:** to say that you are annoyed or not satisfied about something or somebody.

**Object:** means that you disagree with or disapprove of something.

**Protest** is to disagree or disapprove, especially publicly protest against petrol price rise.

**Grumble:** to complain about something on a bad-tempered way.

**Moan:** to complain in an annoying way.

**Whine:** to complain in a crying voice.

**Whinge:** to complain about something in an annoying way.

## 46. Complement – Compliment

**Complement:** to add to something in a way that improves it. If one thing complements another, both work or look better. *They are complementary to each other.*

**Compliment** is to make nice rewards to someone: *He complemented me on my Maths.* It can also mean free: *complimentary passes.*

## 47. Condition – State

**Condition** refers to the appearance, quality or working order of something. It is used with an adjective: *good/bad/perfect condition.*

**State** is used for the condition that something is in at a particular time. It can be used with or without adjective: *mental state, gaseous state.*

## 48. Consist — Comprise

**Consist of:** to be formed from things, activities or people.

**Comprise:** to be formed from things or people mentioned. Usage: comprises or is comprised of.

**Make up:** to be the parts of people that form something: *Girls make up 45 per cent of the student members of the college club.*

**Constitute:** is the same as make up.

**Composed:** to be formed of people or things mentioned: *is composed of.*

## 49. Continual – Continuous

**Continual** describes an action that is repeated again and again. It is used with words: change, fear, pain, problems, questions, updating, complaints, interruptions.

**Continuous** describes something that goes on without stopping. It is used with the words: *employment, flow, supply, speech, process.*

## 50. Cut – Slash – Downsize, etc.

**Cut** is to reduce something especially the amount of money that is demanded, spent, earned, etc: *tax cut, wage cut.*

**Slash:** used often in newspapers as to cut by a large amount: *The workforce has been slashed by nearly 30 per cent..*

**Scale back** is to reduce especially the money in business. It is also used to reduce growth predictions, etc.

**Rationalise** is to make changes to increase efficiency in business, etc.

**Downsize** is to make the company or organisation smaller by reducing the workforce/workplace.

**Scale down** is to reduce the number, size and other dimensions.

## 51. Damage – Harm – Hurt – Impair

**Damage** is to cause physical harm to something — making it less useful, valuable or attractive: *The fire damaged the new building*. It is also used as a noun.

**Harm** is to have a bad effect on something/somebody's life, health, happiness, success: *Oil spills harm aquatic animals*.

**Hurt:** is synonymous with **harm**. Further, it is used for feelings/praise: *She hurt (not harm) my feelings*. Also used as an adjective: *a hurt look*.

**Impair** is to damage somebody's health, abilities or chances: *Fog impairs our vision*. ○ *Alcoholic drinks impair driving*.

## 52. Difficult – Hard – Challenging, etc.

**Difficult:** not easy, needing some effort or skill to do or understand: *difficult task/situation*.

**Hard:** not easy, also tough: *hard to understand, hardwork*.

**Challenging:** difficult, something that will test your ability.

**Demanding:** difficult to deal, needing a lot of effort: *a demanding situation*.

**Taxing:** used in a negative sense — difficult — putting pressure on you: *a taxing job.*

**Testing:** difficult — needing special strength and abilities to do: *testing times.*

### 53. Disables – Handicapped

**Disabled** is used for people with a permanent illness or injury.

**Handicapped:** people with one permanent or temporary disadvantage. Now considered offensive; terms like physically challenged, partially slighted, perons with special needs, etc. are used.

### 54. Discussion – Dialogue – Conversation, etc.

**Discussion:** a detailed discourse about something considered important.

**Dialogue:** conversation in a book, play, movie or TV serial. Also a formal discussion between two groups.

**Conversation:** a private or informal talk.

**Talk:** discussion about some problem.

**Chat:** a friendly, informal conversation.

**Gossip:** conversation about other people's private lives.

### 55. Disease – Illness – Infection – Disorder

**Disease:** some medical problem affecting humans, animals, plants.

**Illness:** a medical problem or a period of suffering: *a brief illness.*

**Infection:** illness caused by bacteria affecting some particular part of the body: *throat infection.*

**Ailment:** an illness that is not very serious.

## 56. Disgusting – Repulsive – Offensive – Nauseating

**Disgusting:** very unpleasant, making you slightly ill: *disgusting smell.*

**Repulsive:** unpleasant in a way that offends you, puts you back.

**Offensive:** extremely unpleasant.

**Nauseating:** something that makes you feel like vomiting: *nauseating smell.*

## 57. Distrust – Mistrust

**Distrust** is the stronger word of the two. It is used when one is sure that the other person is acting dishonestly.

**Mistrust** is used when you have doubts and suspicions that someone is dishonest.

## 58. Double – Dual – Duel

**Double** is used to describe something that has two parts and these parts are very similar. It is used with words: *bed , door,* etc. Double standard means hypocracy.

**Dual** is used when something has two parts, aspects or uses. It is used with words: *approach, citizenship, use,* etc.

**Duel** means a fight between two persons.

## 59. Each – Every

**Each** is used before a singular noun and is followed by a singular verb: *Each candidate has been given a roll number.* But, *Each of the candidates has ....*

When used after a plural subject it has a plural verb: *They each have their own identity.* But *each of them has...*

**Every** is always followed by a singular verb: *Every Indian player is capable of winning a medal.*

## 60. Economic – Financial – Commercial – Monetary

**Economic** is connected with industry, trade and development, use of money, etc.

**Financial** is related to money and finance: *financial position of a company.*

**Commercial** is connected with buying and selling of goods and services.

**Monetary** is connected with all the money in the country: *Monetary measures taken by RBI.*

**Economical** means spending money in a careful manner, avoiding waste.

## 61. Electric – Electrical

**Electric** is used to describe something that produces or uses electricity. It is used with words: *chair, drill, guitar, shock, light.*

**Electrical** is used with more general nouns like appliances, wiring, engineer, shock, signal.

## 62. Entertainment – Recreation – Relaxation – Fun, etc.

**Entertainment** includes TV, cinema, music, etc.: *live entertainment.*

**Recreation** (formal) things people do to enjoy themselves: *recreation club.*

**Relaxation:** things people do to relax, rest and enjoyment.

**Fun** denotes activities that people do, not seriously but from a sense of enjoyment.

**Amusement:** the fact of being entertained by something.

**Pleasure:** the activity of enjoying yourself — in contrast to working.

## 63. Environment – Surrounding – Backdrop, etc.

**Environment** denotes prevailing conditions in a place that impact the behaviour and development of something or somebody: *working environment.*

**Surrounding:** everything that is near or around somebody/something: *Mystery surrounding the murder.*

**Backdrop:** the scenery surrounding an event: *against the backdrop of Himalayan mountains.*

**Background:** the scene or area that is behind or around the main object of focus.

## 64. Especially – Specially

**Especially** is used to mean particularly.

**Specially** means for a particular purpose.

The adjective for both these adverbs is **special.**

## 65. Essential – Crucial – Indispensable, etc.

**Essential** is extremely important and totally necessary, which cannot be overlooked: *Knowledge of Java is essential for this job.*

**Crucial** is extremely important because of a particular situation: *It is crucial that we win this game.*

**Indispensable:** essential — too important to be ignored: *indispensable requirements for sanctioning a loan.*

## 66. Excellent – Outstanding – Superb, etc.

**Excellent** is extremely good. It is used to denote standards of service, etc.: *excellent value.*

**Outstanding** expresses how well somebody does something: *outstanding performance.*

**Superb:** is extremely impressive: *superb shot* (cricket).

**Marvellous/Marvelous** (informal) extremely good.

**Exceptional** is used to express somebody's unusual ability to do something.

**Wonderful:** extremely good, that gives you great pleasure.

## 67. Excited – Ecstatic – Elated, etc.

**Excited:** showing happiness, enthusiasm: *excited about the foreign trip.*

**Ecstatic:** very happy and enthusiastic.

**Elated:** happy and emotionally charged because something good has happened.

**Euphoric:** happy and excited (for a short period of time).

**Rapturous:** express extreme pleasure: *rapturous applause.*

**Exhilarated:** happy and excited — particularly after an exciting physical activity like driving, wind surfing, or a good stage performance.

## 68. Farther – Further

**Farther** is beyond something in distance. In superlative form farthest it is used to denote beyond thought: *Farthest from my mind.*

**Further** means after something. *He further stated that....*

## 69. Fast – Quick – Rapid – Swift – Speedy

**Fast** is something that moves or is able to move at great speed: *fast car.*

**Quick:** denotes something that is done in a short time: *The batsmen took a quick single.* As an adjective it also means a person who is nimble-footed: *He is quick on his feet.*

**Rapid** describes the speed at which something changes: *rapid growth/recovery; rapid pulse/heartbeat.* The word is not used to describe speed.

**Swift:** something that is done or happens quickly: *a swift action.*

**Speedy:** something that happens quickly: *speedy recovery.*

## 70. Fear – Alarm – Apprehension – Fright – Scare

**Fear:** is a bad feeling one has when one is in some danger.

**Alarm:** fear or worry that something dangerous or unpleasant might happen.

**Apprehension:** a worry in anticipation of something bad. Less intense than fear or alarm.

**Fright:** a feeling of fear due to something that happens suddenly.

**Scare:** a situation in which a lot of people are anxious: *bomb scare.*

### 71. Fight – Clash – Scuffle, etc.

**Fight:** a situation in which two or more people try to defeat each other, using physical force: *fight with sticks.*

**Clash** is a short fight between two groups.

**Brawl** is a noisy and violent fight involving a group of people.

**Scuffle** is a short and less violent fight or struggle.

**Tussle** is a short fight or argument in order to get something: *tussle for the rugby.*

**Struggle** is a fight between two people or groups of people when one is trying to get something from the other: *struggle for freedom.*

### 72. Force – Strength – Power – Authority

**Force** is generally used to denote collective strength. It can be violent physical action.

**Strength** is power and influence: *inner strength.*

**Power** is the ability to control people or things: *political power.*

**Authority** denotes power with legal sanction: *sanctioning authority.*

### 73. Frighten – Scare – Intimidate – Startle

**Frighten:** to make somebody feel afraid, generally suddenly.

**Scare:** to make animals, etc. feel afraid: *scare the monkey away.*

**Intimidate:** to frighten or threaten somebody to make him/her nervous.

**Startle** is to make someone feel suddenly frightened or surprised: *A sudden noise startled us.*

## 74. Funny – Amusing – Comic – Hilarious, etc.

**Funny:** something that makes you laugh: *funny fellow.*

**Amusing:** funny and enjoyable: *amusing story.*

**Comic:** (used in literature): *comic elements in the novel, a comic scene.*

**Hilarious:** extremely funny, that makes you laugh heartily.

**Humorous:** funny and entertaining: *humorous look.*

**Witty:** amusing and clever: *witty remark.*

## 75. Glad – Happy – Pleased – Delighted, etc.

**Glad** (not before noun) happy about something: *I was glad to see my old friend.*

**Happy:** pleased about something nice that has happened: *We're happy to announce the engagement of our son.*

**Pleased:** (not before noun) happy about something that has happened: *pleased with one's exam result.*

**Delighted:** is very pleased about something.

**Thrilled:** (informal) extremely pleased and excited about something.

**Overjoyed:** extremely happy about something.

## 76. Great – Awesome – Brilliant, Fantastic, etc.

**Great** is good, giving a lot of pleasure.

**Awesome:** very good and impressive: *The opera was just awesome.*

**Fantastic:** giving a lot of pleasure: *fantastic time.*

**Fabulous:** extremely good: *My mother is a fabulous cook.*

**Terrific:** very good, wonderful: *to do a terrific job.*

**Brilliant:** extremely good, dazzling.

## 77. Half – Whole – Quarter

**Half** can be a determiner, noun, adjective or adverb: *Half the job is already done.* ○ *Cut the board into two equal halves.* ○ *He gave me only half of bread.* ○ *This dish is only half cooked. (Adverb)*

**Whole** means full, total: *Tell me the whole story.*

**Quarter** is one-fourth. The word makes certain idioms: *from close quarters; quarter final; quarter master,* etc.

## 78. Happy – Content – Contented – Satisfied

**Happy:** satisfied with something, not worried: *a happy marriage.*

**Content:** satisfied and happy with what you have.

**Contented:** happy and comfortable with what you have.

**Satisfied:** pleased because you have achieved something.

## 79. Hardly – Barely – Scarcely

**Hardly, barely** and **scarcely** are negative words and they should not be used with negatives—no, not.

They all can be used to say that something is/was just

possible: *The old man could hardly walk.* ○ *We could scarcely believe our eyes.* ○ *The family barely managed to make both ends meet.*

## 80. Hate, Hatred, Dislike, Despise, etc.

**Hate** and **hatred** express a strong feeling of dislike. Hate is a strong feeling of dislike and is used in a general way. Hatred is used to express dislike for a particular person.

**Dislike** is not to like something/someone.

**Despise** is to dislike and have no respect for someone or something: *I despise gossip.*

**Loathe:** to hate somebody very much.

**Detest:** synonymous with **loathe.**

## 81. Hide – Conceal – Cover – Disguise, etc.

**Hide** is to place something/someone in a place where others cannot find it/them.

**Conceal** is to keep something secret.

**Cover** is to place something over it to hide something: *Cover the face with hands.*

**Disguise** is to hide or change the nature of something so that it cannot be recognised: *disguised attack, disguise the fact, disguise himself as a girl, etc.*

**Camouflage** to make the appearance look like surroundings or like something else to deceive others.

## 82. High – Tall

**High** is used to denote the measurement of something from the bottom to top: *The fence is six feet high.*

**Tall** is used to talk about people: *My brother is over six feet tall.*

However, the factory chimneys or columns in a building can be **high** or **tall**.

### 83. Historic – Historical

**Historic** is used to express something very important: *historic deal/treaty.*

**Historical** is used to refer to something that is connected with the past or the study of history: *historical building.*

### 84. Hold – Cling, Grasp, etc.

**Hold** is to have something/somebody in your hands/ arms.

**Cling:** to hold something/someone tightly.

**Clutch** to hold something tightly in your hand, suddenly.

**Grip:** to hold something tightly with your hand.

**Grasp:** to take hold of something firmly: *He grasped my hand and shook it firmly.*

**Clasp:** to hold something tightly in your hand: *She clasped the child in her hands.*

### 85. Holiday(s) – Vacation

They express the regular period of time when you are not at work or at school/college.

**Holiday** denotes single off-day from work. **Holidays** in Am. E. refer to Christmas holidays — December end- early January.

**Vocation** is mainly used to mean the period when schools/colleges/universities are officially closed for students: *summer vacation.*

## 86. Honest, Direct, Straight, Open, etc.

**Honest:** not hiding the truth: *honest confession.*

**Direct:** saying exactly what you mean whether others like it or not: *I like his direct manner of saying things.*

**Straight:** honest and direct.

**Open**: is a person who does not hide his/her feelings/thoughts.

**Outspoken:** one who says what he thinks even if it offends others.

**Blunt:** saying exactly what you think without trying to be polite or polished: *She bluntly told me that ....*

Blunt and direct people consider making honest statements to be more important than being polite.

## 87. Identify – Discern – Distinguish – Recognize, etc.

**Identify:** to be able to tell what/who something/somebody is.

**Discern** is to see or recognize something which is not obvious.

**Distinguish** (formal) usually used in negative statements — to manage to see or hear something that is not very clear: *He could not distinguish her words.*

**Pick:** to recognize something/somebody from among other things/people.

## 88. Imagine – Envisage – Envision – Visualize, etc.

**Imagine:** to form some idea in your mind about something/somebody.

**Envisage** is to imagine what will happen in future.

**Envision:** the word is used in Am. E in place of **envisage**: *I do not envisage/envision staying in this hotel again.*

**Visualize:** to form a picture of something/somebody in your mind.

## 89. Infer – Imply

**Infer** and **imply** can describe the same thing but from different points of view.

If we **infer** something from what the speaker says we come to the conclusion that this is what he/she means.

If the speaker implies something he/she suggests it without saying it directly.

## 90. Intelligent – Smart – Brilliant – Clever, etc.

**Intelligent** is someone who is good at understanding things and thinking in a logical way.

**Smart** means quick at learning, having the ability to make good business and take right decisions: *smart person, smart move.*

**Brilliant** and **bright** are very intelligent and skilful.

**Clever** is quick at understanding things: *a clear person.* The word is also used in a negative sense: *He tried to be clever with me.*

**Overclever, oversmart** are also negative words.

## 91. Interest – Hobby – Pastime, etc.

**Interest:** an activity or subject that someone does or studies for pleasure in their spare time.

**Hobby** is something done for pleasure in spare time: *Gardening is my hobby*. A hobby is more active than interest.

**Pastime** is used while talking about people in general: *Reading is the national pastime of the English.*

## 92. Interesting – Fascinating – Absorbing – Compelling – Gripping, etc.

**Interesting** is something that attracts your attention because it is special, exciting or unusual: *an interesting story*.

**Absorbing:** interesting and enjoyable: *absorbing match*.

**Compelling:** very interesting and exciting: *Vikram Seth's travelogues make a compelling reading*

**Gripping:** so interesting that it engages your attention completely: *A gripping drama was enacted on the college stage.*

**Stimulating** is full of exciting ideas: *a stimulating discussion*.

## 93. Kind – Sort – Type

**Kind:** a group of people/things that are same in some way.

**Sort** is a particular type: the sort of behaviour/things.

**Type** a class or group of people or things that share some particular features: *the type of weather/work.*

### 94. Lastly – At last

**Lastly** is used to mention the last thing in a list or to make the final point: *Lastly, I wish to...*

**At last** is used to mention something which has happened after a long time: *At last the two countries signed a treaty.*

### 95. Late – Lately

**Late:** near the end of a period of time; not in time: *late afternoon; ... arrived late.*

**Lately** is used in the sense of recent times: *He has not been keeping a good health lately.*

### 96. Love – Like – Adore – Be fond of

**Love:** to like or enjoy something very much.

**Like:** to find something attractive, pleasant.

**Adore:** to like or enjoy something/someone very much.

**Be fond of** to like or enjoy something/someone very much: *My father is fond of playing chess.*

### 97. Restriction – Restraint – Constraint, etc.

**Restriction:** a rule or law that limits what you may do.

**Restraint:** a rule, idea or decision that limits what you can do: *moral restraint.*

**Constraint** is some limiting thing/factor that exists rather than something which is made: *resource constraint.*

**Limitation:** the act or process of limiting something: *limitation of power.*

## 98. Look – Watch – See – Observe, etc.

**Look:** to turn your eyes on a specific direction: *He looked at her and she smiled.*

**Watch** is to look at something for a time, paying attention to what happens: *to watch a movie/match/TV serial.*

**See:** to become aware of something by using your eyes.

**Observe:** to watch something carefully especially to learn more about it.

**View:** to look at something carefully: *view somebody's work/paintings.*

## 99. Loud, Loudly, Aloud

**Loud:** making a lot of noise.

**Loudly** is in a loud manner: *He called out loudly so that someone could hear him.*

**Aloud** (formal) is also a loud manner. A voice that other people can hear: *The secretary read the order aloud.*

## 100. Luck – Chance – Coincidence – Fortune, etc.

**Luck:** the force that causes good or bad things to happen: *good luck; bad luck.*

**Chance:** something that happens without any apparent cause: *chance happening/acquaintance.*

**Coincidence:** happening of two things by chance at the same time: *It was a coincidence that I was travelling in the same train as my friend.*

**Accident:** an unexpected happening. An unpleasant event that occurs unexpectedly and causes injury and/or death.

**Fortune:** luck or chance as it affects people's lives.

**Fate:** the power that controls everything.

**Destiny:** the power that is believed to control the course of events: *I wanted to start a business but destiny willed it otherwise.*

**Providence:** God Almighty — the force that controls human lives.

## 101. Main – Major – Chief – Prime, etc.

**Main** is major, largest or most important: *main character in a story/novel play; main road.*

**Major:** most important: *major concern.*

**Chief:** most important: *chief cause of poverty.*

**Prime:** most important, to be considered first: *prime objective, prime concern.*

**Principal:** mainly used for statements of fact: *the principal reason; principal city.*

**Central:** the key issue: *central issue.*

## 102. Many – A lot of — Lots of

**Many** means several. It is used with countable nouns: *many people; many mistakes.*

**A lot of** or **lots of** also means many but is more informal.

**Many** or **a large number of** is preferred in written statements and reports.

## 103. Mark – Stain – Blot – Spot, etc.

**Mark:** a small spot of dirt or stain on a surface, cloth or substance.

**Stain:** a dirty mark on something which is difficult to remove.

**Blot:** a dirty spot left on a surface by ink or paint, etc.

**Spot** is a small dirty mark on something.

**Streak** is a thin mark or line that is different from the surface: *a streak of golden in black hair.*

**Smear:** a mark made, spread or rubbed by oil or paint on a substance.

## 104. Mentally ill – Insane – Neurotic, etc.

**Mentally ill** is one who is suffering from illness of the mind.

**Insane** (not before noun) suffering from serious mental illness.

**Neurotic:** a mental illness in which the person has strong feelings of fear and worry.

**Psychotic:** a mental illness in which the person loses connection with outside reality.

**Disturbed:** mentally ill or deranged because of some shocking happening.

**Unstable:** having behaviour that is not stable, and has sudden and unexpected changes.

## 105. Mistake – Error – Slip, etc.

**Mistake:** a fact, figure or word not spoken or written correctly: *a spelling mistake.*

**Error** also means the same and is more formal: *grammatical error; an error of judgment.*

**Slip** is a small mistake.

**Howler** is a major mistake/error that can lead to embarrassment.

**Type** is a typing mistake in a text.

**Inaccuracy** (formal) a piece of information that is not exactly correct. Mistakes in data, facts and figures, etc.

### 106. Mix – Mingle – Stir – Blend

**Mix:** to combine two or more substances, ideas, feelings or even attributes such that they can't be easily separated.

**Mingle** is actually mixing of sounds, colours or some abstract things like laughter.

**Stir:** to move a liquid or beverage using spoon to mix it completely: *stirred martini.*

**Blend** is to mix two flavours together to create a unique taste.

### 107. Naked – Bare – Stark

**Naked** is used for a person or body not covered with clothes. It is used with words: *man, fear, aggression, truth.*

**Bare** is used for parts: *bare feet/arms/walls/branches.*

**Stark** (formal) used for describing an unpleasant fact that is obvious: *stark reality* or *poverty.*

### 108. Near – Close

**Near** and **close** often have the same meaning. However, **close** is more often used to describe a relationship between people: *close relative/friend.*

**Near** is used in phrases like: *near future/neighbour* and **close** in *close contest, close encounter.*

## 109. Nervous – Neurotic – Edgy, etc.

**Nervous** is easily frightened or worried.

**Neurotic** is someone who does not behave in a reasonable way because they are worried that something will happen: *neurotic about keeping the food clean.*

**Edgy** is frightened worried and bad tempered.

On edge is also nervous, e.g. before an interview.

**Jittery** and **nervy** mean anxious and nervous. *He was jittery when the share market began to tumble.* Nervy is used for being worried about boy, child, etc.: *She was nervy about her baby.*

## 110. Next – Nearest

**Next** means after something in place or turn: *sitting next to someone; the next item is ....*

**Nearest** means closest in space: Kitty is sitting nearest to the window (of all the others).

## 111. Noise – Sound

**Noise** is unpleasant sound: *Don't make a noise.*

**Sound** is something that you hear: *I can hear the faint sound of rustling of leaves.* You don't use words like much, a lot of, etc. with sound.

## 112. Notice – Note – Detect, etc.

**Notice** is to note, become aware of something or somebody.

**Note** is to pay careful attention to some fact or situation.

**Detect** is to discover or notice something that is not easy: *detect a disease through tests.*

**Observe** is to notice something by constant watch.

**Witness:** to see something happen: *witness to a crime.*

**Perceive** is to notice or become aware of something: *We perceived a positive change in his behaviour.*

### 113. Old – Elderly – Aged

**Old:** no longer young; having lived for a long time: *an old man.*

**Elderly** is a polite word for **old:** *elderly lady/relative.*

**Aged:** very old: *an aged relative.*

**Mature** is used for no longer young; someone who is experienced.

**Note:** Older and Elder: *My brother is older than me.* But, ... *my elder brother.*

### 114. Option – Choice

**Option** is something one can choose to have or do.

**Choice** is freedom to choose what you do.

**Alternative** means one instead of the other.

**Alternate** has a different meaning — happening one after the other regularly: *every alternate day* but *alternative medicine.*

**Possibility** is one of the different things that one can do in a particular situation.

### 115. Order – Tell – Instruct – Direct

**Order:** use your position/authority/power to tell someone to do something.

**Tell** is to say somebody that he/she must do something: *I had told you to clean the table*.

**Instruct:** to tell someone to do something, officially, in a particular way: *The letter instructed her to join the Mumbai office*.

**Direct:** to give an official order: *The board directed the CEO to ....*

**Command** is to use your position to dictate your way something must be done: *The General commanded his men to attack*.

## 116. Partly – Partially

Both these words mean 'not completely'.

**Partly** is used to express reason and is followed by *because* or *due to*.

Partially is used while talking about physical conditions: *partially blind*.

## 117. Persuade – Convince

**Persuade** is to try to make someone agree to do something by giving convincing reason: *The salesman persuaded me to buy a watch*.

**Convince** is to make someone believe that something is true: *She convinced me that she was right*.

## 118.  Place – Site – Location, etc.

**Place:** a particular point, building, city, town, etc. *a nice place to visit*.

**Site:** a place where some building will be constructed: *site for mall*.

**Location:** a place where something happens: *a location for shooting a film*.

**Scene:** a place where something unpleasant has happened: *the scene of crime/accident/mishap*.

**Spot:** a specific place in a city or area having some particular character: *picnic spot*.

**Venue:** where people meet for a pre-organized event: *venue of cricket match*.

## 119. Plain – Simple – Unequivocal

**Plain:** simple and direct in way that others may not like.

**Simple** (not before noun) used to express a fact or plain truth: *The simple truth is that our hockey team is weaker than that of Australia.*

**Unequivocal** (formal): expressing one's opinion clearly and firmly: *an unequivocal no.*

**Bold:** used to express some unpleasant fact without any extra explanation: *bold statement*.

## 120. Pleasure – Delight – Joy

**Pleasure:** something that brings you enjoyment. Also enjoyment derived from something.

**Delight:** something that brings great enjoyment. Also great enjoyment and happiness.

**Joy:** a thing or person that brings us great enjoyment: *the joys of youth*.

## 121. Poor – Destitute – Disadvantaged – Deprived, etc.

**Poor:** having very little money — not enough to satisfy basic needs.

**Destitute:** without money, food and other things necessary for life.

**Disadvantaged:** having less money and fewer opportunities than most people.

**Impoverished:** poor, made poor by circumstances.

**Deprived:** those who are denied basic amenities.

**Penniless:** having no money, very poor.

**Hard up:** having not enough money — for a short period: *I am hard up these days.*

**Marginalized:** not given any importance; having no say.

## 122. Pressure – Stress – Tension – Strain

**Pressure:** feelings of anxiety caused by the need to do or advise something: *pressures of work*, etc.

**Stress:** pressure or anxiety caused by problems in someone's life.

**Tension:** anxiety and worry that make it difficult to relax: *nervous tension.*

**Strain:** pressure caused by much work that one has to do or manage.

## 123. Prisoner – Detainee – Hostage – Captive

**Prisoner:** a person who has been kept in a prison.

**Detainee:** a person kept in prison for political reasons, often without trial.

**Hostage:** a person captured and held prisoner by a person or group like terrorists.

**Captive** is also a person who is kept as prisoner. But

this is used in historical context ... kings, queens, slaves, etc.

## 124. Product – Commodity – Goods – Merchandise, etc.

**Product** is something that is produced or grown, usually to be sold: *food products*.

**Produce:** used for things grown in farms — grain, pulses, etc.

**Commodity:** something that can be bought and sold.

**Merchandise:** goods that are for sale in a shop or store; also goods that can be bought or sold, particularly connected with an event/region: *Asian/Commonwealth merchandise*.

**Goods:** things that are produced to be sold.

**Wares** are things sold at a market. Also used for goods which do not have much value.

## 125. Purpose – Aim – Intention, etc.

**Purpose** is what something (plan or effort) is supposed to achieve. Purpose is of something.

**Aim** what something/someone is trying to achieve; aim is of someone.

**Intention** is what you intend to do: *good/bad intention.*

**Plan** is to do something over a longer period of time: *Five-year Plan*.

**Point** (informal) purpose or aim of something: *There is no point in waiting now, let's move.*

**Idea:** somebody's aim: *What's the idea behind....?* (Genuine question). ◯ *What's the point....* (negative, suggesting there is no point).

## 126. Rare – Exceptional

**Rare** denotes something which is not usually found: *rare species; Such questions are rarely asked*.

**Exceptional** means extraordinary, of high quality, and is an appreciative word.

## 127. Reason – Grounds – Excuse – Pretext, etc.

**Reason** is the cause or explanation of something that has happened.

**Grounds:** a valid reason for doing or saying something.

**Excuse:** a reason or explanation, true or false, given for defending a behaviour/doing or not doing something.

**Pretext:** a false reason given for doing something: *on the pretext of....*

**Cause:** a reason based on some fact, scientific explanation: *cause and effect.*

**Motive** is the hidden reason behind some action.

**Justification** is a good reason that exists behind some action.

## 128. Regretfully – Regrettably

Both these words are used to express that the situation has not been on the expected lines: *Regretfully/Regrettably, there will be no pay rise this year.*

Regretfully shows some disappointment or sadness.

## 129. Rely – Depend – Count on

**Rely:** the need to depend entirely on something/somebody: *The small baby relies on milk.*

**Depend:** (always followed by a on/upon) to be sure or

expect that something will happen: *The farmers depend on rain.*

**Count on:** in an assuring way: *You can count on me.*

## 130. Return – Come back – Go back – Get back, etc.

**Return:** to come or go back from some place to the original place: *return to home town.*

**Come back:** relates to the person or place: *Come back soon.*

**Go back** is used from the point of view of the place: *Go back to work.* (The place of work).

**Get back** is used in the sense of contacting or taking up something later after finishing the matter in hand: *We shall get back to you soon.*

## 131. Rich – Wealthy – Affluent – Well off, etc.

**Rich** is someone having a lot of money, possessions, prosperity, etc.

**Wealthy** also means rich but is less used in phrases.

**Affluent:** rich with a high standard of living: *the affluent class.* The word is used in contrast with poor/destitute classes.

**Well-off:** (not frequently used) rich, living comfortably.

**More:** used in negative sense: *not very well-off.*

**Prosperous:** rich and successful, adding to their wealth.

## 132. Right – Correct

**Right:** something that is appropriate or correct to do

in a particular situation: *right decision*. It is more used for beliefs: *wrong and right*.

**Correct:** is used for decision, method, opinion. (It is more formal).

## 133. Rise – Raise – Arise

Rise is used for self and without an object. It denotes a self movement: ○ *I rise* (myself). *She rose from poverty* (herself) [Rise rose risen].

**Raise** is used for other things and with an object: *raise the bar* (something else). [Raise raised raised].

**Arise:** a problem or difficult situation to start to exist: *A new crisis has arisen because of ....* [Arise arose arisen]

## 134. Satisfying – Rewarding – Pleasing – Gratifying, etc.

**Satisfying:** that which gives you pleasure.

**Rewarding** is used for an activity or experience that makes you happy.

**Pleasing:** that which gives you pleasure especially when you look at it, hear or think about it: *pleasing to the eye*.

**Gratifying:** a feeling of pleasure after having done something well.

**Fulfilling:** a happy feeling when your talents are recognized.

## 135. Save – Rescue – Bail out – Redeem

**Save:** to prevent someone/something from dying, embarrassment, harm, etc.: *The doctor saved the patient with....*

**Rescue** is to save from a dangerous situation like natural calamity, disaster: *Rescued from the sinking ship.*

**Bail out** is used for saving someone/something from a difficult situation: *The company was bailed out by the Government with financial help.* Also *a bail-out* package.

**Redeem**: to save from the clutches of evil. In Accounts it is used to convey getting back shares (mortgaged) by making payment.

### 136. Sensible – Sensitive

**Sensible:** having the ability to make good judgments: *a sensible person.*

**Sensitive** is someone who is easily affected by actions/situations/weather changes, etc.

### 137. Serious – Grave – Earnest – Solemn

**Serious:** needing to be thought about carefully; something that must be treated as important.

**Grave:** serious in manner that may be sad or worrying: *grave danger.*

**Earnest:** serious and sincere about something.

**Solemn:** looking or seeming serious, without smiling: *solemn manner/promise.*

### 138. Shine – Glean – Glow – Sparkle, etc.

**Shine:** to brighten, reflect light. Also perform brilliantly.

**Gleam:** to shiene with a clear bright light.

**Glow** is to produce a dull but steady light. Also glow of happiness on someone's face.

**Sparkle:** to shine with flashes of light. Also sparkle of brilliance (performance).

**Glisten:** to shine, reflecting the sunlight, etc.

**Shimmer** is to shine with soft light.

**Glitter:** shine brightly with flashes of light.

**Twinkle:** to shine brightly and softly alternately — like stars.

**Glint:** small flash of light — glint of knife's blade.

**Radiance** is brightness of happiness on someone's face.

## 139. Shock – Horrify – Sicken – Repel, etc.

**Shock:** surprise and upset someone: *shocking news.*

**Horrify:** to make somebody extremely shocked, upset or even frightened: *horrified by terrorists' attack.*

**Sicken** is to make feel very shocked and angry giving a sickening feeling.

**Disgust:** shocked at something unpleasant.

**Repel:** to make feel like turning away due to foul smell, etc.

**Appal** is to shock and upset very much: *an appalling decision by the umpire.*

## 140. Sign – Indication – Signal – Symptom, etc.

**Sign:** an action or event that shows that something exists: *sign of good health.*

**Indication:** a remark or hint about something: *indication of company's new strategy.*

**Signal:** an action that shows what is happening or may happen in future: *signal the arrival of flight/train.*

**Symptom** is a change in our mind or body showing that something is wrong: *symptoms of asthma/malaria.*

**Indicator:** a sign of change: indicators of economic development.

### 141. Sit – Perch – Be seated, etc.

**Sit** is to be seated in a chair. It is also used to mean not doing anything or for players not in the playing eleven: *sitting on the bench* (football, hockey, cricket).

**Perch** is to sit on the end of something: *bird perching on a tree branch.*

**Be seated:** formal way of saying sit down: *Please be seated.*

**Take a seat** is a polite way of inviting someone to sit down.

### 142. Stare – Gaze – Peer – Glare

**Stare:** look at something/someone for a long time.

**Gaze:** a steady look at something/somebody especially with surprise or love.

**Peer:** to look carefully or from a position where you cannot see something properly: *peer through the window.*

**Glare:** look angrily for a long time.

### 143. Storey – Floor

**Storey** is used while talking about the number of levels in a high rise building: *seven storey high.*

**Floor:** is used when you talk about a particular level: *Our flat is on the third floor.*

## 144. Structure – Framework – Composition, etc.

**Structure** is used to talk about how parts are connected together: *structure of atoms in a compound; social structure; wooden structure.*

**Framework** is a set of rules, ideas beliefs that underlie a society.

**Composition:** the different parts that form something: *composition of workforce in a company.*

**Construction:** the way something has been built: *cement/steel construction.*

**Fabric:** the basic structure of society or community.

**Make-up:** different things or people that combine to form something.

## 145. Sure – Certain – Confident, etc.

**Sure** (not before noun): something you have no doubt about.

**Certain:** bound to happen.

**Confident:** completely sure that something will happen the way you want: *confident of victory/success.*

**Convinced:** sure about something because of certain facts or reasons: *From his statement, the judge was convinced that he was innocent.*

## 146. Surprise – Astonish – Astound – Startle, etc.

**Surprise:** a feeling given by some unexpected happening.

**Astonish:** to surprise someone very much: *The news astonished everyone.*

**Astound:** to surprise or shock very much.

**Startle:** to surprise suddenly: *startling behaviour.*

**Stun:** is to shock someone so that they are speechless.

**Amaze:** greatly surprise. Used with some news or behaviour: *The results of elections amazed many.*

**Taken aback:** surprised and docked — by some violent/hostile action.

## 147. Terrible – Awful – Horrible – Dreadful, etc.

**Terrible:** very bad or unpleasant that makes you feel upset and unhappy.

**Awful:** very bad and unpleasant, an action or thing that you immediately disapprove.

**Horrible** is very unpleasant: *horrible taste.*

**Dreadful:** something which you do not approve of: *dreadful weather.*

**Vile** is something bad or unpleasant: *vile smell.*

**Malicious** is full of malice and ill will.

## 148. True – Right – Correct – Exact

**True:** connected with facts: *It is true that....*

**Right:** something which cannot be doubted: *right time/ decision/perspective, way.*

**Correct:** without any mistakes: *grammatically correct.*

**Exact:** giving all details correctly: *exact description.*

**Precise:** to the point; giving whatever required but containing nothing extra.

**Accurate:** correct in every detail: *accurate note.*

**19**

# CHECKING YOUR PROGRESS
## COMPREHENSIVE TEST—3

**(Synonyms – Antonyms – Paronyms – Doublets –
Words Often Confused)**

If you have carefully gone through Chapter No. 14 to 18 you have learnt the following:

1. Over 500 expressive words.

2. Over 500 synonyms of important words.

3. About 200 antonyms of important words.

4. Over 100 paronyms and nearly 150 doublets.

5. All this makes nearly 1500 words which have different shades of meaning and their proper context and usage.

If you have worked diligently, you have come closer to the aim of building a wide and emphatic vocabulary. Not only your verbal and written expression have become more polished, but others around you must have noticed a perceptible change in the way you talk and write now. You must have earned some accolades already.

But you don't have to stop here. There is still much more to learn and achieve. It is necessary to review what you have been able to imbibe in your personality. This chapter is aimed primarily to check your progress of learning what has been given in the previous chapters. You must consult the correct answers given at the end of this chapter and check your score. Further course of action in achieving the objective of building excellent vocabulary should be taken as suggested.

## 1. Expressive Words

**A.** *Fill in the blanks with appropriate collective names:*

1. A _____ of flags.
2. A _____ of worshippers.
3. A _____ of flowers.
4. A _____ of dried plants.
5. A _____ of wine.
6. A _____ of girls/ladies.
7. A _____ of advisers.
8. A _____ of bees.
9. A _____ of bells.
10. A _____ of merchants.

**B.** *Mention the names of places where the following things are made or kept:*

11. Wild animals      _____
12. Bricks      _____
13. Grapes      _____
14. Bees      _____

15. Weapons          _____

16. Provisions       _____

17. Leather goods    _____

18. Iron goods       _____

19. Fish             _____

20. Clothes          _____

**C.** *Fill in the blanks with appropriate comparisons:*

21. As _____ as a butterfly.

22. As _____ as a lark.

23. As _____ as a doorpost.

24. As _____ as a bone.

25. As _____ as an oath.

26. As _____ as a daisy.

27. As _____ as a partridge.

28. As _____ as gossamer.

29. As _____ as a magpie.

30. As _____ as the gospel.

**2. Synonyms and Antonyms**

   **D.** *Mention two synonyms each of the following words. The first letter of each synonym is given for your convenience.*

   1. Abandon     r_____     f_____

   2. Complain    r_____     g_____

   3. Deceit      f_____     t_____

   4. Destroy     d_____     r_____

   5. Grant       c_____     a_____

6. Intrepid      b_____      f_____
7. Implore      e_____      b_____
8. Obstinate    s_____      w_____
9. Penitent     r_____      r_____
10. Prudent      w_____      d_____

**E.** *Mention the antonyms of the following words. The first letter of the word has been given to give you a start:*

11. Scarcity a_____
12. Ancestor d_____
13. Danger s_____
14. Glory s_____
15. Enrich i_____
16. Wane w_____
17. Persuade d_____
18. Repulsive a_____
19. Extravagant f_____
20. Frequent o_____.

## 3. Paronyms and Doublets

**F.** *Given below are the pairs of paronyms followed by four sets of options marked (a), (b), (c) and (d). Find the option that correctly matches the meaning of pairs of paronyms:*

1. **Ale, Ail**
   (a) sick, beverage
   (b) a beverage, to be sick
   (c) fair, pledge

(d) dirty, sweet

**2. Gilt, Guilt**
   (a) sword, dim
   (b) crime, covered with gold
   (c) skill, glad
   (d) covered with gold, crime

**3. Faint, Feint**
   (a) dim, pretence     (b) pretence, dim
   (c) gladly, bright     (d) healthy, image

**4. Wrath, Wroth**
   (a) sharpen, feeble     (b) to squander, lead
   (c) anger, angry     (d) angry, anger

**5. Wet, Whet**
   (a) moist, to sharpen    (b) to sharpen, moist
   (c) drown, valley     (d) white, while

**6. Cite, Site**
   (a) to quote, situation    (b) situation, to quote
   (c) to see, scale     (d) care, observe

**7. Naughty, Knotty**
   (a) nothing, zero
   (b) middle, suffering
   (c) complex, badly behaving
   (d) badly behaving, complex

**8. Raze, Raise**
   (a) lift, destroy     (b) beams, pull up
   (c) destroy, lift     (d) pull up, beams

**9. Lightning, Lightening**
   (a) making light, flash from clouds
   (b) flash from clouds, making light
   (c) making less, electricity
   (d) increasing, power

**10. Tear, Tier**
  (*a*) row, drop from the eye
  (*b*) run, destroy
  (*c*) drop from the eye, row
  (*d*) join, tale

**G.** *Write doublets of the following sets of meanings.*

11. Happening unexpectedly, belonging to the west

    _____, _____

12. Of marriage, a curb or restraint

    _____, _____

13. Glaring, sweet smelling

    _____, _____

14. Falsehood, begging  _____, _____

15. praiseworthy, showily attractive

    _____, _____

16. having virtue, in effect, not real

    _____, _____

17. roomy, plausible  _____, _____

18. very hot, sluggish  _____, _____

19. meddling, pertaining to an office

    _____, _____

20. disrespectful, vague  _____, _____

## 4. Words Often Confused

**H.** *Answer the following in 'Yes' or 'No'.*

1. *Above* is used in relation to a minimum level while *over* is used with numbers, age, etc.

    _____

2. *Current* and *present* are synonyms but *current* suggests a temporary situation. _____

3. *Economics* means spending money carefully, while *economical* relates to trade and industry.
   _____

4. *Despise* means to dislike and have no respect for someone.
   _____

5. You *begin* a journey not *start* _____

6. *Authority* denotes power with legal sanction.
   _____

7. *Historic* and *historical* mean exactly the same.
   _____

8. *Late* means not in time, *lately* means in recent times.
   _____

9. *Howler* means a major mistake while *slip* is a small mistake.
   _____

10. *Perch* means sitting in the middle of something.
    _____

I.  *Choose the appropriate word to match the meaning/statement:*

11. Bad smell : appalling, unpleasant, terrible.

12. Hit hard creating a noise : batter, pummel, pound.

13. Lack of trust on the basis of doubts :
                          mistrust, distrust, untrust

14. Change the nature of something so that it cannot be recognized : conceal, hide, disguise.

15. A line on a surface that is different from the surface : blot, smear, streak.

16. Sitting nearer the window as compared to all other persons : nearest, nearer, next.

огற

17. Suspicious of other people : paranoid, afraid, scared.

18. Alone and sad : lone, lonely, alone.

19. Pleasant to look at, having small delicate features : handsome, beautiful, pretty

20. Say something loudly without thinking carefully : blurt, divulge, call

**J.** *Mention the word that goes with the given word to make a meaningful expression/phrase:*

21. *admit/acknowledge* the mistake.

22. bad *affect/effect.*

23. Sitting *beside/besides* someone.

24. An *irate/furious* letter.

25. *Ask/demand* an explanation.

26. *Avenge/revenge* something.

27. *Back door/rear exit* of the aeroplane.

28. *Go/turn* bald.

29. *Respite/rest* from pain.

30. *Complementary/complimentary* passes.

## ANSWERS

1. **(A)** 1. bunting; 2. congregation; 3. bouquet/garland; 4. herbarium; 5. cellar, 6. bevy; 7. council; 8. swarm/hive; 9. peel; 10. syndicate.

   **(B)** 11. menagerie; 12. kiln; 13. vineyard; 14. apiary; 15. arsenal; 16. pantry; 17. tannery; 18. smithy; 19. aquarium; 20. wardrobe.

**(C)** 21. blithe; 22. cheerful; 23. deaf; 24. dry; 25. familiar; 26. fresh; 27. plump; 28. slender; 29. talkative; 30. true.

**2. (D)**

1. renounce — forsake
2. remonstrate — grumble
3. fraud — trickery
4. devastate — raze
5. concede — admit
6. bold — fearless
7. entreat — beseech
8. stubborn — wilful
9. repentant — remorseful
10. wise — discreet

**(E)** 11. abundance; 12. descendant; 13. safety; 14. shame; 15. impoverish; 16. wax; 17. dissuade; 18. attractive; 19. frugal; 20. occasional.

**(F)** 1. (*b*); 2. (*d*); 3. (*a*); 4. (*c*); 5. (*a*); 6. (*a*); 7. (*d*); 8. (*c*); 9. (*b*); 10. (*c*).

**(G)** 11. accidental, occidental; 12. bridal, bridle; 13. flagrant, fragrant; 14. mendacity, mendicant; 15. meritorious, meritricious; 16. virtuous, virtual; 17. spacious, specious; 18. torrid, torpid; 19. officious, official; 20. irreverent, irrelevant.

**(H)** 1. (Yes); 2. (Yes); 3. (No) *Economic* is connected with trade and industry while *Economical* means to spend the money carefully; 4. (Yes); 5. (No) You *start* a journey not *begin*; 6. (Yes); 7. (No). *Historic* means very important like 'historic deal' while *historical* means connected with past or the study of history; 8. (Yes); 9. (Yes); 10. (No) *Perch* means sitting on the edge of something.

**(I)**   11. unpleasant; 12. pound; 13. mistrust; 14. disguise; 15. streak; 16. nearest; 17. paranoid; 18. lonely; 19. pretty; 20. blurt.

**(J)**   21. admit; 22. effect; 23. beside; 24. irate; 25. demand; 26. avenge; 27. rear exit; 28. go; 29. respite; 30. complimentary.

## *Suggestions*:

1.   The total marks are 100. If your score is below 50, the progress is not up to the mark. You need to work hard and read the chapters 14 to 18 again, before going further.

2.   If your score is around 60 you need to work harder. Re-reading the chapters is recommended.

3.   If your score is around 70, you may revise the study of main parts of the said chapters.

4.   If your score is above 75 the progress is O.K. However, keep on glancing the chapters and also go for further study.

**20**

# THE POWER OF PREFIXES

It is said that a prefix sits in the driver's seat. It determines where the word is going—forward or backward, up or down, in or out. A prefix can herald the turn the word will take for better or worse. It can diminish, enlarge, and count the ways. That a prefix so often controls the destiny of a word can be gauged from the following set of words where substituting one prefix by the other completely changes the meaning of the word.

| attract | distract | software | hardware |
|---------|----------|----------|----------|
| export | import | inhibit | exhibit |
| assent | dissent | overstate | understate |
| converge | diverge | subjective | objective |
| inflate | deflate | introvert | extrovert |
| promote | demote | presence | absence |
| prospect | retrospect | include | exclude |
| epilogue | prologue | constructive | destructive |
| maternal | paternal | inward | outward |
| microeconomics | | macroeconomics | |
| antemeridian | | postmeridian | |

Some main prefixes that drive the meaning of words are discussed below:

## 1. Prefixes that give direction -in, on, upon, into, within:

**In:** It must be clearly understood that *in* as a prefix means *not* or *opposite to*. For example, *inexperienced*, *inaction*, *indecent*, *incorrect*, etc.

It changes to *im* before *m, p* and *b* as in *immediate*, *impatient* and *imbibe*. In words of French origin it appears as *en* as in *encroach* (intrude) *encumber* (load down) and *engender* (beget), etc. It also changes to *em* in certain French words such as *emblem* and *empathy* and *el* in *elliptical*.

Some other words with prefix *in* in its changed form or otherwise are:

| | |
|---|---|
| immure | — wall in, enclose |
| inject | — throw in |
| inscribe | — write in or on |
| invade | — go into, enter in a hostile manner. |

**Epi:** is a prefix which conveys the meaning 'upon' as in:

| | |
|---|---|
| *epigraph* | — an inscription, a quotation at the head of a work or a chapter/(graph) to suggest the theme |
| *epitaph* | — an inscription on a tomb (taph) |
| *epicentre* | — on the centre of an earthquake |
| *epilogue* | — a speech, etc. at the end of a play (logus). |

**Intra:** conveys the meaning 'within' as in:

*intracity, intranet, intravenous,* etc.

Intro is also a prefix conveying the same meaning 'within' as in:

*introspection*— careful examination of one's own thoughts

*introvert*     — a quiet person who is interested in his own thoughts.

**Endo** is another prefix that conveys 'within', as in:

*endocrine*   — internal secretions

*endogamy*   — the custom of marrying within your community

*endoscopy*   — seeing/checking the internal parts of the body.

## 2. Prefixes that give direction — to towards

**Ad:** This prefix changes to *ac, af, ag, al, an, ap, ar, as,* etc., as in:

*accord, accustomed, accounts, accredited, affable, affiliate, affirmative, aggresive, aggregate, aggravate, alleviate, allegation, alliance, annotate, announcement, appalling, apparel, apparaturs, arrogant, arrogate, attract, attentive.*

## 3. Prefixes conveying – away, from, out of

**Ab:** is a prefix used in the following words:

*abnormal*    — away from the normal

*abstain*     — keep away from something (*abstention, abstinence*).

**Apo:** is used in:

*apocryphal*  — hidden away, false, spurious

*apogee*      — the point in the orbit of a satellite at the greatest distance away from (*apo*) the centre of the earth. (Its opposite is perigree).

**Ex:** means out of, and is used in :

*exorbitant* — out of usual track, excessive
*extirpate* — eradicate, wipe out
*Ex* is changed to *ef* in *effective, effluents.*

Prefixes **ec, ex, eco** mean out of, outside of and are used in the words:

*ecstasy* — a state of rapturous delight in which one is standing (stas) outside (ec) oneself — a state of transport or exaltation (altus = high)
*exultation* — in which one has jumped (sult = jump)
*exorcise* — to swear out to drive away evil spirit.

**Extro:** meaning outside, outward is used in:

*extrovert* — turned outward – one who is chiefly concerned with what is happening outside oneself (opposed to introvert).

**Se :** conveys away, aside, apart as in:

*secede* — go away, withdraw from
*seclude* — hide away, withdraw from others
*sedulous* — without, or apart from guile or deccept, i.e. diligent, industrious, assiduous.

4. **Prifixes conveying the meaning — below, down.**

**De** means down as used in:

*dejected* — thrown down – downcast, depressed
*depository* — place where things are put down for safe keeping.

**Cata, cath** mean down and are used in:

*cataclysm* — a washing down – tremendous flood, catastrophe, disaster
*catapult* — to hurl down or against.

**infra** means 'below, lower' as in :

| | |
|---|---|
| *Infrared* | — lying outside or below the red end of the visible spectrum |
| *infrasonic* | — below the level of human audibility. |

Prefix **sub** means 'under'. It occurs as **suc, suf, sug, sup** and **sur** as in:

    *succeed, succint, succumb*
    *suffer, suffuose*
    *suggestion* or *suggestive*
    *support, suppose*
    *surrogate, surrender*

| | |
|---|---|
| *subliminal* | — below the normal, influencing thought below the level of personal awareness |
| *surreptitious* | — seized from under, taken away suddenly and secretly, marked by stealth |
| *subterranean* | — below the earth |
| *subalteran* | — below the rank of a captain |
| *subdue* | — to put under control. |

**Hypo** means 'under' as in:

| | |
|---|---|
| *hypodermic* | — a medical instrument with a long needle to give injection below the skin. |

## 5. Prefixes meaning — above, over, outside of, beyond.

**Extra :** as in:
    *extraordinary, extrasensory, extravagant* (wandering beyond/spending beyond what is necessary).

**Ultra:** as in:

| | |
|---|---|
| *utrasonic* | — beyond the limit of human audibility. |

**super** as in:
*supernatural* — beyond natural human limits
*superhuman*, *superglue*, *superfine*, *superimpose*, etc.

In words derived from French *super* may appear as *sur* as in surplus, surrealist (above realist).

**Hyper** : as in:
*hyperbole* — an exaggeration – a throwing beyond
*hypersensitive* — extremely sensitive to something
*hypertension* — high tension.

## 6. Prefixes meaning across, through

**Meta:** as in:
*metamorphosis* — change of form or shape
*metaphor* — one thing denoted as another.

**Inter:** as in:
*interstate*, *intercoastal*, *intercontinental*, *intercomm*, *interdependent* (mutually dependent).

## 7. Prefixes meaning before, forward, in front of

**Ante:** as in:
*antechamber*, *antemeridian*.
**Pre:** as in:
*predilaction*, *preposition* (positioned before).
**Pro:** as in:
*propal* — drive forward
*prolong*, *promote*, *pronoun*, etc.

## 8. Prefixes meaning around, about

**circum:** as:
*circumlucution* — talking around
*circumambient* — going around
*circumnavigate* — to sail all the way around something.

## 9. Prefixes meaning – after, behind, back, backward

**Re:** as in *recede*, *recount* (narrate)
**Retro:** as in *retrogress, retrospect.*

## 10. Prefixes showing magnitude and quantity

Such prefixes have a set, fixed meaning

**Macro** (large) is used in:
    *macroeconomics, macrocosm* (the large world—universe)
    *macrobiotic* (whole grains, vegetables grown without chemical treatment).

**Micro** (small) is used in:
    *microeconomics, microfinance, microscope*
    *microcosm* — miniature world, etc.

**Meg, mega** are used in:
    *megalith*       — great/huge stones found in prehistoric structures
    *megalomania* — disease characterised by delusions of grandeur;
    *megabyte, megahertz, megastar, megawatt, etc.*

**Multi**—many is used in:
    *multicoloured, multifaceted, multifunctional, multilateral, multilingual* (speaking or using several languages), *multimillionaire, multinational, multiplex, multifaceted, multiplex, etc.*

**Poly**—many is used in:
    *polyglot* — knowing using or written in many languages;
    *polyclinic, polymer, polyester, polytechnic, etc.*
    *Omni* — all or everywhere as in:
    *Omnipotent* — all-powerful
    *Omnivorous* — all-devouring

*Omniscient* — knowing all
*Omnipresent* — present everywhere.

**Pan-** all as in:
*panacea* — healing all
*pan American* — all American.

**Holo-** whole, wholly, entirely, as in:
*holocaust* — complete destruction, widespread devastation
*holograph* — wholly written in the hand of the author.

## 11. Prefixes of time, age, period

Such prefixes comprise combined forms that come at the beginning of a word. Some forms like *phil* may come at the beginning of some words, or at the end of some others.

**Arch, archae, archaeo,** as in:
*archaeology* — study of remains of old civilisations
*archaic* — belonging to an earlier time.

**New**—new, revival of interest, etc. as in:
*neo-classic* — reviving interest in old arts, etc.
*neo-natal* — relating to a child just born
*neophyte* — a person who has recently started an activity – also called new-shoot, novice.

**Pre**—before, is used in:
*prelude* — before the play
*preface* — before the book;
*precursor, predetermined, pre-exist, pre-historic, premeditated* — thought beforehand.

**Pro**—before, **Post**-after, **Re-** again, as in:

| | |
|---|---|
| *prognosis* | — forecast, projection, the act of foretelling the progress of a disease |
| *probate* | — a legal document that tells what is to happen to a person's property when they die |
| *probable* | — likely to happen |
| *postcript* | — written after |
| *posthumous* | — after demise |
| *posterior* | — located behind something |
| *recapitulate* | — to repeat the main points |

*reconsider, remind, reconnect*

*retract* — to say something you have said earlier.

## 12. Prefixes underlining the negative sense

Such prefixes denote the sense 'no'. They may come from Latin such as *contra, dis* and *non,* or Greek like *ante* and *dys*. Prefixes like *a, in* and *un* also convey a negative meaning:

**'A'** - 'not', appears as *an* before words having a vowel pronunciation. Examples are given below:

| | |
|---|---|
| *ahistorical* | — not related to history |
| *amorphous* | — shapeless, formless |
| *anaerobic* | — not existing in air—bacteria, etc. found in media other than air, i.e. water |
| *atheist* | — non-believer in God (opp. of theist) |
| *anomaly* | — different from/not normal |
| *anodyne* | — without pain. |

**In** appears in several words giving them a negative meaning. Some examples are given below:

| | |
|---|---|
| *inexorable* | — inflexible, unyielding, agressive — not to be moved by prayer or entreaty |

*intangible*    — having no physical substance
*inability*     — not having ability to do something
*inaccessible* — which cannot be approached
*inaccurate*   — not accurate
*inauspicious* — not auspicious, ominous
*inane*        — having no meaning
*inadvertently*— without intention.

**Non** and **un** also convey a negative meaning as in:
*nonage*       — not of an age required under law to perform some action or have some right
*nonentity*    — having no importance, value or say
*nonpartisan*  — not partial, politically independent
*unstinting*   — not holding back, giving generously
*undivided*    — not divided
*unpack, unpaid, unofficial, unoccupied, unnecessary, unparalleled, unpardonable, unlucky, unpleasant,* etc.

**Anti**—against, as in:
*anticlockwise, antibacterial, anticlimax, antipathy.*

This prefix is also used as *anta, anto* as in:
*antagonism* and *antonym.*

**Contra, contro, counter**—against, as in:
*contravene*        — come against, contradict
*controversy*       — disagreement, dispute
*counterproductive*— opposing producing the desired result
*countervailing*    — putting an equal opposite force.

**With**—against
*withstand* — stand against/opposite, resist
*withhold*  — hold information against something/ somebody — refuse to give information.

**Dis**—apart, away, as in:
*disclose, disagree, disrespect*
*discrepancy* — a rattling differently
*disparate*   — different, not made equal
*disperse*    — scatter, cause to break up.

**Dis** changes to *dif* in words starting with *f* as in diffusion and *difference,* and loses *s* in words starting with *l, g* and *v* as in *dilute, digression* and *diversion.*

**Ob-** against, as in:
*obstruct*    — block, hinder, impede - build against
*obfuscate*   — against being understood.

**Mal(e)**—bad, badly, as in:
*malefactor*  — evil doer, criminal, felon
*malfunction* — to work badly or imperfectly;
*malnutrition, malpractice.*

**Dys**—badly, as in:
*dyspepsia*   — bad digestion.

**Caco**—bad, **mis-** hate, badly, wrongly, **hetero-** unlike, **pseudo-** false. The examples are:
*cacophony*    — harsh discordant sound - opposite of euphony
*misogymist*   — one who hates women
*misogamist*   — one who hates marriage
*misfortune*   — bad fortune
*mismatch*     — wrong match
*heterogenous* — dissimilar, unlike, made of different parts that are not unified opposite to homogenous
*pseudonym*    — a false/pen name
*pseudopodia*  — false feet (of an amoeba; podia-feet).

## 13. Prefixes conveying positive sense

**Co, com, con**—together with, as in:

| | |
|---|---|
| *coagulate* | — gather together in a mass, cuddle, clot |
| *collaborate* | — (here prefix = col) – work together |
| *collusion* | — the act of playing together, secret arrangement for some illegal purpose |
| *combat* | — work to gether to check some enemy or disease |
| *commisserate* | — to sympathise with somebody |
| *compensate* | — to make up the loss |
| *concomitant* | — attending, accompanying. |

**Syn, sym**—together, as in:

| | |
|---|---|
| *synthesis* | — the act of putting together, combination of parts to form a whole |
| *syndicate* | — a group of people |
| *synthetic* | — combining chemical substances |
| *symmetrical* | — measuring together, harmonious, balanced. |

**Bene, eu**—well, **phil** - love, **homo** - like, **ortho-** staight, right, true, **rect, recti-** straight. The example:

| | |
|---|---|
| *benevolent* | — kind, sympathetic |
| *benediction* | — the act of saying well, best wishes, benison |
| *beneficent* | — doing well, performing acts of kindness |
| *euphony* | — a pleasant sound |
| *euphoria* | — a feeling of well-being |
| *philanthropist* | — one who loves mankind |
| *homogeneous* | — orthodox—conforming to practices and opinions. |

*rectitude*     — rightness
*rectilinear*   — having straight lines.

## 14. Prefixes with general/multiple meaning

**Auto**—self as in:

*automatic, autochlothonous* (native, aboriginal, indigenous)

*autocrat, autonomous* (independent), *autograph*

*autotrophs*   — living things that are able to make their own food.

**Be**—is used in a number words:

*bedevil, befriend, belittle* (meaning 'make')

*beside* means 'by' as in bystander

*berate* — to scold or criticize severely.

**crypto**—hidden, as in:

*cryptogram*   — message with a hidden or secret meaning

*cryptic*      — hidden, occult, secret (as in cryptic puzzle).

**Para, par**—alongwith, nearby as in:

*paramilifary* — close to being military

*paranoia*     — close to having an overactive brain (nons) that is marked by delusions of persecution

*paradigm*     — a typical example of or pattern of something

*paralegal*    — like a lawyer, a person who is trained to help a lawyer

*paramount*    — like a mountain—of more importance than anything else

*paraphrase*   — to get close to the original by stating it in one's own words *parasite*      — taking food alongside—a person/ organism that lives on someone else.

**Quasi**—as if, almost but not quite the thing that is mentioned after it.
*quasi-judicial, quasi-stellar* — almost like a star.

**Vice**—in turn, instead of, in place of, as in:

*vicar*         — a substitute, deputy—acting as representative of God on earth, a parish priest

*vicarious*     — experienced imaginatively through someone else

*viceroy*       — in place of the king, a monarch's representative

*vicissitudes* — the turns of fortune, change of circumstances in life.

**Vice**—next to somebody in rank or position:
*vice-president, vice-admiral, vice-chancellor.*

**Xeno**—strange, foreign.
*xenophile*    — one who is friendly to foreigners
*xenophobia* — a strong feeling of dislike or fear of people from other countries.

Reading the various types of prefixes must have given you a clear idea how they govern the meaning of words. Such knowledge is very handy in understanding the words, their origin and meaning. Whenever you come across the words with such prefixes, you have some idea as to what their connotation might be. It also increases one's curiosity to know more and more words formed with various prefixes. This curiosity and quest helps in enhancing one's vocabulary.

It is also necessary to review what you have grasped

about prefixes. Take the following review tests sincerely to know where you stand and what amount of effort you need to put in to achieve the objective of acquiring an impressive level of vocabulary:

## Review Test 1

*Can you recall 15 words that are made by prefixes in, im, epi, intra, intro and endo—meaning in, on, upon, into, within.*

**Answers:**

1. inaction, 2. imbibe, 3. immediate, 4. inject, 5. invade, 6. encumber, 7. encroach, 8. epigraph, 9. epicentre, 10. epilogue, 11. intranet, 12. intravenous, 13. introspection, 14. introvert, 15. endoscopy.

## Review Test 2

*Match the statements/meanings with words:*

| | |
|---|---|
| 1. write in or on | (*a*) introspection |
| 2. intrude | (*b*) endogamy |
| 3. careful examination of one's own thoughts | (*c*) inscribe |
| 4. the custom of marrying within the community. | (*d*) immure |
| 5. wall in, enclose | (*e*) encroach |

**Answers:**

1. (*c*); 2. (*e*); 3. (*a*); 4. (*b*); 5. (*d*).

## Review Test 3

*Mention 20 words made with prefixes ab, af, ap, apo, ex, ec, se, cata, sup, sur.*

**Answers:**

1. abnormal, 2. abstain, 3. apogee, 4. exorbitant,

5. extirpate, 6. ecstasy, 7. exultation, 8. extrovert, 9. secede, 10. seclusion, 11. depository, 12. dejected, 13. cataclysm, 14. catastrophe, 15. succint, 16. suffuse, 17. support, 18. sublime, 19. subaltern, 20. subdue.

## Review Test 4

*Mention the words that match with the following statements/words:*

1. used to                  ac_____
2. keep away from      ab_____
3. hide away            se_____
4. out of usual tract excesive   ex_____
   (in price, etc.)
5. without guide of deception   se_____

## Answers:

1. accustomed, 2. abstain, 3. seclude, 4. exorbitant, 5. sedulous.

## Review Test 5

*Complete the words with given prefixes:*

1. hypo_____       2. extra_____
3. ultra_____       4. super_____
5. sur_____         6. hyper_____
7. meta_____       8. inter_____
9. ante_____        10. pre_____
11. circum_____     12. re_____
13. macro_____      14. micro_____
15. mega_____       16. multi_____
17. poly_____        18. omni_____
19. pan_____         20. holo_____

286

WORD POWER MADE EASY

**Answers:**

1. hypodermic, 2. extraordinary, 3. ultrasonic, 4. supernatural, 5. surreptitious, 6. hyperbole, 7. metaphor, 8. interdependent, 9. antenatal, 10. predilection, 11. circumspect, 12. recede, 13. macrocosm, 14. microeconomics, 15. megabyte, 16. multiplex, 17. polyglot, 18. omnipotent, 19. panacea, 20. holocaust.

## Review Test 6

Mention 10 words with prefixes **pre, pro, post** (before, after).

**Answers:**

1. prelude, 2. predetermined, 3. prehistoric, 4. premeditated, 5. prognosis, 6. probate, 7. postscript, 8. posthumous, 9. posterior, 10. postdated.

## Review Test 7

Write 10 words that convey a negative meaning, made with the prefix **in** (not):

**Answers:**

1. inexorable, 2. intangible, 3. inability, 4. inaccessible, 5. inauspicious, 6. inadvertently, 7. indecent, 8. inane, 9. indelible, 10. insane.

## Review Test 8

Write 10 words that convey a positive meaning, made with the prefixes **co, com, col, syn** and **sym** (together with):

**Answers:**

1. coagulate, 2. collusion, 3. collaborate, 4. combat, 5. concomitant, 6. compensate, 7. synthesis, 8. syndicate, 9. symmetrical, 10. synthetic.

## 21

# SOME IMPORTANT WORD ENDINGS

Suffixes come at the end of the words and often help us to distinguish them as verbs, nouns, adjectives and adverbs.

Things are *identified;* microscopic objects have to be *magnified;* rules are *notified* while people are *satisfied* if they get proper reward for their efforts. Salt is *iodized;* people are *hypnotized;* thoughts, plans and beliefs are *crystallized* to make them clear and fixed; systems are *computerized* while star performers are *idolized.*

The italicized words in the above paragraph ending with *ied* and *ized* are past/past participles of 'doing words' called verbs. Now have a look at the following:

The aspirants seek *admission* in reputed institutions; some seek *remission* of fee; we have a *passion* for our motherland; workers expect an upward *revision* of their salary; *fission* is a chemical process; the parliament is in *session;* some politician have *vision.* Here, the italicized words ending in *sion* are nouns. Similarly, the words ending in *ous* like *ravenous, nervous, frivolous, fabulous,* etc. are adjectives, and those ending with *ly* like *cleverly, hastily, officially,* etc. are adverbs.

It is necessary to make it clear that we cannot totally depend on suffixes to classify words as verbs, nouns, adjectives and adverbs. Some important suffixes/word endings are given below:

## 1. Verb Endings

**Ate** is used in several verbs such as:

| | |
|---|---|
| *abate* | — to make less |
| *ameliorate* | — to make better, improve |
| *consummate* | — to bring to the highest (summus) point |
| *placate* | — to pacify, to make feel less angry |
| *decimate* | — to kill in large number |
| associate | — to join, become a part of |
| *desiccate* | — to dry up, dehydrate |
| *importunate* | — to demand insistently, annoyingly. |

This suffix is also a part of some adjectives like:

| | |
|---|---|
| *disparate* | — different, unlike |
| *unfortunate* | — unlucky. |

**Esce** — to begin to, become, as in :
*effervesce* — to begin to boil over, to bubble.

Adjective and noun suffixes from it are *escent* and *escence*, as in:
*effervescent* and *effervescence* respectively
*coalesce* — to grow together.
Here, the noun is *coalition*.

**En** is used as suffix in the following words:

| | |
|---|---|
| *dishearten* | — to discourage |
| *broaden* | — to make bigger in size/dimension |
| *enlighten* | — to bring to light, instruct, inform, illuminate. |

*awaken* — to become aware, make someone aware, to wake up

*soften* — to become soft, be less rigid

*weaken* — to make weak

*hearken* — to listen, to heed.

Please note that *often* and *sudden* do not belong to this category.

**Fy** is used in:

*defy* — not to obey, violate.

**Ize** is used in several words like:

*canonize, vulcanize, criticize, authorize, galvanize, ionize, concretize, hypothesize, pressurize, visualize.*

## 2. Adjective Endings

Most of the objective endings convey the meaning—marked by, pertaining/relating to, tending to be, having to do with, resembling, like, as, etc. Some main adjectival word endings are mentioned below:

**Al /ical** is used in:

*empirical* — based on experience and experiment, not theory

*umblical* — of the navel

*connubial, conjugal, nuptual* — relating to marriage

*inimical* — hostile, unfriendly

*logical* — as per rules of logic; and

*natural, reasonable, noval, mental,* etc.

**An, ane** are used in:

*sylvan* — wooded, belonging to the forest

*germane* — relevant, pertinent to what is being discussed.

**Ar, ary** as in:

| | |
|---|---|
| *angular* | — having an angle, twisted |
| *annular* | — ring shaped |
| *vehicular* | — pertaining to movement of vehicles |
| *circular* | — round, like a circle |
| *modular* | — consisting of separate parts |
| *sanguinary* | — blood thirsty |
| *stationary* | — still, not moving |
| *tutelary* | — watching over, serving as a guardian. |

Some nouns are also formed by *ary*, like:

*apiary* (a place where bees are kept), *aviary* (a place where birds are kept), *notary* (where documents are attested) and *treasury* (where securities are kept).

**Fic, ic** are used in:

| | |
|---|---|
| *specific* | — particular |
| *terrific* | — excellent, wonderful |
| *malefic* | — exerting evil or unfavourable influence |
| *soporific* | — inducing sleep |
| *horrific* | — extremely bad, shocking or frightening |
| *ascetic* | — austere, practising rigorous self-denial |
| *kinetic* | — pertaining to motion |
| *didactic* | — teaching moral lessons |
| *hectic* | — very busy, full of activity |
| *sporadic* | — happening in intervals, not regularly. |

**Id** as in:

| | |
|---|---|
| *insipid* | — dull, drab, unsavoury |
| *sapid* | — savory, relishable |
| *lipid* | — not dissolving in water |
| *limpid* | — clear and transparent. |

**Ine** as in:

*bovine* — like a cow, laid back, dull

*vulpine* — like a fox, crafty
*canine* — concerned with dogs.

**Ish, ive, ory** as in the following words:

*childish, boyish, womanish*

*brackish* — salty, not drinkable (of water)
*impish* — showing a lack of respect (in an amusing sense, not serious)
*prudish* — very easily shocked by things connected with sex
*mawkish* — expressing or sharing emotion in an exaggerated way
*hawkish* — preferring to use military action rather than peaceful discussion to solve a political problem
*furtive* — stealthy, like a thief
*active* — always busy doing things
*palliative* — like a clock, acting to soothe pain, alleviating
*innovative* — introducing or using new ideas
*dilatory* — tending to put off, causing delay.

Many nouns are also formed by the suffix *ory* such as *laboratory*, *refractory* (a dining hall) *repertory* (the type of work of a theatre company).

### 3. Noun Endings

Such noun endings give the meaning of the result of, the act of, the condition or quality of:

**Age,** as in:

*bondage* — the state of being a slave
*montage* — a process of combining several pictures to produce a single composition
*hermitage* — a place where hermits live

*arbiterage*   — the practice of buying shares, etc. in one place and selling them in another

*barrage*      — continuous firing of a large number of guns.

**Ance, ence,** as in:

*appurtenance* — accessory to or derived from something more important

*attendance*   — presence in a place

*confidence*   — belief or trust in something or someone

*vigilance*    — watchfulness, carefulness in noticing any danger.

Adjective forms are *ant* and *ent* as in *vigilant, attendant, confident, potent, resplendent, defendant, respondent, delinquent, conversant,* etc.

**Ion** is used in several nouns such as:

*admission, vacation, notion, anticipation, assertion* (claim, a statement that you strongly belief something to be true) *vocation* (work, way of occupancy) *vituperation* (abuse), *summation* (summary, collection) *specification* (detailed description of how something is).

**Ism-** 'a doctrine or system' — this suffix can be attached to any national, political or religious entity.

Some examples of words ending in *ism* are given below:

*jingoism*     — a strong belief that your country is the best

*favouritism*  — favouring certain persons/classes

*universalism* — treating all people equal, preaching love for all humanity *totalitarianism*     — a system/government in which one political party has complete power

*monism, monotheism* — the belief that there is only one God

*aphorism*     — a concise statement containing wisdom of truth, maxim, adage.

The word *schism* meaning strong disagreement with a religious organisation does not belong to this category.

**Ity, iety** equivalent to 'ness' or 'hood', as in:

*amenity*     — some feature that makes a place pleasant confortable

*spontaneity* — the state of something happening naturally and suddenly

*propriety*     — acceptable and correct moral behaviour

*sobriety*     — the state of being sensible, sober

*affinity*     — rapport, close relationship

*serendipity* — the state of something pleasant happening by chance

*profundity* — depth.

**Ment** 'ness', as in:

*merriment*     — fun and enjoyment

*enforcement* — implementation of some law

*endowement* — money that is given to an institution, etc.

*enhancement* — increase, augmentation

*enbankment* — wall, boundary

*statement*     — assertion

*assessment* — evaluation, opinion or judgement about something.

**Ry, ary,** as in:

| | |
|---|---|
| *bigotry* | — extreme intolerance |
| *mimicry* | — the act of imitating |
| *riboldry* | — coarse indecent language |
| *corollary* | — an argument or a situation which is the natural and direct result of another one. |

Remember that *ary* is more an adjective ending as in *literary, sanguinary, tutelary, solitary,* etc.

**Tude, ture** also mean 'ness/hood', as in:

| | |
|---|---|
| *beautitude* | — happiness, blessedness |
| *attitude* | — mindset |
| *turpitude* | — baseness, vileness |
| *gratitude* | — gratefulness |
| *departure* | — going away |
| *suture* | — a surgical sewing |
| *tonsure* | — a clipping, shaving of head |
| *aperture* | — an opening |
| *legislature* | — a body of people who have the power to make/change law. |

## 4. Adverbial Endings

Adverbs are verbs that adds more information about place, time, manner, cause, degree to a verb, adjective, phrase or another adverb. Some main adverbial endings are given below:

**Ly, ally, ully** as in:

*friendly, saintly, leasurely, mainly, lately, additionally, naturally, accidentally, beautifully, gratefully, truthfully,* etc.

**Ward, wards,** appear in

backward(s), forward, upward(s), sideward(s), homeward(s), toward(s), etc. Some of these, especially without s are adjectives.

Untoward is an adjective meaning unfavourable, inconvenient.

**Wise** meaning in the manner, as in:

likewise, lengthwise, areawise, categorywise, otherwise.

## 5. General Suffixes

Apart from the above, there are some other word endings, which are given below:

### A. Showing Capability
**Able, ible, ile,** as in:

capable — having the ability to do a certain thing
feasible — workable, practicable
formidable — powerful, strong
comprehensible — easily understood
prehensile — adapted for grasping.

### B. Related to Medical

**Ma, oma, osis,** as in:

trauma — a mental condition caused by severe shock
carcinoma — a type of cancer
hypnosis — induced sleeplike condition
neurosis — nervous disorder characterised by anxiety.

### C. Persons with Special Characteristics Skills

**Ary, ard, er, eur, ist, ite, nik** as in the following:

antiquary — one who studies ancient things
lapidary — one who cuts precious stones
notary — one who attests court documents
dastard — cowardly, mean

| *laggard* | — lazy, sluggish |
| *broker* | — one who negotiates contracts |
| *banker* | — a professional banker |
| *usurer* | — a person who lends money to people at very high rate |
| *jurer* | — member of jury |
| *amateur* | — one who participates for love of sport, not money; |

*physician, magician, statistician, tactician,* etc.

| *hedonist* | — one who believes that pleasure is the chief goal of life |
| *anchorite* | — one who withdraws from the world, a religious recluse |
| *imposter* | — pretender, one who deceives |
| *sputnik* | — satellite. |

## D. Feminine Connotations

**Ette, euse, ine, ster** as in:

| *coquette* | — a female who tries to attract attention of men |
| *suffragette* | — a female fighter for right to vote, or right of equality |
| *masseuse* | — female masseur |
| *spinster* | — an (elderly) woman who has not married |
| *aviatrix* | — female flier. |

## E. Words of Plenty

**acious, icious, ful, ious, ose, ous, some** as in:

*voracious* — having great capacity for devouring food
*loquacious* — one who talks a lot
*bountiful* — abundant, bounteous
*guileful* — full of deceit
*adipose* — full of fat

*impecunious* — not having pockets full of money
*numinous* — filled with divine presence
*awsome* — full of awe
*wholesome* — good, fresh, clean.

## Grammar Aspect

Since we have talked about nouns, verbs, adjectives and adverbs in this chapter, it is pertinent to provide these parts of speech in respect of various words with specific word endings. Going through the following will prove highly beneficial.

### A. Nouns and adjectives of verbs

| | Verb | Noun | Adjective |
|---|---|---|---|
| 1. | analyze | analysis | analytical/analytic |
| 2. | acquire | acquisition | acquisitive |
| 3. | antagonize | antagonism | antagonistic |
| 4. | corrode | corrosion | corrosive |
| 5. | contend | contention | contentious |
| 6. | subvert | subversion | subversive |
| 7. | eulogize | eulogy | eulogistic |
| 8. | resent | resentment | resentful |
| 9. | pursue | persual | pursuant |
| 10. | reveal | revelation | revealing |

### B. Language interchange in certain words

| | | |
|---|---|---|
| 1. | brotherhood | — fraternity |
| 2. | motherhood | — maternity |
| 3. | falsehood | — mendacity |
| 4. | fewness | — paucity |
| 5. | extreme frugality | — parsimony |
| 6. | greediness | — cupidity |
| 7. | harshness | — asperity |
| 8. | hardihood | — temerity |

|     |                |                                    |
| --- | -------------- | ---------------------------------- |
| 9.  | likelihood     | — possibility                      |
| 10. | liveness       | — vivacity                         |
| 11. | neighbourhood  | — vicinity                         |
| 12. | holiness       | — sanctity                         |
| 13. | boldness       | — audacity                         |
| 14. | thickness      | — density                          |
| 15. | fatness        | — obesity                          |

## C. Types of Rules — by

|     |               |                                    |
| --- | ------------- | ---------------------------------- |
| 1.  | autocracy     | — privileged class                 |
| 2.  | aristocracy   | — one person with absolute power   |
| 3.  | bureaucracy   | — officials & administrators       |
| 4.  | plutocracy    | — wealthy class                    |
| 5.  | theocracy     | — God or religious officials       |
| 6.  | timocracy     | — principal of love of honour      |
| 7.  | ochlocracy    | — mob                              |
| 8.  | kakistocracy  | — worse people                     |
| 9.  | gerontocracy  | — elders                           |
| 10. | gyneocracy    | — women                            |

## D. Specialists — in

|     |                |                    |
| --- | -------------- | ------------------ |
| 1.  | entomologist   | — insects          |
| 2.  | etymologist    | — origin of words  |
| 3.  | orthodontist   | — teeth            |
| 4.  | horologist     | — time, timepieces |
| 5.  | neurologist    | — nerves           |
| 6.  | opthalmologist | — eyes             |
| 7.  | dermatologist  | — skin             |
| 8.  | ornithologist  | — birds            |
| 9.  | otologist      | — ears             |
| 10. | paleontologist | — fossils          |
| 11. | seismologist   | — earthquakes      |
| 12. | toxicologist   | — poisons          |

SOME IMPORTANT WORD ENDINGS

## E. Manias — about

1. kleptomania — impulse to steal small things
2. bibliomania — books
3. arithmomania — preoccupation with numbers
4. dipsomania — craving for alcoholic drinks
5. megalomania — delusion of grandeur
6. dromomania — running about, wandering
7. monomania — irrationality on one subject
8. pyromania — dread of fire
9. mythomania — lying and exaggerating
10. schizophrenia — unable to link thought, emotion and behaviour.

## Review Test 1

Mention 10 word endings in verbs with *ate.*

**Answers:**

1. abate, 2. placate, 3. ameliorate, 4. associate, 5. desiccate, 6. importunate, 7. consummate, 8. obviate, 9. narrate, 10. negate.

## Review Test 2

Mention 10 adjectives with word endings *ar, ary.*

**Answers:**

1. circular, 2. modular, 3. tabular, 4. regular, 5. vehicular, 6. cellular, 7. popular, 8. sanguinary, 9. ancillary, 10. transitory.

## Review Test 3

Mention 15 nouns with word endings *age, ance, ion.*

**Answers:**

1. bondage, 2. hermitage, 3. stoppage, 4. barrage, 5. arbitrage, 6. brokerage, 7. montage, 8. vigilance, 9. appurtenance, 10. countenance, 11. mutation,

12. anticipation, 13. alteration. 14. suffocation. 15. vituperation.

## Review Test 4

*Find words that match the given statement:*

1. A strong belief that your country is the best     j_____
2. The state of something happening naturally and suddenly     s_____
3. Acceptable and correct moral behaviour     p_____
4. to pacify, make less angry     p_____
5. Different or unlike     d_____
6. Relevant, pertinent to what is being discussed     g_____
7. Watching over, serving as a guardian     t_____
8. Happening in intervals, not regularly     s_____
9. Crafty, like a fox     v_____
10. Showing a lack of interest     d_____
11. Close relationship     r_____
12. The state of something pleasant happening by chance     s_____
13. Control of one country over another     h_____
14. Coarse indecent language     r_____
15. A situation that is the direct result of another     c_____

16. Adapted for             p_____

17. Very busy, full of activity     h_____

18. Causing delay          d_____

19. Dry up, dehydrate       d_____

20. To give relief, make better.    a_____

**Answers:**

1. jingoism, 2. spontaneity, 3. propriety, 4. placate, 5. disparate, 6. germane, 7. tutelary, 8. sporadic, 9. vulpine, 10. impish, 11. rapport, 12. serendipity, 13. hegemony, 14. ribaldry, 15. corollary, 16. prehensile, 17. hectic, 18. dilatory, 19. desiccate, 20. ameliorate.

## Review Test 5

*Match the words with their meanings:*

| | | | |
|---|---|---|---|
| 1. | certitude | (a) | loneliness |
| 2. | beatitude | (b) | gratefulness |
| 3. | aptitude | (c) | sureness |
| 4. | pulchretude | (d) | wickedness |
| 5. | quietude | (e) | sainthood |
| 6. | rectitude | (f) | likeness |
| 7. | verisimilitude | (g) | comeliness |
| 8. | solitude | (h) | righteousness |
| 9. | turpitude | (i) | stillness |
| 10. | gratitude | (j) | mindset. |

**Answers:**

1. (c); 2. (e); 3. (j); 4 (g); 5. (i); 6. (h); 7. (f); 8. (a); 9. (d); 10. (b).

## Review Test 6

*Match the following words of some or ful endings with words conveying a similar meaning:*

| | |
|---|---|
| 1. awesome | (a) scornful |
| 2. burdensome | (b) deliberate |
| 3. fretful | (c) salubrious |
| 4. gruesome | (d) solitary |
| 5. loathsome | (e) grievous |
| 6. doleful | (f) querulous |
| 7. wholesome | (g) victorious |
| 8. winsome | (h) hideous |
| 9. wilful | (i) magnificent |
| 10. lonesome | (j) onerous |

**Answers:**

1. (i); 2. (j); 3. (f); 4 (h); 5. (a); 6. (e); 7. (c); 8. (g); 9. (b); 10. (d).

# 22
# FOREIGN WORDS IN ENGLISH

English is unarguably the most dominating language in the world today. One of the reasons is that it draws, distills and assimilates words from other langages like French, Spanish, Italian, Dutch and even—Arabic, Chinese and Hindi—though to a smaller degree. This way it keeps on adding to its vast reportoire of vocabulary and makes it even bigger. Some words, of course, become redundant with the passage of time and slowly and slowly slip out of usage just as many of the words pertaining to 18th century English society of warfare, armed duels, etc. are rarely used these days. On the other hand, as the society is progressing, new discoveries are being made in science and technology, wider applications of computers and other machines are in vogue, new terminology is being added to English.

Another phenomenon that has facilitated the spread of English language to hitherto uncharted areas and interchange of a few words from English to other languages and vice-versa has been globalization. It has brought in its wake, economic liberalization, growth of trade and exchange of latest technologies between countries. The number of meetings, conferences and discussions between delegates of participating nations has increased. The interractions between businessmen are becoming more frequent. The result is that languages get enriched as the trade is expanded.

The service industry has made inroads into foreign territories. Several multi-national companies (MNCs) are outsourcing their businesses abroad. Several Asian engineers, business managers and other professionals are serving in several European and American countries. In nut shell, interractions are regularly taking place at several levels which are enriching English language as prominent and frequently used words in other languages are finding a place in established English dictionaries.

In this chapter we concentrate on some main words that have been taken in English from various other languages. A knowledge thereof is essential for building a powerful vocabulary.

## FRENCH WORDS

English has been quite hospitable to the inclusion of French words. Some of them are being used so often that they appear to be regular English words. For example we use words like *ballet, chauffeur, connoisseur, costume, facade, matinee, menu, personnel, rendezvous, repertoire, sabotage, souvenir,* frequently in our speech.

Some important French words and phrases which are being regularly used in English, and are now, for all intents and purposes, a part of English tongue are given below. Their meaning and usage, wherever thought necessary, have also been given.

| | |
|---|---|
| *a la carte* | — a list of dishes that have separate prices, not included in the complete meal. |
| *adieu* | — goodbye. |
| *aplomb* | — poise, complete confidence, self-assurance. |
| *avant-garde* | — creator(s) of new ideas, vanguards (used for writers, etc.) |
| *bête noir(e)* | — person or subject that is detested — an aversion, bugbear. |
| *canard* | — a false report or piece of news. |
| *carte blanche* | — the complete authority or freedom to do whatever you like. |
| *cartridge* | — a tube or case for an explosive. |
| *coup ,* | — a sudden, illegal, often violent change of government. |
| *coup de grâce* | — an action or event that ends something that had been getting weaker: *My disastrous final year exam results proved to be a coup de grâce to my university career.* |
| *coup détat* | — a change of government by sudden forcible takeover of an opponent, junior or other political leader. |
| *denoument* | — unravelling of the plot (in literature); generally, it means the final outcome of a situation, the way things work out. |
| *déjà vu* | — the feeling that you have previously experienced something. |
| *de-rigueur* | — considered necessary if you wish to be socially accepted. |
| *detente* | — an improvement in the relations of two or more countries. |

| | |
|---|---|
| *deterrent* | — something that prevents/checks some action. *Punishment acts as a deterrent to stop crimes.* |
| *detour* | — diversion, a longer route taken to avoid a problem. |
| *entente* | — understanding, an agreement between two nations that is not so formal as an alliance. |
| *egalitarian* | — a belief that everyone is equal and all should have the same rights and opportunities. |
| *entracte* | — interval, the time between the different parts of play or show. |
| *ensemble* | — a small group of dancers, performers. |
| *en suite* | — (bathroom) joined into a bedroom. |
| *errant* | — not behaving in an acceptable way. |
| *esprit de corps* | — feelings of pride, care, support for each other. |
| *facile* | — easy to obtain. |
| *facsimile* | — an exact copy of something. |
| *fait accompli* | — something that has already been done or has happened that you cannot change, accomplished fact or deed. |
| *faute de miux* | — for want of a better way. |
| *faux* | — artificial but intended to look or seem real. |
| *faux pas* | — social error, egregious blunder. |
| *fin de siéde* | — end of the century, particularly the 19th century marked by decadence, escapism in literature. |
| *haute couture* | — highly rated establishments that make women's clothes, literally 'high sewing'. |
| *haute cuisine* | — high kitchen or cooking. |
| *haute monde* | — high world/society, upper class. |

| | |
|---|---|
| *laissez-faire* | — 'let do', doctrine that the government should regulate as little as possible. |
| *manqué* | — 'missed', failing to achieve the desired goal. |
| *menagerie* | — a collection of wild animals. |
| *noblesse obligé* | — nobility obliges — has its obligations. |
| *nom de guerre* | — a false name (used in a non-official military organization). |
| *nom de plume* | — a name used by a writer instead of his/her real name. |
| *raison d'être* | — reason for the existence of some action or policy. |
| *nouveau riche* | — newly rich. |
| *novella* | — a short novel, e.g. Ernest Hemingway's *Old Man and the Sea*. |
| *nuisance* | — a thing, person or situation that causes annoyance, irritation or problems. |
| *obelique* | — indirect, not expressed or done in a direct manner. |
| *parlour* | — a shop/store that provides particular goods or services. |
| *par avion* | — by air |
| *parley* | — a discussion between people who disagree. |
| *parlance* | — a particular way of using words or expressing yourself. |
| *savoir faire* | — to know how to do, an instinctive ability to act appropriately in a given situation. |
| *savoir vivre* | — to know how to live well. |
| *tour de force* | — turn of strength, an extremely skillful performance. |
| *tête-à-tète* | — head of head, a private conversation between two people. |
| *vis-à-vis* | — face to face, directly opposite. |

Some other common French words/expressions and their meanings are given below:

*bon mot*     — well said
*bon voyage*— happy journey
*confier*     — colleague
*cul-de-sac*  — dead end, blind alley
*en masse*    — in large number, all together
*forte*       — strength
*idé fixé*    — obsession
*malausé*     — vague feeling of disgust
*métier*      — trade, occupation
*nonchalant*  — carefree, lacking concern
*parti pris*  — prejudice, bias, preconceived motion
*sans*        — without
*volte face*  — change of opinion, about-turn.

## SPANISH WORDS

English language has been enriched by many Spanish words. Some major ones are given below, alongwith their meanings:

*armada*      — a fleet of ships.
*bonanza*     — a huge profit, a source of great riches.
*desperado*   — a man who does dangerous and criminal things without caring about himself.
*flotilla*    — a group of small boats/ships sailing together.
*guerrilla*   — a member of a small group of soldiers who are not part of official army, who fight against official soldiers.

| | |
|---|---|
| *gusto* | — force, strength. |
| *incommunicado* | — without means of communication. |
| *junta* | — *'joined'*, a council or committee, group of plotters, a closely knit group of persons. |
| *piccadilly* | — a place that is very busy or crowded. |
| *peccadillo* | — a small sin, a transgression. |

## PORTUGUESE WORDS

| | |
|---|---|
| *auto-da-fà* | — act of faith. |
| *fetish* | — excessive attachment for something, the fact of spending too much time doing or thinking about a particular thing. |
| *persona-non-grata* | — a non-entity, someone who has no saying in a certain matter. |

## ITALIAN WORDS

| | |
|---|---|
| *bravura* | — bravedo, bravery, daring act. |
| *chiaroscuro* | — a sketch of black and white |
| *dilettante* | — 'delighting', delectable, charming; an admirer or lover of arts. |
| *de facto* | — existing as a fact, though not legally accepted. |
| *de jure* | — according to law. |
| *diminuendo* | — with gladly diminishing intensity or volume. |
| *imbroglio, embroglio* | — a violent and complicated quarrel, an embroil. |
| *lingrua franca* | — a common language. |
| *presto* | — quickly, rapidly. |

| *punctillio* | — a nice point of behaviour, etiquette. |
| *punctillious* | — being attentive to small, fine points. |
| *virtuoso* | — virtuous. |
| *nostro* | — our (of bank accounts). |
| *vostro* | — your (of bank accounts). |

## GERMAN WORDS

German words are often archaic and tongue-twisters. Some of them which are used in English are given below:

| *angst* | — anguish, pain, dread, a feeling of anxiety. |
| *blitzkrieg* | — a sudden military attack intended to achieve a quick victory. |
| *ersatz* | — substitute or replacement. |
| *kaffee klatsch* | — coffee and gossip, a party where talk is exchanged over cups of coffee. |
| *denizen* | — inhabitant, native of a place. |
| *kitsch* | — low quality production (in literature, drama, art), designed for popular appeal. |
| *liet motif* | — leading motive or theme. |
| *putsch* | — a sudden secret plot and attempt to overthrow a government. |
| *strafe* | — to punish. |
| *wunderkind* | — wonderful child, a prodigy. |

## WORDS FROM OTHER LANGUAGES

Apart from French, Spanish, Italian and German, some other languages have also contributed words to English language. Some prominent among them are listed below:

| | | |
|---|---|---|
| *apartheid* | — | has been taken from South Africa. It means the policy of racial discrimination against the blacks. |
| *trek* | — | (Africa) — journey, migration. |
| *hegiri* (Arabic) | — | flight, exodus, a mass migration. |
| *safari* | — | a trip or journey. Some people attribute this word to Afrikaans, others to Arabic. |
| *gung ho* | — | is of Chinese language. It means 'everybody work together.' |
| *kibbutz* | — | has Hebrew origin. It means 'a gathering', particularly a collective farm under communal ownership and management. |
| *sabra* | — | (Hebrew) native born Israelis. |
| *banzai* | — | ten thousand years, a cheer of enthusiasm and triumph. It is a Japanese word. |
| *haibu* | — | (Japanese) a delicate form of Japanese poetry consisting of a stanza of three lines. |
| *tycoon* | — | (Chinese/Japanese) a businessman of tremendous influence and wealth. |
| *samurai* | — | (Japanese) professional soldier. |
| *amuck, amok* | — | furious attack; charge in a violent manner; frenzied; out of control; berserk. |
| *satrap* | — | (*Persian*) protector of the kingdoms. |
| *atoll* | — | (Maldive Islands) — small ring-shaped coral reef. |

## INDIAN LANGUAGES WORDS

Several words from various Indian languages — Hindi, Sanskrit, Urdu, Tamil, etc. have found a place in English. Some of them are mentioned below:

| | |
|---|---|
| *brahman, brahman* | — a person of high priestly caste. |
| *juggernaut* | — taken from Jaganath - lord of the world. |
| | — an irresistible strong force that has the power to subdue anything that comes its way. |
| *nirvana* | — salvation, freedom from pain and passion, complete freedom from the cycle of births and deaths. |
| *pariah* | — an outcast, a person rejected by society. |
| *faquir, fakir* | — an ascetic, a holy man without possessions. |
| *dharma* | — religion. |
| *dharna* | — a form of protest in which a group of people refuse to leave a public place, factory, etc. |
| *gurdwara* | — a place of worship for the Sikhs. |
| *bandobast* | — arrangement particularly to maintain law and order. |

## SOME OTHER FOREIGN WORDS

| | |
|---|---|
| *dossier* | — file |
| *penchant* | — strong inclination |
| *incognito* | — under an assumed name |
| *harakiri* | — ritual suicide |

| | | |
|---|---|---|
| *fracas* | — | noisy dispute |
| *vendetta* | — | bloody feud |
| *entourage* | — | retinue |
| *insonciance* | — | freedom from care |
| *concierge* | — | housekeeper |
| *ennui* | — | weariness/boredom |
| *tableau* | — | picture |
| *comouflage* | — | disguise |
| *manqué* | — | not successful |
| atelier | — | workshop |
| milieu | — | environment. |

## Review Test-1

*Find words that match the given statement:*

1. freedom to do whatever you like       c _____
2. creator of new ideas in literature     a _____
3. an improvement in relations between   d _____
   two or more countries.
4. a small group of dancers.              e _____
5. unraveling of plot in a play, story.   d _____
6. an agreement but not alliance          e _____
7. high fashion, women's clothes          h _____
8. absence of state intervention          l _____
9. social error                           f _____
10. easy to obtain                        f _____
11. a collection of wild animals          m _____
12. not expressed directly                o _____
13. a particular way of using words       p _____

14. dead end                                    c _____
15. vague feeling of disgust                    m _____

**Answers :**

|  |  |
|---|---|
| 1. carte blanche | 2. avant garde |
| 3. detente | 4. ensemble |
| 5. denouement | 6. entente |
| 7. haute coutour | 8. laissez-faire |
| 9. faux pas | 10. facile |
| 11. menagerie | 12. obelique |
| 13. parlance | 14. cul-de-sac |
| 15. malouse | |

## Review Test 2

*Match the given foreign words with their meanings:*

1. group of small boats                         (a) angst
2. a closely knit group of persons              (b) gung ho
3. excessive attachment for something           (c) fetish
4. a busy, crowded place                        (d) junta
5. quickly, rapidly                             (e) flotilla
6. anguish, pain                                (f) imbroglio
7. a sudden military attack                     (g) piccadally
8. a violent and complicated quarrel            (h) presto
9. everybody work together                      (i) apartheid
10. policy of racial discrimination             (j) blitzkrieg

**Answers :**

1. (e); 2. (d); 3. (c); 4. (g); 5. (h); 6. (a); 7. (j); 8. (f); 9. (b); 10. (i).

.. 

# 23

## CHECKING YOUR PROGRESS
### COMPREHENSIVE TEST—4

In the previous three chapters we have introduced 180 emphatic words. Their meanings and, in many cases, their synonyms as well as their usage have also been given. You must have gone through them carefully. We have avoided etymology—root words governing them and their pronunciation. Etymology serves little purpose and pronunciation does not pose much problem if you have learnt the spellings. What one needs to do is to retain the words in one's memory, know the meanings thereof correctly and be able to use them as per demands of the situation.

There is no magic formula through which one can immediately add these words in one's vocabulary. Nor it is possible for anyone to suddenly start using all these words in their talks and write-ups. Building vocabulary is a gradual process. Repeated reading and usage of words is what brings them into one's repertoire over a period of time. A repeated reading of the chapters is advised. Just one or two readings will not help you learn all these words and their meanings. However, what it will do is that if you happen to come across these words in a newspaper, article or book, they will not sound unfamiliar. Many times your memory and the context in which the word has been used will help you figure out the correct meaning.

Don't be put back if some of these words slip out of your mind. Only those words will be retained which are read, spoken or written regularly. What is required is sincere and persistent efforts.

It is necessary to assess whatever you have learnt. Given below are six tests. Take them sincerely and assess your progress. If your score is below average or average, read the previous three chapters again. If above average onwards you may proceed further but keep glancing these chapters. Best of luck for the following tests:

## TEST 1

*Write the word that matches the meaning/statement:*

1. Unfocused, going from one thing to another

1. d_____

2. appaling, causing disgust

2. a_____

3. outrageous, completely unreasonable

3. p_____

4. full of energy & confidence

4. e_____

5. making angry and cruel criticism

5. v_____

6. growing or developing rapidly

6. b_____

7. having tendency to cry easily

7. l_____

8. obscure, unknown

8. r_____

9. something pleasant/interesting happening by chance

9. s_____

10. last but one                          10. p_____
11. punishment/defeat that is deserved    11. n_____
    and unavoidable
12. not showing respect for others        12. i_____
13. refusing to obey                      13. d_____
14. talented at young age                 14. p_____
15. very large number of something        15. m_____
16. destroy in large number               16. d_____
17. appropriateness or relevance          17. p_____
18. dull, without taste                   18. i_____
19. very immoral behaviour                19. t_____
20. using low and abusive language        20. r_____

**Answers:**

| | | |
|---|---|---|
| 1. desultory | 2. abominable | 3. preposterous |
| 4. ebullient | 5. vituperative | 6. burgening |
| 7. lachrymose | 8. recondite | 9. serendipitous |
| 10. penultimate | 11. nemesis | 12. impudent |
| 13. defiant | 14. precocious | 15. myriad |
| 16. decimate | 17. propriety | 18. insipid |
| 19. turpitude | 20. ribald | |

## TEST 2

*Each of the following words is followed by four options (a), (b), (c) and (d) only one out of which conveys the meaning of the key word. Pick the right option:*

**1.** histrionic    (a) theatrical    (b) famous
             (c) erudite    (d) deluded

**2.** immanent    (a) prominent    (b) departing
             (c) inherent    (d) impending

**3.** incarcerate    (a) burn complete    (b) imprison
                    (c) torture    (d) imperil

**4.** plaudits    (a) praise    (b) delicacies
             (c) unpleasant    (d) implications

**5.** blatant    (a) aweary    (b) stylish
           (c) flagrant    (d) concealed

**6.** mollification    (a) slight change
                  (b) washing with soap
                  (c) dressing expensively
                  (d) softening of ruffled feelings

**7.** palpable    (a) excited    (b) persuasive
            (c) obvious    (d) subtle

**8.** perfunctory    (a) complete in all details
                (b) superficial
                (c) noble done
                (d) well mastered

**9.** profligacy    (a) wastefulnesss
               (b) forward motion
               (c) productivity
               (d) affluence

**10.** reprehensible    (a) easy to grasp
                  (b) deferential
                  (c) returnable
                  (d) blameworthy

**11.** rhapsodic    (a) fervent    (b) ecstatic
             (c) scattered    (d) isolated

**12.** subsume    (a) include    (b) undermine
           (c) suffer    (d) reject

**13.** supercilious    (a) foolish    (b) eminent
              (c) respectful    (d) haughty

**14.** symbiotic
    (*a*) evoluitonary
    (*b*) living in close association
    (*c*) unreal
    (*d*) tactful

**15.** upbraid
    (*a*) chide
    (*b*) escalate
    (*c*) cause to tremble
    (*d*) raise

**16.** virulent
    (*a*) sudden   (*b*) manly
    (*c*) venomous   (*d*) overpowering

**17.** flippancy
    (*a*) levity
    (*b*) clumsiness
    (*c*) adroitness
    (*d*) lack of understanding

**18.** fecundity
    (*a*) depth   (*b*) fertility
    (*c*) poverty   (*d*) validity

**19.** capitulate
    (*a*) repeat   (*b*) execute
    (*c*) summarise   (*d*) surrender

**20.** arraign
    (*a*) serve on jury
    (*b*) put in order
    (*c*) convict
    (*d*) bring before a court

**Answers:**

| 1. (*a*) | 2. (*c*) | 3. (*c*) | 4. (*a*) | 5. (*c*) |
| 6. (*d*) | 7. (*c*) | 8. (*b*) | 9. (*a*) | 10. (*d*) |
| 11. (*b*) | 12. (*a*) | 13. (*d*) | 14. (*b*) | 15. (*a*) |
| 16. (*c*) | 17. (*c*) | 18. (*b*) | 19. (*d*) | 20. (*d*) |

## TEST 3

*Match the following words with their synonyms/ meanings.*

1. fugacious        (a) frivolty
2. deleterious      (b) quiet, isolated
3. corollary        (c) damaging
4. levity           (d) relentless
5. palatable        (e) ramshakle
6. insoucient       (f) short-lived
7. sequestered      (g) connivance
8. inexorable       (h) relishable
9. ostentatious     (i) consequence
10. specious        (j) insult
11. attenuate       (k) deceptive
12. furtive         (l) nonchalant
13. dilapidated     (m) showy
14. complicity      (n) make less effective
15. affront         (o) stealthy

**Answers:**

| 1. (f) | 2. (c) | 3. (i) | 4. (a) | 5. (h) |
|--------|--------|--------|--------|--------|
| 6. (l) | 7. (b) | 8. (d) | 9. (m) | 10. (k) |
| 11. (n) | 12. (o) | 13. (e) | 14. (g) | 15. (j) |

## TEST 4

*Match the words with their synonyms/meanings:*

1. plaudits        (a) hateful
2. jettison        (b) protection
3. insinuation     (c) criminal
4. quixotic        (d) implication
5. abjure          (e) immaculate
6. resonant        (f) renounce
7. abominable      (g) measure
8. redoubtable     (h) outrageous
9. aegis           (i) accolades
10. preposterous   (j) determined

11. benchmark          (k) punishment
12. nefarious          (l) resounding
13. pristine           (m) impractical
14. tenacious          (n) formidable
15. nemesis            (o) discard

**Answers:**

| | | | | |
|---|---|---|---|---|
| **1.** (i) | **2.** (o) | **3.** (d) | **4.** (m) | **5.** (f) |
| **6.** (l) | **7.** (a) | **8.** (n) | **9.** (b) | **10.** (h) |
| **11.** (g) | **12.** (c) | **13.** (e) | **14.** (j) | **15.** (k) |

## TEST 5

*Give synonyms of the following words:*

1. ephemeral        e_____
2. execrable        t_____
3. defiant          d_____
4. abashed          e_____
5. mollify          p_____
6. myopic           s_____
7. reproof          r_____
8. inexorable       r_____
9. indoctrinate     b_____
10. innuendo        n_____
11. dichotomy       s_____
12. abnegation      r_____
13. relevant        g_____
14. erudite         l_____
15. convoluted      c_____

**Answers :**

1. evanescent
2. terrible
3. disobedient
4. embarrassed
5. placate
6. shortsighted
7. reprimand
8. relentless
9. brainwash
10. nuance
11. separation
12. rejection
13. germane
14. learned
15. complicated

## TEST 6

*Give antonyms of the following words:*

1. attenuate      s_____
2. myriad      h_____
3. insipid      l_____
4. disseminate      c_____
5. comprehensible      a_____
6. plaudits      u_____
7. inveigle      c_____
8. palatable      u_____
9. diffident      a_____
10. succint      c_____
11. commensurate      i_____
12. emancipate      i_____
13. mollify      a_____
14. profligacy      t_____
15. reprehensible      a_____
16. insoncient      e_____

17. veteran          a_____
18. unabashed        e_____
19. furtive          f_____
20. dolorous         e_____

## ANSWERS

| | |
|---|---|
| **1.** strengthen | **2.** handful |
| **3.** lively | **4.** confine |
| **5.** abstruse | **6.** upbraids |
| **7.** capitulate | **8.** unsavoury |
| **9.** audacious | **10.** comprehensive |
| **11.** impertinent | **12.** incarcerate |
| **13.** augment | **14.** thrift |
| **15.** appreciable | **16.** earnest |
| **17.** amateur | **18.** embarrassed |
| **19.** flagrant | **20.** elated. |

### ASSESSMENT

**Test 1, 2 & 6**

| | |
|---|---|
| Less than 10 | not up to the mark |
| 10–13 | average |
| 14–16 | above average |
| 17–18 | excellent |
| 19–20 | superior |

**Test 3, 4 & 5**

| | |
|---|---|
| Less than 8 | not up to the mark |
| 8–9 | average |
| 10–11 | above average |
| 12–13 | excellent |
| 14–15 | superior |

# 24

# FOREIGN PHRASES/TERMS IN ENGLISH

The range of English language is phenomenal. It has been further enriched by several phrases, terms and words from some foreign languages like Latin, French, Greek and Italian. Many key terms from these languages are freely used in newspaper editorials, articles, papers and other write-ups in anthologies and magazines. These phrases carry specific meanings and are therefore used to exactly describe a situation, an action or an emotion. They not only hit the nail on the head but also lend beauty to the expression. Another advantage of using these phrases is that they make the expression terse and say much in a few words. They also bear testimony to the writer's erudition.

You must have read or heard several such words— an *interim* government, an *ad valorum* duty, *prima facie* evidence, maintenance of *status quo,* a complete *ignoramus*, an *im-promptu* performance, *obiter dictum* of a judge, and *quid pro quo* action. Theses phrases convey the exact meaning intended or represented by the situation or action but since they govern the sentences in which they are used, it is difficult to comprehend such sentences unless one knows the meaning and purport of these phrases. It is therefore necessary to know the major phrases of foreign languages used in English. Given below are most of the major terms alongwith their meanings. Reading them just once may not be sufficient to learn, understand and assimilate these terms in your vocabulary. Therefore, read this chapter again and again and use these terms in your discourses and write-ups.

*ad hoc:* 'for this purpose', temporary, for the present situation. For example an *ad hoc* committee whose existence is limited to the period of time it takes to dispose of the matter in hand.

*ad libitum:* 'at pleasure, at will'. Ad lib is shortened form and is used both as a verb and as a noun – it means to improvise, to add meaning extemporaneously to a script.

*bona fide:* 'in good faith'. It is used to modify some other word – bonafide intention. The expression *bonafides* (singular) is used as the subject or object of a verb (meaning evidence that somebody is who they say they are) as in: *Her bonafides is above reproach.*

*malafide:* the expression is antonym to *bonafide* and means having bad intention.

*post facto:* 'after the fact or event', retroactive.

*in extremis:* 'in extreme circumstances', in desperate straits, near death.

*magnum opus:* a great work, a masterpiece; also a crowning achievement.

*modus operandi:* 'manner of operating', a working method or arrangement.

*modus vivendi:* 'manner of living', a way of life; also a temporary arrangement. The term is used these days to talk of peaceful coexistence, a way of getting alongwith other nations or persons in spite of basic differences.

*obiter dictum:* 'said/stated by the way' – an incidental remark or opinion by a judge that is not binding on the final judgement.

*persona grata:* 'an acceptable person', a welcome person.

*persona non grata:* 'an unacceptable person', a person who is not welcome or has no say in any matter.

*prima facie:* 'on first appearance' or at first glance, apparent or self evident. In law it is considered sufficient to establish a fact unless refuted.

*per se:* 'by himself/herself/itself/themselves', of its own accord, independently.

*post bellum:* 'after the war'.

*ante bellum:* 'before the war'.

*pro forma:* 'for the sake of the form', to be used as a form, for the record.

*pro tempore:* 'for the time being', generally used as the short term – *pro tem.*

*pro rata:* 'for the sake of rate', at the rate of.

*quid pro que:* 'tit for tat' or 'something for something', something given for something received.

*sine qua non:* 'without which not', a prerequisite or an essential.

*status quo:* 'the condition in which', the present condition, the state of affairs upto the present time – to maintain the status quo – to leave things as they were before the start of current action.

*sui generis:* 'of his/her/its/their own kind', unique, of a class apart.

*ad infinitum:* endlessly, ceaselessly, for ever.

*dramatis personae:* 'persons of the drama', cast of characters.

*ex officio:* by virtue of one's office or position.

*facsimile:* 'make like', an exact copy.

*id est* short form *i.e.:* 'that is', a phrase giving an explanation of what has just been written or stated.

*in extenso:* 'in detail, at full length'.

*inter alia:* 'among other things'.

*interim:* meanwhile, in the meantime, provisional or temporary, e.g. an *interim government.*

*in toto:* 'totally', entirely.

*ipso facto:* 'by the fact itself'.

*lingua franca:* a shared language of communication used between people whose main languages are different. English has become the lingua franca in many parts of the world.

*lapsus linguae:* 'slip of the tongue'.

*lapsus calami:* 'slip of the pen.'

*literate:* 'lettered', men of letters, learned men.

*sanctum sanctorum:* 'holiest of the holies', a sacred place.

*summum bonum:* the highest good.

*terra firma:* solid ground, also dry land.

*terra cotta:* a reddish brown clay that has been baked but not glazed.

*verbatim:* 'word for word', exactly as said or written.

*viva voce:* 'with the living voice', orally.

## Some Foreign Expressions used in English

A large number of foreign expressions are used in English. Such words are generally kept in *italics* in English write-ups. Some main such expressions are given below alongwith their meanings:

*ab initio:* from the beginning.

*ab intra:* from within.

*absit invidia:* let there be no ill will.

*ad finem:* to the end.

*ad idem:* to the same point.

*ad interim:* in the meanwhile.

*adsum:* I'm present here.

*ad valorum:* according to value.

*affreaux:* fearful, frightful.

*agenda:* (official) list of things to be done.

*alma mater:* a foster mother, the university or college in which one is receiving or has received education.

*alter ego:* one's second self, a friend.

*alter idem:* precisely similar another thing.

*Anno Christi (AC):* in the year of Christ.

*Anno Domini (AD):* in the year of our Lord.

*Ante Meridium (AM):* before noon.

*a paribus:* from equals.

*apres coup:* to late.

*arc-en-ciel:* rainbow.

*argent compatant:* ready money.

*au fait:* well instructed.

*au mieux:* on the best of terms.

*au revoir:* till we meet again, adieu, goodbye.

*a volente:* at pleasure.

*bal pare:* a dress ball.

*basta:* enough.

*beati pacifici:* blessed are the peacemakers.

*ben venuto:* welcome.

*bien entendu:* of course, sure.

*bourgeoisie:* middle class.

*bon ami:* good friend.

*carte blanche:* unlimited authority.

*cause celebre:* a peculiarly notable trial.

*caveat emptor:* let the buyer beware.

*corrigenda:* corrections to be made.

*de novo:* anew.

*deo voleute:* God willing.

*de profundis:* out of the depth.

*dolce:* soft and agreeable.

*dulce domum:* sweet home.

*e contrario:* on the contrary.

*enfant terrible:* a difficult child.

*en masse:* in a body; together.

*en route:* on the way.

*espirit de corps:* the animating spirit of a collective body.

*exceptio probat regulam:* the exception proves the rule.

*exempli gratia:* for instance; for example (abbreviated to e.g.).

*facile princeps:* evidently pre-eminent.

*fait accompli:* a thing already done.

*feu de joie:* firing of guns in token of joy; bonfire.

*fiat lux:* let there be light.

*fortuna fortes adjuva:* fortune aids the brave.

*fortuna favet fatuis:* fortune favours fools.

*fortuna favet fortibus:* fortune favours the bold.

*grand merci:* many thanks.

*idem:* the same.

*id est:* that is (abbreviated to i.e.).

*in nomine*: in the name of.

*in nuce:* in nutshell.

*in pleno:* in full.

*inter alia:* among other things.

*in toto:* in the whole; entirely.

*ipso facto*: in the fact itself; virtually.

*janius clausis:* with closed doors; in secret.

*l'allegro:* the merry, cheerful man.

*lingua franca:* the common language.

*lis litem generate:* strife begets strife.

*lite pendente:* during the trial.

*lucidus ordo:* a clear arrangement.

*lucri causa:* for the sake of gain.

*mala fide:* with bad faith, treacherously.

*mali exampli:* a bad example.

*mea culpa:* by my own fault.

*memento mori:* remember death.

*memorabilia:* things to be remembered.

*mens legis:* the spirit of law.

*mirabilia:* wonders.

*modo et forma:* in manner and form.

*modus operandi:* plan of working.

*mutatis mutandis:* with necessary changes.

*mutuas consensus:* mutual consent.

*nota bene:* mark well, take notice.

*octroi:* duties paid at the gate of a city.

*post restante:* to remain until called for.

*post mortem:* after death.

*prima facie:* on the first view.

*pro tanto:* for so much.

*quantum libet:* as much as you please.

*quantum meruit:* as much as he deserved.

*quasi:* in a manner.

*quo vadis?* whither goes thou?

*repondez s'il vous plait:* (r.s.v.p.) reply, if you please.

*salvo pudore:* without offence to modesty.

*satis, superqua:* enough, and more than enough.

*secundum artem:* according to rule.

*so defendeno:* in self-defence.

*sine die:* indefinitely.

*status quo:* the same position as before.

*sub judice:* under consideration.

*summum bonum:* the chief good.

*summ cique:* give every man his due.

*tabula rasa:* a smooth or blank tablet.

*tempora mutantur, nos el mutamur in illis:* the times are changed, and we are changed with them.

*tempora pareudum:* we must move with the times.

*terra incognita:* an unknown country.

*totes quoties:* as often as.

*toto coelo:* by the whole heavens; diametrically opposite.

*vis-a-vis:* opposite; facing.

*vis inertiae:* the power of inertia; resistance.

*viva voce:* by oral testimony.

*anathema:* something devoted to evil. Someone condemned as an evil doer. Something detested or accursed.

*antipodes:* something diametrically opposed to some other thing.

*apotheosis:* ascension from earthly existence to heavenly glory, also an exalted position.

*ethos:* the word has wide meanings – disposition, demeanor, the spirit that influences/animates the moral values of people. Synonymous with *mores.*

*eureka:* literally means 'I have found it'. It is a cry of triumph after an accomplishment.

*hoi polloi:* 'the many', the term is used to denote common people, ordinary people, and has a derogatory overtone.

*kudos:* fame, glory, prestige. It is a singular noun.

*ergo:* therefore, hence, so, accordingly.

*mores:* customs, moral attitudes, manners and habits of a group, community.

## Literal Meanings of some Latin Words and their Connotation in English Usage

*aura:* 'breeze' – radiant atmosphere, a subtle feeling or a sensation.

*affidavit:* 'a statement by someone upon his faith' – sworn statement.

*condominium:* 'control together' – the word is applied to mean a type of apartment ownership.

*congeries:* a 'heap or pile' – a collection of forces, an aggregation or agglomeration.

*consortium:* 'a sharing together'. These days it is used to mean a group working together: a number of banks joining together to finance a huge project are called a consortium; it also means an international banking agreement like a cartel.

*crux:* 'cross', a crucial or critical point; the crux of the matter is the point that has to be decided to clear up the situation.

*deficit:* 'something is wanting/lacking' – amount by which a sum is less than required.

*emeritus:* 'having earned' (A Roman soldier was called *emeritus* after he had completed his service, and he deserved stipends alongwith his discharge. Today, the word is used as a title especially in the academic world to be bestowed upon a person who has served well.

*habitat:* 'where someone/something dwells' – native environment.

*ignoramus:* 'not knowing something' – a dullard or dunce.

*mandamus:* ordered, ordered by us – writ requiring something to be done.

*memento:* something to remember – a souvenir.

*placebo:* 'something that will please' – medicine given to humour patient.

*recipe:* 'to take' – direction in cooking.

*tenet:* 'something that holds' – a tenet.

*adnauseum:* 'to seasickness' – to a sickening degree.

*a priori:* based on theory rather than experience.

*per capita:* 'by heads' – for each one.

*post factum:* after the deed.

*sine die:* without setting a day for meeting again.

*docorum:* good taste, manner, order.

*folio:* a book made with large sheets of paper, especially as used in early printing; a single sheet of paper from a book.

*impromptu:* 'in readiness'; immediately, on the spur of the moment.

*locus:* 'a place', the exact place where something happens or which is supposed to be the centre of something.

*nimbus:* 'halo', also a large grey rain cloud.

*regimen:* prescribed diet for keeping health.

*requiem:* a 'rest', a dirge.

*rostrum:* speaker's platform.

*tandem:* 'at length', one behind another. These days the word is used to mean – in unison.

*acumen:* mental keenness.

*colloquium:* conference.

*conspeitus:* a brief survey.

*errata:* errors, a list of errors.

*interregnum:* rule during a temporary vacancy.

*lacuna:* literally 'gap'. Now used in the sense of a short-coming.

*nonplussed:* baffled.

*odium:* hatred, scorn.

*propaganda:* spreading of ideas.

*scintilla:* very slight trace.

*antithesis:* exactly opposite.

*apotheosis:* deification.

*chaos:* utter confusion.

*climax:* culmination.

*cosmos:* universe, also the name of flower.

*dogma:* doctrine.

*ellipsis:* omission of words.

*enigma:* riddle, an extremely complicated problem or situation.

*epitome:* embodiment, a perfect example of something.

*lexicon:* dictionary.

*canon:* a body of laws.

*phalanx:* full range of voice or instrument.

*proboscis:* the long flexible nose of some animals like elephant and tapir, etc.

*stigma:* mark of disgrace, blot.

## Review Test 1

*Find the terms that match the given statements/words/ meanings:*

1. a masterpiece                        m_____
2. an unacceptable person               p_____
3. on first appearance                  p_____
4. the present condition                s_____
5. by virtue of one's office            e_____
6. the highest good                     s_____
7. by the fact itself                   i_____
8. according to value                   a_____
9. one's second self                    a_____
10. among other things                  i_____

**Answers:**

1. magnum opus            2. persona non grata
3. prima facie            4. status quo
5. ex officio             6. summum bonum
7. ipso facto             8. ad valorum
9. alter ego             10. inter alia

## Review Test 2

*Match the following Latin expressions with their meanings in the given column:*

1. ordinary                    (a) exempli gratia
2. based on theory             (b) fait accompli

3. without setting a day            (c) sine die
   for meeting again
4. after the deed                   (d) mutatis mutandis
5. for example                      (e) terra firma
6. a thing already done             (f) hoi polloi
7. the same                         (g) malafide
8. with necessary changes           (h) a priori
9. with bad faith                   (i) idem
10. solid earth/footing             (j) post facto

**Answers:**

| | | | | |
|---|---|---|---|---|
| **1.** (f) | **2.** (h) | **3.** (c) | **4.** (j) | **5.** (a) |
| **6.** (b) | **7.** (i) | **8.** (d) | **9.** (g) | **10.** (e) |

## Review Test 3

*Mention the meaning of the following phrases/words:*

1. *lingua franca*      _____
2. *ipso facto*         _____
3. *interim*            _____
4. *alma mater*         _____
5. *carte blanche*      _____
6. *anathema*           _____
7. *ethos*              _____
8. *aura*               _____
9. *consortium*         _____
10. *impromptu*         _____

**Answers :**

1. shared language of communication.
2. by the fact itself.
3. provisional or temporary.
4. college or university in which one has studied.
5. unlimited authority.
6. devoted to evil.
7. the spirit that influences.
8. radiant atmosphere.
9. a sharing together.
10. in readiness, immediately.

# 25

## ADJECTIVAL PHRASES, ADVERBIAL PHRASES, PREPOSITIONAL PHRASES AND CONJUNCTIONAL PHRASES

English language is not just about words. Though the words are extremely important, there is so much else that is involved in the web of expression. Moreover, the words are not used in isolation, they have to be properly framed into meaningful sentences.

As stated in the previous chapter, some key words form phrases in combination with some other words and convey special meanings. We have already seen some important phrasal verbs. Now it is the turn of some other phrases such as adjectival, adverbial, prepositional and conjunctional phrases. They are given below in that order:

### ADJECTIVAL PHRASES

Adjectives as you know are the words that describe a

person or thing, such as *red* rose, *intelligent* boy and *exciting* prospect. Adjectival phrases are those formed with adjectives. Some main adjectives followed by prepositions alongwith some examples of descriptions giving their usage are given below:

## Adjectives Followed by Prepositions

A number of adjectives take certain specific prepositions that follow them to connect them with nouns in the sentence. Some of the commonly used adjectives and the prepositions that go with them are listed below:

| Adjective | Preposition | Description |
|---|---|---|
| acceptable | to | someone |
| accomplished | in | music, painting, etc. |
| accustomed | to | something |
| acquainted | with | a person, a subject, etc. |
| addicted | to | a habit, etc. |
| affectionate | to | children, relatives |
| afraid | of | something |
| alarmed | at | the news, etc. |
| alive | to | a danger, etc. |
| allied | with | a country, party, etc. |
| angry | with | a person |
| annoyed | at | something |
|  | with | someone |
| answerable | to | someone |
|  | for | something |
| anxious | for | something or someone |
|  | about | something |
| applicable | to | someone or something, |
| ashamed | of | something, e.g. one's conduct, etc. |

| | | |
|---|---|---|
| astonished | at | something |
| averse | to | something, e.g. hard work, etc. |
| bent | on | doing something |
| beset | with | difficulties, dangers, etc. |
| born | to, of | rich, poor, parents |
| bound | for | a place |
| busy | with | something |
| capable | of | something, e.g. hard work etc. |
| careful | of | one's health, money, etc. |
| | with | one's work, driving, etc. |
| certain | of | something, e.g. success, victory |
| comparable | to | something |
| concerned | about | something or someone |
| confident | of | success, etc. |
| conscious | of | something, e.g. one's defects |
| contented | with | something |
| contrary | to | something, e.g. a rule, expectations |
| deaf | to | advice, pleading, etc. |
| deficient | in | something |
| delighted | with | one's success etc. |
| devoid | of | something, e.g. good sense, etc. |
| engaged | in | something, e.g. some work etc. |
| | with | someone |
| entitled | to | something |
| envious | of | someone, something |
| essential | for | happiness, success etc. |

| | | |
|---|---|---|
| exhausted | with | work, etc. |
| familiar | to | a person |
| | with | a situation |
| famous | for | something |
| fascinated | by | something, e.g. ornaments, beauty |
| gifted | with | an ability, etc. |
| given | to | a habit, etc. |
| good | at | something, e.g. painting |
| grateful | to | someone |
| | for | something |
| greedy | for | something |
| hopeful | of | success, gain, etc. |
| ignorant | of | something, e.g. law |
| inclined | to | something, e.g. lying |
| indebted | to | someone |
| | for | something, e.g. help |
| indifferent | to | something, some result, happenings |
| infested | with | something, e.g. rats, worms |
| intimate | with | someone |
| jealous | of | somebody or something |
| liable | for | something, e.g. someone's debts |
| | to | a fine, punishment |
| negligent | in | work, etc. |
| | of | duties, etc. |
| obliged | to | someone |
| | for | something |
| occupied | with | some work, etc. |
| offended | with | someone |
| peculiar | to | someone or a place |

| preferable | to | something else |
| prepared | for | something, e.g. test, situation |
| proficient | in | something, e.g. music, English |
| proud | of | something, e.g. one's learning |
| ready | for | something, e.g. an action, |
| responsible | to | someone |
| | for | something |
| satisfied | with | something, e.g. position |
| short | of | something, needed, e.g. money |

## ADVERBIAL PHRASES

Adverbs are words that add more information about place, time, manner, cause, degree to a verb, adjective, a phrase or another verb. Some major adverbial phrases are given below alongwith their meanings:

*above all:* first and foremost.

*above board:* honest, straightforward.

*after all:* inspite of all the facts to the contrary.

*again and again, time and again, over and over again:* repeatedly, frequently, several times.

*all along:* throughout.

*all at once, all of a sudden:* suddenly.

*anything but:* certainly not.

*as a matter of fact:* actually, in reality.

*as such:* therefore; also as before.

*as far as, so far as:* regarding something.

*as long as:* while.

*so long as:* if some given condition is fulfilled.

*as luck would have it:* by sheer chance.

*at all:* in the least.

*at once:* immediately.

*at length:* at last; also in detail.

*at the most:* in the maximum.

*at worst:* taking the worst view.

*at best:* taking the best view.

*at his best:* in the best form or touch.

*at any rate:* in any case, whatever may happen.

*at all costs:* in any eventuality.

*at the eleventh hour:* quite late, at the last moment.

*at an arm's length:* away, at a distance.

*at large:* free; also taken collectively: *the world at large.*

*at odds:* at a disadvantage.

*at the outset:* at the very beginning.

*at random:* not in a particular order.

*at times:* occasionally.

*behind the scene:* internally supportive.

*by no means:* in no way.

*by all means:* definitely, certainly.

*by and by:* gradually.

*by far:* decidedly.

*ever and anon:* now and then.

*ever so:* to the extent.

*far and wide, far and near:* from all directions.

*far and away, out and out:* decidedly, completely.

*fair and square:* just, impartial; also completely.

*few and far between:* limited in number, few.

*first and foremost:* of greatest importance, takes precedence over other things.

*for sure:* certainly.

*for good:* for ever.

*from time immemorial:* since a very long time.

*hard and fast:* strict, definite (rule).

*in time:* eventually, at proper time, punctual.

*in good time:* early.

*in the long run:* sooner or later, eventually.

*in the dark:* ignorant.

*in the course of:* in due time or after the taking place of some events.

*in right earnest:* seriously.

*in good faith:* unsuspectingly.

*in kind:* in other terms than money.

*in the least:* in the minimum.

*in no time:* very soon.

*in the nick of time:* just when the time was about to elapse for some action; just at the right time.

*in the bargain:* additional benefit.

*many a time:* often, frequently.

*now and then, every now and then:* sometimes.

*off and on:* now and then, occasionally.

*on and on:* continuously.

*of late:* recently, lately.

*off hand:* without previous preparation.

*once and for all:* finally.

*on the whole:* considering all aspects.

*over and above:* in addition to something.

*of one's own accord:* of one's free will.

*on its last legs:* about to fail.

*on the contrary:* conversely, in opposite to something.

*of course:* as a natural consequence of something.

*once in a while:* rarely.

*safe and sound:* unhurt.

*to and fro:* backwards and forwards.

*through and through:* completely.

*then and there:* on the spot.

*to the backbone:* thoroughly.

*on the morrow:* on the following day, in the next morning.

*the other day:* recently.

*for all intents and purposes:* really.

*to all appearances:* apparently.

*to one's heart's content:* fully.

*to the letter:* exactly.

*in letter and spirit:* following its true/real meaning.

*without fail:* certainly.

*without much ado:* without any fus.

## PREPOSITIONAL PHRASES

A preposition is a word or a group of words such as *in, on, out, of, over, etc.* used before a noun or pronoun to show place, position, time or method. Phrases made with such words are known as prepositional phrases.

Some major such phrases and their meanings are given below:

*according to, in accordance with:* as per.

*as regards, as for:* relating/concerning something.

*at home:* comfortable, easy doing something: *at home in Mathematics.*

*at the beck and call of:* to be receiving somebody's orders.

*at the discretion of:* will or power of.

*at variance with:* opposed to.

*at the instance of:* at the request of.

*at loggerheads:* be hostile to.

*at the threshold of:* being near to happening, doing or achieving something.

*but for:* except.

*by dint of:* by force of.

*by means of:* through.

*by virtue of:* by the authority of.

*for the sake of:* for the purpose of.

*for want of:* on account of not having.

*in connection with:* pertinent to, relating to.

*in consequence of:* as a result of.

*in the course of:* during.

*in defence of:* in support of.

*in the event of:* in case of.

*in exchange for:* in return for.

*in the guise of:* posing as.

*in cognizance of:* recognizing the fact.

*in the good books of:* in the favour of.

*in harmony with:* in agreement with.

*in lieu of:* instead of.

*in the light of:* considering some points/facts.

*in proportion to:* equal in proposition or degree to.

*in the quest of:* seeking something.

*in the teeth/face of:* despite opposition or amidst opposition.

*in the throes of:* undergoing suffering caused by.

*in the wake of:* following something.

*on the brink/verge of:* just near, about to.

*on the part of:* by someone's doing.

*on the eve of:* only a short time before.

*on the pretence of:* in the guise of.

*on an errand of:* on a message.

*on the plea of:* on the pretext of.

*on tiptoe for:* in eager expectation of.

## CONJUNCTIONAL PHRASES

Conjunctions are words which join two words or sentences. They are also called sentence connectors or simply connectors. Conjunctional phrases also perform the same function. Some major conjunctional phrases alongwith their meanings are given below:

*As long as, until*—Until expresses 'time before'; *as long as* expresses time 'how long':
  1. Do not go away *until* I come back.
  2. Wait here *as long as* it rains.

*As well as, no less ... than* – These phrases emphasize the first of the two words or sentences which they join.
  Tom *as well as* you is to pay this.
  Peter is *no less* guilty *than* you are.

*As ... so* – *As* you sow, *so* shall you reap.

*As, so ... as* – Richard *is* as brave *as* he is wise.

    Tom is *as* tall *as* his father.

    John is not *so* (or as) brave *as* he is wise.

**Note:** *As – as* is used in both affirmative and negative sentences.

*So ... as* is used in negative ones only.

*Both ... and* – Johnson is *both* a writer *and* a thinker.

    Tina is *both* dull *and* lazy.

*But for* – *But for* timely rains, the crops would have failed.

*Either ... or* – *Either* Garth *or* Sam has got the prize.

*Neither ... nor* – I can *neither* beg *nor* borrow.

    Susan is *neither* a fool *nor* a knave.

    *Neither* did he feel sad *nor* complain.

    *Neither* he *nor* his father is present.

*In order that* – I work from morning till evening, *in order* that I may save some money.

*In as much as* – Navita is very simple and religious in her habits *in as much* as her private life is concerned.

    She suffered *in as much* as she neglected her work.

*Indeed ... but* – Robert was *indeed* found guilty *but* could not be convicted.

*In case* – *In case* I go to Delhi, I shall inform you.

*In so far as* – My boss paid me *in so far as* I demanded.

*In so much that* – It rained all day *in so much* that the match had to be called off.

*In that* – *In that,* he confessed his fault, he should be forgiven.

*Hardly or scarcely ... when* – Ricky had *hardly* gone out of the house *when* it began to rain.

*No sooner than/as soon as* – *No sooner* did the chief guest stand up to speak *than* he was garlanded.
The principal was garlanded *as soon as* he stood up to speak.

*Not only ... but* also – She *not only* passed the examination *but also* won a scholarship.
James is *not only* a good teacher *but also* a great scholar.

*Not to speak of* – *Not to speak of* cold drink, even plain water was not available there.

*Nay* – Vic was fined, *nay* imprisoned.

*Now that* – *Now that* I have arrived, you need not wait.

*No less ... than* – Vivian is *no less* responsible *than* you.

*Rather ... than* – I would *rather* starve *than* beg.
She would *rather* go without food *than* beg.

*So ... that* – The old man is *so* weak *that* he cannot walk.
She is *so* weak in English *that* she cannot write a single sentence correctly.

*Such ... as or that* – *Such* man *as* do not take care of their health fall ill.
Suresh behaved in the class in *such* a manner *that* the teacher became angry with him.

*The same ... as* – This *is the same story as* you told him yesterday.
Dehradun does *not have the same climate as* Mussoorie.

*Unless ... if* – She will fail *if* she does not work hard.
She will fail *unless she works hard.*
She will pass *if she works hard.*
She cannot pass *unless she works hard.*

## Review Test 1

*Mention the adverbial phrases of the following meanings/statements:*

1. honest, straight forward    a_____
2. frequently    t_____
3. at a distance    a_____
4. free    a_____
5. strict, fast    h_____
6. ignorant    i_____
7. additional benefit    i_____
8. unsuspectingly    i_____
9. really    f_____
10. following in true sense    i_____

### Answers:

1. above board, 2. time and again. 3. at an arm's length, 4. at large, 5. hard and fast, 6. in the dark, 7. in the bargain. 8. in good faith, 9. for all intents and purposes, 10. in letter and spirit.

## Review Test 2

*Match the following prepositional phrases with their meanings in the two columns:*

1. at variance with    (a) on account of not having
2. at logger heads    (b) undergoing suffering caused by
3. but for    (c) seeking something
4. for want of    (d) opposed to
5. in lieu of    (e) on a message
6. in the throes of    (f) as a result of

 7. on an errand of          (*g*) hostile
 8. in the quest of          (*h*) posing as
 9. in consequence of        (*i*) instead of
10. in the guise of          (*j*) except, without which

**Answers :**

   **1.** (*d*)     **2.** (*g*)     **3.** (*j*)     **4.** (*a*)     **5.** (*i*)
   **6.** (*b*)     **7.** (*e*)     **8.** (*c*)     **9.** (*f*)     **10.** (*h*)

# 26

## WORDS ABOUT PEOPLE AND THINGS AROUND US—I

It's a vast world with many types of persons and things around us. These persons and things have specific characteristics or attributes which need to be described with relevant words. Everyday new or different situations develop around us, which also need to be properly understood and analysed to initiate proper response wherever required. It is not easy to comprehend different people, situations and actions unless we have a decent vocabulary which puts everything before us in the right perspective.

Mass media is working 24×7 to bring before us all the major national as well as international events. Many of these attract our attention as per our tastes, needs and desires. To the students of Management or Civil Services aspirants the daily newspaper is a first-hand source of information about the latest happenings to keep them up to date in General Knowledge and Awareness. One thing which can prove to be a roadblock in the way of properly understanding various aspects of given information is the lack of adequate vocabulary. For example, if somebody does not know the meaning of 'detente' or 'rapprochment', he/she cannot understand where the relationships of two countries—about whom these words have been used in an article or report—are heading.

It is necessary to build a vocabulary to understand people, situations and actions. There are some specific words which aptly describe particular emotions or feelings, without which the innermost throes of human mind cannot be conveyed to others. The print media which includes newspapers, books, magazines, journals and brochures thrives on our knowledge of language and its vocabulary. By working regularly and systematically we can attain a level of knowledge of words, their meanings and usage whereby we can avail of the plethora of literature created by erudite scholars and experts in various fields and work their knowledge to our advantage in an examination, profession or any other task that we undertake to benefit ourselves, our family, friends or society at large. Some commonly used words that appropriately describe things, situations, emotions and actions are given in this and the next chapter:

**accolade:** originally the word meant embrace but now its meaning has swung to convey 'crowning praise' — used in place of award, praise, honour to denote something more than *ovation.*

**ambience:** the word has taken over some connotation of milieu or environment, and means an aura, a setting or pervading atmosphere.

**bevy:** a large group of people or things of the same kind: *a bevy of beauties.*

**burgeon:** to begin to grow or develop rapidly: a *burgeoning population, burgeoning demand, India's burgeoning private sector.*

**cachet:** generally used to mean the seal of approval, the status that goes with complete acceptance. The word must be distinguished from *cache* which means a hidden treasure of something normally used for weapons *a cache of arms.*

**detente:** is relaxation of tension, rapproachment (between nations), being the next step towards friendlier co-existence.

**demented:** behaving in a crazy way because of being extremely upset or worried.

**echelon:** a rank or position of authority in an organisation or a society: the *lower/upper/top/higher echelons.*

**eclectic:** not following one style or set of ideas but choosing from a wide variety: *He has eclectic tastes in music/literature.*

**expertise:** the word is used showily when only knowledge or expertness is to be conveyed. It means expert knowledge in a special field—not only know—how but also know—what.

**mystique:** it implies a complex of mysterious beliefs or skills gathered around an idea, a feeling or a person– *the feminine mystique,* the *oriental mystique.*

**panache:** has come to mean a heroic gesture, a splendid swagger, dash, verve, flamboyance, a charming gesture.

**proliferate:** to increase rapidly in number or amount. The word has also come to mean an illegal spread of nuclear technology, etc. to rogue states to make nuclear weapons, etc.

**syndrome:** a running together, an occurrence, a cycle of symptoms or manifestations that occur together.

**salvage:** the act of saving things that have been or are likely to be lost.

**trauma:** it is the Greek word for wounds. But now the word is used to denote emotional wounds–any scarring or scaring emotional experience.

**alienation:** in literature the word means – to be lost in the troubled world and being unable to find true identity in the turmoil inside. The verb *alienate* does not always have this psycho-sociological extension and simply means to make somebody less friendly or sympathetic towards you.

**arcane:** mysterious, hidden, recondite as contrasted with lucid, clear and direct.

**bellwether:** very popular word with financial and sports pages. It identifies the leader in a particular sport or in a stock market trend.

**charismatic:** having personal magnetism, appeal or charm.

**epiphany:** appearance or manifestation. In literature it sometimes means some essential truth or self-discovery.

**escalation:** literally, to go up the ladder, higher and higher, to step up. It is a strong word for increase, heighten, build up, e.g. *escalation of price/costs*. The opposite word *de-escalation* is frequently used for war situation, etc.

**hubris:** put together arrogance, overweening and excessive pride and you get the meaning of hubris.

**hypocrite:** a person who pretends to have moral standards or opinions that they actually do not have.

**ploy:** It is related to the word employ and is used as a synonym for device, tactic, manoeuvre or gambit.

**serendipity:** it means a lucky discovery made while looking for something else. More precisely it means just happy discovery that is emphasized.

**spectrum:** the word has replaced gamut – meaning the whole range or scope of related qualities, ideas, etc.: *a broad spectrum of interests*.

**spinoff:** an unexpected but useful result of an activity that is designed to produce something else: *commercial spinoff of medical research*.

**stardust:** a magic quality that some famous people with great natural ability seem to have. Also stars that are very far from earth and appear like bright dust in the sky at night.

**tendentious:** promoting a particular tendency, hence biased, and often controversial.

**paradigm:** a perfect example or pattern of something. *Paradigm shift* – a great and important change in the way something is done or thought about.

**paranoid:** afraid or suspicious of the people and believing that they are trying to harm you.

### Review Test 1

*Find words that match the given statements:*

1. a setting or pervading atmosphere       a_____
2. a group of people or things             b_____
3. promoting a particular tendency         t_____
4. to begin to develop rapidly            b_____

5. behaving in a crazy way                           d_____

6. a complex of mysterious beliefs         m_____

7. a charming gesture                              p_____

8. relaxation of tension between           d_____
   nations

9. emotional wounds                              t_____

10. a cycle of symptoms or manifestations
    that occur together                            s_____

**Answers:**

   1. ambience           2. bevy

   3. tendencious      4. burgeon

   5. demented         6. mystique

   7. panache          8. detente

   9. trauma           10. syndrome

## Review Test 2

*Match the words with their meanings/synonyms:*

   1. accolade          (*a*) personal magnetism

   2. cache            (*b*) a lucky discovery

   3. mystique        (*c*) ovation

   4. salvage         (*d*) separation

   5. alienation      (*e*) gamut

   6. charisma       (*f*) hidden treasure

   7. spectrum      (*g*) aura

   8. ambience      (*h*) pull back

   9. cachet         (*i*) seal of approval

10. serendipity    (j) hidden charm

**Answers:**

|   |   |   |   |   |
|---|---|---|---|---|
| **1.** (c) | **2.** (f) | **3.** (j) | **4.** (h) | **5.** (d) |
| **6.** (a) | **7.** (e) | **8.** (g) | **9.** (i) | **10.** (b) |

The following words are ubiquitous, i.e., you see them everywhere. It is quite handy to know their meanings and usage.

**ambivalence:** having equally strong pulls in both directions. Showing both good and bad feelings about something. For example a roller coaster ride excites us as well as scares us.

**amenable:** easy to control, willing to be influenced by something.

**bandwagon:** an activity that more and more people are becoming involved in, something very common to do in the hope of getting some profit, advantage. Something very usual, commonplace as contrasted with exceptional.

**castigate:** to criticize severely, reprimand.

**clandestine:** something done in secret or kept secret – used for illegal or unacceptable actions, having evil designs or intentions.

**clamour:** to demand something loudly: *Public began to clamour for the resignation of the corrupt officer.*

**ephemeral:** literally, it means lasting only a day. Now used to denote something that is short-lived.

**exacerbate:** to make something worse, aggravate is a weaker word with almost the same meaning, opposite is *ameliorate.*

**excruciating:** extremely painful or bad: *an excruciating pain in the back.*

**haywire:** to stop working correctly or become out of control.

**hogwash:** an idea or argument that you consider as silly or stupid.

**intransigent:** often used disapprovingly to talk of people who are unwilling to change their opinions in a way that would be helpful to others.

**jettison:** to get rid of something that you no longer need or want, to discard. Also to reject an idea, belief or plan.

**minuscule:** extremely small. The word is used to denote a scale or magnitude that is negligible.

**misappropriate:** to take somebody else's money or property for yourself especially when they have trusted you to take care of it—*embezzle*.

**miscellany:** a group or collection of different kinds of things—*assortment*.

**nostalgia:** a longing for a return. It suggests the pain, albeit a pleasant sentimental one experienced on returning home or in memory of homestead—a haunt of former times.

**naive:** used disapprovingly—lacking experience of life, knowledge or good judgement. Approvingly—innocent and simple.

**nebulous:** vague, unclear: *a nebulous concept.*

**novice:** a person who is new and has little experience in a field, job or situation.

**paradoxical:** a situation that has two opposite features, and therefore seems strange.

**peripheral:** relating to the outer edge of a particular area. Also the less important part of a social or political group.

**polemic:** highly charged controversial argument. A speech or a piece of writing that argues very strongly for or against something or somebody.

**paragon:** a person who is perfect or is the perfect example of a particular good quality.

**prerogative:** a right or advantage belonging to a particular person or group because of their importance or social position.

**schism:** a split, a rift, a division, a wide gulf between two ideologies.

**stockpile:** a large supply of something that is kept to be used in the future if necessary.

**subjugate:** to gain control over somebody or something.

**sub judice:** a legal case which is still being discussed in the court and it is therefore illegal for anyone to talk about it in the newspapers, etc.

**tertiary:** third in order, rank or importance, after primary and secondary, e.g. *tertiary sector.*

**ubiquitous:** seeming to be everywhere or in several places at the same time; very common.

**visionary:** original and showing the ability to think about or plan the future with great imagination and intelligence.

## Review Test 3

*Find words that correctly match the given statements:*

1. a vociferous demand          c_____
2. short-lived                  e_____
3. extremely painful            e_____
4. extremely small              m_____

5. a stupid idea                             h_____

6. a longing for return to homeland          n_____

7. highly charged argument                   p_____

8. a split or rift                           s_____

9. to criticize                              c_____

10. easy to control                          a_____

**Answers:**

| | |
|---|---|
| 1. clamour | 2. ephemeral |
| 3. excruciating | 4. minuscule |
| 5. hogwash | 6. nostalgia |
| 7. polemic | 8. schism |
| 9. castigate | 10. amenable |

**Review Test 4**

Match the words with their opposites:

| | |
|---|---|
| 1. accolade | (a) central |
| 2. amenable | (b) receding |
| 3. exacerbate | (c) salvage |
| 4. peripheral | (d) lucid |
| 5. burgeoning | (e) expert |
| 6. arcane | (f) unyielding |
| 7. novice | (g) naive |
| 8. misappropriate | (h) reprimand |
| 9. paragon | (i) ameliorate |
| 10. subjugate | (j) yield |

**Answers:**

**1.** (*h*)  **2.** (*f*)  **3.** (*i*)  **4.** (*a*)  **5.** (*b*)
**6.** (*d*)  **7.** (*e*)  **8.** (*c*)  **9.** (*g*)  **10.** (*j*)

# 27

## WORDS ABOUT PEOPLE AND THINGS AROUND US—II

So many things are happening around us all the time that it becomes difficult at times to keep track even of important occurrences. Mass media is so active that its various manifestations—books, newspapers, TV, radio and internet, etc. keep on putting all sorts of information into our head. It has its advantages but a word of caution is necessary. We must not keep on accepting whatever is dished out to us. It is extremely necessary to be selective in gathering information and confine our collation to what falls within the sphere of our pursuits, never bothering about what is happening beyond the periphery.

Words are so important that some of them become the storehouse of particular type of information. Just learn the word and it will contain relevant information connected with it and store it in your brain. It is also useful to keep some sentences containing key words in the memory to keep pertinent information ready whenever required to be used. Have a look at the following passage:

Something that increases *escalates;* one who does not eat properly *emaciates.* Things don't spread like wild fire, they *burgeon* and *proliferate.* Facts don't *alter* even if they are accepted; not all the people show respect for law, some *flout* it. Small children ask too many questions because they are *inquisitive* and *curious* to know about lots of things. When you *eschew* an idea you avoid it, you are *reticent,* you are reserved and people may call you an *introvert.* Some tasks are *cumbersome*— long, complicated and difficult to carry; your *discomfiture* if you have to complete such tasks is *obvious.*

The above passage gives you the meanings of certain words through association with some characteristic or activity. This technique helps you retain the meaning of key words for long time in the memory.

The present chapter contains 70 key words about things, people's characteristics and emotions. Learn them, use them in your conversation and write-ups, find their synonyms and antonyms and march towards building up an impressive vocabulary.

**unwonted:** not usual or expected: *He spoke with unwonted enthusiasm.*

**translucence:** the act of allowing light pass through but not being transparent.

**innocuous:** not intended to offend or upset anyone— harmless.

**inquisitive:** asking too many questions and trying to find what other people are doing—curious, inquiring.

**flout:** to show that you have no respect for a law, etc. by openly not obeying it—defy.

**impunity:** (disapproving) mischievousness. If someone does something bad with impunity, they often get punished for it.

**vivacious:** (especially of a woman) having a lively, attractive personality.

**vitrolic:** full of anger and hatred — bitter.

**vindicate:** to prove that something is true or that you were right to do something, especially when other people had a different opinion—justify.

**vituperative:** making cruel and angry criticism—abusive.

**eschew:** to deliberately avoid or keep away from some idea, situation, action, etc.

**adulation:** admiration and praise especially when this is greater than is necessary.

**doughty:** brave and strong, capable of coming through a tough situation.

**dour:** (person) giving the impression of being unfriendly and severe. (situation) not pleasant, tough.

**duress:** threats or force that are used to make someone do something.

**imprecation:** a curse, an offensive word that is used to express extreme anger.

**ingratiating:** trying too hard to please somebody; ingratiating smile or action.

**rancour:** feeling of hatred and a desire to hurt other people, especially because you think that somebody has done something unfair to you.

**sinecure:** a job that you are paid for even though it involves little or no work.

**esoteric:** likely to be understood or enjoyed by only a few people with a special knowledge or interest.

**gargantuan:** extremely large, enormous; *a gargantuan appetite.*

**cumbersome:** large and heavy, difficult to carry — bulky; long, complicated and tedious.

**truncated:** made short, especially by cutting off the top end.

**discomfiture:** confusion, embarrassment and distress — uncomfortable feeling.

**tentative:** (an arrangement) not definite or certain because you may want to change it later.

**choleric:** easily made angry, bad-tempered.

**aberration:** an action, fact or way that is not usual, more of an exception than a rule.

**cogent:** strongly and clearly expressed in a way that influences what people believe — convincing.

**evince:** to show clearly that you have a feeling or quality — *evince a desire.*

**ostentatious:** showy in a way that is intended to impress people, done in an obvious way so that people may notice it.

**rumination:** the act of thinking deeply about something — ruminative — tending to do so; verb. — ruminate.

**emaciated:** thin and weak, usually because of illness or lack of food.

**venomous:** producing venom — full of bitter feeling or hatred.

**influx:** the fact of a lot of people, money or things arriving somewhere! *a sudden influx of visitors.*

**collate:** to collect information together from different sources in order to examine and compare it; *to collate data.*

**dilate:** to become or make something larger, wider or more open. Opposite: *contract.*

**derogatory:** showing a critical attitude towards somebody: *derogatory remarks.*

**surrogate:** something used to describe a person or thing that takes the place of or is used instead of something else: *a surrogate advertisement.*

**bellicose:** having or showing a desire to argue or fight — *aggressive, warlike.*

**propensity:** a tendency to a particular kind of behaviour — *inclination.*

**impervious:** not affected or influenced by something: *impervious to criticism.*

**veracity:** the quality of being true; the habit of telling the truth — *truthfulness, truth.*

**honorary:** (of a university degree, rank, etc.) given as an honour, without the person having equal qualification — *honorary doctorate/degree.* Not paid: *honorary president.*

**hawkish:** preferring to use military action rather than peaceful discussion to solve a problem. Opposite: *dovish* — from dove — the symbol of peace.

**havoc:** a situation in which there is a lot of damage, destruction or confusion: *play havoc with; wreak havoc on* something.

**heroics:** talk or behaviour that is too brave or dramatic for a particular situation. Actions that are brave and determined.

**herald:** to mark or signal that something is going to happen: *The talks heralded a new era of peace.* As a noun the word is used to be a sign/signal that shows so.

**hiatus:** a pause in activity when nothing happens; a space especially in a piece of writing or a speech where something is missing.

**leapfrog:** to get to a higher position or rank by going past somebody else or by missing out some stages — jump to a higher position.

**flail:** to move around without control. Also to hit somebody or something very hard especially with a stick.

**melee:** a situation in which a crowd of people are rushing or pushing each other in a confused way.

**flab:** soft, loose flesh on a person's body. The word is used to denote redundant/extra staff which a company likes to shed.

**menacing:** seeming likely to cause you harm or danger — threatening.

**nondescript:** having no interesting features or qualities — dull, insipid.

**ostracize:** to refuse to let somebody be a member of a social group — shun.

**refulgent:** very bright on shining.

**reticent:** unwilling to tell people about things — reserved, uncommunicative.

**sinister:** seeming evil or dangerous, making you think that something will happen.

**stagnant:** still, not moving; not developing, growing or changing.

**munificent:** extremely generous; kind, liberal: *a munificent patron.*

**copious:** in large amounts — abundant.

**fuselage:** the main part of the aircraft in which the passengers and goods are carried.

**furore:** great anger or excitement shown by a number of people usually caused by public event.

**affable:** friendly and easy to talk to, genial.

**hazy:** not clear because of haze, fog; not clear because of lack of memory, detail or understanding.

**improvise:** to use some new method or technique than usual; make or do something using whatever is available because you do not have what you really need.

**imposture:** an act of tricking people deliberately by pretending to be somebody else.

**inimical:** harmful to something, not helping something.

**ironic:** showing that you really mean the opposite of what you are saying. Also strange or amusing because it is very different from what you expect.

## Review Test 1

*Find words that correctly match the given statement or words:*

1. not upsetting or offending anyone      i_____

2. to defy a law, etc.                    f_____
3. lively, attractive                      v_____
4. threat to make someone do something          d_____
5. a desire to hurt others             r_____
6. extremely large                      g_____
7. not certain or definite             t_____
8. easily made angry                  c_____
9. the act of thinking deeply about something          r_____
10. full of bitter feelings             v_____

**Answers:**

1. innocuous            2. flout
3. vivacious             4. duress
5. rancour                6. gargantuan
7. tentative              8. choleric
9. rumination          10. venomous

**Review Test 2**

*Match the following words/statements with their meanings/synonyms :*

1. asking too many question      (*a*) cumbersome
2. full of anger & hatred         (*b*) cogent
3. not usual or expected         (*c*) herald
4. an offensive word expressing anger      (*d*) inquisitive
5. difficult to carry             (*e*) nondescript
6. thin and weak                (*f*) vitriolic
7. strongly & clearly expressed    (*g*) emaciated

8. something used for something else     (h) imprecation

9. to mark or signal something     (i) surrogate

10. dull, insipid     (j) unwonted

**Answers :**

   **1.** (d)   **2.** (f)   **3.** (j)   **4.** (h)   **5.** (a)

   **6.** (g)   **7.** (b)   **8.** (i)   **9.** (c)   **10.** (e)

## Review Test 3

*Can you remember the words from the lesson that are opposite to the following? Write them.*

  1. adulatory        v_____

  2. contract        d_____

  3. culminated        h_____

  4. vivacious        n_____

  5. extrovert        r_____

  6. leapfrog        s_____

  7. meagre        c_____

  8. inimical        a_____

  9. insipid, dull        r_____

10. follow        f_____

11. look forward to        e_____

12. blessing        i_____

13. definite/certain        t_____

14. tricky        v_____

15. frugal        m_____

16. empathy        r_____

17. inimical                          a_____
18. hurtful                           i_____
19. confront                          e_____
20. usual                             a_____

## Answers :

| | | | |
|---|---|---|---|
| 1. vituperative | | 2. dilate | |
| 3. heralded | | 4. nondescript | |
| 5. reticent | | 6. stagnate | |
| 7. copious | | 8. affable | |
| 9. refulgent | | 10. flout | |
| 11. eschew | | 12. imprecation | |
| 13. tentative | | 14. veracious | |
| 15. munificient | | 16. rancour | |
| 17. affable | | 18. innocuous | |
| 19. eschew | | 20. aberration | |

# PEJORATIVE USE OR SENSE OF WORDS

Pejorative means derogatory. A word or remark that is pejorative expresses disapproval or criticism. There are a large number of words in English language that can convey criticism, retribution or negative sense. You have already learnt in the previous chapters that the words like *chide, punish, repudiate, rebuke, reprimand, vitriolic, vituperative, imprecation, bellicose, inimical,* etc. convey criticism, anger and opposition. Besides, you have also learnt that some prefixes and suffixes give direction to the meaning of the words, which at times, is negative. It is necessary to read those chapters again and again to recapture those important elements that slip away from the mind after a period of time, and be on the right track to build a powerful vocabulary and proper word usage.

Here, in this chapter, we are taking up those words which originally did not convey a negative sense, or at least did not carry only the negative meaning. In a nut shell they were, originally, not pejoratives, but over time they have acquired a negative meaning as more and more people started using them pejoratively. For example, the word *egregious* which once meant prominent or distinguished, has now come to carry the meaning extremely bad as in *an egregious blunder.* From a favourable connotation, it has acquired a belittling, derogatory meaning. There are several other words which have undergone such transformation. For example, the word *obsequious* which once meant dutiful or obedient, now carries the meaning servile or subservient. The word *puerile* from the Latin word boy has changed its meaning from boyish to childish or immature.

There are also some words which have retained their favourable meaning, but have also come to be used pejoratively. For example, the word *academic* means connected with education, especially studying in schools and colleges. But it has also come to mean theoretical — a discussion is termed as academic when it does not serve a useful purpose; *of only academic interest* means of little practical value. Many such words are given below alongwith their old and new connotations. Read them carefully so that you are able to figure out the sense in which they are used when you come across them in newspapers, articles, books and other write-ups.

**onerous:** it means a difficult task, requiring great effort and responsibility. It is also used in the pejorative sense — to be taxing, tortuous.

**curt:** concise, laconic, pithy, succinct, terse. It may also mean discourteously short reply, answer, etc.

**didactic:** teaching a moral or lesson. Pejoratively it may mean overburdened with moral emphasis, therefore dull and uninteresting.

**esoteric:** means of interest to particular class or persons. It also denotes too scholarly to be comprehended or enjoyed by laymen.

**doctrinaire:** it means stubborn, maintaining an intransigent attitude towards his views.

**brainwash:** it has come to mean influence someone greatly and make them change even their right opinions to take advantage of this fact.

**docile:** it means easily taught, submissive, obedient and amenable. It also means slow and sluggish.

**epithet:** it is still used as a descriptive term such as 'blood, red wine' and 'the moon was a broken mirror', etc. The word is often used as an abusive characterisation. It is often said that when we wish to be abusive we hurl an epithet.

**erudite:** is used both favourably and unfavourably. A learned scholar can be called an erudite scholar. It may also be used in a derogatory sense to mean bookish, knowing more and more about less and less.

**ancillary:** an addition to something but not as important.

**auxiliary:** similarly, this word means giving help or support to the main group, in itself being secondary, not primary.

**provincial:** pertaining to a region; the word is an adjective to province. Pejoratively, it means limited, sectional, unsophisticated.

**factitious:** made by human skill or art — it conveys the sense of being artificial or made up.

**fulsome:** sometimes it carries the meaning abundant, but more often it is used to convey the meaning — excessive.

**gratuitous:** once it meant — given freely; now it is more frequently used to mean — meddlesome, intrusive, even uncalled for.

**fortuitous:** something given by luck rather than as a result of hard labour or required effort — accidental.

**impute:** to put thoughts into someone's mind; to attribute views or motives to someone else.

**indocrinate:** to brainwash somebody.

**ineffable:** in a religious context it always means unspeakable or inexpressible. But in a general sense it means that there were no vile words to express the intended derogatory feeling about something or somebody.

**notorious:** to be famous for wrong reasons — someone who is unfavourably known.

**innuendo:** a hint, suggestion or nuance; now it has come to mean a sly insinuation, something put across with malicious afterthought.

**invidious:** it means jealous, hateful or obnoxious.

**foreboding:** once the word meant to know beforehand; now it is exclusively used to convey a strong feeling that something unpleasant or dangerous is going to happen.

**jobbing:** doing pieces of work for different people rather than a regular job.

**lurk:** to be present but not in an obvious way (of some danger); to wait somewhere secretively because you are going to do something bad.

**stalk:** (of fear, danger) to be there when people want it to clear away.

**obsequious:** this word once meant dutiful, obedient and dutiful, is now used to mean servile, subservient or sycophantic.

**ominous:** the word derived from omen was used for good or bad sign, but is now used in the negative sense of foreboding some bad happening — literally, to draw back from an ill omen.

**ostensible:** means the given reason for doing something as against the actual or real intention.

**pedantic:** comes from pedant — a teacher and is always used to mean formalistic or pompously learned.

**poetaster:** a writer of inferior verses. In literature it means not as good a poet as the established ones like Wordsworth, Keats, etc. The suffix *aster* is always pejorative — meaning fake or of inferior quality.

**sanctimonious:** is from sanctus, which means holy is now used to convey the meaning of being hypocritically so.

**sententious:** originally meant full of sayings and maxims so that it is pithy and terse giving too much in a few words. Now it carries a negative sense of being verbose, wordy, etc.

**sophistry:** now carries the meaning of arguing deceitfully, attempting to present a poor case as a good one by clever and specious reasoning.

**specious:** once meant pleasing in appearance, but now it means deceptive.

**stricture:** it once meant an incidental remark or comment; now it means severe criticism especially of somebody's behaviour. It is now synonymous with *restriction* — a rule or situation that restricts your behaviour.

**academic:** related to education and learning. Sometimes it conveys the meaning of being remote from reality; it has come to mean theoretical. We often read the term ... *of only academic interest.*

**parochial:** the word means narrow, limited or restricted as in: *parochial consideration* — not of country at large but of a particular area.

**precious:** means valuable as in *precious stones, gems.* For writers it is sometimes used to mean overrefined, even hypocritical.

**qualified:** the word looks in two directions. It means competent as in *a qualified doctor.* It also means with some reservation as in *a qualified success* (not complete); *an unqualified* success means that with no ifs and buts.

**anomalous:** having some anomaly or irregularity; not conforming to the normal, irregular or freakish.

**apocalyptic:** it means describing a very serious damage and destruction in past or future events.

**atavistic:** it means reverting to primitive forms of behaviour.

**avatar:** a Hindi word which means reincarnation or embodiment of god, now means the embodiment of some concept or idea.

**capricious:** unpredictable, erratic or given to whim. This word is often confused with captious which means eager to find others' mistakes.

**feckless:** it means ineffective, helpless or incompetent.

**gristy:** causing fear and shudder.

Some words deceive; they don't carry the meaning what their appearance or pronunciation would have an unwary reader believe they do. Sometimes the base word or the root can be misjudged leading to the wrong conclusion about the meaning of a word. For example, the word *contentious* is not from *content* but *contend* meaning to struggle, therefore it means argumentative or pugnacious (syn. bellicose). Similarly, the word *empirical* has nothing to do with empire. It simply means a practical method that relies on experience, observation and experimentation. The word *enervated* does not mean full of energy but out of it — hence weak, debilitated or enfeebled. There is a famous anecdote about a group of stage performers who took part in a competition. When the judges called their performance *meretricious*, one of them jumped in joy thinking it was an accolade. Obviously he was deceived by the word which he mistook to be synonymous with *meritorious* having the base *merit*. Actually *meretricious* means tawdry, flashy or cheaply gaudy. This can happen with anyone who does not work on his/her vocabulary.

Some tricky words are given below and their meanings are explained:

**dissemble:** it is not the opposite of assemble, but means to pretend or feign.

**fractious:** does not relate to fractions or parts; it means refractory, unruly or breaking the rules.

**lissome:** slender, supple. It also means lithe. *Syn. lithesome.*

**atone:** has nothing to do with either at or one; it means to make good, compensate.

**otiose:** it means idle, sterile or unengaged in anything. It means leisure, ease.

**penury:** is related to pennies or money, but the meaning is extreme poverty — with no money at all.

**putative:** is not related to *put* or *at*; it simply means reputed to be, thought to be.

**restive:** is not at rest or peace with oneself, but restless for a cause.

**cargo:** is not something that goes on a car, but a shipment or merchandise on a ship. *Shipment*, on the other hand is something that necessarily goes on a ship but is often sent to the port, or airport by a car or truck. You may find it strange or funny, but that is how the meaning of these two words goes.

**bemused:** is not 'be amused', it means befuddled, a hypnotized or bewildered.

**contentious:** is not related to content but contend – to struggle or fight against, therefore it means pugnacious, argumentative or bellicose.

**descant:** it should not be confused with descent or decent. It means to discuss a subject at length.

**empirical:** is not related to any empire. I simply describes a practical method that relies on experience and experimentation.

**enervated:** does not mean energetic. On the other hand it means weakened, enfeebled or debilitated.

**enjoin:** does not mean join or support; it means to restrain or forbid—an injunction is a restraining order.

**inchoate:** the word should not be confused with chaotic or measurement by inches. It means incomplete, incipient or amorphous. An incomplete cheque is called an inchoate instrument.

**imaginative** means innovative and inventive not lost in imagination.

**indict:** to bring formal charges against someone. It does not mean condemn or convict.

**meretricious:** does not mean meritorious. It means cheaply gaudy.

**momentous:** does not mean momentary. It means a time or event of great importance.

**noisome:** does not have anything to do with noise. It is a short form of annoy + some. It is used to mean an offensive odour.

**officious:** is not official but meddlesome.

**opprobrium:** means infamy or disgrace.

**prosody:** there is nothing prosaic about this word. On the contrary it means the study of versification, accents, meters and rhythms.

**prosaic:** the word meant to convey related to prose rather than poetry; but nowadays it is used to carry the meaning dull and uninspiring.

## Review Test 1

*Find the word that correctly matches the given word or statement:*

1. concise, pithy               c_____
2. slow, sluggish            d_____
3. an addition to something     a_____
4. excessive, abundant        f_____
5. scholarly                  e_____
6. to brainwash somebody      i_____
7. known for wrong reasons     n_____
8. foreboding some bad happening   o_____
9. formalistic, pompously learned   p_____
10. arguing deceiptfully          s_____

**Answers:**

| | | | |
|---|---|---|---|
| 1. | curt | 2. | docile |
| 3. | ancillary | 4. | fulsome |
| 5. | erudite | 6. | indoctrinate |
| 7. | notorious | 8. | ominous |
| 9. | pedantic | 10. | sophistry |

## Review Test 2

*Match the following words/expressions with their synonyms/meanings:*

1. onerous            (a) servile, subservient
2. docile             (b) apparent, not real
3. fortuitous         (c) difficult, requiring big effort
4. innuendo           (d) deceptive
5. lurk               (e) irregular
6. obsequious         (f) obedient, amenable
7. ostensible         (g) extreme poverty
8. specious           (h) befuddled
9. stricture          (i) accidental
10. parochial         (j) incomplete
11. anomalous         (k) restriction
12. capricious        (l) insinuation, hint
13. penury            (m) erratic, whimsical
14. bemused           (n) narrow
15. inchoate          (o) wait secretly

**Answers:**

| | | | | |
|---|---|---|---|---|
| **1.** (c) | **2.** (f) | **3.** (i) | **4.** (l) | **5.** (o) |
| **6.** (a) | **7.** (b) | **8.** (d) | **9.** (k) | **10.** (n) |
| **11.** (e) | **12.** (m) | **13.** (g) | **14.** (h) | **15.** (j) |

# 29

# CHECKING YOUR PROGRESS
## COMPREHENSIVE TEST—5

### (Chapters 25–28)

You must have read these chapters carefully and assimilated many of the ideas presented about the vocabulary relating to people and things around us. You must have learnt several new words, their meanings and usage. Some of these words may have already been used by you in your talks and write-ups or otherwise in your professional activities or academic preparations. You must also have learnt the pejorative use of some words.

It is necessary to know how much you have retained in your memory. To make a fair assessment of the progress you have made, you must take the following tests sincerely. The answers are given at the end. Check them all to know your score and then follow the assessment.

## TEST 1

*Find words that correctly match the given statements. The first letter of the word has been given to give you a start:*

1.  of interest to particular class        e_____
2.  growing rapidly                        b_____
3.  a hidden treasure of arms, etc.        c_____
4.  mysterious charm, attributes           m_____
5.  a heroic gesture                       p_____
6.  heightening, build-up                  e_____
7.  a lucky discovery                      s_____
8.  a perfect example of something         p_____
9.  unexpected, useful result of an
    activity                               s_____
10. a setting                              a_____
11. full of anger, hatred                  v_____
12. brave and strong                       d_____
13. trying hard to please someone          i_____
14. desire to hurt others                  r_____
15. made short                             t_____
16. easily made angry                      c_____
17. think deeply                           r_____
18. show desire, feeling                   e_____
19. brave, dramatic action                 h_____
20. a pause in activity                    h_____

# TEST 2

*Match the synonyms in the two columns :*

1. accolade                    (*a*) justify
2. demented                    (*b*) exception

| | |
|---|---|
| 3. proliferate | (*c*) derogatory |
| 4. arcane | (*d*) ovation |
| 5. ploy | (*e*) signal |
| 6. flout | (*f*) threatening |
| 7. vindicate | (*g*) dull |
| 8. gargantuan | (*h*) crazy |
| 9. aberration | (*i*) friendly |
| 10. collate | (*j*) curt |
| 11. bellicose | (k) tactic |
| 12. pejorative | (*l*) excessive |
| 13. veracity | (*m*) spread |
| 14. herald | (*n*) collect |
| 15. menacing | (*o*) accidental |
| 16. non-descript | (*p*) recondite |
| 17. affable | (*q*) defy |
| 18. laconic | (*r*) truthfulness |
| 19. fulsome | (*s*) pugnacious |
| 20. fortuitous | (*t*) enormous |

## TEST 3

*Match the following words with their antonyms in the following columns:*

| | |
|---|---|
| 1. accolade | (*a*) dilated |
| 2. arcane | (*b*) impervious |
| 3. unwonted | (*c*) real |
| 4. doughty | (*d*) reprimand |

| | | | |
|---|---|---|---|
| 5. | truncated | (e) | communicative |
| 6. | tentative | (f) | refulgent |
| 7. | choleric | (g) | effective |
| 8. | influx | (h) | lucid |
| 9. | surrogate | (i) | detailed |
| 10. | reticent | (j) | complete |
| 11. | hazy | (k) | offending |
| 12. | succint | (l) | expected |
| 13. | feckless | (m) | exodus |
| 14. | inchoate | (n) | definite |
| 15. | innocuous | (o) | weakling |

## TEST 4

*Given below are 20 pairs of words. Say whether these words are synonyms (S), antonyms (A) or different (D) from each other:*

| | | | | | |
|---|---|---|---|---|---|
| 1. | meretricious | – meritorious | S | A | D |
| 2. | bevy | – collection | S | A | D |
| 3. | mystique | – charm | S | A | D |
| 4. | proliferate | – contain | S | A | D |
| 5. | ploy | – manoeuvre | S | A | D |
| 6. | exacerbate | – aggravate | S | A | D |
| 7. | naive | – novice | S | A | D |
| 8. | minuscule | – gargantuan | S | A | D |
| 9. | emaciated | – obese | S | A | D |
| 10. | embezzle | – misappropriate | S | A | D |

| | | | | | |
|---|---|---|---|---|---|
| 11. | ostentatious | – erudite | S | A | D |
| 12. | cogent | – convincing | S | A | D |
| 13. | veracity | – speciousness | S | A | D |
| 14. | hiatus | – pause | S | A | D |
| 15. | flail | – batter | S | A | D |
| 16. | enjoin | – include | S | A | D |
| 17. | sinister | – menacing | S | A | D |
| 18. | affable | – inimical | S | A | D |
| 19. | copious | – abundant | S | A | D |
| 20. | empirical | – provincial | S | A | D |

## ANSWERS

**Test 1:**

| | | |
|---|---|---|
| 1. esoteric | 2. burgeoning | 3. cache |
| 4. mystique | 5. panache | 6. escalation |
| 7. serendipity | 8. paradigm | 9. spinoff |
| 10. ambience | 11. vitriolic | 12. doughty |
| 13. ingratiating | 14. rancour | 15. truncated |
| 16. choleric | 17. ruminate | 18. evince |
| 19. heroics | 20. hiatus. | |

**Test 2:**

| | | | | |
|---|---|---|---|---|
| **1.** (*d*) | **2.** (*h*) | **3.** (*m*) | **4.** (*p*) | **5.** (*k*) |
| **6.** (*q*) | **7.** (*a*) | **8.** (*t*) | **9.** (*b*) | **10.** (*n*) |
| **11.** (*s*) | **12.** (*c*) | **13.** (*r*) | **14.** (*e*) | **15.** (*f*) |
| **16.** (*g*) | **17.** (*i*) | **18.** (*j*) | **19.** (*l*) | **20.** (*o*) |

**Test 3:**

| | | | | |
|---|---|---|---|---|
| **1.** (*d*) | **2.** (*h*) | **3.** (*l*) | **4.** (*o*) | **5.** (*a*) |
| **6.** (*n*) | **7.** (*b*) | **8.** (*m*) | **9.** (*c*) | **10.** (*e*) |
| **11.** (*f*) | **12.** (*i*) | **13.** (*g*) | **14.** (*j*) | **15.** (*k*) |

**Test 4:**

| | | | | |
|---|---|---|---|---|
| **1.** (D) | **2.** (S) | **3.** (S) | **4.** (A) | **5.** (S) |
| **6.** (S) | **7.** (S) | **8.** (A) | **9.** (A) | **10.** (S) |
| **11.** (D) | **12.** (S) | **13.** (A) | **14.** (S) | **15.** (S) |
| **16.** (D) | **17.** (S) | **18.** (A) | **19.** (S) | **20.** (D) |

## ASSESSMENT

### Test 1, 2, & 4

| | |
|---|---|
| *Less than 10* | *not upto the mark* |
| *10–13* | *average* |
| *14–16* | *above average* |
| *17–18* | *excellent* |
| *19–20* | *superior* |

### Test 3

| | |
|---|---|
| *Less than 8* | *not upto the mark* |
| *8–9* | *average* |
| *10–11* | *above average* |
| *12–13* | *excellent* |
| *14–15* | *superior* |

# 30

## IDIOMATIC USE OF WORDS AND VERBAL PHRASES

Words are used in a number of ways in English language. Actually, words are categorised into different parts of speech such as verbs, nouns, adjectives, adverbs, pronouns and modals, etc. according to the functions they perform in sentences.

However, a number of words are used in relation to or in combination with some other words like prepositions to form phrases to convey a specific meaning. Such meaning is generally, totally different from that conveyed by the words in their normal use. For example, the word *give* in its general use means to hand over something to somebody but in its phrasal use, its meaning gets changed as follows:

The chief guest *gave away* the prizes (distributed). My brother has *given up* smoking (abandoned). Following a fierce attack by the Indian army, the enemy had to *give in* (yield). During a dance programme the stage *gave way* due to excess weight/load (broke, yielded).

Similarly many other words acquire a different meaning when they are used as phrases. The word *take* means to acquire, but the phrase *take after* means resemble, *take up* means to occupy or commence while *taken aback* means greatly surprised. Such use of words is known as idiomatic use.

It is absolutely necessary to learn the idiomatic use of important words and know the meaning of various phrases because they are frequently used at all levels in English write-ups. Apart from the comprehension point of view, learning various idioms that are commonly used also helps us to use them while we write something — an article, essay, research paper, a report or even a letter. They not only provide a variety to our write-ups but also embellish our expression and conversation, and create a favourable impression.

Given below are some important idioms made with some key verbs alongwith their meanings. Read and memorise them and use them in your sentences:

*act on:* produce effect.

*act up:* comply, fulfil.

*act upon:* follow, abide.

*abound in/with:* to be full of something.

*accede to:* sanction, agree.

*account for:* explain, be the reason of.

*accustomed to:* get/be used to.

*agree to*: concur with a proposal.

*agree with:* concur with a person.

*alarmed at:* be perturbed with something.

*admit into:* get admission in a school/college, etc.

*admit of*: accept having done something wrong.

*attend to:* pay attention, do some work.

*attend upon:* be on the service of somebody.

*attribute to:* be the reason of.

*back out:* withdraw from an arrangement or contract.

*back up:* to support or sustain.

*bear with:* endure, tolerate.

*bear out:* support, confirm.

*bear down:* crush by force.

*bear through:* manage.

*blow over:* to pass without causing damage.

*blow up:* explode.

*blow out:* extinguish.

*break down:* (of a machine) to stop working; (health) to become bad; (of people) to lose control of feelings; (of things) to divide into parts.

*break for:* to suddenly run towards something.

*break in/into:* to enter a building by force.

*break off:* to become separated from something as a result of force.

*break out:* (of war, fighting or other unpleasant events) to start suddenly.

*break through:* to make new and important discoveries. Distinguish it from *breakthrough* (noun).

*break up:* to separate into smaller pieces.

*break away:* a political group separated from a larger group.

*break even:* a point where a company stops making losses and starts earning profit.

*bring about:* cause, to make something happen.

*bring forth:* produce.

*bring round:* to restore to a healthy state.

*bring up:* rear (children).

*bring out:* to expose, show.

*bring in:* introduce.

*bring back:* recall, remember.

*bring forward:* present, produce to view.

*call at:* visit.

*call upon:* ask someone to do something important.

*call in:* send for, ask for a visit (a doctor, etc.)

*call off:* put an end to an ongoing activity (strike, etc.)

*call out:* speak aloud.

*carry on:* continue.

*carry out:* follow, execute, accomplish.

*carry away:* be influenced, be taken away (be carried away)

*carry through:* to sustain a work till the end.

*cast away:* throw away.

*cast aside:* reject, not to consider.

*cast up:* count arithmetically.

*cast down:* in low spirits, dejected.

*cast off:* abandon.

*come about:* happen, be caused.

*come by:* get, obtain.

*come off:* emerge, come out, (of a part in a machine) to get separated.

*come out:* become public; also tell something: *come out with the truth.*

*come round:* agree, recover.

*come across:* meet with (by chance).

*come up:* amount to, capture: *come up with an idea.*

*come down:* the prices to decrease.

*come down upon:* to be severe with someone, to scold or reprimand someone angrily.

*concerned with:* connected with.

*concerned about:* worried about something/happening.

*correspond with:* write letters; to match.

*correspond to:* agree, concur.

*count on/upon:* depend on, rely on.

*cry for:* to desire immensely.

*cry out:* to complain loudly.

*cry down:* to condemn or criticize.

*cut off:* disconnect, remove.

*cut out:* to stop or end.

*cut through:* to make a path or passage through something.

*cut in:* to interfere.

*cut across:* to affect different groups.

*cut away:* to remove something from something.

*cut up:* to injure; divide into small pieces.

*deal in:* trade, do business in something.

*deal with:* behave with a person.

*do away with:* to put an end to something undesirable or redundant.

*do for:* serve the purpose of.

*do up:* (be done up) exhausted after strenuous work, etc.

*do without:* dispense with.

*draw up:* arrange, compose, prepare.

*draw back:* retire, recede. This idiomatic use must be distinguished from the word *drawback* (noun) which means a defect or shortcoming.

*draw from:* to take help or inspiration from something: *The writer of this article/book has drawn from Amartya Sen.*

*draw near:* to approach, come near, be imminent (some event like an exam, a tournament).

*drop in:* to come in casually, pay an informal visit.

*drop out:* to retire, disappear from one's place. Also used as a noun — *dropouts from school/college.*

*drop away/off:* fall, decrease.

*at the drop of a hat:* quickly, in no time.

*fall away:* decline, decrease.

*fall in with:* agree with somebody.

*fall on:* attack (a thief, miscreant).

*fall out:* to quarrel. Also used as a noun — fallout — consequence (generally negative).

*fall back:* to withdraw or retreat.

*fall back upon:* have something as the last means of support.

*fall short of:* not to prove equal to the task, to be less than the required.

*fall through:* fail, come to nothing.

*fall for:* to be captivated by.

*fall in line:* to follow something as ordered.

*get at:* come near (a fact).

*get ahead:* advance, prosper.

*get along:* proceed.

*get up:* awake, stand.

*get off:* to deboard a bus or train; also to escape: *He got off with minor punishment.*

*get over:* to overcome or surmount.

*get away with:* to escape or be let off with small damage or no damage at all.

*get through:* pass an examination.

*get on:* to progress or proceed.

*get in:* to enter.

*get out:* to go out unceremoniously.

*give away:* distribute, transfer, give in charity.

*give in:* yield, submit.

*give out:* emit, announce.

*give up:* abandon (a bad habit, etc.)

*give way:* yield to pressure, succumb.

*give back:* restore.

*be given to:* have the habit of.

*go by:* act according to, judge from.

*go down:* (price) to become cheaper; lose: *He went down fighting.*

*go up:* rise in price.

*go into:* examine something deeply: *Going into details ....*

*go off:* to depart, (go off the air); to explode (a bomb).

*go through:* read, suffer. *He is going through a period of suffering.*

*go back on:* fail to keep a word, promise or plan.

*go out:* (for electricity) to be off.

*go about:* to do or execute a plan.

*go for:* seek, prefer.

*go with:* agree.

*hold on:* wait, continue.

*hold out:* resist, not yield to.

*hold over:* postpone; also to have a sway over somebody.

*hold up:* a delay or stoppage in a continuing activity.

*hold together:* to remain united.

*hold to:* stick to something.

*hold with:* to agree with somebody.

*hold back:* to keep back, not disclose.

*keep back:* withhold, reserve.

*keep off:* remain at a distance from something or somebody.

*keep from:* abstain.

*keep out:* check.

*keep up:* maintain, continue: *Keep up the good work.*

*keep in:* confine, restrain.

*keep away:* to be absent or aloof.

*knock out:* beat out, defeat.

*knock off:* to stop doing something.

*knock back:* prevent somebody from achieving something.

*knock down:* to persuade somebody to reduce the price of something.

*knock something down:* to destroy a building by breaking its walls.

*lay by:* put aside, save for future use.

*lay out:* draw a plan; also to knock somebody unconscious.

*lay about somebody:* to attack somebody violently.

*lay down:* put something down or stop using it.

*lay something in/up:* to collect and store something to use in the future.

*lay over at/in:* to stay somewhere for a short time during a long journey.

*an easy lay:* a person who is ready and willing to have sex.

*look after:* take care of.

*look on/upon:* to consider or regard.

*look up:* to find something, to use, progress.

*look up to:* regard with respect, to draw inspiration from.

*look forward to:* expect with pleasure.

*look down upon:* to hate, despise.

*look into:* examine, investigate.

*look for:* search, expect.

*took to:* hope to obtain something from somebody.

*look back:* recall, remember the past events.

*make up:* to form something; to put something together from several different things; to invent a story; to complete a number; to replace something that has been lost.

*make up for something:* to do something that corrects a bad situation: *make up for the lost time.*

*make do:* manage with something.

*make good:* to become rich and successful.

*make it:* to fulfil, be successful.

*make it with somebody:* to have sex with somebody.

*make the most of:* gain as much advantage or enjoyment as you can from something.

*make much of something/somebody:* treat somebody/ something as very important.

*to make or break something:* to be total success or failure.

*make off:* to hurry away.

*make off with something:* to steal something and hurry away with it.

*make out:* understand, comprehend something.

*make-believe:* fantasy, imagining or pretending things to be different and more exciting than they actually are.

*makeshift:* provisional, used temporarily for a particular purpose because the real thing is not available.

*part from:* separate from friends, relatives.

*part with:* give up things, possessions.

*pass away:* die.

*pass for:* pose as.

*pass off:* be gone some event: *The festival passed off peacefully.*

*pass through:* undergo : pass through difficult times.

*put on:* wear.

*put out:* extinguish (fire).

*put down:* suppress; also write.

*put off:* postpone.

*put up:* present, show, lodge.

*put up with:* live, endure, tolerate, accept something that is annoying, unpleasant without complaining.

*put forward:* suggest.

*pick out:* select for something.

*pick up:* gain in health, increase in speed from a still position in vehicles, e.g. *pick up speed.*

*run across:* to meet someone or find something by chance.

*run after:* pursue.

*run around:* (disapproving) to spend a lot of time with somebody: *She is always running around with older men.*

*run away:* to escape from somebody/a place.

*run over:* (of a vehicle) to knock a person or animal down and drive over their body.

*run down:* to lose power or stop working: *The battery has run down;* to gradually stop functioning or become smaller in size/number: *The US manufacturing industry has been running down for the last two years.*

*run somebody in:* to arrest somebody and take them to a police station.

*run into somebody:* to meet somebody by chance.

*run off:* to flow out of a container.

*run on:* to continue without stopping.

*run out:* (for supply of something) to stop.

*run through:* to pass quickly (through a crowd); to discuss, repeat or read something quickly.

*run up against something:* to experience a difficulty.

*run up:* increase, accumulate.

*run short of:* to feel the want of.

*set down:* record, enumerate.

*set off:* depart: *He set off for New York this morning;* decorate: *Manners set off merit.*

*set forth:* exhibit, state clearly.

*set up:* establish, start business.

*set on/upon:* attack, instigate.

*set in:* (of a season) to begin.

*set out:* start on journey.

*set about:* apply oneself to.

*set aside:* reject, desregard.

*set apart:* reserve.

*sit pretty:* to be in a good situation.

*sit tight:* to stay where you are rather than change position.

*sit around/about:* (disapproving) to spend time doing nothing very useful.

*sit back:* to be in a relaxed position.

*sit out:* not to participate while being a member of the team etc.; be on the sideline due to injury or some other reason.

*stick to:* continue doing something despite difficulties; not to change what you are doing or engaged in.

*stick your neck out:* to expose yourself to risk by doing something.

*stick to your guns:* refuse to change your mind about something.

*stick to one's word:* to fulfil one's promise.

*stand by:* support especially during need.

*stand for:* represent some values and ideals.

*stand out:* be prominent.

*stand up:* offer to help some cause.

*stand down:* to leave a job or position.

*stand over:* to be near and watch somebody as they do some work.

*stand up to:* bear, be equal to tough situations.

*strike at:* aim at.

*strike out:* to remove something by drawing a line through it, cross out.

*strike a balance:* to find a way of being fair to two opposing things.

*strike a bargain:* to get an advantage in a deal.

*strike gold:* to find or do something that brings you lot of success or money.

*strike it rich:* to get a lot of money.

*strike while the iron is hot:* to make use of the opportunity immediately.

*within a striking distance:* near enough to be reached or attacked easily.

*strike back:* to harm somebody in return for an attack or injury.

*strike off:* to remove somebody/something's name.

*take after:* resemble.

*take for:* to mistake one thing for another.

*take off:* remove clothes.

*take to:* resort to, start a habit.

*take up:* commence an evocation, consider, choose.

*taken aback:* surprised.

*take over:* take the charge of some position.

*throw away:* waste, lose by neglect or folly.

*throw about:* fling things here and there.

*throw up:* resign; also to be sick.

*turn out:* expel, prove. *Turnout* (noun) means the number of people who vote in a particular election.

*turn down:* reject, refuse to consider.

*turn up:* come, assemble.

*turn off:* close.

*turn away:* dismiss, change the course.

*turn into:* become something.

*turn aside:* to deviate.

*turn around:* change position — from negative to positive — in trade, business, etc. Also used as noun: *a turn around work at* — be engaged in doing something.

*work out:* solve; train the body.

*work up:* to excite.

*work off:* get rid of something; to earn money in order to be able to pay a debt.

*have your work cut out:* to be likely to have difficulty in doing something.

*get down to work/set to work:* to begin, make a start.

## Review Test 1

*Mention the idioms that match the given statement/ meaning:*

1. to be full of something              a_____
2. extinguish                            b_____
3. restore to a healthy state            b_____
4. abandon                               c_____
5. meet somebody by chance               c_____
6. to affect different groups            c_____
7. dispense with                         d_____
8. come to nothing                       f_____
9. yield to pressure                     g_____
10. to remain united                     h_____

## Answers:

1. abound in; 2. blow out; 3. bring round; 4. cast off; 5. come across; 6. cut across; 7. do without; 8. fall through; 9. give way; 10. hold together.

## Review Test 2

*Mention the meanings of following idioms:*

1. knock back _____
2. make do _____
3. look down upon _____
4. make out _____
5. put up with _____
6. run down _____
7. set aside _____
8. stick your neck out _____
9. stand out _____
10. strike it rich _____

### Answers :

1. prevent somebody from achieving something.
2. manage with something.
3. despise.
4. understand.
5. accept something annoying without complaining.
6. lose power or stop working.
7. disregard.
8. expose yourself to risk.
9. be prominent.
10. to get a lot of money.

## Review Test 3

*Match the idioms with their meanings in the given columns:*

1. take after        (*a*) restore to a healthy state
2. taken aback      (*b*) be the reason of

3. work out                    (*c*) depend on
4. account for                 (*d*) delay
5. blow over                   (*e*) resemble
6. bring round                 (*f*) train the body
7. come across                 (*g*) in no time
8. count on                    (*h*) surprised
9. at the drop of a hat        (*i*) pass without causing
                                    damage
10. hold up                    (*j*) meet by chance

**Answers :**

1. (e)      2. (h)      3. (f)      4. (b)      5. (i)
6. (a)      7. (j)      8. (c)      9. (g)      10. (d)

# 31

## WORDS COMMONLY MISSPELT AND SOME SPELLING RULES

Learning the correct spellings of words is as important as knowing words. Using a simple and less emphatic word with correct spellings is obviously better and more rewarding than a powerful but misspelt word. The full advantage of having a good vocabulary can only be obtained if we are particular about knowing the correct spellings of words.

It is said that good spellers are not born but made. Most of us have spelling problems. These can, however, be overcome by adopting a systematic approach and making earnest endeavours in this regard. Given below are some commonly misspelt words and some spelling rules.

### Words commonly misspelt

**A**

| | | |
|---|---|---|
| abandon | abbreviate | abhor |
| abhorrent | absence | absolutely |

absorb
abstentious
accede
accept
accessible
assessible
accuse
acknowledge
acquiesce
acquit
access
adjourn
adulterate
advisable
aeroplane
affiliate
affray
agreeable
alien
allowance
already
ambassador
ambiguous
analysis
angelic
anxiety
appearance
appropriate
argument
ascent

absorption
abundance
acceleration
acceptance
accidentally
accordance
accustomed
acquaint
acquire
across
adhere
administrator
advantageous
advertisement
aesthetic
affirmation
aggrieved
aid-de camp
alliance
allusion
altogether
ambiguity
amiable
ancestor
annually
apology
appreciate
approximate
artificial
athlete

abstain
academic
accent
access
accommodate
accumulate
achieve
acquiantance
acquisition
actually
adherent
admission
adventurous
aerial
affectionately
affluence
agony
alcohol
alliteration
Almighty
amateur
ambitious
ammunition
ancient
antique
apparatus
approach
architecture
ascetic
athletics

attendance
autobiography
available
awesome

audience
autumn
awful
awry

auspicious
average
awkward
axiomatic

## B

balloon
banquet
beggar
behaviour
beneficient
besiege
biscuit
bouquet
buoyant
butcher

banality
barbarous
beginning
benefactor
bequeath
bewitching
blasphemy
breakfast
bureaucracy

bankruptcy
barrier
beguile
beneficial
bereave
bilateral
bosom
bungalow
business

## C

calendar
capricious
caricature
cautious
ceremony
Christmas
children
clearance
commission
competition
condemn
conscious
conquer

candour
career
casualty
cemetery
challenge
chronicle
cigarette
coffee
committee
comparison
condescend
condolence
conscience

canonize
carriage
catalogue
centenary
character
characteristics
circumstances
colleague
comparable
comprehension
conference
confusion
conscientious

consecutive       contemporary      contemptible
correspondence    countenance       controversial
councillor        courteous         co-operation
creature          curiosity

## D

debauchery        debris            daunt
decease           deceit            deliberate
decent            decision          deference
deficiency        degree            defiance
deliberate        delicious         deliverance
delusion          dependence        decend
descent           description       development
diagnosis         desperate         dilettante
dialogue          diarrhoea         discern
difference        dilemma           diminution
discipline        disciplinarian    discuss
disguise          dispensary        drudgery
dysentery         distinguish

## E

earnest           eccentricity      eclipse
ecstasy           efficacious       efficient
echelon           elegance          elementary
eligible          emancipation      embarrassed
embroidery        endeavour         enfranchise
engineer          enthusiasm        envelope
entrance          equilibrium       enmity
ethereal          etiquette         European
exasperate        excellence        eerie

| | | |
|---|---|---|
| elliptical | exclamatory | exhilarate |
| existence | exchequer | exemplify |
| explosion | extinguish | extravangance |
| exorbitant | expedient | exuberant |

## F

| | | |
|---|---|---|
| failure | familiar | fascinate |
| fatigue | flamboyant | federal |
| fallible | favourite | feign |
| felicitous | February | ferocious |
| fervent | forbear | fierce |
| fiery | forfeit | flourish |
| forebode | forecast | forgo |
| foreign | foretell | forward |
| forfeit | foreword | formidable |
| fourteen | fortuitous | freight |
| fruition | frustration | fulfilled |
| flamboyant | fulness | furious |
| funeral | funereal | furlong |

## G

| | | |
|---|---|---|
| gallantry | gallery | gallop |
| gamut | gamble | garrulous |
| garrison | gaudy | gazette |
| generally | generous | generosity |
| genius | gaiety | genuine |
| gesture | garrulous | glorious |
| goddess | gauche | gorgeous |
| gossip | gnaw | governor |
| grammar | grandeur | gratuitous |

guarantee

guardian

gregarious

guidance

gourmet

gymnasium

## H

handkerchief

hideous

haphazard

harass

harbour

hasten

haunt

headache

hereditary

heroine

hierarchy

heterogenous

hinder

hindrance

horrendous

honorary

honour

honourable

horrible

hospitable

humour

humorous

hurricane

hilarious

hurrah

humbug

hygiene

hymn

hyporcisy

hypothesis

## I

ideal

idiosyncrasy

identical

illegible

illiterate

illuminate

immediately

immortal

imposter

incite

indefatigable

independent

indispensable

industrious

inferior

influence

influential

ingenuity

inimical

innings

inoculation

inquiry

instalment

inspector

installation

instead

instruction

intelligence

intentionally

interesting

interview

invasion

invisible

irreparable

irritable

irregular

irresistible

itinerant

inventory

## J

| | | |
|---|---|---|
| janitor | jealous | jeopardize |
| jewel | jewellery | journey |
| juvenile | judgement | jugglery |
| juggernaut | jurisdiction | justice |

## K

| | | |
|---|---|---|
| kitchen | kudos | knot |
| kaleidoscope | kennel | knuckle |

## L

| | | |
|---|---|---|
| laboratory | labour | laborious |
| labyrinth | landscape | language |
| luxuriant | laughter | lawyer |
| luscious | leather | leisure |
| league | leopard | liaison |
| liberate | library | licence |
| lieutenant | liquid | liquor |
| literature | litigious | livelihood |
| litterateur | lodging | lottery |
| lovable | luckily | luxury |
| luxurious | lubricant | lyre |

## M

| | | |
|---|---|---|
| machinery | mammoth | magistrate |
| magnificient | menagerie | maintenance |
| majority | malaria | malaria |
| malignant | manageable | mangoes |
| manoeuvre | manufacture | manifest |
| maelstrom | martyr | marvellous |

| material | Mathematics | maturity |
| --- | --- | --- |
| mausoleum | maximum | meagre |
| memento | medicine | mediocre |
| medium | memories | mercenary |
| merchant | merciful | merriment |
| message | messenger | Messrs |
| military | millionaire | minimum |
| minister | maroon | miracle |
| miraculous | miscellaneous | mischief |
| mischievous | miserable | missed |
| mockery | moderate | modern |
| moisture | momentary | monarch |
| monastery | medieval | monitor |
| monologue | mosquito | motto |
| moustache | municipal | muscle |
| musician | murderer | museum |
| mysterious | mutual | mystery |

## N

| narrative | naturally | naughty |
| --- | --- | --- |
| necessary | necessarily | necessity |
| negligence | negligible | negotiate |
| neighbour | neither | nephew |
| nervous | neuter | niece |
| niche | ninety | nobility |
| naive | ninth | notable |
| noticeable | notorious | notoriety |
| nourish | nonchalant | nowadays |
| nuisance | numerous | nymph |

## O

| | | |
|---|---|---|
| oasis | obedience | oblique |
| obliterate | obscene | obscure |
| observance | obvious | occasion |
| occasionally | occur | occupancy |
| occurrence | ocean | obsession |
| odious | odour | offence |
| offensive | officiate | offspring |
| Olympic | ominious | omitted |
| omission | opinion | opium |
| opponent | opportunity | opposition |
| oppress | orator | orchard |
| ordinary | original | ornament |
| orthodox | outcast | overwhelming |
| oyster | oxidant | |

## P

| | | |
|---|---|---|
| pageant | palace | palatial |
| pamphlet | parachute | parade |
| panacea | panorama | parallel |
| parcel | parliament | partial |
| particular | partner | passage |
| passionate | pastime | pasture |
| pathos | pathetic | patience |
| patient | patriot | patronage |
| pavilion | peaceful | peasant |
| peculiar | pedlar | penalty |
| pension | penetrate | penitent |
| perceive | percentage | perceptible |
| performance | permanent | piety |

| permissible | permission | perpetrate |
| --- | --- | --- |
| perpetual | perpetuate | perplexity |
| persuade | persevere | perseverance |
| persistent | personnel | persuasion |
| petition | philosophy | physician |
| pious | pierce | poignant |
| pilgrimage | pioneer | piteous |
| plague | platform | pleasant |
| pleasure | plough | pneumonia |
| poisonous | politician | portrait |
| possess | possession | possibility |
| potpourri | practice | practicable |
| precede | precious | precis |
| prefer | preferred | preference |
| preferable | prejudice | premium |
| preparation | prescription | pretension |
| prevention | priest | portrayal |
| principal | prior | principle |
| privilege | probability | proceed |
| procedure | procession | profession |
| professor | profited | programme |
| prohibit | prosperous | provision |
| psychology | puncture | pursue |
| pursuit | puerile | pursuance |

## Q

| quarrel | quaint | querulous |
| --- | --- | --- |
| question | quorum | quote |
| quinine | quixotic | quotient |

# R

| | | |
|---|---|---|
| reality | realm | recede |
| receive | receipt | reconciliation |
| recess | reckon | recognize |
| recommend | recruit | referee |
| reference | refractory | register |
| registration | regret | regrettable |
| regular | rehearsal | reign |
| rein | relation | reliable |
| relieve | relief | religion |
| religious | remedy | remembrance |
| repetition | reprieve | rescue |
| resign | resemble | resemblance |
| resistance | resource | responsible |
| responsibility | restaurant | retreat |
| reveal | revelation | reversible |
| review | reverence | rhythem |
| ridiculous | rigorous | righteous |
| riot | rivalry | rumour |
| recipe | redundancy | rugged |

# S

| | | |
|---|---|---|
| sacred | sacrifice | safety |
| sailor | satellite | satchel |
| satisfactory | sturdy | savage |
| saviour | scarcely | scatter |
| scenery | scent | scheme |
| scholar | science | scissors |
| secretary | security | seize |
| separate | sergeant | serious |

| | | |
|---|---|---|
| serviceable | several | severe |
| shepherd | shield | shining |
| shrewd | shyly | siege |
| sieve | signature | simultaneous |
| sincerely | situation | skeleton |
| skirmish | skilful | soldier |
| solemn | sovereign | specimen |
| spectacle | spiritual | splendour |
| squirrel | statue | straight |
| subdue | succeed | sufficiently |
| suggestion | suicide | suitable |
| superficial | superintendent | supersition |
| superstitious | superior | supervision |
| surely | surgeon | susceptible |
| suspicion | suspicious | sweetmeat |
| swimmer | sympathise | sympathetic |
| symptom | synonym | synopsis |
| system | systematic | systemic |

## T

| | | |
|---|---|---|
| tailor | tapestry | technical |
| technique | telephone | temperament |
| temporary | tenant | terrible |
| theatre | thief | thoroughly |
| threaten | tiresome | tobacco |
| together | tolerance | tongue |
| tourist | tournament | tragedy |
| tranquillity | transcend | transferred |
| traveller | treasurer | trespass |
| triumph | trivial | truly |

tuberculosis  throes  tuition
tolerance  twelfth  typical
tyranny  tulelage  tsunami

## U

umbrella  unanimous  underneath
unintelligible  unique  university
unkempt  upbraid  usually
usurer  utterance  upbraid

## V

vacation  vaccum  vague
valley  valuable  vapour
variable  variegated  variety
various  vegetarian  vehicle
venerable  venereal  vengeance
venomous  ventilator  verandah
veteran  viceroy  vicious
victorious  villain  violent
violate  violin  violent
voluptuous  vulgarity  visionary
vulnerable  vogue  voyage
voluntary  volunteer  vitreous

## W

warfare  warrant  weapon
weary  weather  wedding
weight  welcome  welfare
whistle  wholesome  wilderness
wield  wilful  willing

writing              woollen             wrestle
workaholic           worrisome           wraith

# Y

yacht               yearn               yeoman
yield               yonder

# Z

zealous             zoology             zipper

## SPELLING RULES

### Doubling of Final Consonants

1.  When /-ed /-ing, -able / are added to a word of syllable containing one vowel followed by a consonant, the final consonant is doubled.

    fan — fanning; war — warring; bat — batting; occur — occurring; rub — rubbed; pen — penned; run — running; get — getting.

    *Exceptions:* happen — happening; whisper — whispering.

2.  This rule applies to polysyllabic words where the accent falls on the last syllable.

    permit — permitted; forget — forgetting.

    *Exceptions*: rivet — riveted; fidget — fidgeted; benefit — benefited.

3.  This rule also applies to words ending in  *-l.*

    appal — appalling; fulfil — fulfilling; spiral — spiralling. travel — travelling; untrammel — untrammelled.

    *Exception:* parallel — paralleled.

4.  In the case of words ending in *ac* or *ic* the end consonant is not doubled; Instead  *-ck* precedes the suffix.

frolic — frolicking; picnic — picnicking; panic — panicky.

## Change of End — y into — i

1. Words ending in -y which are preceded by a consonant, change -y into -i generally in the plural, and when -ed or -ing is added.

   dissatisfy — disatisfied; beautify — beautified; lady — ladies; pony — ponies; folly — follies; story — stories.

   *Exception:* tidy — tidying.

2. When preceded by a vowel the end -y is retained.

   boy — boys; donkey — donkeys; money — moneys (monies in a legal context); storey — storeys; pray — prayed.

3. With the suffixes -ment and -ness, the end y preceded by a consonant is generally changed into i.

   merry — merriment; ready — readiness; busy — business.

   *Exception:* shyness; dryness; wryness.

## Dropping of Final Silent -e

1. When adding -able -ing -ish -ment, the final silent -e of a word is dropped unless it is preceded by -c or -g.

   acknowledge — acknowledgement; argue — argument; smoke — smokeable; hope — hoping; blue — bluish.

   *Exceptions:* peace — peaceable; courage — courageous; singe — singeing; tinge — tingeing.

   Also: blame — blameable; like — likeable; size — sizeable.

2. Silent end -e is generally retained when adding -ly, vague — vaguely; nice — nicely.

   *Exception:* due — duly.

## Use of Diphthongs *ie* and *ei*

In diphthongs which rhyme with pea, the 'i' precedes 'e' unless the diphthong follows the consonant -*e*.

believe; achieve; aggrieve; field; siege; relieve; alievate.

*Exception:* deceive; receive; seize; weird; either; neither; counterfeit; plebeian.

## Dropping of I In Compound Words

In the formation of compound words, one *l* is dropped as in the following examples:

full + fill — fulfil; skill + full — skilful; all + most — almost.

## The End *Ise* or *Ize*

The verbs noted below are spelt -*se*. The rest may be spelt -se or *ze*.

advertise; apprise; compromise; chastise; comprise; despise; devise; disguise; enterprise; excise; exercise; franchise; improvise; merchandise; paralyse; supervise; summarise; surmise; surprise.

*Exceptions:* deodorize; emphasize; ostracize; specialize; tantalize etc.

## Words Ending -*sion*

| | | |
|---|---|---|
| accession | adhesion | admission |
| agression | apprehension | aspersion |
| collision | collusion | commission |
| compassion | compression | concession |
| confession | confusion | decision |
| depression | dimension | emission |
| erosion | expansion | expulsion |
| illusion | intermission | invasion |

| | | |
|---|---|---|
| mission | obsession | occasion |
| omission | oppression | passion |
| permission | procession | profusion |
| remission | supervision | version |

## Words Ending *-tion*

| | | |
|---|---|---|
| absorption | accleration | accommodation |
| accumulation | acusation | addition |
| administration | affectation | alternation |
| avocation | benefaction | calculation |
| caption | caution | centralization |
| civilization | communication | conciliation |
| confirmation | constellation | contamination |
| decoration | eradication | degradation |
| dejection | designation | discrimination |
| emancipation | evaporation | exaggeration |
| exasperation | fascination | generalization |
| illumination | indemnification | infatuation |
| inflammation | institution | interpretation |
| irritation | orientation | perforation |
| persecution | pollution | precaution |
| predilection | prescription | provocation |
| ramification | reclamation | reincarnation |
| repetition | restitution | substitution |
| suggestion | superstition | transcription |
| unction | vaccination | violation |

## Words Ending *-able*

| | | |
|---|---|---|
| acceptable | admirable | adorable |
| agreeable | answerable | believable |
| comfortable | comparable | culpable |

| dependable | desirable | excusable |
| fashionable | habitable | imaginable |
| impracticable | improbable | inevitable |
| innumerable | irrevocable | manageable |
| practicable | profitable | reliable |
| tolerable | unbelievable | valuable |

## Hyphenated Words

| able-bodied | absent-minded | air-pump |
| air-route | anglo-Indian | anti-aircraft |
| arch-enemy | attorney-General | ball-bearing |
| bi-monthly | bi-weekly | boarding-house |
| book-keeping | bow-string | build-up |
| built-in | bull's-eye | by-election |
| bye-law | by-product | column-casting |
| commander-in-chief | | co-operative |
| co-opt | co-ordinate | cross-grained |
| daughter-in-law | deep-sea | delta-connected |
| dog-tired | double-barrelled | double-dealing |
| dry-clean | dull-witted | easy-going |
| eye-catching | face-mould | far-fetched |
| far-off | far-reaching | fault-finding |
| first-hand | fortune-hunter | foster-parent |
| free-handed | full-fledged | full-sized |
| golden-haired | go-between | go-getter |
| good-bye | good-natured | half-caste |
| half-time | happy-go-lucky | hard-earned |
| hard-drawn | head-dress | heavy-duty |
| heir-apparent | high-class | high-speed |
| house-surgeon | ill-fated | ill-natured |
| infra-red | jam-packed | knick-knacks |

knock-out

lay-off

make-believe

matching-head

much-talked-about

off-hand

passer-by

post-mortem

pre-natal

run-off

set-square

Solicitor-General

star-studded

two-wire (system)

vice-chancellor

well-informed

labour-saving

life-belt

many-sided

mind-blowing

non-availability

old-fashioned

peace-loving

power-point

right-handed

sea-sick

simple-minded

son-in-law

take-off

ultra-violet

vice-president

large-scale

lock-up

marked-out

minute-book

north-east

open-minded

plumb-level

pre-eminent

right-minded

self-sacrifice

single-phase

sparking-plug

two-pin (plug)

up-to-date

well-being

## Words Written as One Word

almost

anyhow

bottleneck

brickwork

cannot

castaway

cockpit

diehard

downstairs

everyday

floorboard

hairspring

hardwood

already

anything

brainwashing

bygone

cartwright

causeway

commenwealth

doorframe

earthenware

extraordinary

footwork

hangman

hazelnut

anybody

bloodthirsty

breakneck

bypass

casement

chairman

cupboard

downright

eyewash

fallout

godown

hardcore

however

| | | |
|---|---|---|
| landlord | landscape | landslide |
| lifelong | lifestyle | likewise |
| meanwhile | moreover | networking |
| nowadays | ourselves | outcome |
| outcry | outlive | outlook |
| outrage | outright | outcast |
| outside | outstanding | outstanding |
| outstretched | outworn | overbear |
| overflow | overlook | oversight |
| overthrow | passbook | password |
| piecemeal | pineapple | playwright |
| postgraduate | postscript | priceless |
| regardless | sawdust | scarecrow |
| schoolboy | screwdriver | searchlight |
| showgirl | skyscraper | sleepwalker |
| software | somebody | somehow |
| someone | sometimes | staircase |
| steamship | sunburnt | throughout |
| toothache | tubewell | turncoat |
| turnover | underfed | undersized |
| understatement | undertone | viewpoint |
| worldwide | | |

## Words Written as Two Words

| | | |
|---|---|---|
| ad hock | all right | all round |
| drunken driving | dust trap | edge cut |
| game plan | greeting card | heavy industry |
| ill will | junk mail | life force |
| life jacket | life insurance | pay packet |
| per cent | power cut | power plant |
| public opinion | slab wool | some time |
| step by step | world view | wall board |

Correct spellings are learnt through hardwork and memory. However, there are certain basic rules that govern them. Learning those rules and knowing about exceptions that go with them can prove quite beneficial for the students.

## Some Other Aspects of Spellings

Some other important aspects of spellings are discussed below:

**1.** In case of monosyllable words ending with a single consonant preceded by a single vowel, the consonant is doubled before adding a suffix like *ed, er, ing, or est.* Examples:

(*i*) beg-begged; peg-pegged; rob-robbed; pat-patted; rig-rigged; jam-jammed; pin-pinned; nab-nabbed.

(*ii*) run-runner; win-winner; cup-cupped.

(*iii*) pun-punning; sob-sobbing; hot-hotting.

(*iv*) big-biggest; fit-fittest; sad-saddest.

**2.** In case of words ending with two consonants or a single consonant preceded by two vowels, the last consonant is not doubled before adding a suffix. Examples are:

(*i*) wish-wished; risk-risked; lift-lifted; gift-gifted; walk-walked; calm-calmed.

(*ii*) cold-colder; mild-milder; hand-handed.

(*iii*) fear-feared, fearing; feed-feeder, feeding; maim-maimed, maiming; fail-failed, failing; head-headed; peer-peered; pain-pained, paining.

**3.** In case of words of two or three syllables ending with single consonant preceded by a single vowel the last consonant is doubled if the last syllable is stressed. Examples:

| (*i*) begin | : | beginner, beginning |
| control | : | controller, controlling |
| remit | : | remitted, remitting |
| incur | : | incurred, incurring |

When the last syllable in such words is not stressed, the last consonant is not doubled as:

| (*i*) suffer | : | suffered, suffering |
| (*ii*) benefit | : | benefited, benefiting |
| (*iii*) intend | : | intended, intending |

But there are certain exceptions to this rule also. In the following words the last syllable is not stressed but their last consonant is doubled before adding a suffix:

| (*i*) handicap | : | handicapped |
| kidnap | : | kidnapper, kidnapped, kidnapping. |
| worship | : | worshipper, worshipped, worshipping. |
| pedal | : | pedalled, pedalling. |
| model | : | modelled, modelling. |

It may be noted that the consonant *l* is doubled, when it comes at the end of a word whether it is stressed or not as shown in the example of pedal and model above. Some more examples are as follows:

| (i) travel | : | travelled, traveller, travelling |
| quarrel | : | quarrelled, quarrelling |
| signal | : | signalled, signalling |
| fulfil | : | fulfilled, fulfilling |
| dispel | : | dispelled, dispelling |
| instil | : | instilled, instilling |
| distil | : | distilled, distilling |

But, there is an exception in case of the word parallel.

| parallel | : | paralleled. |

**4.** In case of words ending in *ll*, the second *l* is dropped while adding the suffix *ful* as in :

| | | |
|---|---|---|
| skill | : | skilful |
| will | : | wilful |

**5.** In words ending with *e* which is silent like: *live, move, prove, dope, note,* etc. the *e* is removed before adding a suffix beginning with a vowel like *ed, ing, er.* For example:

| | | |
|---|---|---|
| live | : | lived, liver, living |
| move | : | moved, mover, moving |
| prove | : | proved, proving |
| dope | : | doped, doping |
| note | : | noted, noting |
| drive | : | driver, driving |
| hope | : | hoped, hoping |
| vacate | : | vacated, vacating |
| erode | : | eroded, eroding |

However, the *e* is not dropped while adding suffix starting with a consonant like *ful, ment* or *ness* as in:

| | | | |
|---|---|---|---|
| (*i*) | dole | : | doleful |
| | hope | : | hopeful |
| | spite | : | spiteful |
| | shame | : | shameful |
| (*ii*) | engage | : | engagement |
| | manage | : | management |
| | state | : | statement |
| (*iii*) | strange | : | strangeness |
| | rude | : | rudeness |
| | appropriate | : | appropriateness |

However, the following exceptions may be noted in this regard,

(*i*)  while adding the suffix *ly* to such words, the *e* is droped as in :

| | | |
|---|---|---|
| true | : | truly |
| due | : | duly |
| whole | : | wholly |
| (but sole | : | solely) |

(*ii*)  while adding the suffix the, *ment* or *ful* in the following words the *e* is dropped.

| | | |
|---|---|---|
| nine | : | ninth (but nine + ty = ninety) |
| awe | : | awful (but awesome) |
| argue | : | argument |
| judge | : | judgement (judgment is also considered correct). |

(*iii*)  The words ending with *ce* or *ge* retain their *e* while adding the suffix *able* or *ous* like in :

(a)

| | | |
|---|---|---|
| notice | : | noticeable |
| peace | : | peaceable |
| place | : | placeable |
| trace | : | traceable |
| service | : | serviceable |

(b)

| | | |
|---|---|---|
| courage | : | courageous |
| gorge | : | gorgeous |
| advantage | : | advantageous |
| outrage | : | outrageous |

Sometimes *e* is retained to avoid confusion with other similar words as:

| | | |
|---|---|---|
| singe | : | singeing (to avoid mixing up with singing) |
| spite | : | spiteful (to avoid mixing up with spitful) |

swinge  : swingeing (to avoid mixing up with swinging)
spine    : spineless (to avoid mixing up with spinless)

**6.** Words ending in *ee* do not drop their *e* while adding a suffix :

| | | |
|---|---|---|
| agree | : | agreed, agreeing, agreement |
| see | : | seeing |
| flee | : | fleeing |
| free | : | freeing, freedom, freeness |
| glee | : | gleeful |

**7.** Words ending in *ie* change their *ie* into *y* before adding a suffix as :

| | | |
|---|---|---|
| lie | : | lying (but lie + ed = lied) |
| die | : | dying (but die + ed = died) |
| tie | : | tying (but tie + ed = tied) |

**8.** Words ending with *y*, change their *y* into *i* before adding a suffix like ly, ful, end, ness, er, ment or age, as in :

| | | |
|---|---|---|
| happy | : | happier, happily, happiness |
| beauty | : | beautiful |
| merry | : | merrier, merriment |
| sloppy | : | sloppier, sloppily, sloppiness |
| lazy | : | lazier, laziness |
| carry | : | carrier, (but carrying) |
| marry | : | marriage, married (but marrying) |
| vary | : | varied (but varying) |

It may be noticed that with suffix *ing,* the last *y* does not change, as shown above. In the following cases too, the last *y* does not change:

| | | |
|---|---|---|
| pray | : | prayed, praying |
| play | : | played, playing |
| stay | : | stayed, staying |

| stray | : | strayed, straying |
| sway | : | swayed, swaying |
| key | : | keyed |
| hackney | : | hackneyed |
| obey | : | obeyed |
| okay | : | okeyed |

But, the final *y* changes to *i* in the following cases:

| (*i*) | say | : | said |
| | lay | : | laid |
| | pay | : | paid |
| (*ii*) | ply | : | plied |
| | fry | : | fried |
| | sky | : | skied |
| | levy | : | levied |
| (*iii*) | day | : | daily |
| | gay | : | gaily |
| (*iv*) | heavy | : | heavily |
| | needy | : | needily, needier. |

**9.** In most of English spellings *i* comes before *e* whenever they come together in a word and their pronunciation is like *ee* as in *keep*. Examples are given below:

| achieve | : | grieve |
| believe | : | field |
| relieve | : | shield |
| retrieve | : | yield |

But when the consonant *e* precedes them, the combination changes to *ei* as in the following :

| receive | : | receipt |
| deceive | : | deceipt |

|          |   |                     |
|----------|---|---------------------|
| conceive | : | conceipt            |
| perceive | : | concierge (exception) |

The exceptions in this case *viz* when *ei* combination is used even if it is preceded by the consonant *c* are given below:

|             |   |             |
|-------------|---|-------------|
| protein     | : | seize       |
| counterfeit | : | seizure     |
| surfeit     | : | weird       |
| plabeian    | : | seine       |
| seismic     | : | seismograph |

**10.** The words ending with a consonant preceded by two vowels however, do not double their last consonant while adding a suffix. Examples are given below:

|        |   |                          |
|--------|---|--------------------------|
| seal   | : | sealed, sealing          |
| sweep  | : | sweeping, sweeper        |
| head   | : | headed, header, heading  |
| befool | : | befooled, befooling      |
| loot   | : | looted, looting          |
| shout  | : | shouted, shouting        |
| seam   | : | seamer, seamed, seaming  |
| float  | : | floated, floating        |

The consonants *h, q, w* and *x* are never doubled while adding any of the suffixes :

|              |   |                            |
|--------------|---|----------------------------|
| (*i*) reach  | : | reached, reaching          |
| bath         | : | bathed, bathing            |
| sigh         | : | sighed, sighing            |
| (*ii*) review | : | reviewed, reviewing        |
| sow          | : | sowed, sowing              |
| show         | : | showed, showing            |
| (*iii*) annex | : | annexed, annexing          |
| fix          | : | fixed, fixer, fixing, fixation. |

**11.** The consonant *q* is always followed by vowel *u* :

| | | |
|---|---|---|
| question | quorum | quene |
| quote | plaque | bequethed |
| quite | opaque | quench |
| quiet | requisition | quarter |
| quarrel | queen | quality |

## Review Test - 1

*The following words are misspelt. Write their correct spellings :*

1. abhorent　　　　　＿＿＿＿＿＿
2. acceed　　　　　＿＿＿＿＿＿
3. asessible　　　　　＿＿＿＿＿＿
4. acquisce　　　　　＿＿＿＿＿＿
5. affray　　　　　＿＿＿＿＿＿
6. accross　　　　　＿＿＿＿＿＿
7. beneficient　　　　　＿＿＿＿＿＿
8. calender　　　　　＿＿＿＿＿＿
9. cemetry　　　　　＿＿＿＿＿＿
10. chronical　　　　　＿＿＿＿＿＿

### Answers:

| | |
|---|---|
| 1. abhorrent | 2. accede |
| 3. assessible | 4. acquiesce |
| 5. affrey | 6. across |
| 7. beneficent | 8. calendar |
| 9. cemetery | 10. chronicle |

## Review Test - 2

*Re-write the following words correctly :*

1. casuality _____
2. ernest _____
3. ettiquete _____
4. exhilerate _____
5. grammer _____
6. hetrogenous _____
7. idiosyncracy _____
8. inning _____
9. jurrisdiction _____
10. pretention _____

### Answers:

1. casualty
2. earnest
3. etiquette
4. exhilarate
5. grammar
6. heterogeneous
7. idiosyncrasy
8. innings
9. jurisdiction
10. pretension.

# 32

# WORDS RELATING TO NUMBERS

According to William Walsh, numbers have a legendary and mystic signification. It is not only the mathematician that has been fascinated by them. The poet, the philosopher and the priest have pondered over the changeless relations of numbers to each other and have come to look upon them and their symbols as in some sort a revelation. Students have been particularly attracted towards numbers when they have been used as elements to form words. Some such words are explained below:

The combining of *uni* with Latin word *unus* (meaning one) can be easily recognized in words like *unit, unity* and *union*—meaning a single thing, the state of being joined together to form one unity (like European unity) and the act/state of joining two or more things/people together, respectively. *Unilateral* action is one-sided, undertaken by one side only, usually to its own advantage. *Unison* means to do or say something at the same time; for people or organisations to work together. *Unique* means the only one of its kind. The *universe* is so called because it is the sum total of existing things—earth and space considered as one.

The word *prime* means main, most important, basic while *prior* means former or preferable. Hence, priority means precedence. *Primacy* is the state of being first while *primitive* and *primeordial* are synonyms of *primeval*—meaning—from the earliest period of history of the world. The words *premier* and *foremost* mean first appearance.

The word *monos* from Greek—meaning single or solitary—has many words conveying the idea of oneness: *monolith* and monolithic give the idea of vastness and enormity; *monarch* means the supreme ruler; monastery which means a residence of monks is from *monachus* (alone); *monism* means a system of thought seeking to deduce all phenomena from a single substance; *monogram* means the first letters of somebody's names that are combined in a design and marked on items of clothing, etc.; *monograph* is a detailed written study of a single subject usually in the form of a short book; *monologue* is a long speech by one person during a conversation that stops other people from speaking, or a long speech in a stage play or film spoken by one actor especially when alone; *monocle* is a glass for one eye; *monomania* is a form of insanity in which the sufferer is irrational on only one subject; *monophobia* is the fear of being left alone; *monopoly* is the complete control of trade in particular goods or services; *monotheism* is the doctrine or belief that only one God exists; *monotonous*—means never changing, repetitious—therefore dull and boring.

The word *sesquicentennial* means pertaining to the 150th anniversary or *sesquicentenary*. *Biannual* means occurring twice a year while *biennial* is happening every two years; *bicameral* is having two houses or chambers; *binary* is consisting of two things or parts; *binomial* is consisting of two terms or names. From Greek we get the combining form *di* meaning twice or double. The two most important words formed with it are *dilemma*—an argument presenting two choices, though in modern usage it has come to mean a difficulty, a course of action that offers no satisfactory solution; and *dichotomy*—two divisions, two opposing schools of thought.

The word elements used to express three come from Greek *tri*, Latin *tri/tier*. Some important such words are given below:

*triad:* a group of three related people or things.

*trilogy:* work of literature or music in three parts.

*triennial:* happening every three years.

*tercentenary:* 300th anniversary.

*trident:* three-pronged spear of sea gods.

*trimester:* a college term where the academic year is divided into three-month terms.

*Trinity:* the union of three gods to form a single godhead.

*triumvirate:* an official group of three powerful people or groups who control something together.

*trivial:* from Latin *trivium*—the place where three roads meet. The meaning was extended to include any crossroad, highway or public square where people indulged in gossip, unimportant talk. Now the word means—not important or serious, not worth considering.

The Latin word for the number four is *quattuor*, its combining form is *quadr*. The words formed with it are:

*quadrangle:* a figure with four sides.

*quadratic:* an equation in which the highest power of the unknown term is a square.

*quadrennial:* held every fourth year.

*quarto:* size of a piece of paper cut four from a sheet.

*quadricentennial:* the 400th anniversary.

The Greek word for five *pente* has a combining form *penta*. The Latin word for five is *quinque*. The words formed with them are:

*pentagon:* a five-sided plane figure.

*pentateuch:* the first five books of the Old Testament.

*quinquennium:* a five year period.

*quintessence:* the fifth sense (above earth, air, water and fire), the highest sense. Now the word has come to mean the perfect example of something. Its synonym is *essence*.

*quintuplets:* five babies born at the same time to the same mother.

The Latin word for six *sex* and its ordinal *sextus* (sixth) have given the following words:

*sexagenarian:* a person between 60 and 69 years of age.

*sestet:* a stanza of six lines.

*sextant:* a navigator's instrument.

*sextant:* a group of six musicians or singers who play or sing together.

*semester:* every six months.

The Latin word *septa* and Greek *hepta* for seven make many words used in the sciences and music. Similarly, *octo* and *octaves* for eight and eighth, *novem* and *nonus* for nine and ninth, and *decem* and *decimus* for ten and tenth respectively make many words as enumerated below:

*septet:* a group of seven musicians or singers.

*septuagenarian:* a person between 70 and 79 years of age.

*octave*: (in music) the eighth full tone above or below any given tone.

*octet*: any composition for eight voices or instruments.

*octopus*: a mollusc with eight arms or tentacles.

*nonagone*: a nine-sided plane figure.

*decade*: a period of ten years.

*decimal*: a number expressed in scales of ten.

*decimate*: originally it meant one chosen by lot out of ten; it now means to kill or destroy totally.

Some other words going beyond the number ten are as under:

*quadragenarian:* forty years old.

*pentagonal:* having five sides.

*octogenarian:* eighty years old.

*nonagenarian:* ninety years old.

*centagenarian:* hundred years old.

*centenary:* the 100th anniversary of an event.

*millennium:* a period of 1000 years.

*myriad:* originally the Greek word for 10000, it now means an extremely large number.

## Review Test 1

*Find words for the following:*

1. an action undertaken by one side          u_____
2. for people to work together               u_____

3. first appearance            p_____

4. exclusive possession or control     m_____

5. happening every two years       b_____

6. a group of three             t_____

7. a perfect example of something    q_____

8. to destroy totally           d_____

9. a period of 1000 years        m_____

10. extremely large in number      m_____

## Answers :

1. unilateral; 2. unison; 3. premier; 4. monopoly; 5. biennial; 6. triad; 7. quintessential; 8. decimate; 9. millennium; 10. myriad.

# 33

## SOME NEW WORDS

English is not only the most vast of all languages, it is also the most dynamic. It has evolved and developed over several centuries to reach its present form. If you read the 16th century poets, like Chaucer and Spencer, you will come across several words which are rarely used these days, and very different spellings of some words from what constitutes modern terminology, e.g. *parfit* for perfect, *queene* for queen, *gentelman* for gentleman, etc. The beauty of English language is that it has marched towards simplicity of spellings and usage and at the same time added to its already vast repertoire of vocabulary.

There are several words that have found their way into English vocabulary rather recently. In some cases the usage and meaning of certain words have acquired new dimensions. It is necessary to know these words because a lack of knowledge thereof can cause problems in properly understanding some texts, reports, articles, etc. Over 120 prominent new words and terms that are frequently used these days in print and electronic media are given below alongwith their meanings and usage:

**acrid:** unpleasantly bitter or sharp—pugent: *acrid smoke from burning tyres*.

**aerobics:** a form of physical exercise designed to increase fitness by any maintainable activity that increases oxygen intake.

***anchor:*** the compere of a TV programme, especially a news show.

**aplomb:** complete confidence, self-assurance, poise, etc. When a person has aplomb, they have figuratively been tested for their ability to face tough situations.

**baleful:** threatening to do something evil or to hurt somebody. A baleful influence is one that is harmful and malicious. A harsher word is baneful.

**biological clock:** used to denote an interior mechanism that regulates the various rhythmic and cyclic activities of humans: *The biological clock is ticking all the time*.

**bivouac:** a makeshift open air camp without tents.

**bodice:** the top part of a woman's dress, above the waist: *Designing a bodice is much more difficult than the lower garments*.

**bonanza:** the word has Spanish origin, it means a rich find, a huge profit, an enormous yield, or a source of great riches: *The announcement of bonus shares was a bonanza for the shareholders*.

**bummer:** an unpleasant experience or a disappointing situation: *It is a real bummer that the match has been washed out*.

**blockbuster:** something very successful, especially a book or film—*a blockbusting* (adj.) *performance*.

**buzzword:** a popular word, phrase or jargon; a word or phrase, especially one connected with a particular subject that has become fashionable, popular and is used a lot in newspapers, etc.

**camaraderie:** a feeling of friendship and trust among people who work or spend a lot of time together: *Camaraderie among colleagues is quite natural.*

**canard:** a hoax; a false, groundless story or fabricated report.

**celebrity:** a famous person: *a TV celebrity.* Also the state of being famous—fame.

**caucus:** a meeting of members of a world body or leaders of nations. Also a group of people with similar interests.

**challenged:** it is a popular euphemism, now widely used in the media for the more pejorative words like crippled or handicapped.

**chiaroscuro:** a combination of chiaro (clear, light) and oscuro (dark, shadowy). A sketch in black and white; a sharp contrast. A situation showing contrasted elements: *chiaroscuro of affluence and destitution in Indian society.*

**cliffhanger:** a situation in a story, film or match which is exciting and you do not known what will happen next: *The first half of the movie ended with a real cliffhanger.*

**cineplex:** a cinema that offers a choice of several screens and auditoria.

**conglomerate:** a large business company formed by joining together different firms: *an IT conglomerate.*

**consumerism:** the belief that it is good for a society or an individual to buy and use large quantity of goods and services. Also the protection of the consumer.

**contraption:** a machine or piece of equipment that looks strange.

**corporatize:** the reverse of nationalize; to put a public institution under private ownership.

**crux:** the crucial or critical point of the matter; the point that must be resolved or decided to clear up the situation.

**cutting edge:** the forefront or the most advanced position in a business, technological development or similar areas of activity.

**cybernetics:** the scientific study of communication and control, especially concerned with comparing human and animal brains with the help of machines and electronic devices.

**decouple:** to end the connection or relationship between two things (of an economy); to remain insulated from the effects on other economies.

**disadvantaged:** said of those suffering from poverty, inadequate parenting, deprivation and are unable to lead normal social life.

**doublespeak:** ameliorative language which makes bad seem good, expensive seem cheap (or vice-versa) and negative seem positive. Example are: *Slums are the inner city; The expensive cars have far less maintenance charges; The poor are fiscal underachievers*, etc.

**downmarket:** market aimed at the lower income consumer.

**downsize:** to reduce the number of people who work in a company, business, etc. to cut down costs.

**fallout:** the bad results of a situation or an action. Any unpleasant side-effect that accompanies a political decision, statement or allied activity. Fallout is not always negative, and can apply to knock-on effects, by-products, contingent ideas and responses.

**footage:** part of a film showing a particular event: *footage of war scenes.*

**footsie:** used (informally) as idiom—to play footsie with somebody—to show an expression of affection or sexual interest towards somebody by touching him/her.

**frontline:** the area where the enemies are facing each other during a war; main, major: *frontline stocks (shares)*; doing work that will have an effect on something: *a life spent on the frontline of sports.*

**funky:** originally a slang meaning smelly; from there it moved to mean messy and dirty. Presently it has shed these pejoratives and is used to mean pleasantly eccentric or unconventional.

**game:** apart from the usual meaning (noun) of sports or activity, it is also used (adj.) to mean ready and willing to do something new, difficult or dangerous: *She's game for anything.*

**gay:** a slang for homosexual. Its opposite is straight.

**gerrymander:** to change the site and borders of an area for voting to give an unfair advantage to one party in the elections.

**glasnost:** the word has Russian origin and now means openness in a country's policies and rules for its citizens.

**glitterate:** the celebrities or glittering stars of fashionable society, particularly from the world of literature and entertainment.

**hiatus:** a gap or interval; also an interruption between two periods of continuous activity.

**hang-up:** a problem or difficulty, usually emotional and often in the form of an inhibition or an obsession.

**hegemony:** control by one country, organization, etc. over other countries within a particular group.

**homophobia:** the hatred of homosexuals.

**hype:** to promote a product, an individual performer or any saleable commodity beyond its intrinsic merits—exaggerate.

**hyper:** an abbreviation for hyperactive—over-intense, obsessive.

**hypermarket:** a large supermarket, usually sited outside a town, possibly in a shopping mall.

**immolation:** originally it referred to the act of spreading the ground grain. Now it covers the meaning sacrifice (self-sacrifice of Buddhist monks and nuns in South Vietnam). Self-immolation now denotes—setting fire to oneself and die in protest against some rule, law, situation, etc.

**janitor:** the caretaker of a building.

**jaunt:** a short trip or excursion taken for pleasure.

**junk bond:** bonds issued to raise money for the takeover of a company on its current value.

**junk food:** refers to fast foods usually sold as takeaways. They provide minimal nutritional value, are rich in harmful fats, etc. but satisfy the taste buds.

**junk mail:** unsolicited commercial advertising posted to millions of homes.

**kitsch:** sensational, slushy, slick writing or art; low quality production designed for popular appeal.

**launder:** to transfer any funds that have been obtained illegally into a bank, usually in a foreign country, and then withdrew those funds through legitimate means.

**leitmotif:** literally, it means leading motive or theme. An idea, theme or phrase that is repeated in a poem, play or opera. The term is used these days to denote any dominant idea.

**leverage:** the ability to influence what people do, especially finances, etc. Leveraged buy out means the act of a small company buying a larger company using money that is borrowed by providing the assets of this larger company as collateral.

**literati:** fashionable members of the literary world including authors, critics, editors and publishers.

**ludicrous:** unreasonable; that you cannot take seriously—absurd, ridiculous: *a ludicrous suggestion.*

**macho:** the word with Spanish origin means masculine, vigorous and virile: *The post-feminist world has come to mock macho men for their strutting muscularity and tough-guy posturing.*

**male chauvinism:** the derogatory term for a man who regards himself and all other men as naturally superior to all women and adopts traditional sexist's attitudes towards them.

**mall:** a covered shopping precinct, usually situated outside a town and having car-parking and other facilities.

**manqué:** failing to achieve the desired goal; frustrated, missed.

**mindset:** an attitude or frame of mind; an unthinking assumption or opinion.

**movers and shakers:** energetic, active individuals who get things done and influence others to act with similar zeal.

**neophyte:** a person who is new to a subject, skill or belief—novice, greenhorn.

**neo-colonialism:** the indirect maintenance of colonial power, often over countries that formerly constituted part of a nation's colonial empire, by using economic and political leverage.

**nihilism:** a belief that nothing (especially religion and moral principles) has any value: *Huxley's plays present a nihilistic view of the world.*

**offshore:** existing at (banks, etc.) or coming (investments, etc.) from outside an individual's or company's home country.

**off-the-wall:** unusual, unconventional.

**op.ed:** (abbr.) opposite the editorial page in a newspaper, which carries regular columnists' features.

**outreach:** extending the government or social services beyond their current or conventional limits. Also the activity of an organization that provides a service to people in the community, particularly those who cannot or are unlikely to come to an office, hospital, etc. for help: *an outreach education programme.*

**panache:** the quality of being able to do things in a confident and elegant way that other people find attractive —flair.

**pariah:** a person who is not acceptable to society and is avoided by everyone—outcast. Also used as adj. these days, e.g. *pariah status of a nation which faces sanctions from international community.*

**payload:** the passengers and goods on a ship or an aircraft for which payment is received; the goods that a vehicle (truck, etc.) is carrying; the explosive power of a bomb or missile; the equipment carried by a spacecraft or satellite.

**penury:** the state of being very poor—extreme poverty.

**perestroika:** from Russian, meaning rebuilding, reconstruction or reform. Originally, the term referred to an attempt spearheaded by premier Mickhail Gorbachev to revolutionize the USSR by a radical overhaul of the republics' bureaucratic and corrupt economic institutions.

**pittance:** a very small or inadequate amount of money.

**roadie:** an abbreviation for road manager; member of the team of assistants—the road crew; those who maintain and operate instruments like amplification, light, etc. required by a rock band for their on-stage performances.

**rock:** the word has several meanings—solid hard material (boulders); to move slowly partly forward, partly backward as in a rock dance. In modern usage it means to be good—something rocks means that it is very good: *Brittany's new album rocks.*

**recce:** reconnaissance; the activity of getting information about an area for military purposes.

**roller coaster:** a situation that keeps changing very quickly.

**rubric:** title or set of instructions written in a book or exam paper; also an ecclesiastical canon, a directive or rule of conduct, etc.

**satiety:** the state of being fully satisfied, especially having had enough food, etc.

**scam:** any form of trick, swindle, racket or fraud, especially involving huge embezzlement of money.

**scion:** a young member of a family, especially famous or important one; also a young shoot, twig or piece of a plant, particularly one cut to make a new plant.

**slag:** to vilify, to denigrate; also (noun) an unpleasant person.

**sledge:** an abbreviation from sledgehammer—the practice of the fielding side in cricket to fire continuous and aggressive insults at the batsman—with the intention of intimidating, provoking or breaking his concentration: *The Australian players kept sledging at the Indian batsmen, but the former were greatly disturbed when the latter gave them a taste of their own medicine.*

**spinoff:** a by-product or an added effect; an unexpected but useful result of an activity designed to produce something else: *commercial spinoff of agricultural research.*

**squat:** the illegal occupation of an uninhabited building, usually by a group of homeless people—squatters (doing so).

**state-of-the-art:** using the most modern or advanced techniques or methods; as good as can be at the present time.

**stonewall:** (in politics) to delay a discussion or decision by refusing to answer questions or by talking a lot; to refuse to compromise.

**symbiosis:** a relationship between people, companies— that works to the advantage of both.

**syndrome:** a set of physical conditions that show that a person has a particular disease. Also a set of opinions or a way of behaving that is typical of a particular type of person.

**synergy:** the extra energy, power, etc. that is achieved by two or more people or companies working together, instead of on their own.

**temperance:** the practice of not drinking alcohol because of religious or moral beliefs; controlling your behaviour, the amount you eat, etc.—moderation.

**theme park:** an amusement park organized on a particular theme or based on a unified idea—each attraction having been linked in some way to the theme.

**time-share:** the system of joint ownership of a holiday home under which the owners take turns in using it at pre-arranged times.

**touchstone:** a criterion by which the genuineness of something is measured.

**tour-de-force:** literally, turn of strength; a feat of skill or strength; also a dramatic or literary trick.

**track record:** all past achievements, successes or failures of a person or an organization: *a proven track record in marketing.*

**trivia:** facts about something; unimportant details or information: *Most ladies spend their evenings discussing domestic trivia.*

**upfront:** not trying to hide what you think or do—honest, frank; paid in advance, before other payments are made: *upfront fee*.

**whistleblower:** a person who informs people in authority that the company they work for is doing something wrong or illegal.

**swoop:** to visit or attack suddenly and without warning: *a CBI swoop*.

**scrutiny:** careful and thorough examination—inspection: *The new government's policies came under close scrutiny*.

**bask:** to enjoy the good feelings in a favourable situation.

**swindle:** to cheat somebody, especially money: *the Satyam swindle*.

**bashing:** very strong criticism of a person or group.

**quandary:** dilemma, a state when you are unable to decide what to do in a difficult situation.

**foolhardy:** reckless; taking unnecessary risks.

**savvy:** having practical knowledge or understanding of something: *computer savvy*.

**snarl:** to speak in an angry or bad-tempered way.

**mired:** in a tough or unpleasant situation.

**reprieve:** to cancel/delay a punishment/plan to close or end something.

**riddance:** said (negatively) when you are pleased that somebody/something has gone: *good riddance*.

**soap opera:** a story about the lives and problems of a group of people on TV/radio.

**grimy:** dirty; covered with dirt: *grimy windows/walls.*

**vicinity:** the area around a particular place.

**learning curve:** period or degree of acquiring a new skill.

**breach:** failure to do something that must be done by law: *breach of contract.*

**slumdog:** a very poor person living in a slum.

**humbug:** a person who is not sincere or honest; a behaviour intended to trick people.

**crunch:** said of a very important meeting or a situation that may decide the future course of events: *a crunch situation.*

## Review Test 1

*Fill in the blanks of following sentences with appropriate words taking clues from the words given in brackets.*

1. Being an _____ of a TV programme requires self-confidence. (compere)

2. It is a _____ that the party has been postponed. (a disapproving situation).

3. Cool and chill have become _____ for being tension free. (popular words)

4. His new-found _____ has encroached upon his private life. (fame)

5. The ODI final was a real _____. (exciting, nobody knew what was to happen next)

6. The _____ of the bilateral relations is that both countries should honour their commitments. (crucial or critical point)

7. The Indian economy is not _____ from global economic slowdown. (disconnected)

8. The marketing companies often resort to _____. (use ameliorative language)

9. Many companies _____ their staff to cut costs. (reduce in number)

10. We need a volunteer for this trial run. Who's _____ to try? (willing)

## Answers:

1. anchor; 2. bummer; 3. buzzwords; 4. celebrity; 5. cliffhanger; 6. crux; 7. decoupled; 8. doublespeak; 9. downsize; 10. game.

## Review Test 2

*Find words that match the given statement/word/term. First letter of the word has been given to give you a start:*

1. complete confidence          a_____
2. a huge profit                b_____
3. unpleasant side-effect       f_____
4. unpleasantly eccentric       f_____
5. a problem or difficulty      h_____
6. transfer funds illegally     l_____
7. leading motive or theme      l_____
8. quality of doing things elegantly  p_____
9. a very small amount          p_____
10. to delay a discussion       s_____

## Answers:

1. aplomb; 2. bonanza; 3. fallout; 4. funky; 5. hang-up; 6. launder; 7. leitmotif; 8. panache; 9. pittance; 10. stonewall

## Review Test 3

*Give the meanings/synonyms of the following words/ terms:*

1. blockbuster
2. caucus
3. cutting edge
4. hegemony
5. junk mail
6. mindset
7. outreach
8. payload
9. recce
10. scion
11. spinoff
12. squatters
13. syndrome
14. track record
15. trivia
16. quandary
17. savvy
18. humbug
19. crunch
20. reprieve

## Answers:

1. something very successful (movie/film)
2. meeting of members
3. most advanced position in a business
4. control by one country/organization
5. unsolicited commercial advertising
6. attitude or frame of mind
7. extending of social services
8. passengers/goods on a ship/aircraft
9. reconnaissance
10. young member of a famous family
11. an added effect
12. those who illegally occupy an uninhabited building
13. a set of physical conditions/opinions

14. all past achievements, successes or failures
15. unimportant details or information
16. a dilemma
17. having practical knowledge of something
18. not sincere or honest
19. a crucial meeting/situation
20. cancellation of punishment

# 34

# WORDS AND EXPRESSIONS

## A DAY WITH A NEWSPAPER

We have discussed so many words in the preceding chapters. Many of you who worked hard must have added to their vocabulary and learnt the meanings of a range of new words. It is, undoubtedly, something appreciable. But learning the meanings of new words is not enough. We have advanced dictionaries and access to computer sites which immediately tell us what a particular word means. What we are aiming to achieve through this book is not just to build a decent vocabulary but to develop the ability to use the appropriate word at the right place to convey the intended meaning and create the desired impact. In other words, we are trying to build emphatic, impressive expression through words.

This, however, is never easy. This book, which is the result of hard work, on the part of the team which created it, can guide you, but your part of hard work has to come from your side to realise the envisaged goal. Let us try a very rewarding exercise.

We know newspapers as a set of large printed sheets of paper containing news, articles, advertisements, etc. published everyday or every week. Since their features are expressed through a medium—a language, the newspapers exhibit a range of latest vocabulary and expression of that language. Thus, spending a day with a standard English newspaper invariably proves highly beneficial. This exercise involves reading the entire or at least major features of a day's standard English newspaper like *The Times of India*, *Hindustan Times* or *The Hindu* or a combination thereof and know the expressions used in editorials, reports, articles and main news items.

We did this exercise and noted certain expressions. Given below are expressions/terms/words used in some newspaper features. Read them and try to understand what they convey. Meanings thereof are provided after each set.

## Set I

1. The *dossier* was handed over to Pakistan High Commission *undercutting Pakistan's alibi* that India has not shared evidence with it to move against the terrorists.

2. A 75-year old *braveheart's scuffle* with a *desperate gun-wielding* man not only *foiled* a robbery but set off a chain of events which led to the robbers walking into a trap three hours later.

3. Even if Elon Musk's (CEO Space X) plans *sound like a pipe dream* to *sceptics*, space X has the *credentials* to back it up.

4. We are well on the way to changing decades-old policies on agriculture and public wealth—*mainstays* of our work in promoting the MDGs.

5. Investment in eco-friendly technology should be part of any global economic *stimulus*.

6. Thomas Reed's (a top US nuke scientist) recent book makes a *startling disclosure* about the extent to which Chinese help to Pak may have gone.

7. Despite *overwhelming* evidence of the Jamaat-ud-Dawa's hand in 26/11 attack, Islamabad has done very little so far in *assuaging* India's concerns.

8. China's nuclear aid to Pakistan could thus have changed South Asia's *strategic calculus.*

9. Beijing has solved its boundary disputes with most of its neighbours. India is the *prominent exception* in this regard.

10. While Beijing's approach to New Delhi is cautious and *calibrated*, the Indian response to China is *effusive* and emotional, with *an undertone of anxiety.*

**Meanings**

1. **dossier:** file, containing important information.
   **alibi:** excuse for something wrong you have done.
   **undercutting Pakistan's alibi:** making Pakistan's excuse weak or less effective.

2. **braveheart:** courageous, not afraid to do dangerous or difficult things to save others.
   **desperate:** something tried when everything else has failed.
   **foiled:** thwarted an evil plan.
   **scuffle:** a short, not very violent fight or struggle.
   **gun-wielding:** holding gun in a threatening manner.
   The expression woven around these words makes a direct impact on the reader.

3. **sound like a pipedream:** pipedream is a plan that is impossible to achieve.

4. **mainstay:** most important part of something.

5. **stimulus:** something that helps something/somebody develop better.

6. **startling disclosure:** a revelation that is extremely unusual and surprising.

7. **overwhelming evidence:** proof that is so compelling that it is difficult to ignore it.
   **assuaging:** making an unpleasant feeling less severe.

8. **strategic calculus:** done as part of a plan.

9. **prominent exception:** most important/glaring exception.

10. **calibrated:** here, in degrees, not all at once.
    **effusive:** showing too much emotion.
    **an undertone of anxiety:** showing/expressing anxiousness.

### Set II

11. New Delhi can *leverage* access to Chinese market.

12. Fog reduces visibility, obstructs sunlight and spreads *dankness*.

13. *On a large canvas*, atmospheric pollutants are contributing to climate change.

14. Financial crisis in the US has *negatively impacted* Asian markets.

15. Friendship between *scions of* two dynasties has helped Omar Abdullah become J&K Chief Minister.

16. ...same *milieu* as the rest of the *junta* ...

17. Let us not *mince* words. The economic situation looks *awful*.

18. Federal Reserve has been supplying liquidity *like an engine crew trying to put out fire.*

19. *...revisiting* both Kaynesian economies and the new deal/package.

20. a *surge* in public spending ....

**Meanings**

11. **leverage:** ability to influence what people do.

12. **dankness:** dampness, coldness and unpleasant feeling.

13. **on a larger canvas:** in a broad sense.

14. **negatively impact:** have a bad influence.

15. **scion:** a young member of an important/famous family.

16. **milieu:** background; the social environment that you live or work in.
   **junta:** here, important and powerful people.

17. **mince words:** not to state clearly or boldly what is reality.

18. Note the use of simile (comparison) to create an impact. One can create similar comparisons by using expressions from appropriate comparisons (Chapter 10 of this book).

19. **revisiting:** returning to an idea and discuss/follow it.

20. **a surge in:** a sudden increase in the amount or number of something.

## Set III

21. All plastic bags banned in Delhi. An *indulgent* official machinery may given you time to find alternatives.

22. Satyam finances may not be as *dire* as feared.

23. ICC's list of greatest batsmen is a *shocker*. As criticism poured in for its lopsided rankings of cricket's all-time greats, the ICC went into damage control mode.

24. ... police has arrested more than 50 hooligans in a *crackdown* on groups allegedly involved in *a spate of* loot and arson in the city.

25. The big guns are getting ready to boom once again in India. The Army is hoping that politics will not *override* national security.

26. Puducherry has *eased out* Kerala from top spot in elementary education to become *numero uno*.

27. FBI investigated Kasab, the *lone* Pakistani terrorist captured alive....

28. After *smashing* the oil employees' strike, the government appears determined to *hang the dog after giving it a bad name*, i.e. to project these employees as the most *pampered* lot.

29. Congress ... chose to demonstrate its friendship with Samajwadi Party by deciding to ease out S. Chaturvedi as AICC spokesman—a move that puts alliance between the two *back on track* after some differences had surfaced earlier.

30. *Stung* by criticism, a *low-key* birthday for Maya. There were no *over-the-top* celebrations that marked ... birthday last year. Instead, her residence looked forlorn without the welcome arches, set in canopies, flower-decked dais and orchid-laden cake. Party workers buzzing with activity were conspicuous by their absence .... Instead of a chirpy and carefree hostess there was a subdued Mayawati.

## Meanings

21. **indulgent:** willing to ignore the weaknesses in somebody/something—patient.

22. **dire:** very serious: *dire consequences*.

23. **shocker:** a piece or news that shocks you; something that is of low quality.

24. **crackdown:** severe action taken to restrict the activities of criminals.
    **a spate of:** a large number of things that are usually unpleasant, that happen suddenly within a short period of time.

25. **override:** to use your authority to reject somebody's decision.
    Also note the expression big guns are ready to boom (create a deep sound).

26. **ease out:** depose, lower down from a prominent position, remove.
    **numero uno:** number one (position, slot).

27. **lone:** the only one, singled out. The word used, here, is better than *only*.

28. **smashing:** causing something to fail miserably (an opposing move).
    **pampered:** taken care of rather too well and therefore spoilt.
    Also note the use of proverb: **Give the dog a bad name and hang him:** project somebody as malicious and then undermine his/her position by taking action against him/her.

29. **back on track:** back on original correct position.

30. **stung:** having a feeling of sharp pain or discomfort by a happening.

**low-key:** not intended to attract a lot of attention.
**over-the-top:** excessive, showy.

## Set IV

31. In a *blunt* message to *perpetrators* of terror, the US President Barrack Obama said, "We will defeat you."

32. A million *brave chill* to watch history unfold.

33. It's a day of celebration and *reflection*.

34. There are so many, like King, who one wishes could have *stayed around* to see this day ....

35. Without Johnson, Obama and so many others would have travelled a much more *circumscribed* path.

36. Johnson's contributions to the betterment of American life were nothing short of *monumental*.

37. If Satyam *dented* the image of India's IT industry globally, the Raza forgery may have damaged the *credibility* of Indian art industry and expressed the *underbelly* of art trade in the country.

38. Newspaper clippings are, according to some, breeding ground for *roaches*.

39. Narendra Modi has received *encomiums* not only from high-ranking *honchos* but also ....

40. Congress opened the pre-poll *head-hunting* by *poaching* three former BJP MPs.

41. There is a *stricture* against government servants expressing political opinion.

42. Prime Minister's *indisposition* at the fag end of a reasonably successful term in office could *impair* the UPA's strategy ....

43. Obama was *categorical* in stating the fact that ....

44. The consistent high-level performance by the participants has *raised the bar* for competition in general.

45. The mind of the wise man is *rapt* in the thought of universality ....

46. The sun bathed in a *sensuous* glow the house of the great writer ....

47. The issue like climate change *spans* multiple sciences even though decision-making is *embedded* in the politics of change.

48. ...adaptations *entail* dealing with rising sea levels.

49. The *broad-based* membership ... *cuts across* party lines and could create a political *compact* on many national issues that have an international *footprint*.

50. The minister *bats for* foreign law firms.

**Meanings**

31. **blunt:** very direct, saying exactly what you think without trying to be polite.

32. **brave:** (here verb) to deal with something difficult or unplesant, to achieve something.

33. **reflection:** careful thought about something.

34. **stayed around:** had been alive.

35. **circumscribed:** restricted; limited (freedom, right or power).

36. **monumental:** huge, very high or big.

37. **dented:** damaged, spoiled, harmed.
    **credibility:** the quality of being trusted, believed.
    **underbelly:** the weakest part.

38. **roaches:** (here) dirty, silly things.

39. **encomium:** high praising speech or writing.
    **honchos:** bosses; incharge of companies, offices.

40. **head-hunting:** finding somebody who is suitable for a senior job.
    **poaching:** (here) using somebody/something that belongs to someone else.

41. **stricture:** severe criticism of somebody's behaviour.

42. **indisposition:** illness.
    **impair:** damage; make something worse.

43. **categorical:** (here) expressed clearly.

44. **raise the bar:** make the standard high.

45. **rapt:** engrossed or focused on one thing.

46. **sensuous:** giving pleasure to your senses.

47. **span:** (here verb) to last through a period.
    **embedded:** fixed firmly on something.

48. **entail:** involve something unavoidable.

49. **broad-based:** wide; not limited.
    **cut across:** to affect different groups.
    **compact:** (here) a formal agreement.
    **footprint:** (here) mark, impact.

50. **bat for:** to give help or support.

## Set V

51. Prabhakaran *cornered* but could *flee*, says Sri Lanka army chief.

52. The minister conveyed that Obama has *extended* greetings to Indian people on Republic day. But he said that India should not see the *underlying* motive in it.

53. Sushil *rues* missing the *prestigious* Padma award.

54. The passengers were *stranded* at Delhi airport as many flights were cancelled due to dense fog.

55. Many Indian MBAs and IITians are getting *lucrative* offers from overseas.

56. Such *proscriptions* have no place in a diverse democracy like ours.

57. ... some good men who are so free with their *diktats* express horror at the Taliban and its *cohorts*....

58. They are not *custodians* of culture, religious or social *mores*.

59. Satyam incident is an *aberration*, not something that happens every now and then.

60. There is an immediate *spike* in the money that a man has in his pocket.

61. If India is on a long-term growth *trajectory*, it matters only *slightly* which specific firm you buy into.

62. Our politicians are *past masters* in the art of firing empty *rhetoric*.

63. Judges have made it *mandatory* for candidates contesting elections to declared their assets.

64. The new US approach includes *inducting* more American troops into Afghanistan.

65. Some people have the *disconcerting* habit of saying exactly what they think.

66. *Unqualified adultation* of corporate leades sometimes proves dangerous.

67. Narayanmurthy is rightly *hailed* as a *trailblazer* in the IT industry.

68. How could a famous *stickler* for grammer have bungled a 35-word passage.

**69.** The *rot* set in against the *backdrop* of *deluded* grandeur.

**70.** The employees felt *disgruntled* at the way they had been treated by the company's top management.

**Meanings**

**51. Cornered:** trapped; about to be caught.
**Flee:** to leave a place or person very quickly, run away from a dangerous situation.

**52. Extended:** (here) expressed, conveyed.
**Underlying:** hidden; existing under the surface of something else.

**53. Rue:** regret; to feel bad about something.
**Prestigious:** respected and admired as very important or of very high quality.

**54. Stranded:** to be left in a place from where you have no way to go.

**55. Lucrative:** producing a large amount of money.

**56. Proscriptions:** (from proscribe) official statement banning something.

**57. Diktats:** (disapproving) an order given by a government.
**Cohorts:** a group of people who share a common feature or aspect of behaviour.

**58. Custodians:** caretaker; a person who takes responsibility for protecting something.
**Mores:** conventical; customs and behaviour typical of a social group.

**59. Aberration:** a fact or action that is not usual.

**60. Spike:** (here) sharpness, power.

**61. Trajectory:** path.
**Slightly:** very little; negligible.

62. **Past masters:** experts.
    **Rhetoric:** (disapproving) a speech or writing intended to influence people.

63. **Mandatory:** compulsory; required by law.

64. **Inducting:** formally giving somebody a job or position.

65. **Disconcerting:** causing anxiety or embarrassment.

66. **Unqualified:** complete; not limited by any negative qualities.
    **Adulation:** admiration and praise.

67. **Hailed:** described as very good or special.
    **Trailblazer:** pathmaking; first to do or discover something for others to follow.

68. **Stickler:** a person who believes in a particular quality or behaviour and expects others to follow.
    **Bungle:** botch; to fail at something.

69. **Rot:** decay, decompose, go bad.
    **Deluded:** deceived into believing something that is not true.

70. **Disgruntled:** annoyed or disappointed.

The above expressions are not only beautiful and appropriate but also very emphatic. You must have realized how helpful reading a standard English newspaper can be. It is hoped that you will make it a regular part of your daily routine, howsoever busy you may be.

We have an exercise for you. Given below are some important expressions frequently used in print media. Find them in the newspapers, magazines and other write-ups you read. Assimilate them, along with all those given in Sets I, II, III, IV and V above and use them in your writings/ conversations.

1. **radical change:** basic and most important change.

2. **paradigm shift:** great change in the way something is done.

3. **raison d' eatre:** reason for the existence of some action or policy.

4. **make a statement:** show strength: *Weather made a chilling statement as mercury fell to sub-zero level.*

5. **go bust:** crumble, break completely.

6. **unbridled criticism:** uncontrolled, extreme criticism.

7. **whacky wishlist:** unrealizable plan.

8. **reality check:** accept/recognize the facts about something/about ourselves.

9. **bubble burst:** unprecedented and unwarranted rise— in share market or in a particular stock or sector or company—to fall.

10. **politically correct:** diplomatic, avoiding controversial statements.

11. **gatecrash:** enter forcibly.

12. **heads rolled:** people in position, etc. were removed.

13. **train guns at:** hold somebody responsible for a serious situation and threaten them with punishment.

14. **carve out a niche:** to work hard and create a market/ position/career for yourself.

15. **prudent:** sensible and careful while making decisions.

16. **cosmetic clean up:** propping something to look presentable/beautiful without making it internally strong.

17. **world view:** a person's way of thinking about and understanding life.

18. **hornet's nest:** a difficult situation in which a lot of people get very angry.

19. **low-profile:** receiving little attention.

20. **navigate:** to find the right way to deal with a difficult situation.

## Review Test 1

*Mention the expression/words/terms that match the following meanings:*

1. excuse for something wrong you have done.
2. a revelation that is extremely unusual and surprising.
3. make an unpleasant feeling less severe.
4. in parts/degrees, not all at once.
5. ability to influence what people do.
6. return to an idea and discuss it.
7. willing to ignore the weakness in somebody/something.
8. severe action taken to restrict the activities of criminals.
9. very serious (consequences, etc.)
10. to úse your authority to reject somebody's decision.

### Answers:

1. alibi; 2. startling; 3. assuage; 4. calibrated; 5. leverage;
6. revisit; 7. indulgent; 8. crackdown; 9. dire; 10. override.

## Review Test 2

*Match the meanings with words/terms/expressions:*

1. having a feeling of sharp pain      a. radical change
   or discomfort.

2. not intended to attract attention.  b. navigate

3. uncontrolled, extreme.               c. shocker
4. basic and most important             d. low-key
   change.
5. sensible and careful while           e. milieu
   making decisions.
6. find the right way to deal with      f. effusive
   a difficult situation.
7. great change in the way              g. stung
   something is done.
8. something that is of                 h. paradigm shift
   low quality.
9. social environment that you          i. unbridled
   live in.
10. showing too much emotion.           j. prudent

**Answers:**

1. g; 2. d; 3. i; 4. a; 5. j; 6. b; 7. h; 8. c; 9. e; 10. f.

# 35

## CHECKING YOUR PROGRESS
## (FINAL COMPREHENSIVE TEST)

During the course of reading this book you have taken a number of Review Tests and a few Comprehensive Tests. The purpose of Review Tests, which are given in almost every chapter, is to revise some of the main words and their meanings. Some words which slip out of your memory, and which is quite normal and happens with everybody, underline in your own mind the need to read at least some part of the chapter again. This effort in itself proves beneficial because while re-reading the chapter or some part thereof you are likely to go through many other words apart from the ones that you primarily wanted to after finding out through the Review Test that you are not sure about their correct meaning.

Comprehensive Tests on the other hand aim at checking your progress of the proceeding four-five chapters from which such particular test is set. These are also more elaborate tests comprising a variety of questions relating to prominent words covered in the chapters. Finding correct words in all the cases in these tests is not an easy affair. The correct answers given to each set of questions helps you check your score. The assessment chart enables you to know your rating and decide whether you need to have a relook at the preceding chapters or go ahead.

It is pertinent to mention here that even an average score in these tests, with around 50 per cent correct answers should not be a cause of worry because it also shows that you have added many important words to your vocabulary. What you need to do is build on what you have achieved. It is also necessary to understand that reading a vocabulary book just once, though it helps a lot, does not enable you to acquire a high range of vocabulary. It requires regular efforts to retain the meaning of words as you keep on adding new words to your repertoire.

Similarly, those who have been able to achieve a high score in these tests, though they can consider themselves to be better placed than those with average scores cannot afford to become complacent.

Words and their meanings tend to slip out of the memory if they are not read, written or spoken regularly. Even their spellings get mixed up at times. That's why we have stated earlier and now re-emphasize that English vocabulary needs to be nurtured. Great spellers are made not born as they say. If you realize this fact and make regular efforts to sustain your present level and build on it you will be on the right course.

This Final Comprehensive Test is slightly different from the previous tests in many ways. The sets of questions are from all the preceding chapters which also makes it more comprehensive. The level of questions/words has also been kept higher than in the previous tests because now you have already made a headway in vocabulary through this book. Take this test sincerely. It will not only work as a revision exercise but also enable you to check your progress and assess your present level of vocabulary. Answers are provided at the end.

## TEST 1

*Find the word that represents the given personality trait or situation:*

1. someone who shows feelings of sympathy for people who are suffering    c_____

2. having both good and bad feelings about something    a_____

3. one who cannot afford luxuries and comforts    a_____

4. talking a lot about oneself    e_____

5. taking too much pride in whatever he/she does    c_____

6. good at something which is quite difficult    a_____

7. one who engages in charitable work.    p_____

8. a noisy argument    a_____

9. hatred of marriage    m_____

10. study of human development    a_____

## TEST 2

*Match the following words with their meanings:*

1. pariah            (*a*) unfocused

2. preposterous      (*b*) weak or uncertain

3. desultory         (*c*) immaculate

4. redoubtable          (d) an outcast
5. pristine             (e) protection
6. recondite            (f) public shame
7. aegis                (g) outrageous
8. ignominy             (h) obscure
9. tenuous              (i) unwise
10. imprudent           (j) formidable

## TEST 3

*Mention the antonyms of the following words:*

1. obedient             d_____
2. germane              i_____
3. flagrant             f_____
4. novice               v_____
5. diurnal              n_____
6. infuriate            m_____
7. truthful             s_____
8. strengthen           a_____
9. adulate              r_____
10. receding            b_____

## TEST 4

*Match the following words with their synonyms:*

1. ephemeral            (a) imprison
2. corollary            (b) mollify
3. blatant              (c) consequence

4. incarcerate          (d) furious

5. alleviate            (e) insurmountable

6. placate              (f) evanescent

7. livid                (g) flagrant

8. insuperable          (h) mitigate

9. deplorable           (i) immature

10. puerile             (j) reprehensible

## TEST 5

*Mention the meanings of the following special words:*

1. to relax                              c_____

2. having femine traints                 e_____

3. a procession                          c_____

4. childish or demonish                  i_____

5. brief appearance                      c_____

6. ordinary, lacking imagination         p_____

7. loud and rowdy                        r_____

8. sharp, penetrating                    i_____

9. prolonged intense sound or effect     r_____

10. partner in some bad deed             a_____

## TEST 6

*Fill in the blanks with appropriate expressive words that go with collection of things:*

1. an _____ of poems

2. a _____ of girls

3. a _____ of flags
4. a _____ of cats
5. a _____ of hired applauders
6. a _____ of lions
7. a _____ of pearls
8. a _____ of merchants
9. a _____ of lies
10. a _____ of bells

# TEST 7

*Give one word substitutes for the following:*

1. one who draws maps, etc.         c_____
2. official incharge of a museum    c_____
3. place where govt./public records are kept    a_____
4. woman hired to clean offices    c_____
5. one who cuts/polishes precious stones    l_____
6. who has suddenly risen to wealth and importance    u_____
7. one who always expects failure.    d_____
8. one who buys a particular product or service    p_____
9. study of births, deaths, population in a particular area    d_____
10. one who is hard to please    f_____

## TEST 8

*Mention the foreign words adapted in English which match the given meaning:*

1. file                                    d_____
2. picture                                 t_____
3. workshop                                a_____
4. housekeeper                             c_____
5. bloody fued                             v_____
6. freedom from care                       i_____
7. noisy dispute                           f_____
8. strong inclination                      p_____
9. attentive to minute details            p_____
10. anguish, pain                          a_____

## TEST 9

*Find words that correctly match the given statement:*

1. scold or criticize severely            b_____
2. delusion of persecution                p_____
3. experienced imaginatively              v_____
4. turns of life                          v_____
5. an official group of three men         t_____
6. baseness, vileness                     t_____
7. course, indecent language              r_____
8. extreme frugality                      p_____
9. easy to control or influence           a_____
10. beginning to exist, not fully developed  n_____

## TEST 10

*Mention the meaning of following phrases/terms:*

1. inter alia                    _____

2. ipso facto                    _____

3. ad hoc                        _____

4. prima facie                   _____

5. quid pro quo                  _____

6. sui generis                   _____

7. sine qua non                  _____

8. per se                        _____

9. ex officio                    _____

10. summum bonum                 _____

## ANSWERS

### TEST 1

1. compassionate    2. ambivalent
3. austere          4. egotistical
5. canceited        6. adept
7. philanthropist   8. altercation
9. misogamy         10. anthropology

### TEST 2

1. (*d*)   2. (*g*)   3. (*a*)   4. (*j*)   5. (*c*)
6. (*h*)   7. (*e*)   8. (*f*)   9. (*b*)   10. (*i*)

### TEST 3

1. defiant          2. irrelevant
3. furtive          4. veteran
5. nocturnal        6. mollify

7. specious
9. reprimand
8. attenuate
10. burgeoning.

**TEST 4**
1. (*f*)　2. (*c*)　3. (*g*)　4. (*a*)　5. (*h*)
6. (*b*)　7. (*d*)　8. (*e*)　9. (*j*)　10. (*i*)

**TEST 5**
1. chill
3. cortege
5. cameo
7. raucous
9. resonance
2. effeminate
4. impish
6. pedestrian
8. incisive
10. accomplice

**TEST 6**
1. anthology
3. bunting
5. clank
7. string
9. tissue
2. bevy
4. clowder
6. pride
8. syndicate
10. peal

**TEST 7**
1. cartographer
3. archives
5. lapidary
7. defeatist
9. demography
2. curator
4. charwoman
6. upstart
8. punter
10. fastidious.

**TEST 8**
1. dossier
3. atelier
5. vendetta
7. fracas
9. punctillious
2. tableau
4. concierge
6. insouciance
8. penchant
10. angst

## TEST 9

| | |
|---|---|
| 1. berate | 2. paranoia |
| 3. vicarious | 4. vicissitudes |
| 5. triumvirate | 6. turpitude |
| 7. ribaldry | 8. parsimony |
| 9. amenable | 10. nascent |

## TEST 10

1. among other things
2. by the nature of thing/fact/situation
3. for some specific purpose
4. apparent, on first appearance
5. tit for tat
6. of his/her their own kind
7. an indispensable condition
8. of its own accord
9. by virtue of one's position on office
10. the highest good

### ASSESSMENT

**Total** 10 × 10 = 100

| | |
|---|---|
| 40 or below | not upto the mark |
| 41-55 | average |
| 56-65 | above average |
| 65-74 | good |
| 75-90 | excellent |
| 91–100 | superior |

# 36

# DICTIONARY OF DIFFICULT WORDS

A dictionary of difficult words is necessary because English vocabulary is infinite. However, hard the author may try to cover all the important words in the word power book, scores of them remain out of focus. Just as there are limitations to human mind, there are constraints of space in print media. The chapters of this book contain thousands of words and constitute a set of highly powerful and emphatic vocabulary, but several words may have been left out as per demands of individual chapters to include the very important and those frequently used.

This word list fills the gap by including all such words which may have been left out in the previous chapters. Besides, it serves many other useful purposes like giving usage of certain words in the shape of sentences or at least phrases or terms, denoting what part of speech each word belongs to, and providing synonyms of many of these words. Coming alphabetically, this chapter works as an exclusive dictionary—a reference source or a word ready reckoner. Reading it will be an icing on the cake for an intelligent user.

# A

**ABASHED** (*adj.*)—embarrassed and ashamed because of something you have done. Its antonym *unabashed* is used more.

**ABATED** (*verb*)—became less strong. Its antonym *unabated* is used more: *The violence continued unabated....*

**ABDICATE** (*verb*)—to give up a position of authority being king or queen: *He was forced to abdicate the throne.*

**ABERRATION** (*noun*)—a fact or action that is not usual: *The expert committing a mistake was an aberration.*

**ABEYANCE** (*noun*)—used as idiom *in abeyance*—being postponed or stopped for a short period of life.

**ABNEGATION** (*noun*)—the act of not allowing yourself to have something you want: *His abnegation of luxuries despite being affluent showed his simplicity.*

**ABOMINABLE** (*adj.*)—extremely unpleasant, appalling, disgusting: *The government rightly described the terrorist attack an abominable act.*

**ABRASIVE** (*adj.*)—(of people) rude and unkind; (of things) rough, used to clean a surface to make it smooth.

**ABSOLVE** (*verb*)—to state formally that somebody is not guilty or responsible for something.

**ABSTENTION** (*noun*)—an act of choosing not to vote.

**ABSTINENCE** (*noun*)—the practice of not allowing yourself something especially alcoholic drinks, sex, etc. for health, moral or religious reasons.

**ABYSMAL** (*adj.*)—extremely bad or of a low standard: *abysmal performance in the match.*

**ACCENTUATE** (*verb*)—to emphasize something or make it more noticeable.

**ACCOMPLICE** (*noun*)—a person who helps another to commit a crime or do something wrong: *The main accused in bank robbery and his accomplice were arrested.*

**ACCORD** (*noun*)—a formal agreement between two organizations, countries, etc. (*verb*) give authority, status: *Our society accords great importance to family.*

---

### QUICK TEST–1

**Match the words with their meanings/synonyms.**

| | | | |
|---|---|---|---|
| 1. | abysmal | a. | rude |
| 2. | abominable | b. | not embarrassed |
| 3. | abrasive | c. | partner in crime |
| 4. | abdicate | d. | low |
| 5. | unabashed | e. | postponement |
| 6. | accentuate | f. | unpleasant |
| 7. | accomplice | g. | exception |
| 8. | abeyance | h. | relinquish |
| 9. | aberration | i. | underline |
| 10. | abstention | j. | not voting. |

---

**ACME** (*noun*)—the highest stage of development, or the most excellent example of something—highest: *The post reform period has seen India reach the acme of economic development.* The word should be distinguished from *acne* which is a skin condition.

**ACQUIESCE** (*verb*)—to consent without arguing even if you do not agree with it.

**ACUMEN** (*noun*)—the ability to understand and decide things quickly and well: *business/commercial acumen.*

**ADMONISH** (*verb*)—to reprimand or reprove: *Maria was admonished for chewing gum in the class.*

**ADVENT** (*noun*)—coming of an important event, person, etc: *the advent of modern technology. Adventitious* is happening by chance.

**ADVERSARY** (*noun*)—opponent or rival, somebody that you are competing with in an argument or battle. Note that the word *adverse* (adj) means negative and unpleasant, and *adversity* (noun) is difficult, unpleasant situation.

**AEGIS** (*noun*)—protection or support of a particular organisation or person (usually in a positive sense): *under the aegis of....*

**AGGLOMERATION** (*noun*)—a group of things put together in a particular order or arrangement. The word should be distinguished from *conglomerate* (noun)—a large company formed by joining together different firms—through mergers and acquisitions; *conglomeration* (noun)—a mixture of different things that are found all together: *Delhi is a conglomeration of buildings, flats, malls and ancient architecture.*

**AMBIENT** (*adj.*)—relating to the surrounding area; on all sides; ambient temperatures/light/conditions; also a relaxed atmosphere (created by light music, etc.).

**AMBIGUITY** (*noun*)—the state of having more than one possible meanings such that it is difficult to assess the facts properly, *inconsistencies and ambiguities.*

**AMOK** (*adv.*)—to suddenly become very angry, excited and start behaving violently, especially in a public place: *The procession ran amok when their leader was arrested.*

**ANCILLARY** (*adj.*)—providing necessary support to the main work or activity of an organisation or company: *an ancillary unit/staff/equipment*—auxiliary.

**ANGST**—a feeling of anxiety and worry about a situation or about your life: *Ezekiel's poetry is full of emotional angst.* **Anguish** is mental suffering or unhappiness: *Tears of anguish filled her eyes.*

**APATHY** (*noun*)—the feeling of not being interested in or enthusiastic about anything: *The voter turnout was poor which bears testimony to widespread apathy among the electorate.*

## QUICK TEST–2

**Match the words with their synonyms/meanings.**

| | | | |
|---|---|---|---|
| 1. | acquiesce | a. | a huge company |
| 2. | admonish | b. | opponent |
| 3. | conglomerate | c. | friendly |
| 4. | amok | d. | auxilliary |
| 5. | adversary | e. | lack of interest |
| 6. | affable | f. | consent |
| 7. | angst | g. | ability |
| 8. | ancillary | h. | rebuke |
| 9. | apathy | i. | enraged |
| 10. | acumen | j. | anguish |

**APLOMB** (*noun*)—the quality of being confident and successful and finding a way in a difficult situation.

**APPORTION** (*verb*)—to divide something among the people: *They apportioned the land among the members of the family.*

**APPRISE** (*verb*)—to tell or inform somebody about something or somebody: *The minister was apprised of the worsening flood situation.*

**ARBITRARY** (*adj.*)—an action, decision, rule not seeming to be based on reason, system or rule and is seemingly unfair; using power without restriction and without considering other people.

**ARDENT** (*adj.*)—very enthusiastic and showing strong feelings about something—passionate: *an ardent supporter of Asian unity.*

**ARMISTICE** (*noun*)—a formal agreement during a war to stop fighting and discuss finding a peaceful solution—ceasefire.

**ARSON** (*noun*)—the crime of deliberately setting fire to something, especially a building.

**ASCRIBE** (*verb*)—to attribute something to somebody: *This novel is usually ascribed to Mario Puzo.*

**ASPIRANT** (*noun*)—someone with a strong desire to achieve a position of importance: *The Civil Services aspirants rejoiced at the news of doubling the intake.*

**ASSIDUOUS** (*adj.*)—working very hard and taking great care that things are done immaculately—diligent.

**ASTOUNDING** (*adj.*)—so surprising that it is hard to believe—astonishing: *There was an astounding increase in the company's profits.*

**ATONE** (*verb*)—to make amends for doing something wrong in the past: *to atone for your sins.*

**ATTENUATE** (*verb*)—to make something weaker or less effective: *Yoga attenuates the effect of several ailments.*

**AVANT-GARDE** (*noun*)—new and modern ideas in art, music or literature; also a group of artists, etc. who introduce new and very modern ideas.

**AWRY** (*adv. adj.*)—not happening as per your plans: *All my plans to host the party went awry as my grandfather fell ill.* A similar word is *haywire* which means (plans or situations) to become out of control.

---

### QUICK TEST–3

**Match the words with their synonyms/meanings.**

| | | | |
|---|---|---|---|
| 1. | attenuate | a. | haywire |
| 2. | apportion | b. | unreasonable |
| 3. | avant-garde | c. | distribute |
| 4. | astounding | d. | enthusiastic |
| 5. | awry | e. | surprising |
| 6. | ardent | f. | attribute |
| 7. | assiduous | g. | weaken |
| 8. | atone | h. | make amends |
| 9. | arbitrary | i. | new, modern ideas |
| 10. | ascribe | j. | diligent |

---

### B

**BACK-BURNER** (*noun*)—something which is put on the back-burner is left to be considered later. The usage is: *to put on the back-burner.*

**BACKDROP** (*noun*)—a painted piece of cloth hung behind the stage in a theatre to be the part of scenery. The word is used these days to denote everything that can be seen around an event that is taking place but which is not a part of that event: *The ethnic clashes need to be analysed in the backdrop of poor economic conditions in the area.*

**Back-pedal** (*verb*)—to change an earlier statement or opinion: *The government has back-pedalled on the promised reduction in tax rates.*

**Bald-faced** (*adj.*)—making no attempt to conceal your dishonest behaviour—blatant, bare-faced: *Politics is full of many bald-faced criminals.*

**Bandwagon** (*noun*)—an activity which more and more people are becoming involved in. The idiom *jump on the bandwagon* is used (disapprovingly) to denote—join others in doing something that is becoming fashionable.

**Banish** (*verb*)—to order somebody to leave a place especially a country, as a punishment: *Napoleon was banished to St. Helena;* to make some idea to away from the mind: *The sight of chocolates banished all thoughts away from the child's mind.*

**Bastion** (*noun*)—a group of people or a system that protects a way of life or a belief when it seems that it may disappear: *a bastion of freedom/universal brotherhood.*

**Baulk** (*verb*)—to be unwilling to do something because it is difficult or dangerous: *Many parents baulked at the idea of paying donation while seeking admission of their wards in the reputed business school.*

**Beacon** (*noun*)—a light that is placed somewhere to guide vehicles, warn them of danger. Used frequently for persons who guide and inspire people: *He was a beacon of hope for....*

BELEAGUERED (*adj.*)—experiencing a lot of criticism and difficulties: *The beleaguered politician was forced to resign;* surrounded by enemies: *beleaguered city.*

BELLIGERENT (*adj.*)—unfriendly and aggressive—hostile: a belligerent attitude.

BEMUSED (*adj.*)—befuddled, confused, unable to think clearly—bewildered.

BENEFACTOR (*noun*)—a person who gives money or other help to persons and/or organisations like schools as charity.

BENEVOLENT (*adj.*)—kind, helpful and generous.

BILATERAL (*adj.*)—involving two groups of people or two countries: *bilateral relations/trade.*

---

## QUICK TEST–4

**Match the words with their synonyms/meanings.**

| | | | |
|---|---|---|---|
| 1. | benevolent | a. | blatant |
| 2. | bemused | b. | light |
| 3. | bald-faced | c. | in dire straits |
| 4. | baulk | d. | bewildered |
| 5. | bastion | e. | aggressive |
| 6. | beacon | f. | from both sides |
| 7. | beleaguered | g. | recoil |
| 8. | belligerent | h. | generous |
| 9. | bilateral | i. | embodiment |
| 10. | benefactor | j. | charitable |

BLATANT (*adj.*)—(disapproving) action (considered bad) done in an open way without caring if people will be shocked.

BLEAK (*adj.*)—(of a situation) not encouraging or giving hope: *bleak prospect/outlook : In the age of malls, the future of small traders looks bleak.*

BLOCKADE (*noun*)—the action of surrounding or closing a place, especially a port to stop peopie or goods from coming or going; a barrier; (*verb*)—to surround a place... The word should be distinguished from *blockage*—an obstruction: *blockage in artery/pipe/drain.*

BLUEPRINT (*noun*)—a plan that shows what can be achieved and how: *a blueprint for rural development.*

BOGEY (*noun*)—a thing that causes fear, often without reason: *the prediction of a devastating hurricane proved to be a bogey.*

BOLSTER (*verb*)—to improve or make stronger: *bolster someone's confidence.*

BONHOMIE (*noun*)—a feeling of cheerful friendship.

BOURGEOIS (*adj.*)—belonging to the middle class; the word *bourgeoisie* (noun) means the middle classes in society.

BRAINSTORMING (*noun*)—a method of making a group of people all think about something at the same time to resolve a problem or create good ideas: *a brainstorming session.*

BRAZEN (*adj.*)—open, without shame, usually something that people find shocking, shameless. As a verb, it is used as *brazen it out*—to behave as if you are not ashamed or embarrassed about something.

BRICKBAT (*noun*)—an insulting remark made in public.

BRITTLE (*adj.*)—hard but easily broken: brittle bones/nails; a brittle mood or state of mind is one that appears strong but is actually nervous.

BROWBEAT (*verb*)—to frighten or threaten somebody in order to make them do something—intimidate: Many landowners were browbeaten into selling their plots.

BUCCANEERING (*adj.*)—enjoying taking risks especially in business: *The buccaneering founder of this company proved lucky to make it a multinational.*

BULWARK (*noun*)—a person or thing that protects or defends something: *a bulwark against exploitation*; also a wall built as a defence.

BUREAU (*noun*)—an office or organisation that provides information on a particular subject: *an employment bureau.*

BUST (*verb*)—to break something; to suddenly enter a place and search or arrest somebody; (*noun*) model of a person's head, shoulders and chest; *busted*—caught in the act of doing something wrong and likely to be punished.

BUZZWORD (*noun*)—something that has become popular and fashionable.

## QUICK TEST–5

**Match the words with their synonyms/meanings.**

| | | |
|---|---|---|
| 1. browbeat | a. | break |
| 2. brittle | b. | fashionable |
| 3. bust | c. | protecting |
| 4. brickbat | d. | frighten |
| 5. buccaneering | e. | untrue |

| | | | |
|---|---|---|---|
| 6. | bleak | f. | venturesome |
| 7. | buzzword | g. | unconcealed |
| 8. | brazen | h. | fragile |
| 9. | bulwark | i. | hopeless |
| 10. | bogey | j. | insulting remark |

## C

CALLOUS (*adj.*)—not caring about other people's feelings or suffering, cruel, unfeeling: *a callous attitude.*

CAMEO (*noun*)—a small part in a movie/play for a famous actor; a short piece of writing that gives a good description of something; a brief impressive performance.

CAMOUFLAGE (*noun*)—a way of hiding soldiers or military equipment using paint, leaves, nets, etc. so that they look like part of their surroundings. The word is generally used to denote behaviour that is deliberately meant to hide the truth.

CANALIZE (*verb*)—to control an emotion or activity so that it is used at a particular purpose, channelize: *If the energy of the youth is canalized towards development, we can achieve the objectives of broad-based growth in a short span of time.*

CANDOUR (*noun*)—the quality of saying what you think openly and honestly, frankness.

CAPITULATE (*verb*)—yield, give in, to agree to do something what you had been refusing to do for a long time; surrender.

CAPRICIOUS (*adj.*)—showing sudden changes of attitude and behaviour, unpredictable, changeable.

**CAPTIVATE** (*verb*)—to keep somebody's attention by being interesting, attractive—enchant: *The children were captivated by the magician's tricks.*

**CAPTURE** (*verb*)—to catch a person or animal and keep them as prisoner or in confinement; to take control of a building, place, by force; to make someone interested in something: *capture one's imagination*; to accurately express a feeling or atmosphere. The word is also used as a noun—the act of capturing.

**CARNAL** (*adj.*)—connected with body or sex: *carnal desire.*

**CARVE** (*verb*)—to make objects, patterns, etc.; to write something on a surface by cutting into it; to work hard in order to have a successful career. The verb *carve out a niche* means to create an opening or position for yourself in trade, business or career.

**CATASTROPHE** (*noun*)—a sudden event that causes many people to suffer—disaster; an event that causes one person or a group of people personal suffering: *Acquisition of a sick unit proved a catastrophe for the company.*

**CAUCUS** (*noun*)—a meeting of members or leaders of a political party to choose candidate or to decide policy; also the members or leaders of a political party or group.

**CAVEAT** (*noun*)—a warning that particular things need to be considered before something can be done.

**CELEBRITY** (*noun*)—a famous person: *sports celebrities;* also the state of a being famous: *His celebrity has curtailed his freedom.*

## QUICK TEST—6

**Match the words with their synonyms/meanings.**

| | | | |
|---|---|---|---|
| 1. | cameo | a. | yield |
| 2. | candour | b. | enchant |
| 3. | capitulate | c. | brief, impressive appearance |
| 4. | catastrophe | d. | make, create |
| 5. | carnal | e. | unpredictable |
| 6. | captivate | f. | meeting |
| 7. | callous | g. | frankness |
| 8. | capricious | h. | not caring |
| 9. | carve | i. | corporeal |
| 10. | caucus | j. | disaster |

CENOTAPH (*noun*)—a monument built in the memory of soldiers killed in war who are buried or cremated somewhere else.

CENSURE (*verb*)—to criticize severely and often publicly because they have not done something—rebuke. Also *noun*—strong criticism: *a vote of censure.*

CESSATION (*noun*)—the stopping of something, a pause: *cessation of hostilities.*

CHAGRIN (*noun*)—a feeling of being annoyed or disappointed: *His chagrin at being left out of the team was obvious.*

CHAOS (*noun*)—a state of complete confusion or disorder: slowdown in America caused a complete chaos in Asian stock markets. *Adj.*—chaotic.

CHARISMA (*noun*)—powerful personal quality of some people to attract and impress other people: *Apart from being a great player Sachin Tendulkar has great personal charisma.*

CHAUVINISM (*noun*)—(diapproving) an aggressive and unreasonable belief that one's own country or class is better than all others.

CHEQUERED (*adj.*)—a person's or nation's past history that contains good as well as bad periods; having a pattern of squares of different colours.

CHORE (*noun*)—a task that you are regularly doing: *household/domestic chores*; an unpleasant or boring task: *shopping for daily needs is a chore for the ladies.*

CHRONIC (*adj.*)—lasting for a long time, difficult to cure or get rid of: chronic asthma/bronchitis/diabetes—acute; also having had a disease for a long time.

CIRCUMSPECT (*adj.*)—thinking very carefully before doing something, considering the risks—cautious: *In test match cricket the batsmen are supposed to be circumspect not flamboyant.*

CLAMOUR (*verb*)—to demand something loudly: *After the corruption charges against the minister, people began to clamour for his resignation.*

CLANDESTINE (*adj.*)—done secretly or kept secret: *a cladestine meeting/relationship/plan/deal.*

COERCION (*noun*)—the action of making someone do something they don't wish to do, using force or threat: *The clerk stated that he changed the documents under coercion.*

COGENT (*adj.*)—strongly and clearly expressed in a way that influences people's thoughts—convincing: *He put forward some cogent reasons to accept the plan.*

## QUICK TEST–7

**Match the words with their synonyms/meanings.**

| | | | |
|---|---|---|---|
| 1. | cogent | a. | wicked, done secretly |
| 2. | clandestine | b. | thinking carefully |
| 3. | clamour | c. | lasting for a long time |
| 4. | chagrin | d. | regular work |
| 5. | chronic | e. | loud demand |
| 6. | charisma | f. | pressurising |
| 7. | circumspect | g. | clearly expressed |
| 8. | chore | h. | not smooth |
| 9. | coercion | i. | annoyance |
| 10. | chequered | j. | charm |

COGNIZANCE (*noun*)—knowledge or understanding of something; (*adj.*) cognizant, *idiom—take cognizance of.*

COHORT (*noun*)—a group of people who share a common feature or aspect of behaviour; (disapproving) a member of a group of people who support another person: *Albert and his cohort were asked to leave.*

COLLAGE (*noun*)—the art of making a picture by sticking pieces of coloured paper, cloth, photographs onto a surface; a collection of things that may be different or similar; *an interesting collage of post-colonial paintings.*

COLLATERAL (*noun*)—property or some other valuable tangible that you promise to give somebody if you cannot pay back borrowed money: *collateral security;*

(*adj.*)—connected with something else, additional but less important.

COLLUSION (*noun*)—(disapproving) secret agreement to do something dishonest or tricky: *Hoarders are operating in collusion with corrupt officials and creating shortage of essential consumables in the market.*

COLOSSAL (*adj.*)—extremely large or big: *a colossal statue; also colossal amount of money.*

COMEUPPANCE (*noun*)—a punishment for something bad that you have done: *The villain got his comeuppance at the end of the movie.*

COMMISERATION (*noun*)—an expression of sympathy for somebody who has had something unpleasant happen to them: *commiseration to the losing team.*

COMPATIBLE (*adj.*)—(of machines, computers) able to be used together: *compatible software*; (of ideas, methods, things) able to exist or be used together without causing problems.

COMPELLING (*adj.*)—so strong that you must do something about it: *compelling desire/need/sense of something/reason/evidence.*

COMPETENCE-COMPETENCY (*noun*)—ability to do something well: *level of competence in English; professional, technical competence;* the power of a court/organisation/person to deal with something: *The judge/court has the competence to....* (*adj.*) competent.

COMPLACENCY (*noun*)—(disapproving) a feeling of satisfaction about yourself or a situation which you think is good and no change is necessary, hence making no efforts to improve: *Despite good results in the terminal exams, the students were told that there was no room for complacency.*

**COMPLEMENT** (*noun*)—a thing that adds new qualities to something making it more attractive; (*verb*) to add something...; (*adj.*) complementary.

**COMPLIMENT** (*noun*)—a remark that expresses praise or admiration of somebody: *to pay somebody a compliment*; (*verb*)—to tell somebody that you admire something they have done; (*adj.*) complimentary.

**COMPREHENSIBLE** (*adj.*)—something that can be easily understood by somebody: *readily comprehensible*.

**COMPREHENSIVE** (*adj.*)—complete, full—including all the items details, facts, information, etc. connected with a particular idea, etc.

---

### QUICK TEST–8

**Match the words with their synonyms/meanings.**

| | | | |
|---|---|---|---|
| 1. | cognizance | a. | secret agreement |
| 2. | comprehensible | b. | enormous |
| 3. | collateral | c. | punishment |
| 4. | collusion | d. | appreciative remark |
| 5. | colossal | e. | easy to understand |
| 6. | comeuppance | f. | add something |
| 7. | complacency | g. | additional |
| 8. | commiseration | h. | sympathy |
| 9. | compliment | i. | laziness due to satisfaction |
| 10. | complement | j. | understanding |

---

**COMPUNCTION** (*noun*)—a guilty feeling about doing something: *He felt no compunction about leaving his job.*

CONCEIT (*noun*)—(disapproving) too much pride in yourself and what you do; also clever expression in writing or speech.

CONCOMITANT (*adj.*)—happening at the same time as something else especially because one thing causes the other; (*noun*)—the thing that happens at the same time as something else.

CONDESCEND (*verb*)—(often disapproving) to do something that you think is below your social or professional position to do—deign; (*adj.*)—condescending.

CONFABULATION (*noun*)—a story that somebody has invented in their mind—also the act of inventing the story in your mind.

CONFISCATE (*verb*)—to officially take something away from somebody especially as a punishment: *The estates of princes were confiscated after India's independence.*

CONFOUND (*verb*)—baffle, complicate, to confuse or surprise somebody: *The subprime problem in the USA has confounded economists worldwide.*

CONFRONTATION (*noun*)—a situation in which there is angry disagreement between people or groups: *The coalition governments of today diplomatically avoid confrontation with coalition partners.*

CONGENIAL (*adj.*)—(of a person) pleasant to spend time with because of similar interests and ideas: *congenial colleague.*

CONGENITAL (*adj.*)—existing as a part of a person's character and not likely to change: *a congenital inability to tell the truth.*

CONJECTURE (*noun*)—an opinion or idea that is not based on definite knowledge and is formed by guesses: *His conjecture on the issue was exposed when the actual report was published;* (verb)—to form an opinion about something even though you do not have much information on it.

**CONNIVE** (verb)—(disapproving) to seem to allow something wrong to happen: *Standing by and not stopping someone doing something wrong is also conniving.*

**CONNOISSEUR** (noun)—an expert in matters involving the judgement of beauty, skill or quality in art.

**CONSCIENCE** (noun)—the part of your mind that tells you whether your actions are right or wrong: clear/guilty conscience.

**CONSECRATE** (verb)—to state officially in a religious ceremony that something is holy, or somebody is now a priest.

---

### QUICK TEST–9

**Match the words with their synonyms/meanings.**

| | | | |
|---|---|---|---|
| 1. | confabulation | a. | affable, friendly |
| 2. | confound | b. | collude |
| 3. | confiscate | c. | showdown |
| 4. | congenial | d. | invented story |
| 5. | connoisseur | e. | contemporaneous |
| 6. | connive | f. | idea |
| 7. | congenital | g. | baffle |
| 8. | confrontation | h. | expert |
| 9. | conjecture | i. | officially take away |
| 10. | concomitant | j. | unchanging characteristic |

**CONSPICUOUS** (*adj.*)—easy to see or notice, likely to attract attention: *Belinda was conspicuous by her absence.*

**CONSTERNATION** (*noun*)—a worried or sad feeling after you have received an unpleasant surprise: *To the consternation of millions of fans, Sachin has wrongly given out.*

**CONSTRAINT** (*noun*)—a thing that limits or restricts something—restriction: *constraints of time/resources/ space,* etc.

**CONSTRUCT** (*verb*)—to make or build something such as road, building, bridge, etc. (*noun*)—an idea or belief that is based on various pieces of evidence which are not always true.

**CONSUMMATION** (*noun*)—the act of making a marriage or relationship complete by having sex; the fact of making something complete or perfect: *Tagore's Gitanjali is the consummation of his poetic genius.*

**CONTEMPLATE** (*verb*)—to think about whether you should do something or not, how you should do it—consider: I have been contemplating to take voluntary retirement.

**CONTEMPORANEOUS** (*adj.*)—happening or existing at the same time—contemporary: *contemporaneous accounts/artefacts/events,* etc.

**CONTENTIOUS** (*adj.*)—likely to cause disagreement between people: *a contentious issue/topic/subject.*

**CONTINENTAL** (*adj.*)—pertaining to the continent of Europe not including Britain and Ireland; following the customs of western Europe.

**CONTINGENT** (*noun*)—a group of people at a meeting or event who have something in common, especially the place they come from, that is not shared by other people in the event: *the contingent for Olympics*; (*adj.*)—depending on something that may or may not happen: *a contingent ability.*

**Continuum** (*noun*)—a series of similar items in which each is almost the same as the one next to it but the last is very different from the first—cline: *The famous publishers Routlege have brought a continuum on Management.*

**Conundrum** (*noun*)—a confusing problem or question that is difficult to solve; a question that usually involves a trick with words that you ask for fun—riddle.

**Convoluted** (*adj.*)—extremely complicated and difficult to follow: *a convoluted argument/explanation.*

**Copious** (*adj.*)—in large amount—abundant: *copious amount of water/sand.*

**Cordial** (*adj.*)—pleasant and friendly: *a cordial atmosphere/ relationship*; (*noun*)—a sweet drink that does not contain alcohol, made from fruits: *lime cordial.*

---

### QUICK TEST–10
**Match the words with their synonyms/meanings.**

| | | | |
|---|---|---|---|
| 1. contemplate | a. | apparent |
| 2. constraint | b. | riddle |
| 3. cordial | c. | restriction |
| 4. conspicuous | d. | not fixed |
| 5. consternation | e. | abundant |
| 6. conundrum | f. | causing disagreement |
| 7. convoluted | g. | think deeply |

| | | | |
|---|---|---|---|
| 8. | copious | h. | complicated |
| 9. | contentious | i. | friendly |
| 10. | contingent | j. | worry |

**CORNERSTONE** (*noun*)—the most important part of something on which something important depends: *This agreement is the cornerstone of trade relation between the two countries.*

**COROLLARY** (*noun*)—a situation, fact or argument that is natural and direct result of another one.

**CORPOREAL** (*adj.*)—that can be touched; physical rather than spiritual: *corporeal needs.*

**CORPUS** (*noun*)—a collection of written or spoken texts: *the whole corpus of romantic poetry.*

**CORROBORATE** (*verb*)—to provide evidence or information that supports a statement, theory, etc.—confirm. *The evidence on the kidney racket was corroborated by several witnesses.*

**COUNTENANCE** (*noun*)—a person's face or their expressions; (*verb*)—to agree to something happening—consent: *The board refused to countenance the proposal.*

**COUNTERMAND** (*verb*)—to cancel an order that has been given by giving a different order: *The drawer of this cheque has countermanded its payment.*

**COVERT** (*adj.*)—secret, hidden, difficult to notice: *covert surveillance/operations/glance.*

**CRAVEN** (*adj.*)—lacking courage, cowardly, timid: *He is craven by nature, don't expect him to do any heroics.* The word *craving* means strong desire.

**CREDENTIALS** (*noun*)—qualities, training or experience that make you suitable to do something: *Your résumé shows that you have all the credentials for this job;* documents like letters, etc. that prove that you are what you claim to be: *credentials of the ambassador.*

**CREDIBLE** (*adj.*)—that can be believed or trusted: *credible explanation/witness*—convincing.

**CREDULOUS** (*adj.*)—one who easily believes others and is therefore easy to trick—gullible.

**CRINGE** (*verb*)—to move back or away from somebody because you are afraid—cower: *Sudden appearance of a bull terrier in the lawn made me cringe in fear.*

**CRONY** (*noun*)—(often disapproving) a person that somebody spends a lot of time with. The word is used these days for nations who support or approve even the clandestine actions or policies of the superpower: *America and its cronies should be criticized for attacking Iraq.*

**CROSS SECTION** (*noun*)—a group or things that are typical of a large group: *a representative cross section of society.*

**CULPABLE** (*adj.*)—responsible and deserving blame for having done something wrong: *culpable homicide.*

**CUMBERSOME** (*adj.*)—large, heavy, difficult to carry; slow and complicated, tiring: *I had to read the whole papers with all its cumbersome details.*

---

## QUICK TEST–11

**Match the words with their synonyms/meanings.**

| | | |
|---|---|---|
| 1. countenance | a. | resultant fact |
| 2. countermand | b. | cower |
| 3. cumbersome | c. | cancel an order |

| | | | |
|---|---|---|---|
| 4. | culpable | d. | tiring |
| 5. | corollary | e. | gullible |
| 6. | cronies | f. | testimonials |
| 7. | cringe | g. | representative group |
| 8. | credulous | h. | face |
| 9. | credentials | i. | supporters |
| 10. | cross section | j. | deserving blame |

## D

**DASTRADLY** (*adj.*)—evil and cruel: *The dastardly acts of terrorists are criticized by civil societies all over the world.*

**DAUNT** (*verb*)—to make somebody feel nervous and less confident about doing something—intimidate. The antonym of the word—*undaunted* (*adj.*)—is more in use: *He remained undaunted despite stiff opposition.*

**DEARTH** (*noun*)—a lack of something; the fact that there is a shortage of something—scarcity: *There is no dearth of foodgrain in India, only the distribution system is not proper.*

**DEBACLE** (*noun*)—an event or a situation that is a complete failure and causes embarrassment: *After India's dismal performance in the World Cup, a committee was constituted to study the reasons of the debacle.*

**DEBUNK** (*verb*)—to show that an idea, a belief, etc. is false: *Many old economic theories have been debunked by recent research.*

**DECIPHER** (*verb*)—to succeed in finding the meaning of something that is difficult to read or understand: *Many scripts of old civilizations have still not been deciphered.*

**DECOUPLE** (*verb*)—to end the connection or relation between two things: *An economic slow down in America and Europe has affected India because it is not possible to decouple from other major economies in the present age of globalisation.*

**DECRIPT** (*adj.*)—very old and not in good condition or health.

**DEFIANT** (*adj.*)—openly refusing to obey something or somebody, sometimes in an aggressive way.

**DEFUNCT** (*adj.*)—no longer existing, operating or being used.

**DÉJÀ VU** (*noun*)—the feeling that you have previously experienced something which is happening to you now: *I had a strong sense of déjà vu when I entered the hall.*

**DELIBERATION** (*noun*)—the process of carefully considering or discussing something: *The bill was passed after long hours of deliberation by the members of parliament.*

**DELINQUENCY** (*noun*)—bad or criminal behaviour usually of young people: juvenile delinquency.

**DEMEANOUR** (*noun*)—the way that somebody looks or behaves: *Public figures have to maintain a professional demeanour in all the functions and meetings because they are people's role models.*

**DEMUR** (*verb*)—to say or show that you do not agree with something: *At first she demurred but finally agreed when he importuned her with his love;* (*noun*): *They accepted the decision without demur.*

**DENIZEN** (*noun*)—a person, animal or plant that lives, grows or is found in a particular place: *Royal Bengal tigers are the deniznes of Sunderbans.*

**DEPLORABLE** (*adj.*)—very bad and unacceptable, often in a shocking way—appalling: *Millions of poor people live in deplorable conditions.*

**DEPOSE** (*verb*)—to remove somebody, especially a ruler from power: *The king was deposed in a bloodless coup.*

**DERELICT** (*adj.*)—not cared for and in a bad condition: *derelict building/land*; (*noun*)—a person without home, job or property: *derelicts living on the pavement. Dereliction* means the fact of deliberately not doing what you are required to do: *dereliction of duty.*

**DERISION** (*noun*)—a strong feeling that something is ridiculous, shown in an unkind way/making unkind remarks—scorn (*adj.*)—derisive.

## QUICK TEST–12

**Match the words with their synonyms/meanings.**

| | | | |
|---|---|---|---|
| 1. | dearth | a. | evil and cruel |
| 2. | decouple | b. | discard |
| 3. | daunt | c. | end the connection |
| 4. | dastardly | d. | deportment |
| 5. | debacle | e. | scorn |
| 6. | debunk | f. | intimidate |
| 7. | defunct | g. | discussion |
| 8. | derision | h. | shortage |
| 9. | deliberation | i. | no longer existing |
| 10. | demeanour | j. | predicament |

**DEROGATORY** (*adj.*)—showing an attitude of criticism towards somebody or something—insulting: *derogatory remarks.*

**DESOLATE** (*adj.*)—empty and without people, lonely (place) making you feel sad or frightened; (*verb*)—to make somebody feel sad, without home.

**DESULTORY** (*adj.*)—going from one thing to another without any definite plan and enthusiasm—unfocussed, wavering: *Till he found guidence from his uncle, Peter wandered about in a desultory fashion after completing his graduation.*

**DETEST** (*verb*)—to hate somebody or something very much—loathe: *I detest TV serials that lack imagination.*

**DETRIMENT** (*noun*)—the act of causing harm or damage: *Several children are working in hazardous factories to the detriment of their health.*

**DEXTEROUS** (*adj.*)—skillful with one's hands: *My younger sister is so dexterous at making clay toys.*

**DICHOTOMY** (*noun*)—the separation that exists between two groups or things that are completely opposite to each other: *male female dichotomy.*

**DIKTAT** (*noun*)—the force that directs you to do something or choose a particular course of action: *dictats of circumstances*; also (disapproving) an order given by a government that the people must obey: *an American diktat from Washington DC.*

**DIMUNITIVE** (*adj.*)—very small, completely dominated by something else present alongside; also word or an ending that shows that something is small, like booklet, drumlet, leaflet.

**DISCERN** (*verb*)—to know, recognize or understand something that is not obvious—detect: *I discerned a little lack of enthusiasm in the class to repeat the exercise.*

**DISCREET** (*adj.*)—careful in what you say or do in order to avoid causing embarrassment—tactful: *You ought to have made some discreet enquires before joining the training institute.*

**DISGRUNTLED** (*adj.*)—annoyed or disappointed because something has happened to upset you: *I felt disgruntled when I was rejected in the interview even after a good performance.*

**DISPARAGE** (*verb*)—to suggest that something or somebody is not important or valuable—belittle: *The critics disparaged the author's new book.*

**DISRUPTIVE** (*adj.*)—causing problems, noise, etc. so that work cannot continue normally: *Disruptive elements in the procession forced the police to take action.*

**DISTRACTION** (*noun*)—the thing that takes your attention away from something you are doing on thinking about: *I could not concentrate on preparing my article because there were so many distractions.*

**DISTRAUGHT** (*adj.*)—extremely upset and anxious so that you cannot think clearly: *When my boss told me that my services were no longer required, I felt distraught and didn't know what to say or how to react.*

**DIVEST** (*verb*)—to take away somebody's belongings by cheating or trick: *The tricksters decided to divest the prince of his rich clothes.*

**DOSSIER** (*noun*)—a collection of documents that contain information about a person, event or subject—file:

*compile a dossier*; *I have a dossier on fashion garments.*

**DRUBBING** (*noun*)—a situation in sports where one team easily beats the other: *We gave the opponents a drubbing in the finals.*

---

**QUICK TEST–13**

**Match the words with their synonyms/meanings.**

| | | | |
|---|---|---|---|
| 1. | detrimental | a. | file |
| 2. | dossier | b. | skillful |
| 3. | divest | c. | lonely, sad |
| 4. | detest | d. | injurious |
| 5. | desultory | e. | annoyed |
| 6. | dexterous | f. | disturbance |
| 7. | desolate | g. | rob |
| 8. | dichotomy | h. | loathe |
| 9. | distraction | i. | separation |
| 10. | disgruntled | j. | unfocused, wavering |

---

# E

**EARNEST** (*adj.*)—very serious and sincere: *earnest endeavours*; Idiom *in earnest* means more seriously and with more force or effort than before: *the preparations for the fair shall start in earnest from tomorrow.*

**EBULLIENT** (*adj.*)—full of confidence, energy and good humour: *The new MD of the company is an ebullient young man.*

**ECCENTRIC** (*adj.*)—considered by other people to be strange and unusual: *eccentric behaviour*.

**ECHELON** (*noun*)—a rank or position of authority in an organisation or society: *higher echelons*.

**EMANCIPATE** (*verb*)—to free somebody especially from legal, political or social restrictions—set free: *Even after more than 60 years of achieving independence we have not been able to emancipate women from exploitation and discrimination.*

**EMPATHY** (*noun*)—the ability to understand another person's feelings, experience, etc.: *Gandhi was rich but he had great empathy for the downtrodden.*

**EMPIRICAL** (*adj.*)—based on experiments and experience rather than ideas or theories: *This article contains a lot of empirical data.*

**EMULATE** (*verb*)—to try to do something as well as somebody else—copy: *Hillary Clinton was trying to emulate her husband—Bill Clinton—the former President of America.*

**ENCROACHMENT** (*noun*)—(disapproving) the act of using somebody else's area, time, rights, etc.: *In Delhi many houses and shops are an encroachment of public land.*

**ENSNARE** (*verb*)—to make somebody or something unable to escape from a difficult situation—trap: *Many young adolescents are ensnared in a life of terrorism and crime.*

**ENVISAGE** (*verb*)—to imagine what will happen in the future about some particular thing or situation: *It was envisaged that the share market cannot sustain itself at such a high level.*

ERSTWHILE (*adj.*)—former, something or somebody that recently was the person or thing described, but is no more: *erstwhile Soviet Union.*

ESCALATE (*verb*)—to become or make something greater, worse, more serious, etc.: *The prices of consumer durables have escalated recently.*

EXACERBATE (*verb*)—to make something worse, especially a disease or problem—aggravate: *Self medication at times exacerbates the ailment.*

EXASPERATE (*verb*)—to annoy or irritate somebody very much—infuriate; (*noun*)—*exasperation.*

EXODUS (*noun*)—a situation in which many people leave a place at the same time: *mass exodus from war-torn Iraq to neighbouring states.*

EXONERATE (*verb*)—to officially state that somebody is not responsible for something they have been blamed for: *Many encroachers of public land are likely to be exonerated under the new master plan.*

EXORBITANT (*adj.*)—(of a price) to be much high: *exorbitant prices/fees/fares/rents, etc.*

EXPEDIENT (*noun*)—an action that is useful or necessary for a particular purpose, though not always fair or right: *Bird flu in West Bengal was controlled by the expedient culling of chickens in many districts in the neighbouring states.*

EXPIATE (*verb*)—to accept punishment for something wrong you have done in order to show that you are sorry: *There is no shame in expiating for your guilt.*

## QUICK TEST–14

**Match the words with their synonyms/meanings.**

| | | |
|---|---|---|
| 1. eccentric | a. | previously existing |
| 2. expedient | b. | rank, position |
| 3. emancipate | c. | aggravate |
| 4. echelon | d. | trap |
| 5. emulate | e. | strange and unusual |
| 6. erstwhile | f. | useful, necessary |
| 7. ensnare | g. | very costly |
| 8. exacerbate | h. | follow, copy |
| 9. exorbitant | i. | increase, heighten |
| 10. escalate | j. | free, liberate |

## F

**FABULOUS** (*adj.*)—extremely good: *That was a fabulous performance;* very good: *fabulous wealth/riches/beauty.*

**FACADE** (*noun*)—the front of a building, the way that somebody/something appears to be, which is different from the way somebody/something really is: *She managed to maintain a facade of indifference.*

**FACILITATE** (*verb*)—to make an action or a process possible or easier: *The new trade agreement should facilitate more rapid economic growth. Structured teaching facilitates learning.*

**FAIR-WEATHER** (*adj.*)—behaving in a particular way or doing a particular activity only when it is pleasant for them: *A fair-weather friend.*

**FAIT ACCOMPLI** (*noun*)—something that has already happened or been done and that you cannot change.

**FASTIDIOUS** (*adj.*)—being careful that every detail of something is correct: *Everything has to be planned in fastidious detail.*

**FATALISM** (*noun*)—the belief that events are decided by fate and that you cannot control them; the fact of accepting that you cannot prevent something from happening.

**FATHOM** (*verb*)—to understand or find an explanation for something: *It is hard to fathom the pain felt at the death of a child;* (*noun*)—a unit for measuring the depth of water, equal to 6 feet or 1.8 metres: *The ship sank in 20 fathoms.*

**FAUX PAS** (*noun*)—an action or a remark that causes embarrassment because it is not socially correct.

**FELICITOUS** (*adj.*)—chosen well; very suitable, giving a good result: *A felicitous turn of phrase.*

**FELONY** (*noun*)—the act of committing a serious crime such as murder or rape.

**FEND** (*verb*)—to take care of yourself without help from anyone else: *His father agreed to pay the rent for his flat but otherwise left him to fend for himself.*

**FEUD** (*noun*)—an angry and bitter argument between two people or groups of people that continues over a long period of time: *A long running feud between the two artists;* (*verb*)—to have an angry and bitter argument with somebody over a long period of time: *Stories of bitter feuding between rival business tycoons.*

**FIASCO** (*noun*)—something that does not succeed: often in a way that causes embarrassment: *The event was a fiasco.*

**FLAMBOYANT** (*adj.*)—different, confident and exciting in a way that attracts attention: *A flamboyant gesture/style/personality.*

## QUICK TEST–15

**Match the words with their synonyms/meanings.**

| | | | |
|---|---|---|---|
| 1. facilitate | | a. | hard to please |
| 2. fiasco | | b. | serious crime |
| 3. fabulous | | c. | causing embarrassment |
| 4. fastidious | | d. | failure |
| 5. fathom | | e. | already happened |
| 6. felony | | f. | gauge |
| 7. feud | | g. | make easy |
| 8. faux pas | | h. | take care of yourself |
| 9. fend | | i. | marvellous |
| 10. fait accompli | | j. | bitter argument |

FLAUNT (*verb*)—to show something you are proud of, to other people, in order to impress them: *One should never flaunt one's wealth.*

FLOUNDER (*verb*)—to struggle to know what to say or do or have to continue with something—fumble: *His abrupt change of subject left her floundering;* (*noun*)—a small flat sea fish that is used for food.

FOIBLE (*noun*)—a silly habit on a strange or weak aspect of a person's character that is considered harmless by other people: *We should learn to tolerate each other's little foibles.*

FOOLHARDY (*adj.*)—taking unnecessary risks: *it would be foolhardy to drive in fog.*

FORBEARANCE (*noun*)—the quality of being patient and sympathetic towards other people, especially when they have done something wrong.

FORTHRIGHT (*adj.*)—direct and honest in manner and speech: *I am a man of forthright views.*

FORTUITOUS (*adj.*)—happening by chance, especially a lucky chance that brings good result—accidental.

FRACAS (*noun*)—A noisy argument or fight, usually involving several people.

FULMINATE (*verb*)—to criticize somebody/something angrily: *The minister's irresponsible statement was fulminated by the whole house.*

FURORE (*noun*)—great anger or excitement shown by a number of persons usually caused by a public event—uproar: *The elections cause a lot of furore in every constituency in India.*

## QUICK TEST–16

**Match the words with their synonyms/meanings.**

| | | | |
|---|---|---|---|
| 1. | flounder | a. | fumble |
| 2. | fracas | b. | criticize strongly |
| 3. | flaunt | c. | taking unnecessary risk |
| 4. | forthright | d. | make a show-off |
| 5. | fulminate | e. | accidental |
| 6. | foible | f. | direct and honest |
| 7. | foolhardy | g. | uproar |
| 8. | forbearance | h. | patience and sympathy |
| 9. | fortuitous | i. | a noisy argument |
| 10. | furore | j. | a silly habit |

# G

**Gaffe** (*noun*)—a mistake that a person makes in public or in a social situation, especially something embarrassing.

**Gainsay** (*verb*)—to say that something is not true; to disagree with or deny something: *You cannot gainsay his claims.*

**Gallows** (*noun*)—a structure on which people, for example criminals are killed by hanging: *to send a man to the gallows.*

**Galore** (*adj.*)—In large quantities: *There will be games and prizes galore.*

**Galvanize** (*verb*)—to make somebody take action by shocking them or by making them excited: *They were galvanized with action by the urgency of her voice.*

**Gambit** (*noun*)—a thing that somebody does or something that somebody says at the beginning of a situation or conversation, that is intended to give them some advantage; a move or moves made at the beginning of a game of Chess in order to gain an advantage later: *an opening gambit.*

**Gamesmanship** (*noun*)—the ability to win games by making your opponent less confident and using rules to your advantage.

**The Gamut** (*noun*)—the complete range of a particular kind of thing: *I have heard, this network provides the gamut of computer services.*

**Gargantuan** (*adj.*)—entirely large: *a gargantuan appetite.*

**Garnish** (*verb*)—to decorate a dish of food with a small amount of another food; (*noun*)—a small amount of food that is used to decorate a layer dish of food.

GAUDY (*adj.*)—brightly coloured in a way that lacks taste: *gaudy clothes.*

GEARED (*adj.*)—designed or organized to achieve a particular purpose, or to be suitable for a particular group of people: *The programme is geared to prepare students for the world of work.*

GENESIS (*noun*)—the beginning or origin of something.

GEOPHYSICS (*noun*)—the scientific study of the earth's atmosphere, oceans and climate.

GEOPOLITICS (*noun*)—the political relation between countries and groups of countries in the world, the study of these relations.

---

## QUICK TEST–17

**Match the words with their synonyms/meanings.**

| | | | |
|---|---|---|---|
| 1. | galore | a. | origin of something |
| 2. | genesis | b. | decorate |
| 3. | galvanize | c. | designed, organized |
| 4. | gainsay | d. | variety, range |
| 5. | garnish | e. | in large quantities |
| 6. | geared | f. | ability to win games |
| 7. | gargantuan | g. | incite |
| 8. | gamut | h. | deny something |
| 9. | gamesmanship | i. | brightly coloured |
| 10. | gaudy | j. | enormous |

---

GESTATION (*noun*)—the time that the young of a person or an animal develops inside its mother's body until it is born, the process of developing inside the mother's body; the process by which an idea or a plan develops:

*The gestation period of a horse is about eleven months.*

**GHETTO** (*noun*)—an area of a city where many people of the same race or background live, separately from the rest of the population: *Ghettos are often crowded, with bad living conditions.*

**GIBBERISH** (*noun*)—words that have no meaning or are impossible to understand: *You are talking gibberish in your sleep.*

**GLAMOUR** (*noun*)—the attractive and inciting quality that makes a person, a job or a place seen special, often because of wealth or status; physical beauty that alone suggests wealth or success: *Bollywood actors and actresses are dazzled by the glamour of hollywood.*

**GLARING** (*adj.*)—very easily seen; very bright and unpleasant; angry, aggressive: *glaring eyes.*

**GLEAN** (*verb*)—to obtain information or knowledge, sometimes with difficulty and often from various different places: *These figures have been gleaned from a number of studies.*

**GLOAT** (*verb*)—to show that you are happy about your own success or somebody else's failure, in an unpleasant way: *She gloated over her cousin's disappointment.*

**GODSEND** (*noun*)—something good that happens unexpectedly and helps somebody/something when they need help: *This benefit is a godsend for low income families.*

**GO-GETTER** (*noun*)—a person who is determined to succeed, especially in business.

**GORGEOUS** (*adj.*)—very beautiful and attractive, giving pleasure and enjoyment: *a gorgeous woman.*

**GRAPEVINE** (*noun*)—by talking in an informal way to other people: *I heard on the grapevine that you are leaving.*

**GRASS-ROOTS** (*noun*)—ordinary people in society or in an organization, rather than the leaders or people who make decisions: *We need support at grass-roots level.*

**GRATIS** (*adj.*)—done or given without having to be paid for: *He gave a gratis copy of a book to me.*

**GRATUITOUS** (*adj.*)—done without any good reason or purpose and after having harmful effects: gratuitous violence on television.

**GRIEVANCE** (*noun*)—something that you think is unfair and that you complain or protest about: *This company has a proper grievance procedure.*

---

### QUICK TEST–18

**Match the words with their synonyms/meanings.**

| | | | |
|---|---|---|---|
| 1. | gibberish | a. | happy over others' failure |
| 2. | gratuitous | b. | period of development |
| 3. | grassroots | c. | meaningless |
| 4. | gloat | d. | something good happening unexpectedly |
| 5. | grapevine | e. | perceptible |
| 6. | gestation | f. | basic |
| 7. | glaring | g. | determined to succeed |
| 8. | godsend | h. | rumour |
| 9. | go-getter | i. | free |
| 10. | gratis | j. | done without reason or purpose |

**GRIMACE** (*verb*)—to make an ugly impression with your face to show pain, disgust etc: *He grimaced as the needle went in;* (*noun*)—an ugly expression made by twisting your face, used to show pain, disgust, etc. or to make somebody laugh: *to give a grimace of pain.*

**GRISLY** (*adj.*)—entirely unpleasant and frightening and usually connected with death and violence: *a grisly crime.*

**GRIT** (*noun*)—very small pieces of stone or sand: *A piece of grit went in my eye;* (*verb*)—to spread grit, salt or sand on a road that is covered with ice; to bite your teeth tightly together: *She gritted her teeth against the pain.*

**GROTESQUE** (*adj.*)—strange in a way that is unpleasant or offensive: *It's grotesque to expect a person of his experience to work for so little money;* (*noun*)—a person who is entirely ugly in a strange way: *a style of art using grotesque figures.*

**GRUMBLE** (*verb*)—to complain about somebody/something in a bad-tempered way: *She's always grumbling about something or the other;* (*noun*)—something that you complain about because you are not satisfied: *Her main grumble is about the lack of privacy.*

**GRUNT** (*verb, noun*)—to make a short low sound in the throat, especially to show that you are in pain, annoyed or not interested: *She grunted something about being late and rushed out.*

**GUNG-HO** (*adj.*)—too enthusiastic about something, without thinking seriously about it, especially about fighting and war.

## QUICK TEST–19

**Match the words with their synonyms/meanings.**

| | | | |
|---|---|---|---|
| 1. | grunt | a. | show disgust |
| 2. | gung-ho | b. | extremely unpleasant |
| 3. | grimace | c. | strange, offensive |
| 4. | grotesque | d. | move in circles |
| 5. | grit | e. | force |
| 6. | grumble | f. | very enthusiastic about something |
| 7. | grisly | g. | sad, disappointed |
| 8. | gusto | h. | determination |
| 9. | gutted | i. | make short low sound |
| 10. | gyrate | j. | complain in a bad tempered way |

GUSTO (*noun*)—enthusiasm and energy in doing something: *The choir sang with gusto.*

GUTTED (*adj.*)—extremely sad or disappointed: *He felt gutted after being rejected in the interview.*

GYRATE (*verb*)—to move in circles: *The dancers gyrated around the fire and took rhythmic steps.*

## H

HABITAT (*noun*)—the place where a particular type of animal or plant is normally found: *The panda's habitat is the bamboo forest.*

HAGGLE (*verb*)—to argue to reach an agreement particularly about the price of something—bargain.

HANDIWORK (*noun*)—work that you do, or something that you have made especially using your artistic skill; something bad or tricky done by a particular person or group: *This sabotage is the handiwork of members of a dissident group.*

HANKER (*verb*)—to have strong desire for something: *He hankered after wealth all his life.*

HARDCORE (*noun*)—the small central group in an organization or in a particular group of people, who are most active or who never change their belief or behaviour: *hardcore terrorists.*

HARD-EDGED (*adj.*)—powerful, true to life and not affected by emotion: hard-edged realism of Jhumpa Lahiri's novels.

HARD-PRESSED (*adj.*)—having a lot of problems such as too much work, too little time or money; having to do something which is quite difficult: *I was hard-pressed to find the lap top desired by my father.*

HARMONY (*noun*)—a state of peaceful existence and agreement: *racial/social harmony;* different notes in music sung together: *Bethoven's fifth harmony;* pleasing combination of related things: *harmony of colours/ designs.*

HAUTE COUTURE (*noun*)—the business of making fashionable and expensive clothes for women.

HAWKISH (*adj.*)—prefering to use military action rather than peaceful discussion to solve a political problem— dovish: *The hawkish attitude of some countries has lead to widespread violence in several parts of the globe.*

**Haywire** (*adj.*)—*go hawire*—to stop working correctly or go out of control—awry: *After the resignation of chairman, things went haywire in the company.*

**Hazard** (*noun*)—a thing that can be dangerous or cause damage: *fire/safety/hazard, health hazard*; (*verb*)—to make a suggestion: *hazard a guess.*

**Heady** (*adj.*)—having a strong effect on your senses, making you feel excited, confident, intoxicating, the heady days of youth; heady mixture of fear and desire; excited in a way that makes you do things without worrying about consequences: *Some people become heady with success.*

**Hegemony** (*noun*)—control by one country, organization, etc. over other countries within a particular group: *hegemonic control.*

**Herald** (*verb*)—to be a sign that something is going to happen: *Indo-US nuclear deal will herald a new era of energy security in India.*

**Heritage** (*noun*)—the history, traditions and qualities that a country or society has had for many years and are considered an important part of its character: *India's rich cultural heritage.*

**Heroics** (*noun*)—actions that are brave and determined: *India won the final, thanks to Dhoni's heroics in the slog overs.*

**Hide Bound** (*adj.*)—having old fashined ideas, rather than accepting new ways of thinking—narrow-minded.

**Hideout** (*noun*)—a place where somebody goes when they do not want anyone to find them: *Many deadly weapons were found in the terrorists' hideouts.*

**HIGH-HANDED** (*adj.*)—using authority in an unreasonable way, without considering the opinion of other people—overbearing: *The high-handed boss was not popular among the employees.*

---

### QUICK TEST–20

**Match the words with their synonyms/meanings.**

| | | | |
|---|---|---|---|
| 1. | haggle | a. | make a suggestion |
| 2. | hard-edged | b. | old-fashioned |
| 3. | hawkish | c. | excited |
| 4. | hazard | d. | awry |
| 5. | haywire | e. | bargain |
| 6. | herald | f. | in difficulties |
| 7. | hegemony | g. | true to life |
| 8. | hidebound | h. | control |
| 9. | heady | i. | dovish |
| 10. | hard-pressed | j. | signal |

---

**HINDRANCE** (*noun*)—a roadblock in some task or work: *Sometimes rain is more of a hindrance than help for the farmer;* also the act of making something more difficult.

**HINDSIGHT** (*noun*)—retrospection about something done in the past, an understanding after reflection about some past action that tells you that it could have been done better, differently: *With hindsight it is easy to say that....*

**HOLISTIC** (*adj.*)—considering the whole thing, rather than a collection of parts: *A holistic approach to peace;* the whole person rather than just the symptoms of a disease: *Yoga's approach to good health is holistic rather than symptomatic.*

**HOMESTEAD** (*noun*)—a house with its surroundings, particularly a farm.

**HONE** (*verb*)—develop and improve something, especially a skill over a period of time: *Many institutions hone the debating skills of the students.*

**HORRENDOUS** (*adj.*)—extremely shocking—horrific; extremely unpleasant and unacceptable: *There is horrendous pollution in several industrial cities.*

**HORSE-TRADING** (*noun*)—discussing business with somebody using clever or secret methods to reach an agreement that suits.

**HUNKY-DORY** (*adj.*)—*everything is hunky-dory* means that there are no problems and everyone is happy.

---

## QUICK TEST–21

**Match the words with their synonyms/meanings.**

| | | | |
|---|---|---|---|
| 1. | hindsight | a. | discussing business using secret methods |
| 2. | hindrance | b. | fine |
| 3. | horrendous | c. | home with surroundings |
| 4. | horse-trading | d. | develop and improve |
| 5. | hunky-dory | e. | total |
| 6. | holistic | f. | obstacle |
| 7. | homestead | g. | horrific |
| 8. | hone | h. | in retrospection |

## I

**ICONOCLAST** (*noun*)—a person who is critical of popular beliefs, established customs or ideas.

**IDIOSYNCRASY** (*noun*)—somebody's unusual way of behaving or thinking; an unusual feature—eccentricity: *I was surprised at the idiosyncrasies of our new teacher.*

**IDYLL** (*noun*)—a happy and peaceful place, event or experience, particularly the one connected with the countryside; also a short poem or piece of writing that describes a happy, peaceful scene: *Shelley's idylls are remarkable.*

**IGNOBLE** (*adj.*)—not good or honest, something that makes you feel shame—base: *if ignoble thoughts come to your mind, the best thing is to pray.*

**IGNOMINIOUS** (*adj.*)—an act or situation that makes you feel ashamed—humiliating: *The champion suffered an ignominious defeat at the hands of an unseeded player.*

**ILLUSTRIOUS** (*adj.*)—very famous, admired because of some high accomplishments—distinguished: *Sachin has established several world records in his illustrious career.*

**IMBECILE** (*noun*)—a rude way to describe an idiotic person—stupid.

**IMBIBE** (*verb*)—to absorb something, especially an idea or information: *Education is about imbibing noble and practical information on the given topics.*

**IMBROGLIO** (*noun*)—a complicated situation that causes confusion or embarrassment: *Both Republicans and Democrats were involved in the imbroglio over Presidential elections.*

IMPETUOUS (*adj.*)—done in haste and without thinking carefully about the possible consequences—rash, impulsive: *Impetuous acts often have us repenting later.*

IMPINGE (*verb*)—to have a noticeable effect on something or someone—encroach: *It is difficult not to let failures in work impinge on one's family life.*

IMPONDERABLE (*noun*)—something that is difficult to measure or estimate: *As there were too many imponderables, we could not foresee the impact of Annual Budget on the equity market.*

INCINERATE (*verb*)—to burn until it is completely destroyed: *High temperatures incinerate delicate plants.*

INCRIMINATE (*verb*)—to make seem that someone has done something illegal or offensive: *In a lie detector, wrong answers incriminate the accused.*

INDIGENOUS—(person) belonging or (thing) produced in a particular place (local) rather than brought from outside—native: *indigenous people/language/goods.*

## QUICK TEST–22

**Match the words with their synonyms/meanings.**

| | | | |
|---|---|---|---|
| 1. | idiosyncrasy | a. | local |
| 2. | illustrious | b. | critical of popular beliefs |
| 3. | imbecile | c. | humiliating |
| 4. | impinge | d. | wicked, base |
| 5. | indigenous | e. | absorb an idea |
| 6. | iconoclast | f. | eccentricity |

| 7. impetuous | g. encroach |
| 8. ignominious | h. admired |
| 9. ignoble | i. impulsive |
| 10. imbibe | j. stupid |

INDIGNANT (*adj.*)—very angry and surprised because of unfair treatment: *Many employees of the MNC were indignant when they were given the pink slips (asked to leave the job).*

INDULGENCE (*noun*)—(disapproving) the act or state of having or doing whatever you want to: *a life of indulgence; excessive indulgence in fast food; Grandparents often show limitless indulgence to their grandchildren.*

INEXORABLE (*adj.*)—that which cannot be stopped or changed—relentless: *There has been an inexorable decline in moral values in modern society.*

INEBRIATED (*adj.*)—drunk, unable to talk or conduct themselves properly: *He lost her love when he appeared before her in an inebriated condition.*

INFRINGE (*verb*)—(of an action) to break a law or rule: *The author has not infringed the copyright rules.*

INGRAINED (*adj.*)—that has existed for a long time and is therefore difficult to change—deep-rooted: *ingrained orthodoxy.*

INNOCUOUS (*adj.*)—not intended to offend or upset anyone—harmless: *Sometimes even innocuous remarks are mistaken to be offending.*

INNUENDO (*noun*)—an indirect remarks about something or somebody which are bad or rude: *This piece of writing is full of sexual innuendoes.*

**INSCRUTABLE** (*adj.*)—inscrutable expression of a person means it is hard to know what he/she is thinking or feeling; not showing any emotion.

**INSIDIOUS** (*adj.*)—(disapproving) spreading gradually or without being noticed, but causing serious harms: *The effects of obesity are often insidious and are realized later.*

**INSINUATE** (*verb*)—to suggest indirectly that something unpleasant is true—imply; to succeed in gaining somebody's respect, etc. to use it to your advantage.

**INSULATE** (*verb*)—to protect something with a material that prevents heat, electricity, cold, sound, etc. from passing through it; also to protect from unpleasant experiences: *The Indian stock market is not fully insulated from economic slowdowns in other countries.*

**INTIMIDATE** (*verb*)—to frighten or threaten somebody to make him/her do what you want: *They were accused of intimidating people into voting for their party.*

**IVORY TOWER** (*noun*)—disapproving a plea or situation where you are isolated from problems and practical aspects of life: *The protagonist of this novel remains in an ivory tower and is not aware of the realities of life.*

## QUICK TEST–23

**Match the words with their synonyms/meanings.**

| | | | |
|---|---|---|---|
| 1. | inexorable | a. | not showing any emotion |
| 2. | indignant | b. | threaten |
| 3. | innuendo | c. | relentless |

| | | | |
|---|---|---|---|
| 4. | ingrained | d. | break a rule |
| 5. | inscrutable | e. | drunk |
| 6. | insulate | f. | enraged |
| 7. | intimidate | g. | hint |
| 8. | ivory tower | h. | an isolated place |
| 9. | infringe | i. | deep-rooted |
| 10. | inebriated | j. | protect |

## J, K, L

**JEOPARDISE** (*verb*)—to put something or somebody in risk—endanger: *Gross indiscipline in college can jeopardize one's career.*

**JETTISON** (*verb*)—to throw something out of a moving plane or ship to make it lighter; get rid of something that is not required—discard; to reject an idea, belief or plan—abandon.

**JINGOISM** (*noun*)—(disapproving) a strong belief that your own country is the best.

**JITTERS** (*noun*)—the feeling of being anxious and nervous, especially before an important event or before having to do something difficult like an exam, an interview, etc.

**JUDICIOUS** (*adj.*)—careful and sensible, showing a balanced approach and judgement: *A judicious person scores over a flamboyant one in practical life.*

**JUNK MAIL**—(disapproving) advertising material that is sent to people without asking for it: *Junk mail and pesky calls are big headaches these days.*

**KALEIDOSCOPE** (*noun*)—a situation, pattern containing a lot of different parts that are always changing: *The book is virtually a kaleidoscope of Indian culture and society.*

**KICKSTART** (*verb*)—to do something to help a process start quickly: *The economic reforms have kickstarted the Indian economy.*

**KNOW-HOW** (*noun*)—knowledge of how to do something properly, particularly involving technology: *technical know-how.*

**KUDOS** (*noun*)—the respect and admiration that goes with a particular position/prestige: *Few persons get the kudos of playing for their country.*

**LABYRINTH** (*noun*)—a complicated series of paths through which it is difficult to find a way: *a labyrinth of rules and regulations for exporting goods.*

**LACONIC** (*adj.*)—using only a few words to say something—terse.

**LACUNA** (*noun*)—a place where something is missing in a piece of writing or in an idea or plan—gap. The word is also used to denote a shortcoming in an idea or theory.

**LAISSEZ-FAIRE** (*noun*)—the policy where there is little or no government control, and private businesses are allowed to develop freely.

**LAVISH** (*adj.*)—large, impressive and usually costing a lot of money—extravagant: *lavish gifts/celebrations/lifestyle;* doing or giving something generously: *lavish praise.*

**LEGACY** (*noun*)—money or property that is given to you by somebody (your forefathers) when they pass away; a situation that exists now because of the events, actions of the past: *a legacy of rich culture.*

**LEIT MOTIF** (*noun*)—an idea or a phrase that is repeated often in a book or work of art or is typical of a particular group or person.

LEVERAGE (*noun*)—the ability to influence what people do: *Diplomatic leverage by India and America has brought the two countries closer.*

LOQUACIOUS (*adj.*)—talking a lot—talkative, a chatterbox: *Anne Frank was a loquacious girl.*

LUMINARY (*noun*)—a person who is an expert or a great influence in a special area of activity: *Many luminaries in the field of education have been guiding the students through their lectures and books.*

LURKING (*adj.*)—something who is around in a stealthy way to do something bad or illegal: *I could sense the lurking danger in that farmhouse.*

---

### QUICK TEST–24

**Match the words with their synonyms/meanings.**

|     |            |     |                    |
| --- | ---------- | --- | ------------------ |
| 1.  | lurk       | a.  | repeated often     |
| 2.  | leverage   | b.  | abandon            |
| 3.  | leit motif | c.  | gap                |
| 4.  | jitters    | d.  | skulk              |
| 5.  | loquacious | e.  | web                |
| 6.  | jettison   | f.  | ability to improve |
| 7.  | lacuna     | g.  | shivering in anxiety |
| 8.  | legacy     | h.  | inheritance        |
| 9.  | labyrinth  | i.  | terse              |
| 10. | laconic    | j.  | talkative          |

---

## M

MAELSTROM (*noun*)—a situation full of strong emotions or confusing events that is hard to control and makes you feel frightened; also a strong current of water that moves in circles—whirlpool.

**Mainstay** (*noun*)—a person or thing that is the most important part of something and enables it to exist or be successful: *In two decades, industry not agriculture shall be the mainstay of India's economy.*

**Malaise** (*noun*)—the problem affecting a particular situation or a group of people: *economic/social malaise*; a general feeling of being ill, unhappy or unsatisfied—unease.

**Malice** (*noun*)—a feeling of hatred for somebody that causes a desire to harm them: *He sent her a threatening e-mail out of malice.*

**Manoeuvre** (*verb*)—a movement performed with care and skill; a clean plan, action or movement that is used to get an advantage: *Nano is easy to manoeuvre through narrow roads and busy traffic.*

**Mantle** (*noun*)—the role and responsibilities of an important person or job: *After Dhirubhai Ambani the mantle fell on his two sons Mukesh and Anil Ambani*; a cover around a flame of a gas lamp; also a loose piece of clothing.

**Maroon** (*adj.*)—dark brownish red in colour; (*verb*)—to leave somebody in a place that they cannot escape from, e.g. an island: *After the shipwreck they were marooned in an unknown island in the Pacific Ocean.*

**Maverick** (*noun*)—a person who does not behave like or think like anyone else but who has many independent options; also *adj.*: *maverick filmmaker.*

**Mayhem** (*noun*)—confusion and fear, usually caused by a violent behaviour or a sudden shocking event: *After the* *fire broke out in the hotel, there was a mayhem as everyone wanted to get out first.*

**MEANDER** (*verb*)—(of a river or stream) to move in curves rather than flow straight; (of persons) to walk slowly and change directions frequently—wander.

**MELANCHOLY** (*noun*)—a deep feeling of sadness that lasts for a long time and often without explanation; (*adj.*)—very sad and making you feel despondent—mournful.

**MEMENTO** (*noun*)—a thing that you keep or give somebody to remind you or them of a place, person, event, occasion, etc.—souvenir.

**MENIAL** (*adj.*)—not skilled or important, and often boring and lowly paid: *menial job/work/task.*

**MERCENARY** (*noun*)—a soldier who is ready to fight for any group of country that offers payment; (*adj.*)—only interested in making or getting money.

**MISANTHROPE** (*noun*)—a person who hates and avoids other people.

**MISGIVING** (*noun*)—feeling of doubt or anxiety about what may happen: *I have misgivings about visiting Jaipur in such hot weather.*

**MITIGATE** (*verb*)—to make something less harmful, serious, etc.—alleviate: *The National Employment Guarantee Scheme aims to mitigate the effect of poverty in rural areas.*

**MONOTONOUS** (*adj.*)—very boring and dull; repetitious: *monotonous work/diet/routine.*

**MUNDANE** (*adj.*)—not interesting or exciting—dull, ordinary: *a mundane job*; also worldly, belonging to the ordinary affairs of life.

**MYSTIQUE** (*noun*)—the quality of being mysterious or secret that makes something or somebody seem attractive or interesting: *The mystique surrounding the novels of J.K. Rowling.*

---

### QUICK TEST–25
**Match the words with their synonyms/meanings.**

| | | | |
|---|---|---|---|
| 1. | mayhem | a. | alleviate |
| 2. | mundane | b. | souvenir |
| 3. | mitigate | c. | confusion |
| 4. | mercenary | d. | whirlpool |
| 5. | memento | e. | most important part |
| 6. | melancholy | f. | dull/worldly |
| 7. | malice | g. | an ill-feeling |
| 8. | mainstay | h. | only interested in getting money |
| 9. | maelstrom | i. | mournful |
| 10. | mantle | j. | responsibility |

---

## N & O

**NAGGING** (*adj.*)—continuing for a long time and difficult to stop, cure or remove: *a nagging pain/doubt.*

**NAIVE** (*adj.*)—(disapproving) lacking experience of life, good judgement or knowledge; innocent and simple—artless: *His first novel was a naive attempt to capture the realities of life.*

**NASCENT** (*adj.*)—beginning to exist, not fully developed: *The research for the cure of AIDS is only at the nascent stage.*

**NONCHALANT** (*adj.*)—behaving in a calm, relaxed way; feeling no anxiety—casual, carefree.

**NURTURE** (*verb*)—to care for and protect somebody or something while they are growing and developing—foster; (*noun*)—care and support given to something or somebody: *nurture the idea of peaceful to existence.*

**OBDURATE** (*adj.*)—refusing to change your mind or your actions—stubborn.

**OBLITERATE** (*verb*)—to remove all signs of something by destroying or covering it: *The snow has completely obliterated the road.*

**OBNOXIOUS** (*adj.*)—offending, extremely unpleasant: *obnoxious behaviour.*

**OBVIATE** (*verb*)—to remove the need or necessity for something: *Recent rain has obviated the need for watering the fields in this area.*

**OFFICIOUS** (*adj.*)—eager to tell people what to do, self-important, meddlesome: *Officious colleagues though sometimes helpful, are a source of annoyance.*

**OMINOUS** (*adj.*)—suggesting that something bad is going to happen in the future—foreboding: *Ominous winds started blowing before the tornado.*

**ONEROUS** (*adj.*)—needing great effort, causing worry and trouble: *The world economy is faced with the onerous task of achieving inclusive growth.*

**OPPORTUNE** (*adj.*)—suitable for doing a particular thing so that it succeeds—favourable: *opportune time/moment*; (of an action) done or happening at the appropriate time: *an opportune remark.*

**OSTRACIZE** (*verb*)—to turn someone out of a social group, refuse to meet or talk to—shun: *The union leader was* *ostracized by the workers for not supporting the proposed strike.*

**OVERARCHING** (*adj.*)—extremely important, because it includes or influences many things: *Developing non-conventional sources of energy is the overarching need of modern times.*

---

### QUICK TEST–26

**Match the words with their synonyms/meanings.**

|   |   |   |   |
|---|---|---|---|
| 1. | ostracize | a. | protect, develop |
| 2. | naive | b. | arduous |
| 3. | nonchalant | c. | carefree |
| 4. | nurture | d. | remove the need |
| 5. | overarching | e. | stubborn |
| 6. | onerous | f. | initial, not developed |
| 7. | obnoxious | g. | most important |
| 8. | obviate | h. | turn out of a social group |
| 9. | nascent | i. | offending, damaging |
| 10. | obdurate | j. | artless |

---

## P

**PAINSTAKING** (*adj.*)—needing a lot of care, effort and attention to details—thorough: *The Union Budget has been prepared with painstaking attention to look after all aspects of economic development.*

**PALATABLE** (*adj.*)—(of food, drink) having a relishable taste; pleasant or acceptable: *The story of this film—an adaptation from a famous novel—has been slightly changed to make it palatable to cinegoers.*

**PALPABLE** (*adj.*)—that is easily noticed by the senses or the mind: *The tension in the examination hall was almost palpable.*

**PANDEMIC** (*noun*)—a disease that spreads over a whole country or the whole word: *We must take necessary precautions before AIDS becomes pandemic.*

**PARANOIA** (*noun*)—a mental disease in which a person starts behaving that other people are trying to harm him/her; fear or suspicion of other people when there is no reason/evidence to do so.

**PARLANCE** (*noun*)—a particular way of using words or expressing by a group: *legal/common parlance.*

**PAROCHIAL** (*adj.*)—(disapproving) only concerned with small issues of local/regional area, not interested in more important issues—*narrow*: *The broad-based development demands that we should come out of parochial considerations.*

**PARTISAN** (*adj.*)—(often disapproving) showing too much support for one group, idea or person without considering it carefully: *Even the partisan crowd of spectators applauded when Yuvraj played a blinder of an innings;* (*noun*)—a person who strongly supports a particular group....

**PEDANTIC** (*adj.*)—(disapproving) too worried about small details or rules.

**PEEVISH** (*adj.*)—easily annoyed by unimportant things—ill-tempered.

**PEJORATIVE** (*adj.*)—a remark that expresses disapproval or criticism: *the word used in a pejorative sense.*

**PERFUNCTORY** (*adj.*)—(of an action) done as a duty, without real interest, attention or feeling: *a perfunctory nod/smile.*

**PITTANCE** (*noun*)—a very small amount of money that somebody receives as a wage and is hardly enough to live on: *I'm working for a pittance.*

**PLAUSIBLE** (*adj.*)—(of an excuse or explanation) reasonable and likely to be true: *He could not offer any plausible excuse for his long absence from duty.*

**PLUMMET** (*verb*)—to fall quickly and suddenly from a high position or level: *The share prices plummeted at Dow Jones following the news of recession in American economy.*

**PORTEND** (*verb*)—to be a sign of warning of something bad or unpleasant that is going to happen in the future—foreshadow.

**PRECEDENT** (*noun*)—an official action or decision that has happened in the past: *a set of precedents for future cases of cybercrime*; a similar action or event that has happened earlier.

**PRE-EMPTIVE** (*adj.*)—done to stop somebody taking action especially action that is considered harmful to yourself: *pre-emptive action.*

**PREPOSTEROUS** (*adj.*)—totally unreasonable in a way that is shocking—outrageous: *Politicians use preposterous methods to grind their axe.*

**PREVARICATE** (*verb*)—to avoid giving a direct answer to the question to hide the truth—beat about the bush.

**PRIMORDIAL** (*adj.*)—existing from the beginning of the world—primeval; a basic feeling or desire: *primordial impulses.*

**PUNTER** (*noun*)—a person who buys or uses a particular product or service: *In today's market, advertisement is necessary to sustain a clientele of punters.*

## QUICK TEST–27

**Match the words with their synonyms/meanings.**

1. prevaricate
2. preposterous
3. palatable
4. paranoia
5. partisan
6. parochial
7. pejorative
8. perfunctory
9. plausible
10. parlance

a. fear of harm by others
b. supporting a particular group
c. beat about the bush
d. done without interest
e. reasonable
f. outrageous
g. particular way of using words
h. easily noticeable
i. expressing disapproval
j. narrow-minded

## Q & R

**QUAGMIRE** (*noun*)—an area of soft wet ground—bog; difficult or dangerous situation—morass.

**QUALM** (*noun*)—a feeling of doubt or worry about whether you are doing something right—misgiving: *Confident people have no qualms about their deeds.*

**QUANTIFY** (*verb*)—to describe or express something as an amount or a number: *Risk to health due to environmental pollution cannot be quantified.*

**QUARANTINE** (*noun*)—a period of time when an animal or person that has or may have a disease is kept away from others to prevent the disease from spreading.

**QUEST** (*noun*)—a long search for something especially a quality like happiness, peace of mind: *quest for knowledge.*

**QUINTESSENCE** (*noun*)—the perfect example of something; the most important feature of something—*essence: The book captures the quintessence of Indian society.*

**QUIXOTIC** (*adj.*)—involving plans or ideas that show imagination but are usually not practical.

**RADICAL** (*adj.*)—concerning the most basic and important parts of something; thorough and complete—far-reaching: *radical changes*; new, different and likely to impact something: *radical solution/proposals.*

**RAMIFICATION** (*noun*)—large and unexpected results of an action or decision: *social ramification of economic policies.*

**RAVISHING** (*adj.*)—extremely beautiful, gorgeous: *a ravishing beauty.*

**RECALCITRANT** (*adj.*)—unwilling to obey rules or follow instruction; difficult to control: *The UNO has problem with recalcitrant nations which are proliferating nuclear technology.*

**REDOUBTABLE** (*adj.*)—having very strong qualities that make you respect a person or feel afraid of them—formidable.

**REMNANT** (*noun*)—a part of something that is left after other parts have been used, destroyed or removed—remains: *Those trees are remnants of a big grove that existed till the last decade.*

**REMONSTRATE** (*verb*)—to protest or complain about something or somebody: *The importers have remonstrated about the sudden increase in tariff.*

RESTIVE (*adj.*)—unable to stay calm, restless; wanting some excitement.

RETROGRESSIVE (*adj.*)—(disapproving) returning to old-fashioned ideas or methods instead of making progress: *The legislation to reduce import duty was a retrogressive step.*

RHETORIC (*noun*)—(often disapproving) a writing or speech that is intended to influence people but is not completely true or honest: *the rhetoric of India shining.*

RUKUS (*noun*)—a situation where there is a noisy activity.

---

## QUICK TEST–28

**Match the words with their synonyms/meanings.**

| | | | |
|---|---|---|---|
| 1. | quagmire | a. | noisy situation |
| 2. | rhetoric | b. | difficult to control |
| 3. | rukus | c. | effect |
| 4. | quest | d. | difficult situation |
| 5. | ravishing | e. | thorough, far-reaching |
| 6. | recalcitrant | f. | speech/writing intended to influence people |
| 7. | restive | g. | protest, complain |
| 8. | ramification | h. | very beautiful |
| 9. | radical | i. | search |
| 10. | remonstrate | j. | restless |

# S

**SABOTAGE** (*noun*)—the act of doing deliberate damage to equipment, transport, machines, etc. (*verb*)—to prevent something from being successful: *The dissidents tried to sabotage the new plan.*

**SAGACIOUS** (*adj.*)—showing good judgement and understanding—wise, discreet.

**SANGUINE** (*adj.*)—cheerful and confident about the future—optimistic: *I am sanguine about the India's share market.*

**SATURATION** (*noun*)—the state of progress when no more of something can be accepted, where no further improvement or addition is possible: *My pay-scale has reached saturation point, no further increment can be given to me.*

**SCRUPULOUS** (*adj.*)—careful about paying attention to every detail—meticulous; careful about being honest and knowing and doing what is right.

**SEDENTARY** (*adj.*)—(work, activity, etc.) in which you spend a lot of time sitting down; involving very little physical exercise/activity: *sedentary job/lifestyle.*

**SEMINAL** (*adj.*)—very important and having a strong influence on later developments: *a seminal study/article.*

**SERVITUDE** (*noun*)—the condition of being a slave or being forced to obey another person—slavery.

**SKULK** (*verb*)—(disapproving) to hide or move around quickly, especially when you are planning something bad: *Someone was skulking behind the railings of the park.*

**SLANDER** (*noun*)—a false statement (spoken) intended to damage the good opinion people have of somebody: *a vicious slander on company's products.*

**SNEAK** (*verb*)—to go somewhere secretly, trying to avoid being seen: *sneaked into the gathering*; to do something or take something or somebody secretly, without permission.

**SOLACE** (*noun*)—a feeling of emotional comfort when you are sad or disappointed—comfort: *After losing money in gambling he found solace in wine.*

**SUCCOUR** (*noun*)—help that you give to somebody who is suffering or having problem.

**SUMPTUOUS** (*adj.*)—very expensive and looking very impressive: *a sumptuous meal.*

**SUPERFICIAL** (*adj.*)—not looking or studying deeply or thoroughly; seeing only what is obvious; appearing to be true, real or important until you look at it more carefully; only affecting the surface.

**SURFEIT** (*noun*)—an amount of something that is too large—excess.

**SYNERGY** (*noun*)—extra energy, power, success, etc. that is achieved by two or more people or companies working together.

---

## QUICK TEST–29

**Match the words with their synonyms/meanings.**

| | | | |
|---|---|---|---|
| 1. | surfeit | a. | very careful |
| 2. | sumptuous | b. | relief |
| 3. | sanguine | c. | expensive & impressive |

| 4. scrupulous | d. deliberate damage |
| 5. servitude | e. extra energy achieved by working together |
| 6. succour | f. excess |
| 7. sagacious | g. discreet |
| 8. sabotage | h. optimistic |
| 9. synergy | i. false statement |
| 10. slander | j. slavery |

# T, U, V, W, X, Y & Z

**TANTRUM** (*noun*)—a sudden short period of angry, unreasonable behaviour: *Australian cricketers' tantrums in the ground irked Indian spectators.*

**TEMPESTUOUS** (*adj.*)—full of extreme emotions—stormy: *a tempestuous relationship/behaviour.*

**TEMPORAL** (*adj.*)—connected with real, physical world rather than spiritual.

**TENACITY** (*noun*)—the state or quality of being determined: *She completed with skill and tenacity.*

**THRIVE** (*verb*)—to become and continue to be strong, healthy and successful: *Animals do not thrive well in captivity.*

**TRANQUIL** (*adj.*)—quiet and peaceful—serene: tranquil waters of Dal lake.

**TRANSITION** (*noun*)—the process or period of change from one state or condition to another: *Last two decades have been of great transition in Indian society.*

**TRANSITORY** (*adj.*)—lasting only for a short period of time—fleeting, evanescent.

**ULTERIOR** (*adj.*)—(of a reason for doing something) that which is hidden and not admitted: *ulterior motive*.

**UNABASHED** (*adj.*)—not ashamed, embarrassed or affected by people's disapproval.

**UNDERMINE** (*verb*)—to make something (somebody's authority, confidence) gradually weaker or less effective.

**VANGUARD** (*noun*)—the leaders of a movement in society, e.g. in politics, art, industry, etc.: *vanguard of scientific progress*.

**VULNERABLE** (*adj.*)—weak and easily hurt physically or emotionally: *Illiterate persons are more vulnerable to exploitation*.

**WEIRD** (*adj.*)—strange, unusual difficult to explain, strange in a mysterious way—*eerie*.

**XENOPHOBIA** (*noun*)—a strong feeling of dislike or fear of people from other countries.

**YONDER** (*adj.*)—over there, at a distance: *yonder tree/rock*.

**ZEALOT** (*noun*)—a person who is extremely enthusiastic about something especially religion or politics—fanatic.

---

## QUICK TEST–30

**Match the words with their synonyms/meanings.**

| | | | |
|---|---|---|---|
| 1. | tranquil | a. | determination |
| 2. | zealot | b. | fleeting |
| 3. | tenacity | c. | calm, quiet |
| 4. | tantrum | d. | weaken |

| | | | |
|---|---|---|---|
| 5. | transitory | e. | strange |
| 6. | undermine | f. | extremely enthusiastic |
| 7. | vanguard | g. | hidden |
| 8. | weird | h. | angry unreasonable behaviour |
| 9. | transition | i. | change |
| 10. | ulterior | j. | protection of a cause |

# ANSWERS

## QUICK TEST–1

1 — d; 2 — f; 3 — a; 4 — h; 5 — b; 6 — i; 7 — c; 8 — e; 9 — g; 10 — j.

## QUICK TEST–2

1 — f; 2 — h; 3 — a; 4 — i; 5 — b; 6 — c; 7 — j; 8 — d; 9 — e; 10 — g.

## QUICK TEST–3

1 — g; 2 — c; 3 — i; 4 — e; 5 — a; 6 — d; 7 — j; 8 — h; 9 — b; 10 — f.

## QUICK TEST–4

1 — h; 2 — d; 3 — a; 4 — g; 5 — i; 6 — b; 7 — c; 8 — e; 9 — f; 10 — j.

## QUICK TEST–5

1 — d; 2 — h; 3 — a; 4 — j; 5 — f; 6 — i; 7 — b; 8 — g; 9 — c; 10 — e.

## QUICK TEST–6

1 — c; 2 — g; 3 — a; 4 — j; 5 — i; 6 — b; 7 — h; 8 — e; 9 — d; 10 — f.

## QUICK TEST–7

1 — g; 2 — a; 3 — e; 4 — i; 5 — c; 6 — j; 7 — b; 8 — d; 9 — f; 10 — h.

## QUICK TEST–8

1 — j; 2 — e; 3 — g; 4 — a; 5 — b; 6 — c; 7 — i; 8 — h; 9 — d; 10 — f.

## QUICK TEST–9

1 — d; 2 — g; 3 — i; 4 — a; 5 — h; 6 — b; 7 — j; 8 — c; 9 — f; 10 — e.

## QUICK TEST–10

1 — g; 2 — c; 3 — i; 4 — a; 5 — j; 6 — b; 7 — h; 8 — e; 9 — f; 10 — d.

## QUICK TEST–11

1 — h; 2 — c; 3 — d; 4 — j; 5 — a; 6 — i; 7 — b; 8 — e; 9 — f; 10 — g.

## QUICK TEST–12

1 — h; 2 — c; 3 — f; 4 — a; 5 — j; 6 — b; 7 — i; 8 — e; 9 — g; 10 — d.

## QUICK TEST–13

1 — d; 2 — a; 3 — g; 4 — h; 5 — j; 6 — b; 7 — c; 8 — i; 9 — f; 10 — e.

## QUICK TEST–14

1 — e; 2 — f; 3 — j; 4 — b; 5 — h; 6 — a; 7 — d;
8 — c; 9 — g; 10 — i.

## QUICK TEST–15

1 — g; 2 — d; 3 — i; 4 — a; 5 — f; 6 — b; 7 — j;
8 — c; 9 — h; 10 — e.

## QUICK TEST–16

1 — a; 2 — i; 3 — d; 4 — f; 5 — b; 6 — j; 7 — c;
8 — h; 9 — e; 10 — g.

## QUICK TEST–17

1 — e; 2 — a; 3 — g; 4 — h; 5 — b; 6 — c; 7 — j;
8 — d; 9 — f; 10 — i.

## QUICK TEST–18

1 — c; 2 — j; 3 — g; 4 — a; 5 — h; 6 — c; 7 — e;
8 — d; 9 — g; 10 — i.

## QUICK TEST–19

1 — i; 2 — f; 3 — a; 4 — c; 5 — h; 6 — j; 7 — b;
8 — e; 9 — g; 10 — d.

## QUICK TEST–20

1 — e; 2 — g; 3 — i; 4 — a; 5 — d; 6 — j; 7 — h;
8 — b; 9 — c; 10 — f.

## QUICK TEST–21

1 — h; 2 — f; 3 — g; 4 — a; 5 — b; 6 — e; 7 — c;
8 — d.

### QUICK TEST–22

1 — f; 2 — h; 3 — j; 4 — g; 5 — a; 6 — b; 7 — i;
8 — c; 9 — d; 10 — e.

### QUICK TEST–23

1 — c; 2 — f; 3 — g; 4 — i; 5 — a; 6 — j; 7 — b;
8 — h; 9 — d; 10 — e.

### QUICK TEST–24

1 — d; 2 — f; 3 — a; 4 — g; 5 — j; 6 — b; 7 — c;
8 — h; 9 — e; 10 — i.

### QUICK TEST–25

1 — c; 2 — f; 3 — a; 4 — h; 5 — b; 6 — i; 7 — g;
8 — e; 9 — d; 10 — j.

### QUICK TEST–26

1 — h; 2 — j; 3 — c; 4 — a; 5 — g; 6 — b; 7 — i;
8 — d; 9 — f; 10 — e.

### QUICK TEST–27

1 — c; 2 — f; 3 — h; 4 — a; 5 — b; 6 — j; 7 — i;
8 — d; 9 — e; 10 — g.

### QUICK TEST–28

1 — d; 2 — f; 3 — a; 4 — i; 5 — h; 6 — b; 7 — j;
8 — c; 9 — e; 10 — g.

### QUICK TEST–29

1 — f; 2 — c; 3 — h; 4 — a; 5 — j; 6 — b; 7 — g;
8 — d; 9 — e; 10 — i.

### QUICK TEST–30

1 — c; 2 — f; 3 — a; 4 — h; 5 — b; 6 — d; 7 — j;
8 — e; 9 — i; 10 — g.